بسم الله الرحمن الرحيم

اللهم صل على محمد وآل محمد

The Muhammadan *Light*

صلى الله عليه وسلم

in the Qur'an, Sunna, and Companion-Reports

From the Teachings of Mawlana al-Sayyid Shaykh Muhammad Nazim al-Haqqani and His Deputy al-Sayyid Shaykh Muhammad Hisham al-Kabbani

GIBRIL FOUAD HADDAD

THE MUHAMMADAN LIGHT
IN THE QUR'AN, SUNNA, AND COMPANION-REPORTS

ISBN: 978-1-938058-00-4

Published by:

Institute for Spiritual and
Cultural Advancement (ISCA)
Silver Parkway, #201
Fenton, MI 48430 (USA)
Tel: (888) 278-6624
Fax: (810) 815-0518

Printed in the United States.

Typesetting and cover design by Author and Faryal Naveed.

Pictures and Illustrations:

Covers: Green Dome of the Prophetic Mosque in Madina; Door to Mawlana Shaykh Nazim's house, Lefke, Cyprus. Calligraphy: *Basmala* and *Ṣalawāt*, http://www.khamis.ws; Mawlana Shaykh Nazim al-Haqqani (top L) in his 20s with his teacher Mawlana Shaykh ʿAbd Allah Fa'iz al-Daghistani and 60 years later with his deputy Shaykh Hisham Kabbani (bottom L). Qur'ān (anti-clockwise from top): 2:144, 4:113, 33:56, 68:4. Poetry: 1st line: ʿAbd al-Raḥmān b. al-Daybaʿ; 2nd line: ʿAbd al-Raḥīm al-Barʿī; bottom: Ḥassān b. Thābit's quatrain at his first sight of the Prophet *When I beheld his lights*, see page 48; couplet at the end of the book from Aḥmad al-Dardīr, *Manẓūmat Asmā' Allāh al-Ḥusnā*. Lithographs: pages 31-32 of the 1281/1864 edition of Aḥmad al-Ṣāwī's *Sharḥ al-Ṣalawāt al-Dardīriyya* where he cites the earliest known wording of the "hadith of Jābir" on the creation of the Prophet's Light, from al-Taftāzānī's (722-792/1322-1390) commentary on the *Burda*; first page of the 1283/1866 edition of al-Diyārbakrī's (d. 966/ 1559) 1,000-page *Tārīkh al-Khamīs fī Akhbār Anfasi Nafīs* which opens with a mention of the Light of the Prophet as the first creation.

بسم الله الرحمن الرحيم

قَدْ نَرَىٰ تَقَلُّبَ وَجْهِكَ فِي ٱلسَّمَآءِ

وَتِلْـكَ الْقُبَّـةُ الخَضْرَاءُ فِيهَـا ... نَبِيٌّ نُـورُهُ يَجْلُـو الْغَيَاهِـبَ

وَخُصَّ بِأَدْنَى قَابَ قَوْسَينِ رِفْعَةً ... وَبِالحَوضِ فِي بَحْرِ السَّنَا المُتَهَلِّلِ

وَإِنَّكَ لَعَلَىٰ خُلُقٍ عَظِيمٍ

وَكَانَ فَضْلُ ٱللَّهِ عَلَيْكَ عَظِيمًا

لَمَّا نَظَرْتُ إِلَى أَنْوَارِهِ سَطَعَـتْ ... وَضَعْتُ مِنْ خِيفَتِي كَفِّي عَلَى بَصَرِي

خَوْفاً عَلَى بَصَرِي مِنْ حُسْنِ صُورَتِهِ ... فَلَسْـتُ أَنْظُرُهُ إِلَّا عَـلَى قَـدَرِي

الأَنْـوَارُ مِنْ نُـورِهِ فِي نُـورِهِ غَـرِقَـتْ ... وَالْوَجْـهُ مِنْهُ طُلُوعُ الشَّمْـسِ وَالْقَمَـرِ

رُوحٌ مِنَ النُّورِ فِي جِسْـمٍ مِنَ الْقَمَـرِ ... كَحِلَّـةٍ نُسِجَـتْ بِالْأَنْجُـمِ الزُّهُـرِ

صَلُّوا عَلَيْهِ وَسَلِّمُوا تَسْلِيمًا

صفحتان من شرح الصلوات الدرديرية للإمام أحمد الصاوي رحمه الله

٢١

شجرة الاصل) الاضافة للبيان اى الشجرة التى هى الاصل وهو صلى الله عليه وسلم اصل العوالم على الاطلاق واساس شرفها بالاتفاق (النورانية) بضم النون نسبة الى النور ويحتمل ان يراد به الرب سبحانه وتعالى فانه قد ورد تسميته تعالى بالنور في الكتاب والسنة وحقيقة النور هو الظاهر بنفسه المظهر لغيره ونسب اليه تعالى لانه صلى الله عليه وسلم نشأ من حضرة الله بدون واسطة مادة ويحتمل انه اراد بالنور خلاف الظلمة وجمعه انوار فقد ورد ان ذات النبى صلى الله عليه وسلم كانت نورا حتى انه لا يظهر له ظل فى الشمس * وعن عائشة رضى الله عنها انها قالت بينما انا اخيط ثوبا فى السحر فوقعت الابرة منى وانطفأ المصباح اذ دخل على رسول الله صلى الله عليه وسلم فالتقطت الابرة من نور وجهه فقلت يا رسول الله ما ابهى وجهك وما انور طلعتك فقال يا عائشة الويل كل الويل لمن لم يرنى يوم القيمة فقلت ومن ذا الذى لا يراك يوم القيمة فقال البخيل فقلت وما البخيل فقال الذى ذكرت عنده فلم يصل على فعليه فنسبة الشئ لنفسه على سبيل المبالغة وزيادة شرف والنون لزيادة الفه وعلى كل هو معنى الحديث الوارد عن جابر بن عبد الله الانصارى رضى الله عنه قال سألت رسول الله صلى الله عليه وسلم عن اول شئ خلقه الله فقال هو نور نبيك يا جابر خلقه الله ثم خلق منه كل خير وخلق بعده كل شر وحين خلقه اقامه قدامه فى مقام القرب اثنى عشر الف سنة ثم جعله اربعة اقسام فخلق العرش من قسم والكرسى من قسم وحملة العرش وخزنة الكرسى من قسم واقام القسم الرابع فى مقام الحب اثنى عشر الف سنة ثم جعله اربعة اقسام فخلق القلم من قسم واللوح من قسم والجنة من قسم واقام القسم الرابع فى مقام الخوف اثنى عشر الف سنة ثم جعله اربعة اجزاء فخلق الملائكة من جزء وخلق الشمس من جزء وخلق القمر والكواكب من جزء واقام

الجزء الرابع في مقام الرجاء اثني عشر الف سنة ثم جعله اربعة اجزاء
فخلق العقل من جزء والحلم والعلم من جزء والعصمة والتوفيق من
جزء واقام الجزء الرابع في مقام الحياء اثني عشر الف سنة ثم نظر
اليه فترشح النور عرقا فقطرت منه مائة الف وعشرون الفا
واربعة الاف قطرة فخلق الله تعالى من كل قطرة روح نبي اورسول
ثم تنفست ارواح الانبياء فخلق الله من انفاسهم نور ارواح
الاولياء والسعداء والشهداء والمطيعين من المؤمنين الى
يوم القيمة فالعرش والكرسي من نوري والكروبيون والروحانيون
من الملائكة من نوري وملائكة السموات السبع من نوري
والجنة وما فيها من النعيم من نوري والشمس والقمر والكواكب
من نوري والعقل والعلم والتوفيق من نوري وارواح الانبياء
والرسل من نوري والشهداء والسعداء والصالحون من نتايج
نوري ثم خلق الله اثني عشر حجابا فاقام النور وهو الجزء الرابع
في كل حجاب الف سنة وهي مقامات العبودية وهي حجاب الكرامة
والسعادة والرؤية والرحمة والرأفة والحلم والعلم والوقار والسكينة
والصبر والصدق واليقين فعبد الله ذلك النور في كل حجاب
الف سنة فلما اخرج النور من الحجب ركبه الله في الارض فكان يضيء
بين المشرق والمغرب كالسراج في الليل المظلم ثم خلق الله آدم من
الارض وركب فيه النور في جبينه ثم انتقل منه الى شيث ولده
وكان ينتقل من طاهر الى طيب الى ان وصل الى عبد الله بن عبد المطلب
ومنه الى وجه امي آمنة ثم اخرجني الى الدنيا فجعلني سيد المرسلين
وخاتم النبيين ورحمة للعالمين وقائد الغر المحجلين هكذا
كان بدء خلق نبيك يا جابر اهـ ذكره شيخنا الشيخ سليمان الجمل
في اول شرحه على الشمايل عن سعد الدين التفتازاني في شرح
بردة المديح عند قوله * وكل آي اتى الرسل الكرام بها * فانما اتصلت من نوره بهم *

الصفحة الأولى لسيرة تاريخ الخميس للعلامة الدياربكري

الله

الجزء الاول من تاريخ الخميس فى أحوال أنفس نفيس

(بسم الله الرحمن الرحيم)

الحمد لله الذى خلق نور نبيه قبل كل أوائل * ثم خلق منه كل شئ من الاعالى والاسافل * ثم أودعه فى الاصلاب الطيبة الجلائل * ورباه فى الارحام الطاهرة من الرذائل * فقلبه فى الآباء والامهات الجزائل * حتى أظهره من أطهر بيت من خير الشعوب والقبائل * محمد المخصص بأبين السير وأحسن الشمائل * المؤيد بأثبت المعجزات وأوضح الدلائل * صلى الله عليه وعلى اخوانه المصطفين أولى أكمل الفضائل * وعلى آله وأصحابه المقتدين ذوى أجمل الخصائل * (أما بعد) فيقول المستوهب من الله ذى المنن العبد الضعيف حسين بن محمد بن الحسن الدياربكرى غفر الله له ولوالديه * وتولهم كرامة لديه * هذه مجموعة فى سير سيد المرسلين وشمائل خاتم النبيين صلى الله عليه وعلى آله وأصحابه أجمعين * انتخبتها من الكتب المعتبرة تحفة للاخوان الكرام البررة وهى التفسير الكبير والكشاف وحاشيته للشريف الجرجانى والكشف والوسيط ومعالم التنزيل وأنوار التنزيل ومدارك التنزيل وتفسير القشيرى وبحر العلوم والنهر ولباب التأويل وتفسير الحدادى وعمدة المعانى وزاد المسير لابن الجوزى وتفسير الينابيع وتبصير الرحمن وتفسير أبى الليث السمرقندى وصحيحا البخارى ومسلم وسنن الترمذى وشمائله وسنن أبى داود والنسائى وابن ماجه والمصابيح وشرح السنة والمشكاة وشرحها للطيبى ومشارق الانوار للصغانى والموطأ وشرحا صحيح البخارى لابن حجر والكرمانى ومسند الامام أحمد ومستدرك الحاكم وجامع الاصول لابن الاثير والنهاية له وأسد الغابة والكامل له والشفاء وشعب الايمان للبيهقى ودلائل النبوة له واحياء العلوم والتلقيح لابن الجوزى وصفوة الصفوة له وشرف المصطفى له والحدائق له والوفاء له وخلاصة الوفا للسمهودى

وايضاح

Know that Allah was unknown in His pre-eternity since there was no one created that might know Him. He loved to be known, so *He seized a Handful of His Light*, that is, He seized it Himself. *Of* here stands for *with* and the Light stands for the Essence. So *of His Light* is a clarification of *He seized a Handful*, to mean that He Himself caused it to appear without the intermediary of any material.

That Handful which He seized is what is known as the Muḥammadan Light, the Soul of Souls, the Muḥammadan Secret, the Greater Throne of Allah, the First Adam, the Greater Forefather, the Perfect Man, the Secret of Secrets, the Pupil of the Eye of Existence, the Tree of Origins, and other names that are familiar to the gnostics.

—al-Ṣāwī, *Sharḥ al-Ṣalawāt al-Dardīriyya*

قال الإمام الصاوي رحمه الله في شرح الصلوات الدرديرية: إِعْلَمْ أَنَّ اللهَ كَانَ فِي أَزَلِهِ لَمْ يُعْرَفْ لِعَدَمِ وُجُودِ مَنْ يَعْرِفُهُ فَأَحَبَّ أَنْ يُعْرَفَ فَقَبَضَ قَبْضَةً مِنْ نُورِهِ أَيْ بِذَاتِهِ فَـ(مِنْ) بِمَعْنَى الْبَاءِ وَالنُّور بِمَعْنَى الذَّاتِ وَالْإِضَافَهُ لِلْبَيَانِ، وَالْمُرَادُ: أَبْرَزَهُ بِقُدْرَتِهِ مِنْ غَيْرِ وَاسِطَةِ مَادَّةٍ. وَهَذَا الْمَقْبُوضُ هُوَ الْمُسَمَّى بِالنُّورِ الْمُحَمَّدِيِّ وَبِرُوحِ الْأَرْوَاحِ وَبِالسِّرِّ الْمُحَمَّدِيِّ وَبِعَرْشِ اللهِ الْأَكْبَرِ وَبِآدَمَ الْأَوَّلِ وَبِالْأَبِ الْأَكْبَرِ وَبِالْإِنْسَانِ الْكَامِلِ وَبِسِرِّ الْأَسْرَارِ وَبِإِنْسَانِ عَيْنِ الْوُجُودِ وَبِشَجَرَةِ الْأَصْلِ وَغَيْرَ ذَلِكَ مِنَ الْأَسْمَاءِ الْمَشْهُورَةِ بَيْنَ الْعَارِفِينَ.

Preface

All praise belongs to Allah Almighty Who created the universe from absolute nothingness; Who brought the creations into existence and illumined them with His Light, adorning them with His Names and Attributes; and Who caused them to be reflected in the mirror of His Reality. Praise belongs to Him, and through this Praise, I ask that He open to us the doors of His Heavenly Goodness, thanking Him with gratitude scented with the perfume of the roses of His Divine Names.

I bear testimony that Allah is the Only One to be worshipped, and I bear witness that His Messenger, our supporter Muhammad is His sincere and loyal Servant whom He chose to be His Divine Beloved.

Our beloved Prophet Muhammad is the Sun from the unseen Light of the Divine Presence, who came forth and outshone the light of all suns. There is none brighter than the one who shines upon all creation. His existence preceded all others, and his name preceded the Pen, because he was before all that is, the Master of this creation. As he perceived he informed, and as he discovered he described. With him, the Light of Prophecy shone forth, and the lights of prophets and messengers thereby appeared.

Allah sent him as the representative created from His Light as a sincere servant to His Creation, raising him up to His Divine Presence and putting his name besides His Name, where He said, in His Divine Uncreated Word: *wa kafā billāhi shahīdan Muḥammadun Rasūlullāh – sufficient is Allah as Witness that Muhammad is the Messenger of Allah.* (48:28-29) He was a prophet when Adam was between water and clay.

May Allah reward our son, Shaykh Gibril Haddad, for his dedication, forbearance and perseverance in seeking out the source-works of Classical Islam to present in this precious volume, the diamonds and gems of Prophetic Narrations and Luminous Quranic Commentaries revealing the unimaginable, utterly unfathomable and inestimable grandeur of our beloved Prophet, about whom in reality we understand only the merest fraction.

In performing this service of love for Allah and His Prophet, Shaykh Gibril has bulwarked and upheld, in the face of ongoing viral attacks, the reality that *Sayyidunā* Muḥammad is the First Creation, a reflection of the Divine Attribute an-Nur, the Light, and the locus of manifestation of the Divine Names and Attributes. He has brought out and shone a spotlight on heretofore hidden and purposely-veiled knowledge about the Essence of our Prophet (*salla Allahu 'alayhi wa-'ala Alihi wa-Sahbihi wa-Sallam*) and his limitless perfections. He has extracted from the parchments of the classical scholars witness-accounts that clarify and authenticate the true pure *'aqida* of *Ahl as-Sunna wa'l-Jama'a*, whose foundations were laid by none other than the Prophet himself under the guidance of the Lord of creation, whose walls were built by the Pious Predecessors, *as-Salaf al-ṣāliḥīn*, and whose roof was erected by *al-Khalaf al-ṣādiqīn*, the Truthful Successors, up to the present age. May Allah reward Dr. Haddad in this world, and far more, in the next, for his exertion to elucidate realities of the greatness of our Prophet, about whom we say: "Our life is our Prophet, our breath is our Prophet, our death is our Prophet, we are for him and he is for us, and without him, we would never have come to know our Lord, the Creator."

The Perfumed Prayers of Allah and His Angels, Peace and countless Blessings be on the Master of the Firsts and the Lasts, Sayyidunā Muḥammad and on his family and companions, from now until the Hour of Rising.

Shaykh Muhammad Hisham Kabbani
Fenton, Michigan
Rajab 20, 1433/ June 8, 2012

CONTENTS

Preamble 1-20

"The tongue is incapable of speech" (Shaykh Hisham) 1
Dedication and Supplication 3
Mawlana Shaykh Nazim's Life and Teachings 4
The Daghistani-Haqqani chain of transmission 11-12
Shaykh Hisham's Life and Teachings 16
The use of weak hadiths in support of excellent works 19

I The Prophet as the First Creation 21-39

I am the first of those who surrender (6:163) 21
"He is the first of Muslims on the Day of Promises" (al-Samarqandī) 21
"He was the first one to say *Yes, verily!*" (Muḥammad al-Bāqir) 22
"He precedes everything and everyone in existence" (Rūzbahān) 23
"There is no first other than Muḥammad" (al-Qurṭubī) 24
"I was the first of the Prophets created and the last to be sent" (Hadith) 25
The Prophet's status and title of Beloved of Allah 25-29
"Allah has made me the Opener and the Seal" (Hadith) 25
"I made you the first Prophet created and the last sent" (Hadith Qudsī) 26
"Behold, I am the Beloved of Allah" (Hadith) 27
"The sequence of Prophets began with me ahead of them" (Hadith) 29
"I was a Prophet when Adam was between spirit and body" (Hadith) 30
"He received Qur'ān and all his knowledge at that time" (Kattānī) 31
"This is your son Aḥmad; he is the First and the Last" (Hadith Qudsī) 33
"Adam and everyone after him are under my flag" (Hadith) 35
The All-Beneficent taught the Qur'ān (55:1-2) to the Prophet 36
"Allah Himself addressed him with Qur'ān directly" (al-Sulamī) 36
"Everything became manifest to me and I knew" (Hadith) 37

II The Prophet as a Light in Qur'ān and Sunna 41-76

The ten referents of *nūr* in the Qur'ān 41
"His Light is more than abundantly visible east and west" (al-Qārī) 42
One who calls to Allah by His leave and a Luminous Lamp (33:45-46) 43
There has come to you from Allah a Light (5:15) 44
The crystal resembles a star of diamond... Light upon Light (24:35) 44
The description of the Prophet as a light by over 40 Companions 45

"It was as if the sun was running its course in his face" (Abū Hurayra) 45
"His face was like the sun and the moon" (Jābir b. Samura) 46
"If you saw him you saw the sun rising" (Rubayyiʿ bint Muʿawwidh) 47
His Light overwhelmed beholders 47-52
"I could not bear to take my fill of looking at him" (ʿAmr b. al-ʿĀṣ) 47
"I feared for my eyes due to his beauty, I barely looked at him" (Ḥassān) 48
"Humble woman, do not tremble!" (Hadith) 49
"I felt as if I were looking at Allah" (Ubay b. Kaʿb) 50
"His *bāṭin* reflects the All-Exalted; his *ẓāhir* the All-Loving" (Ḥalabī) 51
al-Dārimī's "Chapter on the Beauty of the Prophet" 52-53
"I swear he was more beautiful to me than the moon" (Jābir b. Samura) 52
"When he spoke you could see light coming out" (Ibn ʿAbbās) 52
"I never saw anyone more luminous or lustrous" (Ibn ʿUmar) 53
"His face was like the moon" (al-Barāʾ b. ʿĀzib) 53
"We saw as if light was coming out of his mouth" (Abū Qirṣāfa) 53
Like the Sun and the Moon, not Like the Sword 54
"His face was like a piece of the moon" (Kaʿb b. Mālik) 55
"His face was like the halo of the moon" (Kaʿb b. Mālik) 55
"His face was like the crescent moon" (Jubayr b. Muṭʿim) 56
"I saw the face of a man like the full moon" (an unnamed woman) 56
"The full moon has risen over us" (the Madinans) 57
"His forehead shone like the moon" (Ḥassān b. Thābit) 58
"They saw his forehead as if it were the light of the moon" (ʿĀʾisha) 58
"Like the moonlight dispelling darkness" (Abū Bakr al-Ṣiddīq) 59
"If you were not human you would be moonlight" (ʿUmar al-Fārūq) 60
"My eyes! Weep Hāshim's full moon" (ʿĀtika bint ʿAbd al-Muṭṭalib) 60
"You are a light from the Almighty" (al-ʿAbbās b. ʿAbd al-Muṭṭalib) 60
"He dispelled darkness with light" (ʿAbd al-Raḥmān b. ʿAwf) 61
"He is the light that dispels blindness past or future" (Abū al-Ṭufayl) 61
His Knowledge of the Unseen 62-65
"If he says anything unseen it is confirmed sooner or later" (Ḥassān) 62
"At your wish he foretells you the morrow" (Mālik b. ʿAwf) 63
"Nothing is left but I was shown it" (Hadith) 64
Seeing the Prophet in one's grave (Ibn Abī Jamra) 66
"His sweat shone like pearls" (ʿĀʾisha, Anas, ʿAlī, Hind b. Abī Hāla) 67-72
"His face beamed like a white lightning-cloud" (ʿĀʾisha) 67
"Fairer than you my eye never saw, no woman ever bore" (Ḥassān) 68
"No woman has conceived nor given birth to one like him" (Ḥassān) 69
"Women cannot give birth to a second Muḥammad" (Abū Dahbal) 69
"Woe to whoever is deprived of looking at this Face" (Hadith) 70
"He was rosy-colored (*azhar al-lawn*)" (Anas) 71
The meaning of *azhar* 72-74
"That tawny man" (Hadith) 73

"Bless me on the radiant night and the rosy day (Jumu'a)" (Hadith) 74
The Long Hadiths of Hind b. Abī Hāla and 'Ā'isha 74-76

III The Intercession of His Face & Grave 77-101

"**A fair one by whose face rain-prayers reach the clouds**" (Abū Ṭālib) 77-81
"Where can people flee except to the Messengers?" (a Bedouin) 79
"Through him the clan of Hāshim seek refuge from evil" (Abū Ṭālib) 79
"Through him Allah waters us with rain" (unnamed Companion) 79-80
"His gifts are sought when Allah holds up rain" (Aswad b. Mas'ūd) 82
"Let there be no ceiling between him and the sky for rain" ('Ā'isha) 83
"70,000 angels daily surround his grave" (Ka'b al-Aḥbār) 84
"I travelled to you so you will intercede for me" (Māzin al-Ṭā'ī) 85
"Pillar relied on, surety of refugees, resort of the parched" (Ḥassān) 85
The Prophet as a Light in the Companions' Funeral Elegies 86-101
"When he entered Madina everything lit up" (Anas b. Mālik) 86
"He who in our midst was the source of our light" (Ḥassān) 87
"May you be blessed, Grave of the Messenger!" (Ḥassān) 88
How the Early Muslims Acted at the Prophet's Grave 89-101
"What loss does one bear after the scent of Aḥmad's grave?" (Fāṭimā) 89
"I came to the Prophet, not to a stone or a room" (Abū Ayyūb) 90
"O Grave of the Prophet and his two Friends, help us!" (al-Nābigha) 91
"My soul be sacrificed for a grave you inhabit" (A Bedouin) 92-93
"Whoever stands at the grave of the Prophet" (Ibn Abī Fudayk) 94
"Why should I not travel on my eyes to his Grave?" (al-Dahhān) 95
"Even if we rode to him on our eyes every day" (Ibn al-Dayba') 96
Tabarruk with the Grave is the way of the *Salaf* (Isḥāq b. Rāhūyah) 97
"Houses and plains and dwelling quarters and his *mawlid*" (Ḥassān) 98
"My soul be sacrificed for you and your body" (Abū Bakr al-Ṣiddīq) 100
"You are pure in life and you are pure in death" (Abū Bakr, 'Alī) 100-101

IV Prophet as Light from the Light of Allah 103-137

There has come to you from Allah a Light and a manifest Book (5:15) 103
"His light makes truth (*al-ḥaqq*) manifest" (al-Ṭabarī) 104
"The *ṣirāṭ mustaqīm* is the Prophet Muḥammad" (Makkī al-Qaysī) 104
"Allah used the Greatest Name and said *from Allah a Light*" (Biqā'ī) 105
"He is the Light of lights" (al-Ālūsī) 106
"Both *the Light* and *the Manifest Book* are the Prophet" (Qārī, Ālūsī) 106
"Truly his character was the Qur'ān" ('Ā'isha) 107
"I.e. his character was the character of Allah" (al-Suhrawardī) 108

"He is the mirror for the Essence and Attributes" (al-Wartujabī) 109
His face resembled the Qur'ān (Anas) 110
The similitude of the Divine Light is the Prophet (Muqātil, Ka'b) 111-118
Allah is the Light of the heavens and the earth 111
His appearance revealed his Prophethood (Ibn Rawāḥa, Nafṭawayh) 114
"Light upon Light" means the two *Shahādas*" (Shaykh Hisham) 115
The *mishkāt* is Muḥammad, *al-miṣbāḥ* his heart, *al-zujāja* his chest 115
Mishkāt as "backless aperture" and "source" 116-117
Three canonical variants for the Verse of Light 117
Allah created in darkness then cast His light on creation (Hadith) 118
"Souls are a light from the Light of Allah" (Mughulṭāy) 118
"Each receives that light in the heart and the limbs" (Ibn al-'Arabī) 119
"*Taqwā* is obedience on Light from Allah's Light" (Ṭalq b. Ḥabīb) 119
The Covenant taken from creation (Hadith) 120
Meaning of *nūr al-Nabī min nūrih* (Prophet's light from His light) 121-132
"The first light-made reality is the Muḥammadan Reality" (Sirāj al-Dīn) 121
"He created Prophet's Light from His own Essence" (Shabrāmallasī) 122-123
Prophet is in you (49:7) i.e. nothing is without his light (Shaykh Hisham) 123
How all lights are extracted from the Muḥammadan Light (Sukayrij) 124-128
Only Allah Most High truly knows the Prophet 128
"Allah derived the Prophet's Name from His own Name" (Ḥassān) 132
"Allah based love on you by naming you Glorified" (Ibn Mirdās) 133
"There is no *muḥammad* except Muḥammad" ('Abd al-Raḥmān Bisṭāmī) 134
"He is a light whose illumination is sought" (Ka'b b. Zuhayr) 136

V The Progression of His Light in Time 139-177

More reports on the Prophet as the first Light created 139-146
"I was a light in front of my Lord for 14,000 years" 139
"Allah created His servants' spirits 2,000 years before them" 140
"Allah wrote the *qadar* of creatures 50,000 years before creation" 141
"The first thing Allah created is the Pen which is made of light" 141
"Allah created the light of Prophet 424,000 years before creation" 142
"Quraysh was a light standing before Allāh for 2,000 years" 145
al-'Abbās b. 'Abd al-Muṭṭalib's "Light of *Mawlid*" poem 147-158
When the waters rose We carried you upon the ship (69:11) 148
We bore their offspring in the laden ship (36:41) 148
And your translation among the worshippers (26:219) 148
"Aḥmad progressed as a great light" (Ibn Nāṣir al-Dīn) 149
His visible light in the foreheads of his ancestors 150-156
The blessings of his light in history (Shahrastānī) 152
The light of 'Abd Allāh b. 'Abd al-Muṭṭalib 155-156

The Prophetic Light as a marker of selection and refinement 157-165
He is the quintessence of human beings 160
ʿAlī al-Ḥabshī's "Necklace of Pearls" (*Simṭ al-Durar*) 160
The light of his *mawlid* as witnessed by his mother 162
"She gave birth to a light that lit the universe" (Ḥassān) 165
The splittings of the chest and his immersion in light 166
The body of the Prophet in the Holy Qur'ān 168-175
The Light of the Prophet in early Scriptures 175-177

VI His Pre-Existent Universal Intercession 179-224

"Angels were created from light…" (Hadith) 179
"Prophets are intermediaries between Allah and creation" (ʿIyāḍ) 180
"Prophets' spirits have superhuman, angelic qualities" (ʿIyāḍ) 180
"The Prophet is the Ultimate Purpose of creation" (Ibn Taymiyya) 182
"But for him, I would not have created creation" (Hadith Qudsī) 184
Intermediacy is the meaning of Prophethood and Messengership 185
The Prophet has authority over us in all things (al-Tustarī) 186
The Prophet has priority before all other souls (Ibn Diḥya) 186
"Every good in my life is on account of the Prophet" (al-Subkī) 188
"He is the means and root of every mercy in creation" (al-Bakrī) 189
His exalted status before Adam's creation 189
"Adam repented and sought intercession with my Name" (Hadith) 190
"*We exalted your fame* means: through Prophet's Name" (al-Rāzī) 191-192
The meaning of "I was a Prophet when Adam…" (al-Subkī) 194-196
The reality of the Prophet exists since the beginning of time 195
The lights of all Prophets are from his Light (Ibn Marzūq) 198
The Prophet's light and his name fill creation (al-Dabbāgh) 200-202
The Prophet intercedes for hundreds of billions 204-221
- Narration of ʿĀ'isha "Three lights came and filled our house" 204
- Narrations of Abū Umāma 205-206
- Narration of Abū Saʿīd al-Anmārī 206
- Narration of ʿUtba b. ʿAbd 207-208
- Narration of Faltān b. ʿĀṣim 208
- Narration of Anas 209
- Narration of Abū Hurayra 210
- Narration of ʿAbd al-Raḥmān b. Abī Bakr 211

He does not make any difference who he intercedes for (Kalābādhī) 212
- Two other narrations of Abū Hurayra 213-214
- Narration of Abū Ayyūb 215
- Narration of Abū Bakr and ʿAmr b. Ḥazm 216
- Another narration of ʿĀ'isha 217

The meaning of *Umma* (al-Kalābādhī) 218
"70,000" and its multiples denote over-abundance 220
"Three lights filled Madīna from end to end" (ʿAmr b. ʿAwf, Salmān) 222-224

VII His Light Overpowers All Lights 225-254

"The Prophet had no shadow that could be seen" (Hadith) 225-226
"Light does not have a shadow" (al-Zurqānī) 227
His shadowlessness in Shāfiʿī and Ḥanbalī *fiqh* books 227
The Prophet Mūsā's Hand of Light 228
The sun and the moon obeyed the Prophet Muḥammad 228
"I felt I could touch the top of the sky" (ʿAlī b. Abī Ṭālib) 230
His splitting of the moon 231
Invocations of blessings by his light as the source of all lights 232-240
Ṣalāt al-Asrār wal-Anwār (Mashīshiyya) 232
Ṣalāt Nūrāniyya (Badawiyya) 232
The different names of the Muḥammadan Light (al-Ṣāwī) 233
Ṣalāt Nūr al-Abṣār (Ṭibbiyya) 235
Ṣalāt Nūrika al-Sārī 236
Ṣalāt Nūr al-Nūr 236
Ṣalāt al-Nūr al-Awwal (Ṭaybāniyya Khaḍiriyya) 237
Ṣalāt al-Kāmila (Tāziyya=Nāriyya) 237
Ṣalāt Nūr Wajhillāh (ʿĀẓīmiyya) 238
Ṣalāt Tājiyya 239
Ṣalāt Bahī al-Anwār (Ibn al-Daybaʿ) 240
Every *ṣalāt* on the Prophet takes you to the Throne (Shaykh Hisham) 240
The Unfathomability of the Prophet's Rank I 241-248
"Comprehension shrank from attaining his reality" (al-Ṣāwī) 242
"None comes near or far from him, they all fall short" (al-Būṣīrī) 242
"His station is unattainable, unmatchable, unknowable" (Ibn ʿAjība) 244
"He made all helpless, minds capitulate" (Ibn Mashīsh) 244
"How can even Prophets ascend such as your ascent?" (al-Būṣīrī) 245-246
"You are the supreme Vicegerent assisting creation" (al-Haytamī) 247
The Unfathomability of the Prophet's Rank II 249-254
O Believers! Bless and salute him abundantly 249
"Say: O Allah, bless Muḥammad and his Household…" (Hadith) 249
"No one can repay the Prophet except Allah" (al-Kattānī) 250
"Whoever invokes blessings on me once…" (Hadith) 251
"Even if his heart is elsewhere" (Abū al-Mawāhib al-Shādhilī) 251
"Whoever says: May Allah recompense Muḥammad…" (Hadith) 252
Invoking blessings on the Prophet is better than paying *zakāt* (al-Raṣṣāʿ) 252
Each trait of his encapsulates all his perfection (al-Būṣīrī) 253

He is exempt of any partner in his perfection (al-Būṣīrī) 254
The totality of his beauty was not revealed to us (al-Haytamī) 254

VIII The Light of the Prophetic Inheritors 257-281

The three types of progeny in *alastu bi-Rabbikum* (al-Tustarī) 257
Prophets and *Awliyā* drank deepest from his light (al-Dabbāgh) 259
Creation is under *Awliyā*, and they are under the Prophet (al-Tustarī) 261
The visible light of the *Awliyā* here and hereafter 261-281
  Hadith of Usayd b. Ḥuḍayr and ʿAbbād b. Bishr's light 261
  Hadith of al-Ḥasan and al-Ḥusayn's light 262
  Hadith of the light of the Companions making *duʿāʾ* 263
  Hadith of al-Ṭufayl b. ʿAmr al-Dawsī's light 264
"Allah has transfigured Muḥammad with beauty" (Ṭufayl b. ʿAmr) 265
"I shall certainly know my Community by their light" (Hadith) 265
"They will come with light on their faces and limbs" (Hadith) 266-267
"When will I meet my beloved ones?" (Hadith) 267
"Prophet has as many lights as he has hairs on his body" (Kaʿb) 268
The Prophet's definition of the *Awliyā* 269
"*Awliyā* are the very purpose of all that exists" (Ibn al-Jawzī) 270
"The host of the unseen has hailed from the unseen" (al-Rawwās) 271
The Prophet's humanity is visible in the *Awliyā* of his House 272
The hadith of the *Awliya* on pulpits of lights 270-280
  Narrations of Muʿādh b. Jabal 274
  Narration of Abū Muslim al-Khawlānī 275
  Narration of Abū Umāma al-Bāhilī 276
  Narration of Abū Hurayra 276
  Narration of Abū Mālik al-Ashʿarī 277
  Narration of ʿAbd Allah b. ʿAmr b. al-ʿĀṣ 279
"The *walī* is a light from the light of Allah" (Ibn ʿAjība) 280

IX Epilogue 283-285

"My heart nearly flies off with unbearable longing" (ʿAlī al-Ḥabshī) 283
Final Prayer 285

Bibliography 287-301

بسم الله الرحمن الرحيم

The Muhammadan Light

in the Qur'ān, Sunna, and Companion-Reports

النّورُ المحمّدي في القرآن والحديث وآثار خير العصور

"None of us can imagine the glory of the glorious Prophet in the sight of Allah.... Even the vault of heaven is like zero before his Dome." –Mawlana al-Shaykh Muhammad Nazim al-Haqqani.

"Glory, praise and thanks be to Allah the Lord of the worlds; abundant blessings and peace on our master Muḥammad, the master of all Prophets and Messengers, all human beings, and all angels, the one upon whom Allah Most High Himself has sent blessings since pre-eternity and without end. The tongue is incapable of speech; the pen is incapable of writing; the mind is incapable of reflection; the heart bleeds and weeps in longing to see the Beloved. Allah Himself is the One Who has honored him, brought him respect, exalted him, made him powerful and made him reach the Station of *Two Bows' Lengths or Nearer Yet* (53:9). He created his light—upon him blessings and peace—before the creation of the universes and before the creation of the constellations and galaxies and before the creation of anything whatsoever. The Light of Muḥammad was the first of all creations in the presence of Allah Almighty. It was created as a droplet, a tear, so to speak, out of the Light of Allah Most High as He said: *The similitude of His light is like a niche in which is a lamp, the lamp is in a crystal, the crystal resembles a star of diamond* (24:35), and in another verse He named him *a Luminous Lamp* (33:46) and in another *a Light from Allah* (5:15). This creation was explicitly related in the report of ʿAbd al-Razzāq that when the Prophet was asked about the first creation before any other creation he replied: 'O Jābir, truly Allah created before all things the Light of your Prophet from His own Light.'"

Thus did the internationally celebrated Sufi master, our teacher Shaykh Muhammad Hisham Kabbani begin his speech on the birth of the Prophet Muḥammad before a large gathering in Madura, Indonesia, on December 26, 2011.[1] His statement about the Light of the Prophet takes up the three overarching themes of the great *mawlid* panegyrics: its firstness before all creation, its being made of light, and its being created "from" or "out of" Allah's own light (*min nūrih*). These themes are spelled out in the above statement attributed to the Prophet known as the hadith of Jābir:[2]

عَنْ جَابِرِ بْنِ عَبْدِ اللهِ قُلْتُ: يَا رَسُولَ اللهِ بِأَبِي أَنْتَ وَأُمِّي، أَخْبِرْنِي عَنْ أَوَّلِ شَيْءٍ خَلَقَهُ اللهُ قَبْلَ الأَشْيَاءِ؟ قَالَ: يَا جَابِرُ إِنَّ اللهَ تَعَالَى خَلَقَ قَبْلَ الأَشْيَاءِ نُورَ نَبِيِّكَ مِنْ نُورِهِ الحديث كما ذكره القسطلاني في المواهب وعزاه لعبد الرزاق. قال السيوطي في الحاوي: لا يُعرف له سند. وقالت جماعة: معناه صحيح.

Each of these themes is independently confirmed in the Qur'an, the Sunna, poetic testimonials of the Companions and other early reports. This book presents the textual evidence for these three aspects.

By the blessing of Allah this book, begun on 13 Dhūl-Ḥijja 1432, was finished on 1 Rajab 1433 (10 November 2011-21 May 2012).

[1] media.islamicsupremecouncil.org/Good_Tidings_for_Lovers_of_the_Prophet_s_-4025.html

[2] The report "O Jābir…" is part of a longer text cited by Shihāb al-Dīn al-Qasṭallānī (d. 923/1517) in *al-Mawāhib al-Ladunniyya* (1:36-37) where he sources it to "'Abd al-Razzāq narrated with his chain." The report is not found in any earlier source and al-Suyūṭī in *al-Ḥāwī lil-Fatāwā* (1:323-325, *tafsīr* of Sūrat al-Muddaththir) said there is no extant chain of transmission for it. Another version of it is found in *Talqīḥ al-Adhhān wa-Miftāḥ Ma'rifat al-Insān* attributed to Shaykh Muḥyī al-Dīn Ibn 'Arabī (561-638/1165-1240); however, the Syrian Ibn 'Arabī specialist Maḥmūd Maḥmūd Ghurāb considers the attribution of the *Talqīḥ* to Ibn 'Arabī spurious and said its oldest manuscript is dated 946, three centuries after his time. Nevertheless the first phrase of the report—"The first thing Allah created is my light"—is mentioned in Rūzbahān's (d. 606/1210) *Tafsīr* (see further down) and—with its long continuation—in al-Taftāzānī's (722-792/1322-1390) *Sharḥ al-Burda* according to Sulaymān al-Jamal in the beginning of his commentary on al-Tirmidhī's *Shamā'il* entitled *al-Mawāhib al-Muḥammadiyya bi-Sharḥ al-Shamā'il al-Tirmidhiyya* and his student al-Ṣāwī in his *Sharḥ al-Ṣalawāt al-Dardīriyya* (p. 31-32). *Qabla al-ashyā'* "before all things" is sometimes dot-corrupted and letter-corrupted to *qabla al-anbiyā'* "before Prophets" (الأشياء → الأنبياء).

Dedication and Supplication

The debt of gratitude we owe to our teachers – our spiritual parents – in this book and in our life is indescribable. They are our father and mother who fostered us, our guardians and mainstays who raised us, our lighthouses and compasses who guided us. They have embodied for us the wisdom and devotion of the ancient Knowers of God, the Prophets, whose hearts trembled and whose faces fell prostrate, weeping at the mention of their Lord. They have illuminated and illustrated for all people the form and spirit of the Paragon of all Prophets and Saints in this world and the next, and in all the uncountable worlds created and yet to be created from before the beginning of existence until the Day of Resurrection: our Master and Liegelord, the Life of our spirits and the Light of our eyes, the Best of Creation without end, *Sayyidunā* Muḥammad who was already Prophet before existence began.

Descend on him, O our Lord, a blessing of grandeur, exaltation and praise such as will reveal to all beings the inexpressible lights of his beauty and majesty which You Yourself have bestowed on him alone in creation by naming him Glorified – and repair, O our Lord, our broken, bankrupt hearts with a kind Gaze from that Light after which loss is replaced with plenty and thirst is quenched, never to return again; and upon the Guarantors of his Religion and the Stars that point the way to him: his Family and his Companions one and all, and the rest of his Inheritors to the Day of Judgment, most particularly our Guide and Helper Mawlana al-Shaykh Muhammad Nazim al-Haqqani, and Shaykh Muhammad Hisham al-Kabbani who is his Deputy and the Deputy of *Sulṭān al-Awliyā'* Mawlana al-Shaykh 'Abd Allah al-Fa'iz al-Daghistani.

Grant us such closeness to them and to Your Prophet as you have done when You joined body and soul, life and breath, the drop and the ocean, and Light with Light.

Mawlana Shaykh Nazim's Life and Teachings

Mawlānā al-Shaykh Muḥammad Nāẓim ʿĀdil b. al-Sayyid Aḥmad b. Ḥasan Yashīl Bāsh al-Ḥaqqānī al-Qubrusī al-Ṣāliḥī al-Ḥanafī – may Allah sanctify his soul and bless his ancestors and descendants – was born on 23 Shaʿbān 1340/April 21, 1922 in the city of Larnaca, Cyprus (Qubruṣ) to a family of Arab origin with Tatar roots. His father descends from Shaykh ʿAbd al-Qādir al-Jīlānī and his mother from Mawlānā Jalāl al-Dīn al-Rūmī. This makes him a descendant of the Holy Prophet Muḥammad, upon him blessings and peace, on his father's side and a descendant of Abū Bakr al-Ṣiddīq, Allah be well-pleased with him, on his mother's side.

After finishing school in Cyprus, Mawlana went to college in Istanbul and graduated in chemical engineering. There, he studied Arabic and *fiqh* under al-Ḥājj Jamāl al-Dīn al-Ālṣūnī (d. 1375/1955) the head preacher in Jāmiʿ Bāyazīd in Istanbul, and received *ijāza* from him. He took *taṣawwuf* and the Naqshbandi *Ṭarīqa* from Shaykh Sulaymān Arḍarūmī (d. 1368/1948) who eventually sent him to Shām (Syria).

Mawlana continued his *Sharīʿa* studies in Ḥalab (Aleppo), then Ḥamā, then Ḥimṣ, also known as Homs, before moving to Damascus. He studied at the shrine and mosque school of the great Companion Khālid b. al-Walīd in Ḥimṣ under its great Ulema and obtained *ijāza* in Ḥanafī *fiqh* from Shaykh Muḥammad ʿAlī 'Uyūn al-Sūd and Shaykh ʿAbd al-Jalīl Murād, and *ijāza* in hadith from the *Muḥaddith* Shaykh ʿAbd al-ʿAzīz b. Muḥammad ʿAlī ʿUyūn al-Sūd al-Ḥanafī.

The latter is one of the ten great hadith teachers of the late Rifāʿī *Ḥāfiẓ* of Aleppo, Shaykh al-Islām ʿAbd Allāh Sirāj al-Dīn who sat on his knees for two hours at the feet of Mawlana Shaykh ʿAbd Allāh when the latter visited Aleppo in 1959 and who gave *bayʿa* in the Naqshbandī *Ṭarīqa* to Mawlana Shaykh Nazim during the latter's last visit to him in Aleppo in 2001 as narrated to this writer by *Ustādh* Muḥammad ʿAlī b. Mawlānā al-Shaykh Ḥusayn ʿAlī al-Shaykhānī from Shaykh Muḥammad Fārūq ʿItqī al-Ḥalabī who was present at the latter event.

Mawlana also studied under Shaykh Sa'īd al-Sibā'ī who sent him to Damascus after receiving a sign related to the coming of Mawlana Shaykh 'Abd Allāh Fā'iz al-Dāghistānī (1294-1393/1877-1973) to Syria. After his initial arrival in Syria from Daghistan in the late thirties, Mawlana Shaykh 'Abd Allāh lived mostly in Damascus but often visited Aleppo and Ḥimṣ. In the latter city he got to know Shaykh Muḥammad Sa'īd al-Sibā'ī who was director of the Khālid b. Walīd School. Shaykh Sa'īd wrote him, "We have a remarkable student from Turkey studying with us." Mawlana Shaykh 'Abd Allāh replied to him, "That student belongs to us; send him over!" That student was our teacher Mawlana Shaykh Nazim who, although he intended to move to Madina for settling (*mujāwara*), came to the *zāwiya* of Shaykh Ḥasan al-Jibāwī in Damascus with Shaykh Sa'īd and gave his *bay'a* to our Grandshaykh there between 1940 and 1944:

> We came with him [al-Sibā'ī], knocked on Hazrat Shaykh's door. It opened. I saw that Shaykh Effendi Hazratleri was in his *mintan* (shirt) with his *takke* (skullcap), according to Sunna. It immediately came to my heart that he was sent from Istanbul. I still remember that day. How many years has it been? 60 years? It has been 70 years. 70 years! *Allāhu akbar al-Akbar*. Shaykh Sibā'ī said: "*Yā Sayyidī,* this young man has been in Homs all this time, he desires to go to Madina al-Munawwara as a *mujāwir*." Shaykh Effendi Hazratleri took one look at me and said: "I will present him tonight in *munājat* (Divine conversation) to the Presence [of the Prophet]. He will do according to what his answer will be. He may come back tomorrow morning." We left him and returned the next morning. I had been unable to sleep all night. We went there early in the morning. He said: "I showed you to the Prophet. He said: 'This is my son. There is nothing he will do here now if he comes to Madina al-Munawwara. Shaykh 'Abd Allah, give him permission to collect my *Umma* and send him to Cyprus.'" It was in 1944. Finished. He said nothing. No words. He said I would know the time to come there. He advised me like this. So I came to Cyprus from there through Beirut. Such astonishing states. And Allah Almighty made me reach this day. Thanks to him.[3]

[3] Mawlana Shaykh Nazim, Turkish *suḥba* of 14 May 2012.

The next year Mawlana al-Shaykh ʿAbd Allāh moved into the house bought for him by his first Syrian Murīd and caliph, Mawlānā al-Shaykh Ḥusayn b. ʿAlī b. Muḥammad 'Ifrīnī al-Kūrkānī al-Rabbānī al-Kurdī al-Shaykhānī al-Ḥusaynī (1336-1429/1917-2008) – Allah bless and sanctify his soul and have mercy on his foreparents – in Qasyoun, the mount overlooking Damascus to which Allah Most High alluded: *By the Fig and the Olive! By Mount Sīnā!* (95:1-2). Qatāda and al-Ḥasan al-Baṣrī said: "The Fig is the Mount on which Damascus sits [i.e. Jabal Qāsyūn] and the Olive is the Mount on which Jerusalem sits." Narrated by ʿAbd al-Razzāq, al-Ṭabarī, al-Wāḥidī, al-Bayḍāwī, Ibn al-Jawzī, al-Qurṭubī, Ibn Kathīr, al-Suyūṭī, al-Shawkānī, etc., all in their *Tafsīr*s.

Mawlana Shaykh Nazim also bought a house near Grandshaykh's house and, together with Mawlana Shaykh Ḥusayn, helped build Masjid al-Mahdī, Grandshaykh's Mosque, which in 2002 was enlarged into a *Jāmiʿ* in the back of which is Grandshaykh's illumined grave and shrine and where, to this day, delicious cereal and chicken soup is prepared in huge vats and continues to be distributed to the poor twice a week.

Mawlana Shaykh Nazim lived in Damascus from the mid-forties to the early eighties, travelling at times to study or on behalf of Grandshaykh, such as his seclusions in Baghdad and Madina, until the latter left this life in 1973. After that Mawlana remained in Damascus for several years then moved to Cyprus. He related: "My Shaykh said like this: 'Nazim Effendi, I made 7,000 *ṣuḥba*s for you.' May Allah sanctify his secret."[4]

Both Mawlana, who is originally Cypriot, and Grandshaykh, who is originally Dāghistānī, became Damascene *"Shāmiyyūn"* and lived in the district of the righteous *(al-ṣāliḥīn)* called Ṣāliḥiyya. No doubt, the reason for the importance of Damascus for Mawlana and Grand-Shaykh is because Shām is blessed and protected through the Prophets and Saints, as was well-known to countless scholars and *awliyā'* who emigrated there from their respective countries. Imām

[4] *Ibid.*

Aḥmad and his student Abū Dawūd narrated with *ṣaḥīḥ* chains that our Holy Prophet said, upon him blessings and peace: "You must go to Shām. It is Divinely chosen by Allah in all His earth. In it He protects His chosen servants; and Allah Almighty has given me a Guarantee concerning Shām and its people!"

Imām al-Nawawī said in his book *Irshād Ṭullāb al-Ḥaqā'iq ilā Ma'rifat Sunan Khayr al-Khalā'iq*: "This hadith is among the huge merits of Shām and is an observable fact."

The general director of Dār al-Fatwā and al-Azhar University in Beirut, Lebanon, Shaykh Ṣalāḥ al-Dīn Fakhrī wrote:

> On the morning of al-Aḥad 20 Rabī ' al-Ākhir 1386 corresponding to Sunday 7 August, 1966, we were granted the privilege of visiting Shaykh 'Abd Allāh al-Dāghistānī – Allah have mercy on him – in Mount Qāsyūn in Damascus on the initiative and in the company of Mawlānā al-Shaykh Mukhtār al-'Alāylī – Allah have mercy on him – the Muftī of the Republic of Lebanon at the time; Shaykh Ḥusayn Khālid the imām of Nawqara Mosque; Ḥājj Khālid Bashīr – may Allah have mercy on both of them; Shaykh Ḥusayn Ṣa'biyya [the director of Dār al-Ḥadīth al-Ashrafiyya in Damascus]; Shaykh Maḥmūd Sa'd; Shaykh Zakariyyā Sha'r; and Ḥājj Maḥmūd Sha'r. The Shaykh received us most kindly, with a warm welcome full of happiness and mirth. This was in the presence of Shaykh Nāẓim al-Qubruṣī – Allah save and keep him!
>
> We sat from nine o'clock in the morning until the *ẓuhr* call to prayer while the Shaykh – Allah have mercy on him – explained and spoke about Shām, its excellence, its extraordinary merits and the fact that it is the site of the Resurrection and that Allah will gather all human beings in it for the final Reckoning. He mentioned things that moved our hearts and minds, imbued with the glorious spirit of the Ṣāliḥiyya district, and he spoke about the indissoluble link – in practice as well as discourse – between *taṣawwuf* and *Sharī'a*. May Allah lead and keep us upon guidance in the company of the righteous Saints. *Āmīn, yā Rabb al-'ālamīn!*

There are many more prestigious names of the Ulema and *Awliyā'* of Shām that loved and associated with our *Shuyūkh* during that golden period such as Shaykh Muḥammad Bahjat al-Bayṭār (1311-1396/ 1894-1976), Shaykh Sulaymān Ghāwjī al-Albānī (d. 1378/1959) the father of our teacher Shaykh Wahbī, Shaykh Tawfīq al-Hibrī, Shaykh Muḥammad al-ʿArabī al-ʿAzzūzī (1308-1382/1891-1962) the Mufti of Lebanon and principal Shaykh of our teacher Shaykh Ḥusayn ʿUsayrān (1329-1426/1911-2005), al-ʿĀrif Shaykh Shahīd al-Ḥalabī, al-ʿĀrif Shaykh Rajab al-Ṭā'ī, Shaykh al-Qurrā' Shaykh Najīb Khayyāṭa al-Faraḍī al-Ḥalabī, al-Sayyid Muḥammad al-Nabhān al-Ḥalabī (1318-1394/1900-1974), Shaykh Aḥmad ʿIzz al-Dīn al-Bayānūnī (1329-1395/1913-1975), al-ʿĀrif Shaykh Aḥmad al-Ḥārūn (1315-1382/1897-1962), Shaykh Muḥammad Zayn al-ʿĀbidīn al-Jadhba, and others – Allah have mercy on all of them!

From that blessed 30-year *ṣuḥba* between Mawlana and GrandShaykh came those unparalleled *Mercy Oceans* that are still lavishing on every seeker their *Endless Horizons*, their *Pink Pearls*, their *Rising Suns*. No doubt, those early transcriptions are milestones of the greatest single-handed call to Islām the US and Europe had seen in the twentieth century, by the grace of Allah.

May Allah bless Mawlana Shaykh Nazim ever more and grant him the highest stations He ever granted to His Friends, near our glorious liege-lord Muḥammad who said, upon him blessings and peace:

> If anyone travels on a road in search of knowledge, Allah will cause him to travel on one of the roads of Paradise, the angels will lower their wings from pleasure with one who seeks knowledge, and the dwellers of the heavens and the earth and the fish in the depth of the sea will ask forgiveness for the person of learning! The superiority of the person of learning over the ordinary believer is like that of the moon on the night when it is full over the rest of the stars! The Ulema are the inheritors of the Prophets, and the Prophets have neither dinar nor dirham, they leave only knowledge; and he who takes it takes an abundant portion!

The first place I ever travelled in search of this Prophetic Knowledge was London in the month of Ramadan 1411 following my witnessing *shahāda: lā ilāha illā Allāh, Muḥammadun Rasūlullāh.* There, I took Mawlana's noble hand for the first time and made *bay'a* to him after having been introduced to *Ṭarīqa* in December 1990 by his son-in-law and American deputy, Shaykh Hisham Kabbani, whom I accompanied until, by his blessing, I moved to Damascus together with my family and lived in Mawlana Shaykh Nazim's house and library there for nine years (1997-2006). I visited Mawlana several times in his home in Cyprus and saw him many times in Damascus as well. Among the gifts of *ṣuḥba* Mawlana gave were the last two weeks of Rajab in the year 1422 – October 2001 – in his house and *zāwiya* in the Turkish Cypriot town of Lefke. A memento of this experience was written in Arabic and English and published under the title *Qubruṣ al-Ṭarab fī Suḥbati Rajab* or *The Joy of Cyprus in the Association of Rajab.*

At that time and also later, during his last two trips to the US, in England, Cyprus, and Damascus, I took from Mawlana the same great directive for every seeker of truth: **OUR GOAL IS THE DEFENSE AND ILLUSTRATION OF THE PROPHET MUHAMMAD AND HIS LOFTY ATTRIBUTES**, upon him and his House and Companions blessings and peace; to which Allah support us!

I understood from this that the true *Murīd* in the Naqshbandī-Ḥaqqānī *Ṭarīqa* is the friend and helper of every defender of *Sayyidinā* Muḥammad and it is his duty to associate with such defenders because they are on Mawlana's path whether they are Naqshbandi or not.

When the late octogenarian Friend of Allah in Johore, Malaysia, al-Ḥabīb 'Alī b. Ja'far b. 'Abd Allāh al-'Aydarūs received us in his home in May 2003, wearing clothes that had not changed since the 1940s, he looked like Mawlana in all respects and even seemed to mimick him when he said to pardon his broken Arabic. To our begging his *du'ā* for our injured lands and people he replied, "The *Umma* is protected and in good hands and you have in Shaykh Nazim Sufficiency!"

Thus has it been for the humble *murīd* of Mawlāna in every encounter with the *Awliyā'* of this *Umma.* They invariably show the highest respect and most fearsome humbleness to Mawlāna and his *silsila* even when they are ostensibly on a different path such as Ḥabīb ʿAlī al-ʿAydarūs (d. 1431/2010) in Malaysia; the late Sayyid Muḥammad b. ʿAlawī al-Mālikī (1367-1425/1948-2004) in Makka; the late *Sharīf* Muṣṭafā b. al-Sayyid Ibrāhīm al-Baṣīr (1360-1427/1941-2006) in central Morocco; the late Grandmuftī of Syria Shaykh Aḥmad Kuftāro b. Mawlānā al-Shaykh Muḥammad Amīn (1330-1425/1912-2004) and his friends the late Shaykh Bashīr al-Bānī (1329-1429/1911-2008), Shaykh Rajab Dīb, and Shaykh Ramaḍān Dīb; the Kattānī Shuyūkh of Damascus who never failed to invite and visit him whenever he resided there; the late Shaykh ʿAbd Allāh Sirāj al-Dīn (1343-1422/1924-2002) and his nephew Dr. Nūr al-Dīn ʿItr; the late Shaykh ʿAbd al-Raḥmān al-Shāghūrī (1331-1425/1913-2004); and the remainder of our teachers and brethren in Damascus and the world. All invariably invoked *taraḍḍī* on Mawlana al-Shaykh Nazim, expressing belief in the loftiness of his *wilāya* and asking for his *duʿā* or that of his followers; *and Allah suffices as Witness that Muḥammad is the Messenger of Allah* (48:28-29).

Al-Rawwās said in *Fadhlakat al-Ḥaqīqa*: "For the people of hearts it is one and the same who comes near and who goes far." It is an agreed-upon rule among the Men of Allah that multiplicity of paths is the theme of the unconnected while those that are *mawṣūl* are all on one path and in one circle and they know each other and love one another. They will be on pulpits of light on the Day of Resurrection. Therefore, we *Murīd*s of those respective paths must also know and love one another for the sake of Allah and His Prophet and His friends so that we may enter that blessed light and belong in the highest circle of *suḥba* and *jamāʿa* away from *furqa* and arrogance.

As Allah Most High said: *O Believers! Beware of Allah and keep [company and loyalty] with the Truthful ones!* and our Holy Prophet said: "I charge you with following my Companions then those that follow them then those that follow; after that, lying will spread... But you must keep to the *Jamāʿa* and beware of separation!"

This *Jamāʿa* is described in the *mutawātir* hadith: "He for whom Allah desires great good, He grants him true understanding in the Religion. I only distribute and it is Allah Who gives! That group shall remain in charge of the Order of Allah, unharmed by those who oppose them, until the coming of the Order of Allah." O Allah, make us thankful forever for what You gave and Your *Rasūl* and *Ḥabīb* distributed!

I heard Mawlānā Shaykh Nāẓim say many times on behalf of his teacher, *Sulṭān al-Awliyā'* Mawlānā al-Shaykh ʿAbd Allāh b. Muḥammad ʿAlī b. Ḥusayn al-Fā'iz al-Dāghistānī *thumma* al-Shāmī al-Ṣāliḥī (ca.1294-1393/1877-1973),[5]
- from Shaykh Sharaf al-Dīn Zayn al-ʿĀbidīn al-Dāghistānī al-Rashādī (d. 1354/1936),
- from his maternal uncle Shaykh Abū Muḥammad al-Madanī al-Dāghistānī al-Rashādī,[6]
- from Shaykh Abū Muḥammad Abū Aḥmad Ḥājj ʿAbd al-Raḥmān Effendī al-Dāghistānī al-Thughūrī (d. 1299/1882),[7]
- from Shaykh Jamāl al-Dīn Effendī al-Ghāzī al-Ghumūqī al-Ḥusaynī (d. 1292/1875),[8]
- also (both al-Thughūrī and al-Ghumūqī) from Muḥammad Effendī b. Isḥāq al-Yarāghī al-Kawrālī (d. 1260/1844),[9]
- from Khāṣṣ Muḥammad Effendī al-Shīrwānī al-Dāghistānī (d. 1254/1838),[10]

[5] There is a variety of opinions over Mawlānā al-Shaykh ʿAbd Allāh's date of birth ranging from 1284 (in Muḥammad Darnīqa's *al-Ṭarīqa al-Naqshbandiyya*) to 1294 according to Shaykh ʿAbd Allāh's oldest student Mawlānā al-Shaykh Ḥusayn (in Muḥammad ʿAlī b. al-Shaykh Ḥusayn ʿAlī, *al-Ṭarīqat al-Naqshbandiyya al-Khālidiyya al-Dāghistāniyya*) to 1303 in Shaykh Adnan Kabbani's *al-Futūḥāt al-Ḥaqqāniyya* to 1309 in Shaykh Hisham Kabbani's *The Naqshbandi Sufi Way*.
[6] He also received the Qādirī *Ṭarīqa* from Shaykh Ibrāhīm al-Qādirī (as did Shaykh Jamāl al-Dīn) with whom he began his *sulūk* until Shaykh Ibrāhīm directed him to Shaykh al-Thughūrī cf. ʿAlī, *Ṭarīqa Naqshbandiyya* (p. 229).
[7] Cf. Shuʿayb b. Idrīs al-Bākīnī, *Hadāyā al-Zamān fī Ṭabaqāt al-Khwājagān al-Naqshbandiyya* (p. 375). He also took directly from al-Yarāghī cf. Ilyās al-Zadqārī, *Sullam al-Wuṣūl* as quoted in *Hadāyā* (p. 378 n.).
[8] Cf. al-Bākīnī, *Hadāyā* (p. 396). He received the Qādirī *Ṭarīqa* from Shaykh Ibrāhīm al-Qādirī and introduced the loud *dhikr* into the Dāghistānī branch of the Naqshbandis through that authorization cf. al-Bākinī, *Hadāyā* (p. 396); ʿAlī, *Ṭarīqa Naqshbandiyya* (p. 229).
[9] And not 1254 as erroneously mentioned in several sources. The correction is thanks to ʿAlī, *Ṭarīqa Naqshbandiyya* (p. 214). Muḥammad al-Yarāghī also took directly from Shaykh Ismāʿīl al-Shīrwānī cf. al-Bākinī, *Hadāyā* (p. 350-351).
[10] From present-day Shirvān in Azerbaijan. He died in Damascus and is buried in Mount Qāsyūn next to Mawlānā Khālid and Mawlānā Ismāʿīl al-Ānarānī who is Mawlānā Khālid's first successor who died seventeen days after the death of Mawlānā Khālid, both of them from the plague – may Allah have mercy on them and all His *shuhadā'*.

- from Shaykh Ḍiyā' al-Dīn Ismā'īl Effendī Dhabīḥ Allāh al-Qafqāzī al-Shīrwānī al-Kurdāmīrī al-Dāghistānī (d. ?)
- from Shaykh Ismā'īl al-Anārānī (d. 1242/1826 or 27),
- from Mawlānā Ḍiyā' al-Dīn Khālid *Dhūl-Janāḥayn* b. Aḥmad b. Ḥusayn al-Shahrazūrī al-Sulaymānī al-Baghdādī al-Dimashqī al-Naqshbandī al-'Uthmānī b. 'Uthmān b. 'Affān *Dhūl-Nūrayn* (1190-1242/1776-1827) with his well-known chain up to Shāh Naqshband Muḥammad b. Muḥammad al-Uwaysī al-Bukhārī who said:

Our *Ṭarīqa* is companionship and goodness is in the group.

Allah be well-pleased with them, have mercy on them, reward them, and benefit us with them, *Āmīn*!

Certain would-be Sufi critics of the Ḥaqqānī *Ṭarīqa* expressed criticism of that path for what they termed "lack of knowledge."[11] A prudent Sufi would be the last person to utter such criticism. They should be the first of people to know that knowledge by itself is not only useless but may form a mortal trap that leads to Satanic pride. Neither the proud nor the ignorant are excused; yet the loving, sincere, and repentent Sufi who suffers even severe gaps in his knowledge and *adab* is closer to Allah Most High and to knowledge of Allah than the knowledgeable Sufi who harbors a speck of pride in his heart. May Allah protect you and us!

Ibrāhīm al-Khawwāṣ said knowledge is not to know much but to obey the Sunna and practice what one knows even if a little. Imām Mālik said knowledge is not to know many things but is a light Allah casts in the heart. Imām al-Shāfi'ī said knowledge is not to merely know proofs but to know what actually benefits. And when someone said of Ma'rūf al-Karkhī, "He is not very knowledgeable," Imām Aḥmad said: "*Mah!* Allah forgive you! Is anything meant by Knowledge other than what Ma'rūf attained?"

[11] Dr. Tawfīq al-Būṭī as stated to this writer in Damascus; and others in Amman and elsewhere.

Other critics object to *Rābiṭa* or "connection," a particular characteristic of the Naqshbandī Ṭarīqa.[12] More precisely, they object to the element of *taṣawwur* or "picturing" in *Rābiṭa* which requires of the Murīd to picture the image of the Shaykh between his closed eyes and in the heart at the beginning of *dhikr* and during it. But Allah Most High said, *Truly in the Messenger of Allah you have a good example* (33:21) and He said to *enter the houses through their doors* (2:189) and so we come to the Prophet through the Ṣiddīq, and to the latter through Salmān, and to the latter through Qāsim, and to the latter through the Sayyid, etc. Since "the Ulema are the inheritors of the Prophets" it follows that the *Murshid* is our examplar of that fact. He must be one of those of whom the Prophet said: "When you see them, you remember Allah."

Others objected to what they termed "novel overemphasis on Mahdī"[13] in Grandshaykh's teachings, a charge unwittingly put to rest by the recent publication of a book in which it is claimed that Grandshaykh's teacher, Shaykh Sharaf al-Dīn, according to his daughter-in-law,

> never gave *ijāza* to any shaykh after him, seemingly because of the imminent expectation of the long-awaited Mahdi, whose name appears on a plaque on the *dergah* wall of their *silsila* [in Güneyköy near Bursa in Turkey] directly after the name of Shaykh Sharaf al-Dīn himself.[14]

Yet others question the prevalence of mercy in Grandshaykh ʿAbd Allah al-Daghistani's teachings, such as his famous statement that "whoever recites the Fātiḥa even one time in their lives will be saved in the hereafter." I asked Mawlana about the comment of one of

[12] The father of the above-named in his book *Hādhā Wālidī*. This objection was rebutted by another Kurdish scholar of Qāmushlī, Shaykh ʿAbd al-Raḥīm al-Shaykh Muḥammad Maʿṣūm al-Khaznawī in his book *al-Rābiṭa: Atharuhā fī Tazkiyat al-Nufūs wa-Aqwāl al-ʿUlamāʾ Fīhā* ([Damascus?:] al-ʿArabī lil-Ṭibāʿa wal-Nashr, 1995.
[13] Hamid Algar.
[14] Nuh Keller, *Sea Without Shore: A Manual of the Sufi Path* (Amana Publications, 2011) p. 99. Shaykh Sharaf al-Dīn did of course give *ijāza* to Shaykh ʿAbd Allāh Fā'iz, even if Shaykh Sharaf al-Dīn's relatives continue to deny it to this day. What is strange is that the reporter keeps mum on the patent assertion of such successorship and seems to dismiss even the remotest possibility that it might be valid and true, and he is or should be aware of the rule that affirmation takes precedence over denial.

those said to be of the *Abdāl* who had attended Grandshaykh's teachings in Damascus and said 30 years later: "Hope overwhelmed [fear] in him."[15] Mawlana Shaykh Nazim simply replied:

> One time our Master Yaḥyā [John the Baptist] met our Master 'Īsā [Jesus] – upon our Prophet and upon them blessings and peace! – and said to him: "It seems you feel safe of Divine punishment!" 'Īsā replied: "It seems you despair of Divine mercy!"

Some even object to the Murīd's self-effacement in the Shaykh or *fanā' fil-Shaykh*. They might say, "Your Shaykh is just a man; let your *fanā'* be in Rasūl Allāh!"[16] This is true for (i) the possessor of a direct connection (such as the speaker of the above statement) and/or (ii) the disciple of an unaccomplished guide – and (iii) by the same token one might say "let your *fanā'* be in Allah!"[17]; but it is false that the true guiding Shaykh (*murshid kāmil*) is just like any other. Rather, he is the marvelous door of opportunity and the rarest helping hand leading wayfarers to the Prophet, without which one faces an impossible task.

Shaykh Aḥmad Sirhindī (971-1034/1564-1624) said – Allah sanctify his soul:

> Know that wayfaring *(sulūk)* in this Most Distinguished Path is by connection *(rābiṭa)* and love for the Shaykh we follow. Such a Shaykh trod this Path steadfastly and was dyed *(inṣabagha)* with all kinds of perfections through the strength of Divine attraction *(jadhba)*. His gaze cures the diseases of the heart and his concentration *(tawajjuh)* lifts away spiritual defects. The owner of these perfections is the Imām of the period and the Khalīfa of that time.... Thus our connection is love and our relationship *(nisba)* is

[15] Shaykh Abū Sa'īd Quwaydir as heard from him by this writer in Sayyid Yūsuf al-Rifā'ī's *dīwān* in Damascus.
[16] Shaykh 'Abd Allāh Sirāj al-Dīn al-Ḥalabī as narrated by Shaykh Nūr al-Dīn 'Itr in his biography.
[17] As advised by Sahl al-Tustarī to a man who declared that he wanted to accompany him: "What if one of us dies? Who will the other accompany then?" The man said: "Allah." Sahl said: "So then, let us accompany Him from now." *Risāla Qushayriyya* (*Bāb al-ṣuḥba*).

mirroring and dyeing regardless of being near or far. Then the *murīd* gets dyed in this Path by the connection of love for the Shaykh, hour by hour, and gets enlightened through the reflection of his lights. In this pattern, knowledge of the process is not a precondition for the giving or receiving of benefit. The watermelon ripens through the heat of the sun hour by hour and warms with the passage of days. It matures, yet what knowledge does it have of this? Does the sun even know that it ripens and warms it?

As mentioned above, objecting to *fanā' fil-Shaykh* is also like objecting to love of the Shaykh. We aim to love our Shaykh and know that he is the worthiest object of love and respect in this world. As the poet said in *Ṭawq al-Ḥamāma*:

وَأَمْحَضْتُكَ النُّصْحَ الصَّرِيحَ وَفِي الْحَشَا لِوُدِّكَ نَقْشٌ ظَاهِرٌ وَكِتَابُ
وَمَـــا لِي غَـــيْرُ الْوُدِّ مِنْـــــكَ إِرَادَةٌ وَلَا فِي سِوَاهُ إِلَيْكَ خِطَابُ

Out of pure and sincere faithfulness to you I say:
Love of you is written inside my heart of hearts,
a patent engraving (naqsh), an ancient writ.
Nor do I have any will (irāda) except your love,
Nor can I say anything to you but that I love you.

On this topic Mawlana said:

We have been ordered to love holy people. These are the Prophets and, after Prophets, their inheritors, the *Awliyā'*. We have been ordered to believe in Prophets and belief gives us Love. Love makes people to follow that beloved one. *Ittibā'* means to love and follow while *iṭā'at* means [only] to follow. An obedient person may be obedient either by force or by love but not necessarily by love.

Now, Allah Almighty is asking for His servants to love Him. And servants can't reach directly to love of their Lord. Therefore, Allah Almighty sends, on behalf of Himself, Prophets that represent Him among His servants. And everyone that loves *Awliyā* and *Anbiyā*, through *Awliyā* are reaching love of Prophets. And through love of Prophets you are reaching to love of Allah Almighty.

Therefore, without love, a person can't be a beloved one in the Divine presence. And if you are not giving your love, how does Allah Almighty love you?

But people that are like wood – dry, dry wood – are denying love. They are such dry ones – no life! A tree, with love, is opening through spring time. But dry ones, even if seventy springs came on them, never open. Love makes nature open and give its fruits, its beauty to people. Without love, it should never be opening, never flowering, never giving its fruits. So *love* is the most important pillar for faith. **No love: no faith**. I may speak on it up to next year, but you must understand, from a drop, an ocean!

Shaykh Hisham's Life and Teachings

Shaykh Muhammad Hisham Kabbani (b. 1364/1945) was born in Beirut, Lebanon to al-Ḥājj Muḥammad Salīm al-Qabbānī al-Ḥusaynī and al-Ḥājja Yusrā ʿUthmān al-ʿAlaylī al-Ḥasaniyya. Like Mawlana Shaykh Nazim, Shaykh Hisham descends from the Prophet, upon him blessings and peace, through both the Ḥasanī and Ḥusaynī sides and from both parents. His family's prestigious lineage is well-known and well-documented in Lebanon and Syria and its genealogical tree is with the descendants of the *muqri'* and *munshid* scholar of Damascus Shaykh Muḥammad ʿArabī al-Qabbānī al-Azharī as he himself informed this writer before he passed away, Allah have mercy on him. The Qabbanīs of the Middle East are also documented in *Muʿjam al-Usar al-Dimashqiyya*, a large dictionary of the families of Damascus by the present rector of Abu al-Nur Institute there, Sayyid Muḥammad al-Ṣawwāf.

Shaykh Hisham met Mawlana Shaykh Nazim and his blessed and venerable teacher our Grandshaykh Sulṭān al-Awliyā' Mawlana Shaykh ʿAbd Allāh Fā'iz al-Dāghistānī (Allah sanctify their souls) in Damascus in 1958 when he was 13 and Mawlana Shaykh Nazim was 36. At that time Mawlana Shaykh Nazim had already been with Grandshaykh for 16 years. Shaykh Hisham as a legally-responsible Muslim (*mukallaf*) thus accompanied Grandshaykh for 15 years and has accompanied Mawlana Shaykh Nazim for over 55 years; after the passing of Mawlana Shaykh Ḥusayn ʿIfrīnī, Shaykh Hisham is therefore the oldest and highest-reaching historical link to Mawlana Shaykh Nazim and Grandshaykh Sultan al-Awliya with a *waṣiyya* from the latter on the face of the earth today. Grandshaykh's *waṣiyya* comprised the order that "Whenever people gather and Hisham is present, let him always be Imam." This was witnessed by Mawlana Shaykh Nazim, Shaykh Adnan Kabbani (Shaykh Hisham's younger brother), and others.

Thus the position of Shaykh Hisham and Shaykh Adnan in relation to Grandshaykh is that of Companion, and in relation to Mawlana Shaykh Nazim that of senior Companion—the viziers of the first hour, the *Awwalūn al-Sābiqūn*; while the position of everyone else with regard to Grandshaykh is either that of junior Companion (such as common disciples, visitors, servants and relatives) or Successor, and with regard to Mawlana Shaykh Nazim that of Companion or junior Companion; and so until the Day of Resurrection. It suffices that the Holy Prophet (upon him blessings and peace) said: "The one who does not know the right of our seniors is not one of us!"

Besides the Prophetic lineage already mentioned, Shaykh Hisham hails from one of the major Sunni families of Beirut. His maternal uncle Shaykh Aḥmad Mukhtār ʿUthmān ʿAlaylī (1316-1404/1899-1984) headed Dar al-Fatwa in Lebanon for 22 years (1962-1984) and was one of the greatest Shāfiʿī jurists of Shām, while his other maternal uncle Shaykh ʿAbd Allāh ʿAlaylī was a leading intellectual figure in the Arab world. Shaykh Hisham's father, Hajj Muhammad Salim, was one of the great landowners and most important cloth merchants in the Middle East and because his house was larger than Shaykh Mukhtār's, the latter often used it to receive prominent visitors to Dar al-Fatwa. This is where Shaykh Hisham was able to sit at the feet of important figures from Lebanon and Syria such as those already mentioned as well as the head of Rābiṭat al-ʿUlamā' Shaykh Abū al-Khayr al-Maydānī (d. 1380/1960), his successor Sayyid Makkī al-Kattānī (1312-1393/1895-1973), Shaykh Ibrāhīm al-Ghalāyīnī al-Naqshbandī (1300-1378/1883-1959) whom Grandshaykh nicknamed "the sincere" (*Ibrāhīm al-mukhliṣ*), and Shaykh Muḥammad Ṣāliḥ Farfūr (1318-1407/1900-1987).

(Most importantly Mawlana disclosed that Grandshaykh had named Shaykh Hisham "Allah's Help" (*Madad al-Ḥaqq*) and "The Devoted Proof of Allah" (*Ḥujjat Allāh al-Mukhliṣ*) among other spiritual titles. In Jumādā 1431 (May 2010) Mawlana himself named Shaykh Hisham *Quṭb al-Mutaṣarrif*, the Arch-Saint in charge of destinies.)

Shaykh Hisham then studied medicine at the university of Louvain (Belgium), after which he moved to Jeddah and worked with his brother the physician Dr. Mahmud Kabbani in administering a hospital there. At that same hospital Shaykh Hisham on occasion worked with famous visitors such as Dr. Sāmer al-Naṣṣ, Shaykh Rashīd Qabbānī the Mufti of Lebanon, and Badr al-Din Aḥmad Ḥassūn the Mufti of Syria. In Mecca he befriended Sayyid Muḥammad b. ʿAlawī al-Mālikī. Dr. Mahmud's initiative in registering the entire Kabbani clan in the US Green Card lottery led to Shaykh Hisham and his family being offered a chance to move to the US which, on the directive of Mawlana Shaykh Nazim, he decided to take, landing in New York in 1990 and moving to California.

It became apparent – and Allah knows best – that by sending Shaykh Hisham to the United States, Mawlana Shaykh Nazim was asking him to assume the spiritual leadership (*quṭbiyya*) of that region – and by extension, naturally, the rest of the world – which he did in a miraculously short time. And just as Mawlānā Khālid al-Baghdādī had done in the wake of his lightning-speed worldwide success in spreading the Sufi Path on his teacher's behalf, Shaykh Hisham was a *furqān* exposing, on the one hand, the true believers in spirituality and, on the other, those who were and remain interested in following other agendas at all levels of the *Umma*. Muslim leaders and even *ṭarīqa* affiliates took sides, ostensibly disputing his methodology but in reality only his authority: "There is no rarer asceticism than the renouncing of leadership" (Sufyān al-Thawrī). The rest is history.

By Mawlana Shaykh Nazim, Allah has made all difficult things easy. We are grateful to know him because he is our shortcut to the Light in this Religion. This *nūr* is the goal of every sane person. It is described in the magnificent verse *He gives wisdom unto whom He will, and he unto whom wisdom is given, he truly has received abundant good! But none remember except people of understanding* (2:269).

May Allah grant us this wisdom and keep us on the path He commands and loves for us. May Allah grant Mawlana Shaykh Nazim, Shaykh Hisham, and all Mawlana's followers long life and health and grant us the rank of true discipleship for the sake of the Most Honored Prophet Muḥammad—upon him blessings and peace.

The use of weak hadiths in support of excellent works

Most of the hadiths contained in this book are of the highest levels of authenticity, either sound (*ṣaḥīḥ*) or fair (*ḥasan*). Some, however, fall short of that level but they all concern the greatness of the Prophet Muḥammad, upon him and his Family and Companions blessings and peace; thus their meaning is supported through other evidence from the Qur'ān and the authentic Sunna. Furthermore, the rule adhered to by the consensus of scholars – and spelled out by Imam al-Nawawī (631-676/1234-1277) in his *Adhkār*, *Bustān*, *Irshād*, *Majmū'*, *Rawḍa*, and *Sharḥ Ṣaḥīḥ Muslim* – is that when it comes to excellent works all hadiths are accepted as long as they are not known to be forged.[18] Lastly and most remarkably, the greater scholars and the elite of the Righteous of the past and present have faithfully transmitted and preserved these hadiths for the *Umma*, leaving no choice for the humble layperson but to accept them as well. The erudite jurist Abū 'Abd Allāh Muḥammad b. Qāsim al-Anṣārī al-Raṣṣā' (d. 894/1489) said in his book *Tuḥfat al-Akhyar fī Faḍl al-Ṣalāt 'alā al-Nabī al-Mukhtār*:

> Some of those who have weak faith might look at certain hadiths and critique them and say "they did not appear in the authentic collections." This type of critique stems from bad belief and is casting aspersions on the *Sharī'a* of the Master of Prophets. The correct way is to receive whatever the scholars have received with acceptance because the uprightness of his Community prevents them from lying about our Master the Messenger, since he said: "Whoever wilfully lies about me, let him expect his seat in the Fire," and far be it from the scholars, who fear Allah, that they should wilfully lie about the Messenger of Allah.[19]

[18] See "The Use of Weak Hadiths in Islam" in our *Sunna Notes I* (p. 100-104).
[19] In al-Nabhānī, *Sa'ādat al-Dārayn* (p. 85).

قال الشيخ أبو عبد الله محمد بن قاسم الأنصاري الرَّصَّاع في تحفة الأخيار في فضل الصلاة على النبي المختار ﷺ:

رُبَّمَا نَظَرَ بَعْضُ ضُعَفَاءِ الإِيمَانِ فِي بَعْضِ هٰذِهِ الأَحَادِيثِ فَيَقْدَحُ فِيهَا وَيَقُولُ إِنَّهَا لَمْ تَرِدْ فِي الصِّحَاحِ. وَهُوَ مِنْ سُوءِ الْعَقِيدَةِ وَالْقَدْحِ فِي شَرِيعَةِ سَيِّدِ الْمُرْسَلِينَ ﷺ. بَلِ الصَّوَابُ: تَلَقِّي مَا تَلَقَّاهُ الْعُلَمَاءُ بِالْقَبُولِ لِأَنَّ عَدَالَةَ أُمَّتِهِ ﷺ تَمْنَعُهُمْ مِنَ الْكَذِبِ عَلَى السَّيِّدِ الرَّسُولِ، وَقَدْ قَالَ ﷺ: مَنْ كَذَبَ عَلَيَّ مُتَعَمِّداً فَلْيَتَبَوَّأْ مَقْعَدَهُ مِنَ النَّارِ. وَحَاشَا أَهْلِ الْعِلْمِ الْخَائِفِينَ مِنَ اللهِ أَنْ يَتَعَمَّدُوا الْكَذِبَ عَلَى رَسُولِ اللهِ ﷺ.

I

The Prophet as the First Creation

The primacy and precedence (*taqaddum*, *asbaqiyya*, *awwaliyya*) of the Prophet Muḥammad's creation is a reflection of his foremost excellence as a servant of Allah from the first moment of creation and the limbo of pre-existence to the eschaton or Resurrection.

I am the first of those who surrender (6:163)

The most literal proof to that effect is the Qur'anic expression which the Prophet is commanded to utter:

1. *And I am the first of those who surrender* (6:163). Abū al-Layth al-Samarqandī (d. 373/983) in his *Tafsīr* glossed this verse to mean "the first of Muslims on the Day of Promises."[20]

﴿ قُلْ إِنَّ صَلَاتِي وَنُسُكِي وَمَحْيَايَ وَمَمَاتِي لِلَّهِ رَبِّ الْعَالَمِينَ ﴿١٦٢﴾ لَا شَرِيكَ لَهُ وَبِذَٰلِكَ أُمِرْتُ وَأَنَا أَوَّلُ الْمُسْلِمِينَ ﴿١٦٣﴾ ﴾ قال أبو الليث السمرقندي في بحر العلوم قِيلَ: أَوَّلُ الْمُسْلِمِينَ يَوْمَ الْمِيثَاقِ.

The latter event is described in a hadith of the Prophet related from Ibn ʿAbbās:

2. Allah took the covenant from Adam's progeny in Naʿmān — meaning ʿArafa—and brought out of his loins every single offspring He created from his seed. He scattered them before Himself like ants then He addressed them, saying: *Am I not your*

[20] Abū al-Layth al-Samarqandī, *Baḥr al-ʿUlūm* (*sub* 6:163).

Lord? They said: Yes, verily! We testify. That was lest you should say on the Day of Resurrection: Truly of this we were unaware; or lest you should say: It is only that our fathers ascribed partners to Allah of old and we were their seed after them. Will You destroy us on account of that which those who follow falsehood did? (7:172-173).[21]

عَنِ ابْنِ عَبَّاسٍ رَضِيَ اللهُ عَنْهُمَا عَنِ النَّبِيِّ ﷺ قَالَ: **أَخَذَ اللهُ الْمِيثَاقَ مِنْ ظَهْرِ آدَمَ بِنَعْمَانَ يَعْنِي عَرَفَةَ فَأَخْرَجَ مِنْ صُلْبِهِ كُلَّ ذُرِّيَّةٍ ذَرَأَهَا فَنَثَرَهُمْ بَيْنَ يَدَيْهِ كَالذَّرِّ ثُمَّ كَلَّمَهُمْ قِبَلًا** ﴿أَلَسْتُ بِرَبِّكُمْ قَالُوا بَلَىٰ شَهِدْنَا أَن تَقُولُوا يَوْمَ الْقِيَامَةِ إِنَّا كُنَّا عَنْ هَٰذَا غَافِلِينَ ﴿١٧٢﴾ أَوْ تَقُولُوا إِنَّمَا أَشْرَكَ آبَاؤُنَا مِن قَبْلُ وَكُنَّا ذُرِّيَّةً مِّن بَعْدِهِمْ أَفَتُهْلِكُنَا بِمَا فَعَلَ الْمُبْطِلُونَ ﴿١٧٣﴾﴾

رواه أحمد والحاكم وغيرهما.

That the Prophet was the first one to say yes is based on the report from Abū Jaʿfar Muḥammad b. ʿAlī b. al-Ḥusayn al-Bāqir (60-118/680-736) when he was asked: "How did Muḥammad precede the Prophets when he was the last one to be sent?" He replied:

> **3.** Truly when Allāh Most High *brought forth from the Children of Adam, from their reins, their progeny, and made them testify of themselves: Am I not your Lord?* (7:172) Muḥammad was the first one to say *Yes, verily!* and that is why he was given precedence over all the Prophets even though he is the last one ever to be sent.[22]

[21] Aḥmad, *Musnad* (4:267 §2455); al-Ḥākim, *Mustadrak* (1:27-28, 2:544), and others.

[22] Narrated in the *Amālī* of Abū Sahl al-Qaṭṭān from Sahl b. Ṣāliḥ al-Hamdānī: al-Suyūṭī in the openings of both his *Khaṣā'iṣ al-Kubrā* and its epitome entitled *Unmūdhaj al-Labīb fī Khaṣā'iṣ al-Ḥabīb*; and al-Qasṭallānī, *Mawāhib* (1:30).

قال السيوطي في الخصائص الكبرى أخرج أبو سهلٍ القطان في جزء من أماليه عن سهل بن صالح الهـمْدَانِي قال سَأَلْتُ أَبَا جَعْفَرٍ مُحَمَّدَ بْنَ عَلِيٍّ: كَيْفَ صَارَ مُحَمَّدٌ ﷺ وَآلِـهِ يَتَقَـدَّمُ الأَنْبِيَاءَ وَهُوَ آخِرُ مَنْ بُعِثَ؟ قَالَ: إِنَّ اللهَ تَعَالَى لَمَّا أَخَـذَ ﴿ مِنۢ بَنِىٓ ءَادَمَ مِن ظُهُورِهِمْ ذُرِّيَّتَهُمْ وَأَشْهَدَهُمْ عَلَىٰٓ أَنفُسِهِمْ أَلَسْتُ بِرَبِّكُمْ ﴾ كَانَ مُحَمَّدٌ أَوَّلَ مَنْ قَالَ ﴿ بَلَىٰ ﴾ وَلِهَٰذَا صَارَ مُتَقَدِّماً عَلَى الْأَنْبِيَاءِ وَهُوَ آخِرُ مَنْ يُبْعَثُ.

Rūzbahān Baqlī (d. 606/1210) said in his *Tafsīr* of the verse *and I am the first of those who surrender* (6:163):

4. It is an allusion (*ishāra*) to the primacy (*taqaddum*) of his [Muḥammad's] spirit and his substance over everything else and everyone else in existence in the Divine Presence when He addressed him with the Message, Friendship, Love, and Intimacy, at which time he followed in surrender at the first of the first in pre-eternal pre-existence. What we mentioned was implied in his saying: "I was a Prophet when Adam was still between water and clay" and his saying: "The first thing Allah created is my light."[23]

قال رُوزْبَهَان البَقْلِيُّ في تفسيره الإشاري المسَمّـى (عرائس البيـان وحقائـق القـرآن): ﴿ وَأَنَا۠ أَوَّلُ ٱلْمُسْلِمِينَ ﴾ إِشَارَةٌ إِلَى تَقَدُّمِ رُوحِهِ وَجَوْهَرِهِ ﷺ عَلَى جَمِيعِ الكَوْنِ وَأَهْلِهِ فِي الْحَضْرَةِ حِينَ خَاطَبَهُ بِالرِّسَالَةِ وَالْوِلَايَةِ وَالْمَحَبَّةِ وَالْخِلَّةِ، فَانْقَادَ فِي أَوَّلِ الأَوَّلِ الأَزَلِيِّ الأَبَدِيِّ.... وَأَشَارَ إِلَى مَا ذَكَرْنَا قَوْلُهُ: كُنْتُ نَبِيّاً وَآدَمُ بَيْنَ الْمَاءِ وَالطِّينِ وَقَوْلُهُ أَوَّلُ مَا خَلَقَ اللهُ نُورِي.

[23] Rūzbahān, *ʿArāʾis al-Bayān* (*sub* 6:163).

Al-Qurṭubī (d. 671/1273) said in his *Tafsīr*:

> **5. There is no first other than Muḥammad**—upon him blessings and peace. If someone asks: Are not Ibrāhīm and the Prophets before him? We reply that he comes first before them because of his primacy in creation over them. Allah said: *And when We exacted a covenant from the Prophets, and from you (O Muḥammad) and from Nūḥ and Ibrāhīm and Mūsā and ʿĪsā the son of Maryam. We took from them a solemn covenant* (33:7). Qatāda said that the Prophet said: "I was the first of the Prophets to be created and the last one to be sent;" and this is the reason he was mentioned first in this verse before Nūḥ and others.[24]

قال القرطبي في التفسير: ﴿ وَأَنَا۠ أَوَّلُ ٱلْمُسْلِمِينَ ﴾ إِذْ لَيْسَ أَحَدُهُمْ بِأَوَّلِهِمْ إِلَّا مُحَمَّداً ﷺ فَإِنْ قِيلَ أَوَ لَيْسَ إِبْرَاهِيمُ وَالنَّبِيُّونَ قَبْلَهُ؟ قُلْنَا إِنَّهُ أَوَّلُهُمْ لِكَوْنِهِ مُقَدَّماً فِي الخَلْقِ عَلَيْهِمْ قَالَ اللهُ تَعَالَى ﴿ وَإِذْ أَخَذْنَا مِنَ ٱلنَّبِيِّـۧنَ مِيثَـٰقَهُمْ وَمِنكَ وَمِن نُّوحٍ ﴾ الآية قَالَ قَتَادَةُ: إِنَّ النَّبِيَّ ﷺ قَالَ: **كُنْتُ أَوَّلَ الأَنْبِيَاءِ فِي الخَلْقِ وَآخِرَهُمْ فِي الْبَعْثِ** فَلِذٰلِكَ وَقَعَ ذِكْرُهُ هُنَا مُقَدَّماً قَبْلَ نُوحٍ وَغَيْرِهِ.

"I was the first of the Prophets created and the last one sent"

As mentioned by al-Qurṭubī, another explicit proof is the Prophetic hadith narrated from Abū Hurayra (d. 58/678):

[24] Al-Qurṭubī, *al-Jāmiʿ li-Aḥkām al-Qurʾān* (*sub* 33:7).

6. I was the first of the Prophets to be created and the last one to be sent.²⁵ Another wording states: "I was the first of people."²⁶

عَنْ أَبِي هُرَيْرَةَ رَضِيَ اللهُ عَنْهُ مَرْفُوعاً كُنْتُ أَوَّلَ النَّبِيِّينَ فِي الْخَلْقِ وَآخِرَهُمْ فِي الْبَعْثِ. مسند الشاميين وفوائد تمام ودلائل النبوة لأبي نعيم وتفسير البغوي. ورواه الطبري في التفسير مرسلا بلفظ كُنْتُ أَوَّلَ الْأَنْبِيَاءِ. وفي رواية ابن سعد عن قتادة مرسلا كُنْتُ أَوَّلَ النَّاسِ.

His Status and Title of "Beloved of Allah"

The above hadith is confirmed by the *hadith qudsī* embedded within the long hadith of *Isrā'* and *Mi'rāj* also narrated from Abū Hurayra in which the Prophet says:

7. Praise be to Allah Who has sent me as a mercy to the worlds sent to all without exception, and as a bearer of glad tidings and a warner; Who has caused to descend upon me the Criterion in which there is a perfect exposition of all things; Who has made my Community the best Community ever brought out for the benefit of mankind; Who has made my Community the Most Virtuous one (*ummatan wasaṭan*); <u>Who has made my Community truly the First and truly the Last of all Communities</u>; Who has expanded my breast and relieved me of my burden and exalted my name; <u>Who has made me the Opener and the Sealer.</u> ...

Allah Most High then said:

8. <u>I have taken you to Myself as My Beloved and Intimate Friend (*ḥabīban wa-khalīlan*), and it is written in the Torah: *Ḥabībullāh*,</u>

---

²⁵ Tammām al-Rāzī, *Fawā'id* (4:207 §1399); al-Ṭabarānī, *Musnad al-Shāmiyyīn* (4:34-35 §2662); Abū Nuʿaym, *Dalā'il* (p. 42 §3); also narrated from Qatāda *mursal* by al-Ṭabarī in his *Tafsīr* (sub 33:7).
²⁶ Ibn Saʿd, *Ṭabaqāt* (1:124).

the Beloved of Allah. I have sent you to all people without exception, a bearer of glad tidings and a warner. I have expanded your breast for you and relieved you of your burden and exalted your name, as I am not mentioned except you are mentioned with Me. I have made your Community the Most Virtuous one, and I have made them truly the first and truly the last of all Communities. I have made public address impermissible for your Community unless they first witness that you are My Servant and Messenger. I have placed in your Community many people whose hearts are their Gospels. I have made you the first Prophet created and the last one sent, and the first one heard in My court. I have given you Seven of the Oft-Repeated which I gave to no other Prophet before you. I have given you al-Kawthar. I have given you eight lots: Islam, Emigration, Jihad, Charity, Prayer, Fasting Ramaḍān, Ordering Good, and Forbidding Evil; and I have made you the Opener and the Sealer."[27]

عَنْ أَبِي هُرَيرَةَ رَضِيَ اللهُ عَنْهُ مَرْفُوعاً في حديث المعراج الحَمْدُ لله الَّذِي أَرْسَلَنِي رَحْمَةً لِلْعَالَمِينَ، وَكَافَّةً لِلنَّاسِ بَشِيراً وَنَذِيراً، وَأَنْزَلَ عَلَيَّ الْفُرْقَانَ فِيهِ تِبْيَانُ كُلِّ شَيْءٍ، وَجَعَلَ أُمَّتِي خَيْرَ أُمَّةٍ أُخْرِجَتْ لِلنَّاسِ، وَجَعَلَ أُمَّتِي وَسَطاً، وَجَعَلَ أُمَّتِي هُمُ الْأَوَّلُونَ وَهُمُ الْآخِرُونَ، وَشَرَحَ لِي صَدْرِي، وَوَضَعَ عَنِّي وِزْرِي وَرَفَعَ لِي ذِكْرِي، وَجَعَلَنِي فَاتِحاً خَاتِماً ... فَقَالَ لَهُ رَبُّهُ: قَدِ اتَّخَذْتُكَ حَبِيباً وَخَلِيلاً وَهُوَ مَكْتُوبٌ فِي التَّوْرَاةِ: حَبِيبُ اللهِ؛ وَأَرْسَلْتُكَ إِلَى النَّاسِ كَافَّةً بَشِيراً وَنَذِيراً، وَشَرَحْتُ لَكَ صَدْرَكَ، وَوَضَعْتُ عَنْكَ وِزْرَكَ، وَرَفَعْتُ لَكَ ذِكْرَكَ، فَلَا أُذْكَرُ إِلَّا ذُكِرْتَ مَعِي، وَجَعَلْتُ أُمَّتَكَ أُمَّةً وَسَطاً، وَجَعَلْتُ أُمَّتَكَ هُمُ الْأَوَّلُونَ وَالْآخِرُونَ، وَجَعَلْتُ أُمَّتَكَ لَا تَجُوزُ لَهُمْ خُطْبَةٌ، حَتَّى

[27] al-Ṭabarī, *Tafsīr* (14:424-435, *sub* 17:1).

يَشْهَدُوا أَنَّكَ عَبْدِي وَرَسُولِي؛ وَجَعَلْتُ مِنْ أُمَّتِكَ أَقْوَاماً قُلُوبُهُمْ أَنَاجِيلُهُمْ، وَجَعَلْتُكَ أَوَّلَ النَّبِيِّينَ خَلْقاً وَآخِرَهُمْ بَعْثاً، وَأَوَّلَهُمْ يُقْضَى لَهُ، وَأَعْطَيْتُكَ سَبْعاً مِنَ الْمَثَانِي، لَمْ يُعْطَهَا نَبِيٌّ قَبْلُكَ، وَأَعْطَيْتُكَ الْكَوْثَرَ، وَأَعْطَيْتُكَ ثَمَانِيَةَ أَسْهُمٍ: الإِسْلَامُ وَالهِجْرَةُ، وَالجِهَادُ، وَالصَّدَقَةُ، وَالصَّلَاةُ، وَصَوْمُ رَمَضَانَ، وَالْأَمْرُ بِالْمَعْرُوفِ، وَالنَّهْيُ عَنِ الْمُنْكَرِ، وَجَعَلْتُكَ فَاتِحاً وَخَاتِماً رواه الطبري.

The Prophet confirmed his title and status of Beloved of Allah in a famous hadith related by Ibn ʿAbbās:

9. Some of the Companions of the Prophet sat waiting for him. He came out until, as he neared them, he heard their discussion. One of them said: "It is astonishing that Allah took one of His creatures as an Intimate Friend: He took Ibrāhīm as His Intimate Friend." Another said: "What is more astonishing than speaking with Mūsā? He spoke with him without intermediary!" Another said: "What about ʿĪsā? The Word of Allah and His Spirit!" Another said: "And Adam: Allah chose him." The Prophet came out and greeted them then he said: "I have heard your discussion and your astonishment. Truly Ibrāhīm is the Intimate Friend of Allah and that is true; Mūsā is the Converser with Allah and that is true; ʿĪsā is the Spirit from Allah and His Word, and that is true; and Adam was chosen by Allah and that is true. Behold, I am the Beloved of Allah and I say this without pride; and I shall hold the Flag of Divine Glory on the Day of Resurrection."[28]

Another version adds:

10. Under it will be Adam and all those after him; and I am the first Intercessor and the first to be given intercession on the Day of Resurrection, and I say this without pride; and I am the first

[28] al-Tirmidhī, *Sunan* (*al-Manāqib ʿan Rasūl Allāh*). Some of its parts are also narrated from other Companions as cited further down.

one to stir the latch of the gate of Paradise, and I say this without pride. Then Allah shall open it and make me enter together with the poor among the Believers, and I say this without pride. And I am the most honored of the First and the Last in the Divine Presence, and I say this without pride.[29]

Another Prophetic report narrated from ʿUmar states:

11. Adam is the Elect of Allah, Ibrāhīm is the Intimate Friend of Allah, Mūsā is the Converser with Allah, ʿĪsā is the Spirit from Allah, and I am the Beloved of Allah.[30]

عَنِ ابْنِ عَبَّاسٍ رَضِيَ اللهُ عَنْهُمَا قَالَ جَلَسَ نَاسٌ مِنْ أَصْحَابِ رَسُولِ اللهِ ﷺ يَنْتَظِرُونَهُ فَخَرَجَ حَتَّى إِذَا دَنَا مِنْهُمْ سَمِعَهُمْ يَتَذَاكَرُونَ فَسَمِعَ حَدِيثَهُمْ فقالَ بَعْضُهُمْ عَجَباً إِنَّ اللهَ عَزَّ وَجَلَّ اتَّخَذَ مِنْ خَلْقِهِ خَلِيلاً إِتَّخَذَ مِنْ إِبْرَاهِيمَ خَلِيلاً. وَقَالَ آخَرُ: مَاذَا بِأَعْجَبَ مِنْ كَلاَمِ مُوسَى كَلَّمَهُ تَكْلِيماً. وَقَالَ آخَرُ: فَعِيسَى كَلِمَةُ اللهِ وَرُوحُهُ. وَقَالَ آخَرُ: آدَمُ اصْطَفَاهُ اللهُ. فَخَرَجَ عَلَيْهِمْ فَسَلَّمَ وَقَالَ قَدْ سَمِعْتُ كَلاَمَكُمْ وَعَجَبَكُمْ. إِنَّ إِبْرَاهِيمَ خَلِيلُ اللهِ وَهُوَ كَذَٰلِكَ، وَمُوسَى نَجِيُّ اللهِ وَهُوَ كَذَٰلِكَ، وَعِيسَى رُوحُ اللهِ وَكَلِمَتُهُ وَهُوَ كَذَٰلِكَ، وَآدَمُ اصْطَفَاهُ اللهُ وَهُوَ كَذَٰلِكَ، أَلاَ وَأَنَا حَبِيبُ اللهِ وَلاَ فَخْرَ، وَأَنَا حَامِلُ لِوَاءِ الحَمْدِ يَوْمَ القِيَامَةِ رواه الترمذي والدارمي والكلاباذي في بحر الفوائد وزاد الأخيران تَحْتَهُ آدَمُ فَمَنْ دُونَهُ وَلاَ فَخْرَ وَأَنَا أَوَّلُ شَافِعٍ وَأَوَّلُ مُشَفَّعٍ يَوْمَ الْقِيَامَةِ

[29] al-Dārimī, *Sunan* (*Muqaddima, bāb mā uʿṭiya al-Nabī min al-faḍl*) and al-Kalābādhī, *Baḥr al-Fawāʾid* (1:440-441 §460).
[30] Ibn Abī Shayba, *Muṣannaf* (16:512-513 §32462) and Ibn Rāhūyah, *Musnad* cf. al-Būṣīrī, *Itḥāf* (7:347-348 §7028) and Ibn Ḥajar, *Maṭālib* (17:111-112 §4179).

وَلاَ فَخْرَ وَأَنَا أَوَّلُ مَنْ يُحَرِّكُ غَلَقَ الجَنَّةِ وَلاَ فَخْرَ فَيَفْتَحُ اللهُ فَيُدْخِلُنِيهَا وَمَعِي فُقَرَاءُ الْمُؤْمِنِينَ وَلاَ فَخْرَ وَأَنَا أَكْرَمُ الأَوَّلِينَ وَالآخِرِينَ عَلَى اللهِ وَلاَ فَخْرَ وجاء في الباب عَنْ عُمَرَ بْنِ الخَطَّابِ رَضِيَ اللهُ عَنْهُ مَرْفُوعاً: آدَمُ صَفِيُّ اللهِ وَإِبْرَاهِيمُ خَلِيلُ اللهِ وَمُوسَى نَجِيُّ اللهِ وَعِيسَى رُوحُ اللهِ وَأَنَا حَبِيبُ اللهِ مصنف ابن أبي شيبة ومسند ابن راهويه.

12. The major imam of the Successors Masrūq (d. 63/683) would say, whenever narrating from ʿĀ'isha: "The truthful woman, daughter of the truthful and trusting Saint and the beloved of the Beloved of Allāh, narrated to me…"[31]

قَالَ الشَّعْبِيُّ كَانَ مَسْرُوقٌ إِذَا حَدَّثَ عَنْ عَائِشَةَ رَضِيَ اللهُ عَنْهَا قَالَ: حَدَّثَتْنِي الصَّادِقَةُ ابْنَةُ الصِّدِّيقِ حَبِيبَةُ حَبِيبِ اللهِ. ذكره الحافظ في الإصابة.

"The sequence [of Prophets] began with me ahead of them"

The Prophet himself used the hadith "I was the first of the Prophets to be created" as an exegetical commentary for the verse *And when We exacted a covenant from the Prophets, and from you (O Muḥammad) and from Nūḥ and Ibrāhīm and Mūsā and ʿĪsā the son of Maryam. We took from them a solemn covenant* (33:7) which he cited then said:

> **13.** I was the first of the Prophets in creation and the last of them to be sent: the sequence began with me ahead of them.[32]

[31] In Ibn Ḥajar, *Iṣāba* (*sub* ʿĀ'isha).
[32] Ibn Abī Ḥātim, *Tafsīr* (10:3116, *sub* 33:7)

﴿ وَإِذْ أَخَذْنَا مِنَ ٱلنَّبِيِّـۧنَ مِيثَـٰقَهُمْ وَمِنكَ وَمِن نُّوحٍ وَإِبْرَٰهِيمَ وَمُوسَىٰ وَعِيسَى ٱبْنِ مَرْيَمَ ۖ وَأَخَذْنَا مِنْهُم مِّيثَـٰقًا غَلِيظًا ﴿٧﴾ ﴾ قَالَ النَّبِيُّ ﷺ كُنْتُ أَوَّلَ النَّاسِ فِي الخَلْقِ وَآخِرَهُمْ فِي الْبَعْثِ فَبُدِئَ بِي قَبْلَهُمْ. تفسير ابن أبي حاتم.

"I was a Prophet when Adam was still between spirit and body"

Another famous hadith expresses the Prophet's primacy in creation in explicit terms:

14. A man asked: "Messenger of Allāh, when did you become a Prophet?" People objected to the question but the Messenger of Allāh said: "Let him ask. I was a Prophet when Adam was still between spirit and body."[33] In another version: "when Adam was still between spirit and body, at which time the Covenant was taken from me."[34] The questioner was Maysarat al-Fajr.[35] The same is also related from Abū Hurayra, Ibn ʿAbbās, and Abū al-Jadʿā'.[36]

قَالَ رَجُلٌ يَا رَسُولَ اللهِ مَتَى كُنْتَ نَبِيّاً فَقَالَ النَّاسُ مَهْ مَهْ فَقَالَ رَسُولُ اللهِ ﷺ دَعُوهُ كُنْتُ نَبِيّاً وَآدَمُ بَيْنَ الرُّوحِ وَالجَسَدِ رواه ابن سعد. وعنده أيضاً رواية قَالَ وَآدَمُ بَيْنَ الرُّوحِ وَالجَسَدِ حِينَ أُخِذَ مِنِّي المِيثَاقُ. وهو ثابت عن جماعة من الصحابة رواه أحمد وغيره عن ميسرة الفجر والترمذي وقال حسن صحيح غريب والطحاوي عن أبي هريرة والطبراني عن ابن عباس وابن سعد عن أبي الجعداء.

[33] Ibn Saʿd, *Ṭabaqāt* (1:123).
[34] *Ibid.*
[35] As narrated by Aḥmad in his *Musnad* (34:202 §20596), al-Ḥākim, *Mustadrak* (2:608-609), al-Ṭabārānī, *al-Muʿjam al-Kabīr* (20:353 §833-834), and others, and its chain was declared strong by Ibn Ḥajar in the *Iṣāba*, chapter on Maysara.
[36] In al-Tirmidhī, *Sunan*, (*Manāqib, faḍl al-Nabī, ḥasan ṣaḥīḥ gharīb*) and al-Ṭaḥāwī, *Sharḥ Mushkil al-Āthār* (15:231 §5976) from Abū Hurayra; al-Ṭabarānī, *al-Muʿjam al-Awsaṭ* (4:272 §4175) and *al-Muʿjam al-Kabīr* (12:92 §12571) from Ibn ʿAbbās; and Ibn Saʿd, *Ṭabaqāt* (1:123) from Abū al-Jadʿā'.

He received Qur'ān and all his knowledge at that time (al-Kattānī)

The above hadith defines both our understanding of the temporal parameters of the Prophet's status and knowledge, and of the extent of that knowledge. The Imam of the Kattānī Path Abū al-Fayḍ Muḥammad b. ʿAbd al-Kabīr al-Kattānī (1290-1327/1873-1909) inferred from it that

> **15.** the Prophet was given, already at that time, all his knowledge of Allah, of His Names, Attributes and Acts, of His Books, of His Prophets and Messengers and their Communities and laws, the Qur'ān, His Angels, and about his own unique levels and stations in His Presence, all of which without the intermediary of Jibrīl. … Neither in the Book nor in the Sunna was it ever said that after knowing all that, he then lost that knowledge. How then can it be claimed that he was given Prophethood only after the age of forty? Then how was he before?[37]

قال الشيخ أبو الفيض محمد بن عبد الكبير الكتاني قدس الله سرّه فيما رواه عنه العلامة عبد السلام بن المعطي السرغيني في كتابه (اللؤلؤة الفَاشِيَة في الرحلة الحجازية) في شرح حديث **كُنْتُ نَبِيّاً وَآدَمُ بَيْنَ الرُّوحِ وَالجَسَدِ** مختصراً:

> النَّبِيُّ ﷺ مُخْبَرٌ مِنْ قِبَلِ الحَقِّ سُبْحَانَهُ فِي ذَٰلِكَ الْوَقْتِ، وَلَا آدَمَ وَلَا سَمَاءَ، وَلَا أَرْضَ وَلَا زَمَانَ وَلَا مَكَانَ، وَالْمُخْبَرُ بِهِ أَضْرُبٌ: أَمَّا الجَنَابُ الْأَقْدَسُ؛ فَقَدْ زُجَّ بِهِ ﷺ فِي بِحَارِ المَعَارِفِ الْإِلٰهِيَّةِ مُحَصِّلاً مِنْ ذَٰلِكَ مَا لَا يَعْلَمُ حَقِيقَتَهُ إِلَّا اللهُ. وَأَمَّا الْأَسْمَاءُ؛ فَقَدْ عَلِمَ كُلَّ إِسْمٍ وَمُقْتَضَاهُ، وَمَفَادَهُ وَمُؤَدَّاهُ. وَأَمَّا الصِّفَاتُ؛ فَقَدْ عَلِمَهَا ثُمَّ تَعَلَّقَ بِهَا، ثُمَّ تَخَلَّقَ بِمَا يَصْلُحُ لِلتَّخَلُّقِ مِنْهَا، ثُمَّ

[37] In al-ʿImrānī, *al-Lu'lu'at al-Fāshiya.* alkettanien.ahlamontada.com/t104-topic. The question shows that what the Prophet received in his maturity was Messengership, while he already had Prophethood from times immemorial, and Allah knows best.

تحَقَّق بِهَا. وَأَمَّا الْأَفْعَالُ فَقَدْ عَلِمَ هُنَاكَ كَيْفَ انْبَجَسَتْ مِنْ حَضْرَةِ الرُّبُوبِيَّةِ، وَأَنَّ الْفَاعِلَ الْحَقِيقِيَّ هُوَ اللهُ تَعَالَى، وَأَنْ لَا فَاعِلَ سِوَاهُ، وَعَلِمَ إِذْ ذَاكَ مِنَ الشُّؤُونِ الْإِلٰهِيَّةِ مَا لَا يَصِلُ إِلَى حِمَاهُ نَبِيٌّ وَلَا رَسُولٌ وَلَا مَلَكٌ. وَأَمَّا مَا يَتَعَلَّقُ بِهِ ﷺ؛ فَقَدْ عَلِمَ هُنَاكَ مَا تُوِّجَ بِهِ، وَتُقُلِّدَ إِذْ ذَاكَ مِنْ حِلَلِ الْإِصْطِفَاءِ وَالتَّخصِيصِ الْإِلٰهِيِّ مَا أُفْرِغَ عَلَيْهِ، وقَرَّتْ عَيْنُهُ إِذْ ذَاكَ بِمَا حُبِيَ بِهِ، وَعَلِمَ كَمِّيَّةَ ذٰلِكَ الْبَحْرِ الطَّامِّ، وَكَيْفِيَّةَ الرُّكُوبِ فِيهِ لِلْخَاصِّ وَالْعَامِّ. وَأَمَّا مَا يَرْجِعُ لِلْأَنْبِيَاءِ وَالْمُرْسَلِينَ: فَقَدْ عَلِمَ طَبَقَاتِهِمْ وَدَرَجَاتِهِمْ وَعَدَدَهُمْ وَتَفَاوُتَهُمْ فِي الْفَضْلِ، وَأَعْدَادَهُمْ وَأَسْمَاءَهُمْ وَأَوْقَاتَهُمْ، وَالْمُتَّبَعَ مِنْهُمْ وَمَنْ لَا، وَعَدَدَ التَّابِعِينَ. وَأَمَّا مَا يَرْجِعُ إِلَى أُمَمِهِمْ؛ فَقَدْ عَلِمَ هُنَاكَ أُمَّةَ كُلِّ رَسُولٍ وَعَدَدَهَا وَمُدَّتَهَا وَالْمُتَّبِعَ مِنَ الْمُعْتَرِضِ وَمَا يَقَعُ لِلرُّسُلِ مَعَهُمْ. وَأَمَّا مَا يَرْجِعُ إِلَى الْكُتُبِ السَّمَاوِيَّةِ؛ فَقَدْ عَلِمَ هُنَاكَ عَدَدَهَا وَأَسْمَاءَهَا وَأَصْحَابَهَا، وَالْأَسْرَارَ الَّتِي انْطَوَتْ عَلَيْهَا. وَأَمَّا مَا يَتَعَلَّقُ بِالْمَلَائِكَةِ؛ فَقَدْ عَلِمَ هُنَاكَ أَصْنَافَهُمْ وَأَعْدَادَهُمْ وَمَقَامَاتِهِمْ وَعِبَادَتَهُمْ وَتَفَاوُتَهُمْ فِي الْمَرَاتِبِ. وَأَمَّا مَا يَرْجِعُ إِلَى الشَّرَائِعِ؛ فَقَدْ عَلِمَ هُنَاكَ الشَّرَائِعَ عَلَى تَفْصِيلِهَا، وَعَلِمَ أَسْرَارَ كُلِّ شَرِيعَةٍ وَأَحْكَامَهَا وَأَهْلَهَا الْعَامِلِينَ بِهَا. وَأَمَّا مَا يَرْجِعُ إِلَى الْكِتَابِ الْعَزِيزِ؛ فَقَدْ تَلَقَّاهُ هُنَاكَ مِنْ لَدُنْ حَكِيمٍ عَلِيمٍ، وَعَلِمَ أَمْرَهُ وَنَهْيَهُ، وَخَبَرَهُ وَوَعْدَهُ وَوَعِيدَهُ، وَنَاسِخَهُ وَمَنْسُوخَهُ. وَذٰلِكَ كُلُّهُ مِنْ غَيْرِ وَاسِطَةِ جِبْرِيلَ وَلَا غَيْرِهِ؛ لِأَنَّكَ قَدْ عَلِمْتَ أَنَّ هٰذَا كُلَّهُ أُخبِرَ بِهِ ﷺ فِي عَالَمِ الْبُطُونِ، وَهُوَ مَعْنَى **كَوْنِهِ نَبِيّاً وَآدَمُ**

بَيْنَ الرُّوحِ وَالجَسَدِ. وَأَمَّا أَنْ يَكُونَ النَّبِيءُ مُشْتَقّاً مِنَ النَبْوَةِ - وَهِيَ الرِّفْعَةُ - وَهِيَ لَا تَحْصُلُ إِلَّا بِحِيَازَتِهِ ﷺ المَعَانِي السَّابِقَةَ. فَهٰذَا المَعْنَى الثَّانِي لَازِمٌ، وَالْأَوَّلُ مَلْزُومٌ. وَمَنْ عَلِمَ هٰذَا وَأَحَاطَ بِهِ خُبْراً، تَبَيَّنَ لَهُ مَا فِي شُيُوخِيَّةِ جِبْرِيلَ لَهُ ﷺ عِنْدَ الْقَائِلِ بِهَا؛ وَكَيْفَ يَكُونُ شَيْخَهُ وَهُوَ خَادِمُهُ؟ وَحَيْثُ أُفْرِغَتْ عَلَيْهِ ﷺ حُلَلُ الْكَمَالَاتِ إِذْ ذَاكَ، وَلَا زَمَانَ وَلَا مَكَانَ، وَلَا مَخْلُوق هُنَاكَ، فَلَمْ يَرِدْ فِي الْكِتَابِ وَلَا فِي السُّنَّةِ المُطَهَّرَةِ أَنَّهُ انْسَلَخَ مِنْ ذٰلِكَ؛ بَلِ الْأَصْلُ هُوَ الْإِسْتِصْحَابُ وَهُوَ أَقْوَى الْأَدِلَّةِ عِنْدَ الْأُصُولِيِّينَ. وَعَلَيْهِ فَكَيْفَ يَصِحُّ الْقَوْلُ بِأَنَّهُ إِنَّمَا نُبِّئَ عَلَى رَأْسِ الْأَرْبَعِينَ سَنَةً؟ يُقَالُ عَلَيْهِ: وَكَيْفَ كَانَ قَبْلُ؟ سِيَّمَا وَقَدْ ضَرَبَتْ طُبُولُ الْكَائِنَاتِ بِهِ قَبْلَ وُجُودِهِ، وَأَوْصَتِ الْأَنْبِيَاءُ أُمَمَهَا بِنَصْرِهِ وَاتِّبَاعِهِ إِنْ أَدْرَكُوهُ.

"This is your son Aḥmad; he is the First and the Last"

Another *ḥadīth qudsī* – narrated from Abū Hurayra with a fair chain – mentions Adam's sighting of the light of the Prophet:

> **16.** When Allah Almighty created Adam He showed Adam the excellence of his offspring. Adam beheld their respective ranks and precedence. Then he saw me, a dazzling light beneath all of them. He said: "O my Lord, who is this?" Allah replied: "This is your son Aḥmad; he is the First and the Last and he is the first intercessor."[38]

[38] al-Sarrāj al-Thaqafī, *Ḥadīth al-Sarrāj* (3:236 §2628) and through him al-Bayhaqī, *Dalā'il* (5:483).

عَنْ أَبِي هُرَيرَةَ رَضِيَ اللهُ عَنْهُ مَرْفُوعًا بِسَنَدٍ حَسَنٍ لَمَّا خَلَقَ اللهُ عَزَّ وَجَلَّ آدَمَ خَيَّرَ لِآدَمَ بَنِيهِ فَجَعَلَ يَرَى فَضَائِلَ بَعْضِهِمْ عَلَى بَعْضٍ فَرَآنِي نُورًا سَاطِعًا فِي أَسْفَلِهِمْ فَقَالَ يَا رَبِّ مَنْ هٰذَا قَالَ هٰذَا إِبْنُكَ أَحْمَدُ ﷺ هُوَ الأَوَّلُ وَالْآخِرُ وَهُوَ أَوَّلُ شَافِعٍ. رواه الحافظ محمد بن إسحاق السَّرَّاج الثَّقَفِي في جزء حديث السَّرَّاج ومن طريقه البيهقي في دلائل النبوّة

What is even more remarkable is that Allah Most High instructed the three most major Prophets after the Prophet Muḥammad to greet him by those very titles during the Night Journey and Heavenly Ascent as narrated from Anas within his long hadith:

17. As he went on he was met by some of Allah's creatures who said "Peace be upon you, O First One! (*yā awwal*). Peace be upon you, O Last One! (*yā ākhir*). Peace be upon you, O Gatherer! (*yā ḥāshir*)." Jibrīl said to him: "Return their greeting," and he did. Then he saw them another time and they said the same thing. Then he saw them a third time and again they greeted him. Then he reached Bayt al-Maqdis. Jibrīl said: "Those that greeted you were Ibrāhīm, Mūsā, and 'Īsā."[39]

عَنْ أَنَسٍ رَضِيَ اللهُ عَنْهُ مَرْفُوعًا في حديث الإسراء والمعراج: فَلَقِيَهُ خَلْقٌ مِنَ الخَلْقِ، فَقَالُوا: السَّلَامُ عَلَيْكَ يَا أَوَّلُ، السَّلَامُ عَلَيْكَ يَا آخِرُ، السَّلَامُ عَلَيْكَ يَا حَاشِرُ، فَقَالَ لَهُ جِبْرِيلُ: أُرْدُدِ السَّلَامَ يَا مُحَمَّدُ، فَرَدَّ السَّلَامَ، ثُمَّ لَقِيَهُ الثَّانِيَةَ، فَقَالَ لَهُ مِثْلَ مَقَالَتِهِ الْأُولَى، ثُمَّ الثَّالِثَةَ كَذٰلِكَ حَتَّى انْتَهَى إِلَى بَيْتِ

[39] al-Bayhaqī, *Dalā'il* (2:362) and Ibn 'Asākir, *Tārīkh* (3:502). al-Ḍiyā' al-Maqdisī included it in *al-Aḥādīth al-Mukhtāra* (6:258-259 §2277), a compilation of good narrations.

الْمَقْدِسِ، فَقَالَ لَهُ جِبْرِيلُ: أَمَّا الَّذِينَ سَلَّمُوا عَلَيْكَ: فَإِبْرَاهِيمُ وَمُوسَى وَعِيسَى عَلَيْهِمُ السَّلَامُ. رواه البيهقي في دلائل النبوة وأورده الضياء المَقْدِسي في المختارة فهو عنده جيّد مقبول ولو كان معلولاً.

"Adam and everyone after him are under my flag"

The Prophet also affirmed his primacy on the Day of Resurrection in the hadith of the "flag of glory" (*liwā' al-ḥamd*) narrated from Abū Sa'īd al-Khudrī (d. 74/693) and Ibn 'Abbās (3BH-68/619-688):

18. I am the lord of the children of Adam on the Day of Resurrection, and this is no vain boast. Adam and everyone after him are under my flag at that time.[40]

أَنَا سَيِّدُ وَلَدِ آدَمَ يَوْمَ الْقِيَامَةِ وَلَا فَخْرَ وَأَنَا أَوَّلُ مَنْ تَنْشَقُّ عَنْهُ الْأَرْضُ وَلَا فَخْرَ وَبِيَدِي لِوَاءُ الْحَمْدِ وَلَا فَخْرَ آدَمُ فَمَنْ دُونَهُ تَحْتَ لِوَائِي وَلَا فَخْرَ رواه أحمد عن ابن عباس وهذا لفظه والترمذي عن أبي سعيد وقال حديث حسن صحيح.

That flag refers to the Prophet's intercession for all nations, at which time all the Prophets and their communities will approach him for help (*istighātha*) as established in other well-known hadiths. These two extremes of primacy—creation and the eschaton—are summed up in another hadith from Jābir:

19. I am the leader (*qā'id*) of the Messengers and this is no vain boast; I am the seal of the Prophets and this is no vain boast; I am the first intercessor and the first to be granted intercession and this

[40] al-Tirmidhī, *Sunan* (*Tafsīr, Sūrat Banī Isrā'īl, ḥasan ṣaḥīḥ*) from Abū Sa'īd and Aḥmad, *Musnad* (4:330 §2546, 4:427 §2692) from Ibn 'Abbās.

is no vain boast.[41] Another version has "I am the leader of Muslims."[42]

وَعَنْ جَابِرٍ رَضِيَ اللهُ عَنْهُ مَرْفُوعاً أَنَا قَائِدُ الْمُرْسَلِينَ وَلاَ فَخْرَ وَأَنَا خَاتَمُ النَّبِيِّينَ وَلاَ فَخْرَ وَأَنَا أَوَّلُ شَافِعٍ وَأَوَّلُ مُشَفَّعٍ وَلاَ فَخْرَ رواه الدارمي والطبراني

وفي رواية أَنَا قَائِدُ الْمُسْلِمِينَ رواه البخاري في التاريخ الكبير

"Allah addressed him with the Qur'ān directly" (al-Sulamī)

Another Qur'anic passage that implicitly expresses the Prophetic primacy is the beginning of Sūrat al-Raḥmān: *The All-Beneficent taught the Qur'ān. He created Man. He taught him speech* (55:1-4).

20. The commentaries concur with Ibn ʿAbbās and Saʿīd b. Jubayr (46-95/666-ca.714) that the implied second direct object of *taught the Qur'ān* in the above verse is the Prophet Muḥammad.[43]

Sufi exegeses mention that among the immense merits entailed by this distinction is the fact that

> **21.** it makes it clear that Allah Most High Himself addressed him with the Qur'ān directly… and He taught Adam the Names and then presented them to the angels, but He taught Muḥammad the Qur'ān and then presented it to Himself, saying: "O Muḥammad, what does the Highest Assembly fight about?"[44]

[41] al-Dārimī, *Sunan* (*Muqaddima, Bāb mā uʿṭiya al-Nabiyyu min al-faḍl*); al-Ṭabarānī, *al-Muʿjam al-Awsaṭ*, (1:61 §170).
[42] al-Bukhārī, *al-Tārīkh al-Kabīr* (*sub* Ṣāliḥ b. ʿAṭā' b. Khabbāb).
[43] Cf. *Tafsīr*s of al-Māwardī, *Nukat*; al-Samarqandī, *Baḥr*; al-Māturīdī, *Ta'wīlāt*; Makkī, *Nihāya*; al-Wāḥidī, *Wajīz*; al-Baghawī, *Maʿālim*; Ibn al-Jawzī, *Zād*; Ibn ʿAbd al-Salām; al-Qurṭubī, *Jāmiʿ*; al-Shawkānī, *Fatḥ*; Ibn ʿĀshūr, *Taḥrīr* (all *sub* 55:1); al-Rāzī, *Mafātīḥ* (*sub* 2:253) and Ibn ʿĀdil, *Lubāb* (4:302).
[44] Cf. al-Sulamī, *Ḥaqā'iq*; al-Qushayrī, *Laṭā'if*; Rūzbahān, *ʿArā'is* (all *sub* 55:1).

﴿ ٱلرَّحْمَـٰنُ ۝١ عَلَّمَ ٱلْقُرْءَانَ ۝٢ ﴾ أي علّم محمّداً القرآن وهو قول الماوردي والماتريدي والسمرقندي ومكي والواحدي والبغوي وابن الجوزي وابن عبد السلام والقرطبي وابن عادل والشوكاني وابن عاشور في تفاسيرهم ويروى عن ابن عباس وسعيد بن جبير. وفي حقائق التفسير للسلمي: عَلَّمَ آدَمَ الْأَسْمَاءَ كُلَّهَا ثُمَّ عَرَضَهُمْ عَلَى المَلَائِكَةِ وَعَلَّمَ مُحَمَّداً الْقُرْآنَ وَعَرَضَهُ عَلَى نَفْسِهِ فَقَالَ فِيمَا يَخْتَصِمُ المَلَأُ الأَعْلَى؟ يعني الملائكة في قوله تعالى ﴿ مَا كَانَ لِيَ مِنْ عِلْمٍ بِٱلْمَلَإِ ٱلْأَعْلَىٰٓ إِذْ يَخْتَصِمُونَ ۝٦٩ ﴾ ص وحديث الترمذي الآتي ذكره. ومثله في تفسير القشيري وروزبهان البقلي.

"Everything became manifest to me and I knew"

The latter phrase is a reference to the verse *I had no knowledge of the Highest Assembly as they disputed* (38:69) which the Prophet glossed in a momentous hadith narrated from Muʿādh:

22. The Prophet was kept away from us one morning at the time of the dawn prayer until we almost saw the sun rise. Then he came out hastily, the last call to prayer was raised and he led us in prayer which he made brief. After giving salam he called out with a loud voice for us to stay where we were. Then he came closer to us and said: "I will tell you what delayed me from coming out to you this morning. I woke up in the night, washed and prayed whatever was ordained for me, then I felt drowsy in my prayer until I dozed off. Lo and behold! I found myself in front of my Lord in the best form. He said: 'O Muḥammad!' I replied: 'At Your service, O my Lord!' He said: 'Over what do the Higher

Assembly (*al-mala' al-a'lā*)[45] compete?' I said: 'I do not know, O my Lord.' This went on three times. Then I saw Him put His palm between my shoulders, and I felt the coolness of His fingers in my innermost, whereupon everything became manifest to me and I knew [*var.* "then everything in heaven and earth became manifest to me and I knew it"[46]]. He said: 'O Muḥammad!' I replied: 'At Your service O my Lord!' He said 'Over what do the Higher Assembly compete? I said: 'Over expiations.' He said: 'What are they?' I said: 'Walking on foot to congregational prayers; sitting in mosques after prayers; and performing a full ablution even in uncomfortable circumstances.' 'And over what else?' I said: 'Feeding people, speaking gently, and praying at night while people are asleep.' He said: 'Ask!' I said: 'O Allah, I ask you the doing of good deeds, the abandonment of reprehensible deeds, love of the poor, and that You forgive me and grant me mercy, and when You intend strife and punishment for a people, cause me to die without strife and punishment, and I ask you Your love, and the love of those who love You, and the love of a deed that brings me closer to Your love.' This is truth, so study it and learn it!"[47]

عَنْ مُعَاذِ بْنِ جَبَلٍ رَضِيَ اللهُ عَنْهُ قَالَ اِحْتبَسَ عَنَّا رَسُولُ اللهِ ﷺ ذَاتَ غَدَاةٍ مِنْ صَلاَةِ الصُّبْحِ حَتَّى كِدْنَا نَتَرَاءَى عَيْنَ الشَّمْسِ فَخَرَجَ سَرِيعاً فَثُوِّبَ بِالصَّلاَةِ فَصَلَّى رَسُولُ اللهِ ﷺ وَتَجَوَّزَ فِي صَلاَتِهِ، فَلَمَّا سَلَّمَ دَعَا بِصَوْتِهِ فَقَالَ لَنَا عَلَى مَصَافِّكُمْ كَمَا أَنْتُمْ ثُمَّ انْفَتَلَ إِلَيْنَا ثُمَّ قَالَ أَمَا إِنِّي سَأُحَدِّثُكُمْ مَا حَبَسَنِي عَنْكُمُ الغَدَاةَ أَنِّي قُمْتُ مِنَ اللَّيْلِ فَتَوَضَّأْتُ فَصَلَّيْتُ مَا قُدِّرَ لِي فَنَعَسْتُ فِي صَلاَتِي حَتَّى اسْتَثْقَلْتُ فَإِذَا أَنَا بِرَبِّي تَبَارَكَ وَتَعَالَى فِي أَحْسَنِ صُورَةٍ فَقَالَ يَا مُحَمَّدُ قُلْتُ لَبَّيْكَ رَبِّ قَالَ فِيمَ يَخْتَصِمُ المَلأُ الأَعْلَى؟ قُلْتُ لَا أَدْرِي رَبِّ قَالَهَا

45 I.e. "the angels brought near" according to Ibn al-Athīr in *al-Nihāya* and others.
46 al-Dāraquṭnī, *al-Ru'ya* (p. 340 §254).
47 al-Tirmidhī, *Sunan* (*Tafsīr, min Sūrat Ṣād, ḥasan ṣaḥīḥ*).

ثلاثاً، قَالَ فَرَأَيْتُهُ وَضَعَ كَفَّهُ بَيْنَ كَتِفَيَّ قَدْ وَجَدْتُ بَرْدَ أَنَامِلِهِ بَيْنَ ثَدْيَيَّ فَتَجَلَّى لِي كُلُّ شَيْءٍ وَعَرَفْتُ – وفي رواية الدارقطني في كتاب الرؤية **عَنْ ثَوْبَانَ مَوْلَى رَسُولِ اللهِ ﷺ: فَتَجَلَّى لِي مَا فِي السَّمٰوَاتِ وَمَا فِي الْأَرْضِ فَعَرَفْتُهُ – فَقَالَ يَا مُحَمَّدُ قُلْتُ لَبَّيْكَ رَبِّ قَالَ فِيمَ يَخْتَصِمُ الْمَلَأُ الْأَعْلَى؟ قُلْتُ فِي الكَفَّارَاتِ، قَالَ مَا هُنَّ؟ قُلْتُ مَشْيُ الْأَقْدَامِ إِلَى الْجَمَاعَاتِ، وَالْجُلُوسُ فِي الْمَسَاجِدِ بَعْدَ الصَّلَوَاتِ، وَإِسْبَاغُ الْوُضُوءِ حِينَ الْمَكْرُوهَاتِ، قَالَ ثُمَّ فِيمَ؟ قُلْتُ: إِطْعَامُ الطَّعَامِ، وَلِينُ الْكَلَامِ، وَالصَّلَاةُ بِاللَّيْلِ وَالنَّاسُ نِيَامٌ. قَالَ سَلْ، قُلْتُ اللّٰهُمَّ إِنِّي أَسْأَلُكَ فِعْلَ الْخَيْرَاتِ، وَتَرْكَ الْمُنْكَرَاتِ، وَحُبَّ الْمَسَاكِينِ، وَأَنْ تَغْفِرَ لِي وتَرْحَمَنِي، وَإِذَا أَرَدْتَ فِتْنَةً فِي قَوْمٍ فَتَوَفَّنِي غَيْرَ مَفْتُونٍ، وَأَسْأَلُكَ حُبَّكَ وَحُبَّ مَنْ يُحِبُّكَ وَحُبَّ عَمَلٍ يُقَرِّبُ إِلَى حُبِّكَ. قَالَ رَسُولُ اللهِ ﷺ إِنَّهَا حَقٌّ فَادْرُسُوهَا ثُمَّ تَعَلَّمُوهَا.** رواه الترمذي وقال حديث حسن صحيح. قال صاحب السيرة الحلبية نقلاً عن الشيخ محي الدين ابن عربي: أَيْ تَجَلَّى لَهُ الحَقُّ بِالتَّجَلِّي الخَاصِّ الَّذِي مَا ذُكِرَ عِبَارَةٌ عَنْهُ.

II

The Prophet as a Light in the Qur'ān and Sunna

Al-Ālūsī (1217-1270/1802-1854) cites ten referents for the word *nūr* (light) in the Qur'ān:

23. Allah has mentioned ten things which He described as a light: (i) His Essence in the verse *Allah is the Light of the heavens and the earth* (24:35); (ii) the Messenger in the verse *There has come to you from Allah a Light and a manifest Book* (5:15); (iii) the Book in the verse *and they follow the Light which was sent down with him* (7:157); (iv) faith in the verse *They seek to extinguish the light of Allah with their mouths* (9:32); (v) Divine justice in the verse *And the earth shines with the light of her Lord* (39:69); (vi) the moon in the verse *And He has made the moon a light therein, and made the sun a lamp* (71:16); (vii) daylight in the verse *and He has appointed darkness and light* (6:1); (viii) manifest proofs in the verses *We did reveal the Torah, wherein is guidance and a light* (5:44), *and We bestowed on him the Gospel wherein is guidance and a light* (5:46); (ix) Prophets in the verse *Light upon Light* (24:35); and (x) gnosis in the verse *The similitude of His Light is like a niche* (24:35).[48]

قال الآلوسي في تفسير سورة طه: قَالَ بَعْضُ النَّاسِ إِنَّهُ تَعَالَى ذَكَرَ عَشْرَةَ أَشْيَاءَ وَوَصَفَهَا بِالنُّورِ. الأَوَّلُ ذَاتُهُ جَلَّ شَأْنُه ﴿ ٱللَّهُ نُورُ ٱلسَّمَـٰوَٰتِ وَٱلْأَرْضِ ﴾ الثَّانِي الرَّسُولُ ﷺ ﴿ قَدْ جَآءَكُم مِّنَ ٱللَّهِ نُورٌ وَكِتَـٰبٌ ﴾. الثالث

[48] al-Ālūsī, *Rūḥ al-Maʿānī* (16:212, *sub* 20:55).

الكتاب ﴿وَٱتَّبَعُوا۟ ٱلنُّورَ ٱلَّذِىٓ أُنزِلَ مَعَهُۥٓ﴾. الرَّابعُ الإِيمَانُ ﴿يُرِيدُونَ أَن يُطْفِـُٔوا۟ نُورَ ٱللَّهِ بِأَفْوَٰهِهِمْ﴾. الخَامِسُ عَدْلُ الله تَعَالَى ﴿وَأَشْرَقَتِ ٱلْأَرْضُ بِنُورِ رَبِّهَا﴾. السَّادِسُ الْقَمَرُ ﴿وَجَعَلَ ٱلْقَمَرَ فِيهِنَّ نُورًا﴾. السَّابعُ النَّهَارُ ﴿وَجَعَلَ ٱلظُّلُمَٰتِ وَٱلنُّورَ﴾. الثَّامِنُ البَيِّنَاتُ ﴿إِنَّآ أَنزَلْنَا ٱلتَّوْرَىٰةَ فِيهَا هُدًى وَنُورٌ﴾. التَّاسِعُ الْأَنْبِيَاءُ عَلَيْهِمُ السَّلَامُ ﴿نُّورٌ عَلَىٰ نُورٍ﴾. الْعَاشِرُ المَعْرِفَةُ ﴿مَثَلُ نُورِهِۦ كَمِشْكَوٰةٍ﴾.

Al-Qārī (d. 1014/1605) said:

24. As for his Light—upon him blessings and peace—it is more than abundantly visible east and west. Indeed, the first thing Allāh created was his Light. In His Book He names him *a Light* (5:15). The Prophet would say in his supplications: "O Allah! Make me a Light."[49] Also in the Qur'ān: *They seek to extinguish the light of Allah with their mouths, but Allah disdains all save that He shall perfect His light* (9:32). Allah Most High also says: *Allah is the Light of the heavens and the earth. The likeness of His Light* (24:35) is in the heart of Muḥammad. Allah Most High also says: *For any to whom Allah gives not Light, there is no Light* (24:40). Nonetheless this light can only be perceived by those endowed with spiritual vision, for *Truly it is not the eyes that are blind but the hearts which are within the breasts* (22:46).[50]

قال المُلّا عليٌّ القارِيُّ في (الأسرار المرفوعة) ما نصه: وَأَمَّا نُورُهُ ﷺ فَهُوَ فِي غَايَةٍ مِنَ الظُّهُورِ شَرْقاً وَغَرْباً. وَأَوَّلُ مَا خَلَقَ اللهُ: نُورُهُ. وَسَمَّاهُ فِي كِتَابِهِ نُـوراً. وَفِي

[49] See below (p. 167 §156).
[50] al-Qārī, *Asrār* (p. 386-387).

دُعَائِـهِ ﷺ **اجْعَلْنِي نُـوراً** [رواه مسلم وأحمد]. وَفِي التَّنْزِيـلِ: ﴿ يُرِيدُونَ أَن يُطْفِـُٔواْ نُورَ ٱللَّهِ بِأَفْوَٰهِهِمْ وَيَأْبَى ٱللَّهُ إِلَّآ أَن يُتِمَّ نُورَهُۥ وَلَوْ كَرِهَ ٱلْكَٰفِرُونَ ﴿٣٢﴾ ﴾ التوبة وَقَالَ اللهُ تَعَالَى ﴿ ٱللَّهُ نُورُ ٱلسَّمَٰوَٰتِ وَٱلْأَرْضِ ۚ مَثَلُ نُورِهِۦ ﴾ فِي قَلْبِ مُحَمَّدٍ ﷺ. وَقَالَ عَزَّ وَجَلَّ ﴿ وَمَن لَّمْ يَجْعَلِ ٱللَّهُ لَهُۥ نُورًا فَمَا لَهُۥ مِن نُّورٍ ﴿٤٠﴾ ﴾ الآية. النور لَكِنْ هَٰذَا النُّورَ لَيْسَ لَهُ الظُّهُورُ إِلَّا فِي عَيْنِ أَهْلِ الْبَصِيرَةِ ﴿ فَإِنَّهَا لَا تَعْمَى ٱلْأَبْصَٰرُ وَلَٰكِن تَعْمَى ٱلْقُلُوبُ ٱلَّتِى فِى ٱلصُّدُورِ ﴿٤٦﴾ ﴾ الآية. الحج.

The Qur'ān explicitly identifies the Prophet Muḥammad, upon him blessings and peace, as a light in a famous passage addressed to him and proclaiming his status as a Prophet sent to mankind as a whole:

> *O Prophet, truly We have sent you as a witness, a herald of glad tidings and a warner, one who calls to Allah by His permission, and a Luminous Lamp!* (33:45-46).

Qadi ʿIyāḍ (471-544/ca.1078-1149) said:

> **25.** He [the Prophet] was named a Luminous Lamp (*sirājan munīran*) because of the clarity of his case and the fact that his Prophecy was made manifest, and also because of the illumination of the hearts of the believers and the knowers of Allah with what he brought.[51]

Al-Qārī also said:

[51] ʿIyāḍ, *Shifā* I.iii.14 (p. 296).

26. *Luminous Lamp* means "luminous sun" since Allah Most High said *and He has placed therein a great lamp and a moon giving light* (25:61). There is in this a warning that just as the sun is the highest of all sensory (*ḥissī*) lights and all other such lights are outpourings from it, likewise the Prophet is the highest of all ideal (*maʿnawī*) lights and all other such lights are taken from it by virtue of their relation to its intermediacy and its towering rank in the universal scheme of creation, as can be inferred from the hadith "The first thing Allah created is my light."[52]

﴿ يَٰٓأَيُّهَا ٱلنَّبِيُّ إِنَّآ أَرْسَلْنَٰكَ شَٰهِدًا وَمُبَشِّرًا وَنَذِيرًا ﴿٤٥﴾ وَدَاعِيًا إِلَى ٱللَّهِ بِإِذْنِهِۦ وَسِرَاجًا مُّنِيرًا ﴿٤٦﴾ ﴾ الأحزاب. قال القاضي عياض: سُمِّيَ بِذَٰلِكَ لِوُضُوحِ أَمْرِهِ وَبَيَانِ نُبُوَّتِهِ وَتَنْوِيرِ قُلُوبِ الْمُؤْمِنِينَ وَالْعَارِفِينَ بِمَا جَاءَ بِهِ. وقال الملا علي القاري في شرح الشفا: ﴿ وَسِرَاجًا مُّنِيرًا ﴾ أَيْ شَمْساً مُضِيئاً لِقَوْلِهِ تَعَالَى ﴿ وَجَعَلَ فِيهَا سِرَٰجًا وَقَمَرًا مُّنِيرًا ﴾ فَفِيهِ تَنْبِيهٌ عَلَى أَنَّ الشَّمْسَ أَعْلَى الأَنْوَارِ الحِسِّيَّةِ وَأَنَّ سَائِرَهَا مُسْتَفِيضٌ مِنْهَا، فَكَذَٰلِكَ النَّبِيُّ ﷺ أَعْلَى الأَنْوَارِ المَعْنَوِيَّةِ، وأَنَّ بَاقِيهَا مُسْتَفِيدٌ مِنْهُ بِحُكْمِ النِّسْبَةِ الوَاسِطِيَّةِ وَالمَرْتَبَةِ الْقُطْبِيَّةِ فِي الدَّائِرَةِ الكُلِّيَّةِ، كَمَا يُسْتَفَادُ مِنْ حَدِيثِ أَوَّلُ مَا خَلَقَ اللهُ نُورِي.

He is also mentioned as a light in Sūrat al-Nisā': *There has come to you from Allah a Light* (5:15) and again in the Verse of Light, *the crystal resembles a star of diamond...* (24:35), both of which are discussed further down, in the fourth section.

[52] al-Qārī, *Sharḥ al-Shifā* (1:505). He may have taken this explanation from his teacher al-Haytamī, since its terms closely resemble what he said in commentary of al-Būṣīrī's *Hamziyya* (see further down) and elsewhere.

The description of the Prophet as a light or a body of light abounds in hadith literature and the testimonials of over forty Companions and other contemporaries of the Prophet; among them:

- al-ʿAbbās b. ʿAbd al-Muṭṭalib
- ʿAbd Allāh b. ʿAbbās
- ʿAbd Allāh b. ʿAmr b. al-ʿĀṣ
- ʿAbd Allāh b. Rawāḥa
- ʿAbd Allāh b. ʿUmar
- ʿAbd al-Raḥmān b. ʿAwf
- Abū Bakr al-Ṣiddīq
- Abū Hurayra
- Abū Ṭālib b. ʿAbd al-Muṭṭalib
- Abū al-Ṭufayl
- Abū Umāma al-Bāhilī
- ʿĀ'isha bint Abī Bakr al-Ṣiddīq
- ʿAlī b. Abī Ṭālib
- Āmina bint Wahb
- Anas b. Mālik
- ʿĀtika bint ʿAbd al-Muṭṭalib
- al-Barā' b. ʿĀzib
- Dhakwān
- Ḥalīma al-Saʿdiyya
- Ḥassān b. Thābit
- Hind b. Abī Hāla
- ʿIrbāḍ b. Sāriya
- Jābir b. ʿAbd Allāh al-Anṣārī
- Jābir b. Samura
- Jubayr b. Muṭʿim
- Kaʿb b. Mālik
- Kaʿb b. Murra
- Kaʿb b. Zuhayr
- Kaʿb al-Aḥbār
- Maysarat al-Fajr
- Rubayyiʿ bint Muʿawwidh
- Samura b. Jundub
- Shaddād b. Aws
- Ṭāriq b. Shihāb
- al-Ṭufayl b. ʿAmr
- ʿUmar b. al-Khaṭṭāb
- ʿUtba b. ʿAbdin al-Sulamī
- ʿUthmān b. Abī al-ʿĀṣ's mother
- Wāthila b. al-Asqaʿ
- Yazīd b. Rumān
- Unnamed Companions

27. [Abū Hurayra:] I never saw anything more handsome than the Messenger of Allah. It was as if the sun were running its course in his face.[53]

عَنْ أَبِي هُرَيْرَةَ رَضِيَ اللهُ عَنْهُ مَا رَأَيْتُ شَيْئاً أَحْسَنَ مِنْ رَسُولِ اللهِ ﷺ كَأَنَّ الشَّمْسَ تَجْرِي فِي وَجْهِهِ. الترمذي وأحمد وابن حبان وبَقِي بن مَخْلَد. وَعَنِ الْبَرَاءِ قَالَ مَا رَأَيْتُ شَيْئاً قَطُّ أَحْسَنَ مِنْ رَسُولِ اللهِ ﷺ متفق عليه.

[53] al-Tirmidhī, *Sunan* (*Manāqib*, *bāb* 45); Aḥmad, *Musnad* (14:258 §8604, 14:506 §8943). The first sentence is also identically related from al-Barā' b. ʿĀzib: al-Bukhārī, *Ṣaḥīḥ* (*Libās, al-thawb al-aḥmar*); Muslim, *Ṣaḥīḥ* (*Faḍā'il, ṣifat al-Nabī wa-annahu kāna aḥsan al-nās wajhan*); Aḥmad, *Musnad* (30:422 §18473).

Al-Ṣāliḥī (d. 942/1536) said the above simile was explained as an affirmation that the Prophet's beauty increased the more one looked at his face; or as a comparison of his face to the sky, as one poet said:

28. *Why would existence not be illuminated by you when its night hails a morning that unveils your beauty?*
Thus with the sun of your splendor every day becomes radiant and with the full light of your face every night is moonlit.[54]

قَالَ الطِّيبِيُّ: شَبَّهَ جَرَيَانَ الشَّمْسِ فِي فَلَكِهَا بِجَرَيَانِ الْحُسْنِ فِي وَجْهِهِ ﷺ. وَمِنْهُ قَوْلُ الشَّاعِرِ:

يَزِيدُكَ وَجْهُهُ حُسْناً ٭ إِذَا مَا زِدْتَهُ نَظَرَا

وَيَحْتَمِلُ أَنْ يَكُونَ فِيهِ تَنَاهِي التَّشْبِيهِ جَعَلَ وَجْهَهُ مَقَرًّا وَمَكَاناً لِلتَّشْبِيهِ. وَلِلَّهِ دَرُّ الْقَائِلِ:

لِمَ لَا يُضِيءُ بِكَ الْوُجُودُ وَلَيْلُهُ ٭ فِيهِ صَبَاحٌ مِنْ جَمَالِكَ مُسْفِرُ

فَبِشَمْسِ حُسْنِكَ كُلُّ يَوْمٍ مُشْرِقٌ ٭ وَبِبَدْرِ وَجْهِكَ كُلُّ لَيْلٍ مُقْمِرُ

ذكره الحافظ الصالحي في سبل الهدى والرشاد

29. [Jābir b. Samura:] His face was like the sun and the moon.[55]

عَنْ جَابِرِ بْنِ سَمُرَةَ رَضِيَ اللهُ عَنْهُ كَانَ وَجْهُهُ ﷺ مِثْلَ الشَّمْسِ وَالْقَمَرِ. مسلم.

30. Abu ʿUbayda b. Muḥammad b. ʿAmmār b. Yāsir said: "I asked al-Rubayyiʿ bint Muʿawwidh: 'Describe for me the Mes-

---

[54] al-Ṣāliḥī, *Subul al-Hudā* (2:11).
[55] Muslim, *Ṣaḥīḥ* (*Faḍāʾil, bāb shaybih ṣallā Allāh ʿalayh wa-sallam*).

senger of Allah.' She replied: 'My son, if you saw him you saw the sun rising.'"[56]

عَنْ أَبِي عُبَيْدَةَ بْنِ مُحَمَّدِ بْنِ عَمَّارِ بْنِ يَاسِرٍ قَالَ قُلْتُ لِلرُّبَيِّعِ بِنْتِ مُعَوِّذِ بْنِ عَفْرَاءَ رَضِيَ اللهُ عَنْهَا صِفِي لَنَا رَسُولَ اللهِ ﷺ فَقَالَتْ يَا بُنَيَّ لَوْ رَأَيْتَهُ رَأَيْتَ الشَّمْسَ طَالِعَةً الدارمي باب حُسْن النبي ﷺ وابن أبي عاصم والطبراني والبيهقي

His Light Overwhelmed Beholders

The above similes of the Prophet's light to the sun were more literal to the Companions than we imagine. This is borne out by Ḥassān b. Thābit's assertion, when he first saw the Prophet, that he needed to shield his eyes from his light (see below) and the hadith of ʿAmr b. al-ʿĀṣ who said on his deathbed that after he entered Islam, the Prophet seemed so resplendent in his eyes that he could not bear to look at him for any length of time. Even more remarkable is ʿAmr's inference, from such sighting, of a spiritual state that he felt guaranteed paradise for him:

31. We were with ʿAmr b. al-ʿĀṣ in his last moments. He wept for a long time and turned his face to the wall … Then he said: "No one was more beloved to me than the Messenger of Allah. No one seemed more majestic in my eyes. I could not bear to take my fill of looking at him because I venerated him too much. If someone asked me to describe him I could not bear to do so, because I never took my fill of looking at him. If I died in that state I would expect to be one of the people of Paradise.[57]

[56] al-Dārimī, *Sunan* (*Muqaddima*, 10: *fī ḥusn al-Nabī*); Ibn Abī ʿĀṣim, *Āḥād* (6:116 §3335); al-Ṭabarānī, *al-Kabīr* (24:274 §696) and *al-Awsaṭ* (4:369 §4458) through trustworthy narrators cf. Haythamī, *Majma*ʿ (8:280); Bayhaqī, *Dalā'il* (1:200).
[57] Muslim, *Ṣaḥīḥ* (*Imān, al-islām yahdimu mā qablah wa-kadhā al-hijra wal-ḥajj*).

حَضَرْنَا عَمْرُو بْنَ الْعَاصِ رَضِيَ اللهُ عَنْهُ وَهُوَ فِي سِيَاقَةِ المَوْتِ فَبَكَى طَوِيلاً وَحَوَّلَ وَجْهَهُ إِلَى الْجِدَارِ إلى أن قال: مَا كَانَ أَحَدٌ أَحَبَّ إِلَيَّ مِنْ رَسُولِ اللهِ ﷺ وَلاَ أَجَلَّ فِي عَيْنِي مِنْهُ وَمَا كُنْتُ أُطِيقُ أَنْ أَمْلَأَ عَيْنَيَّ مِنْهُ إِجْلاَلاً لَهُ وَلَوْ سُئِلْتُ أَنْ أَصِفَهُ مَا أَطَقْتُ لِأَنِّي لَمْ أَكُنْ أَمْلَأُ عَيْنَيَّ مِنْهُ وَلَوْ مُتُّ عَلَى تِلْكَ الْحَالِ لَرَجَوْتُ أَنْ أَكُونَ مِنْ أَهْلِ الْجَنَّةِ. رواه مسلم في الصحيح.

Ḥassān b. Thābit (60BH-40/562-660) expressed the same sublime admiration in memorable lines:

> **32.** *When I beheld his lights shining out,*
>   *I placed in awe my hand before my eyes,*
> *In fear for my sight at the beauty of his frame;*
>   *and now I look at him only to my capacity.*
> *His light has made all lights drown in his lights.*
>   *His face has replaced every sun and moonrise.*
> *He is a spirit of light inside a body of moon*
>   *like a gown that was sewn with sparkling stars.*[58]

لَمَّا نَظَرْتُ إِلَى أَنْوَارِهِ سَطَعَتْ   *   وَضَعْتُ مِنْ خِيفَتِي كَفِّي عَلَى بَصَرِي
خَوْفاً عَلَى بَصَرِي مِنْ حُسْنِ صُورَتِهِ   *   فَلَسْتُ أَنْظُرُهُ إِلَّا عَلَى قَدَرِي
الْأَنْوَارُ مِنْ نُورِهِ فِي نُورِهِ غَرَقَتْ   *   وَالْوَجْهُ مِنْهُ طُلُوعُ الشَّمْسِ وَالْقَمَرِ
رُوحٌ مِنَ النُّورِ فِي جِسْمٍ مِنَ الْقَمَرِ   *   كَحِلَّةٍ نُسِجَتْ بِالْأَنْجُمِ الزُّهُرِ

من شعر حسّان بن ثابت رضي الله عنه

Reciters of *mawlid* echo the above in a famous line:

---

[58] Ḥassān b. Thābit as cited in al-Ṭayyib Ibn Kīrān, *Sharḥ al-Ṣalāt al-Mashīshiyya* (p. 164) and al-Ṭāhir al-Kattānī's *Maṭāliʿ al-Saʿāda* (p. 272).

33. *You are a sun, you are a moon, you are light on top of light.*

أَنْتَ شَمْسٌ أَنْتَ بَدْرٌ   أَنْتُ نُورٌ فَوْقَ نُورِ

Another hadith describes the emotional reaction of a female Companion named Qayla bint Makhrama when she first laid eyes on the Prophet and realized the extent of his humbleness:

34. ʿAbd Allāh b. Ḥassān al-ʿAnbarī narrated from his grandmother and her sister, Ṣafiyya and Duḥayba, the daughters of ʿUlayba bint Ḥarmala – who had both been raised by Qayla bint Makhrama their paternal great-grandmother – from Qayla: "I saw the Messenger of Allah sitting with his two knees drawn up, thighs against his chest and hands on the ground. When I saw him, the Messenger of Allah, sitting so humbly, I began to tremble in fear."[59] Al-Ṭabarānī's version adds: "Someone sitting next to him said: 'Messenger of Allah, the poor woman is trembling!' The Messenger of Allah said to me without looking at me, as I was behind him: 'Woman humble, do not tremble!' (*yā miskīna ʿalayki al-sakīna*). When he said this, Allah took away from me the fear that had entered my heart."

عَنْ عَبْدِ اللهِ بْنِ حَسَّانَ الْعَنْبَرِيِّ قَالَ حَدَّثَتْنِي جَدَّتَايَ صَفِيَّةُ وَدُحَيْبَةُ ابْنَتَا عُلَيْبَةَ بِنْتِ حَرْمَلَةَ وَكَانَتَا رَبِيبَتَيْ قَيْلَةَ بِنْتِ مَخْرَمَةَ رَضِيَ اللهُ عَنْهَا وَكَانَتْ جَدَّةَ أَبِيهِمَا: أَنَّهُمَا أَخْبَرَتْهُمَا أَنَّهَا رَأَتْ رَسُولَ اللهِ ﷺ وَهُوَ قَاعِدٌ الْقُرْفُصَاءَ. قَالَتْ: فَلَمَّا رَأَيْتُ رَسُولَ اللهِ ﷺ الْمُخْتَشِعَ – وَقَالَ مُوسَى بْنُ إِسْمَاعِيلَ: الْمُتَخَشِّعَ – فِي الْجِلْسَةِ أُرْعِدْتُ مِنَ الْفَرَقِ. أبو داود والبخاري في الأدب المفرد

[59] Abū Dāwūd, *Sunan* (*Adab, julūs al-rajul*); al-Bukhārī, *al-Adab al-Mufrad* (*Bāb al-qurfuṣāʾ*); al-Tirmidhī, *Shamāʾil* (*Mā jāʾa fī jilsat Rasūl Allāh*); al-Ṭabarānī, *al-Muʿjam al-Kabīr* (25:9 §1); and al-Bayhaqī, *Sunan* (3:235-236).

والترمذي في الشمائل والبيهقي. والطبراني بزيادة **فَقَالَ لَهُ جَلِيسُهُ: يَا رَسُولَ اللهِ، أُرْعِدَتِ الْمِسْكِينَةُ. فَقَالَ رَسُولُ اللهِ ﷺ وَلَمْ يَنْظُرْ إِلَيَّ وَأَنَا عِنْدَ ظَهْرِهِ: يَا مِسْكِينَةُ، عَلَيْكِ السَّكِينَةُ. فَلَمَّا قَالَهَا رَسُولُ اللهِ ﷺ أَذْهَبَ اللهُ عَنِّي مَا كَانَ دَخَلَ فِي قَلْبِي مِنَ الرُّعْبِ.** قَالَ أَبُو عُبَيْدٍ – القَاسِمُ بْنُ سَلَّامٍ – الْقُرْفُصَاءُ أَنْ يَجْلِسَ الرَّجُلُ كَجُلُوسِ الْمُحْتَبِي وَيَكُونَ احْتِبَاؤُهُ بِيَدَيْهِ وَيَضَعُهُمَا عَلَى سَاقَيْهِ كَمَا يَحْتَبِي بِالثَّوْبِ.

In yet another testimonial, a self-blaming Ubay b. Kaʿb compares his beholding of the Prophet, after the latter forcefully corrected a mistake that had crept into Ubay's heart, to seeing Allah Himself:

35. I was in the mosque when a man came in and prayed. I did not agree with his recitation. Another man entered and prayed yet differently. When we finished praying we all went to see the Messenger of Allah. I said: "This man has recited in a way I disagree with; then that one came in and recited differently yet!" The Prophet ordered them to recite, which they did, and he approved of them completely. A feeling of denial crept up in my mind which never occurred to me before, even during the Days of Ignorance. When the Messenger of Allah saw how I was affected he slapped my chest, whereupon I broke into a sweat and felt as if I were looking at Allah in fear. He said to me: "Ubay! It was revealed to me that I should recite the Qur'ān according to one aspect/dialect (*ḥarf*); I replied to Him: 'Make it easy for my Community.' He said to me the second time: 'Recite it according to two aspects; I replied to Him: 'Make it easy for my Community.' He said to me the third time: 'Recite it according to seven aspects, and for each of My injunctions to you you have a request that will be answered.' I said: 'O Allah, forgive my Community! O Allah, forgive my Community!' and I delayed the third one to the day when all creatures shall seek out my help, including Ibrāhīm."[60]

[60] Muslim, *Ṣaḥīḥ* (*Ṣalāt al-musāfirīn wa-qaṣruhā, bayān anna al-Qur'ān ʿalā sabʿati aḥruf*) and Aḥmad, *Musnad* (35:102 §21171).

عَنْ أُبَيِّ بْنِ كَعْبٍ رَضِيَ اللهُ عَنْهُ قَالَ كُنْتُ فِي الْمَسْجِدِ فَدَخَلَ رَجُلٌ يُصَلِّي. فَقَرَأَ قِرَاءَةً أَنْكَرْتُهَا عَلَيْهِ ثُمَّ دَخَلَ آخَرُ فَقَرَأَ قِرَاءَةً سِوَى قِرَاءَةِ صَاحِبِهِ. فَلَمَّا قَضَيْنَا الصَّلاَةَ دَخَلْنَا جَمِيعاً عَلَى رَسُولِ اللهِ ﷺ فَقُلْتُ إِنَّ هٰذَا قَرَأَ قِرَاءَةً أَنْكَرْتُهَا عَلَيْهِ. وَدَخَلَ آخَرُ فَقَرَأَ سِوَى قِرَاءَةِ صَاحِبِهِ. فَأَمَرَهُمَا رَسُولُ اللهِ ﷺ فَقَرَآ. فَحَسَّنَ النَّبِيُّ ﷺ شَأْنَهُمَا. فَسُقِطَ فِي نَفْسِي مِنَ التَّكْذِيبِ وَلاَ إِذْ كُنْتُ فِي الْجَاهِلِيَّةِ. فَلَمَّا رَأَى رَسُولُ اللهِ ﷺ مَا قَدْ غَشِيَنِي ضَرَبَ فِي صَدْرِي فَفِضْتُ عَرَقاً وَكَأَنَّمَا أَنْظُرُ إِلَى اللهِ عَزَّ وَجَلَّ فَرَقاً. فَقَالَ لِي: يَا أُبَيُّ أُرْسِلَ إِلَيَّ أَنِ اقْرَإِ الْقُرْآنَ عَلَى حَرْفٍ. فَرَدَدْتُ إِلَيْهِ: أَنْ هَوِّنْ عَلَى أُمَّتِي. فَرَدَّ إِلَيَّ الثَّانِيَةَ: إِقْرَأْهُ عَلَى حَرْفَيْنِ. فَرَدَدْتُ إِلَيْهِ: أَنْ هَوِّنْ عَلَى أُمَّتِي. فَرَدَّ إِلَيَّ الثَّالِثَةَ: إِقْرَأْهُ عَلَى سَبْعَةِ أَحْرُفٍ. فَلَكَ بِكُلِّ رَدَّةٍ رَدَدْتُكَهَا مَسْأَلَةٌ تَسْأَلُنِيهَا. فَقُلْتُ: اللّٰهُمَّ اغْفِرْ لِأُمَّتِي! اللّٰهُمَّ اغْفِرْ لِأُمَّتِي! وَأَخَّرْتُ الثَّالِثَةَ لِيَوْمٍ يَرْغَبُ إِلَيَّ الْخَلْقُ كُلُّهُمْ. حَتَّى إِبْرَاهِيمُ ﷺ. مسلم وأحمد.

These four reports reveal the respective *jamālī* and *jalālī* poles of the Prophet's disposition, one of intimate closeness and one of daunting transcendence. A glimpse of this dual nature between intense attractive beauty (*jamāl*) and awesome majesty (*jalāl*) was captured in the following verse by a Shāfiʿī Syrian decendent of ʿAbd al-Raḥmān b. ʿAwf famous for his Prophetic panegyrics, the poet of Fes and maternal ancestor of the Kattānī family, Sirāj al-Dīn Abū al-ʿAbbas Aḥmad b. ʿAbd al-Ḥayy al-Ḥalabī (1050-1120/1640-1708) from his anthology entitled *ʿArāʾis al-Afkār fī Madāʾiḥ al-Mukhtār*:

36. *And in his inward being the All-Exalted has hidden Himself;*

and in his outward being is the manifestation of the All-Loving.[61]

وَبِبَاطِنِهِ اخْتَفَى الْمُتَعَالِي * وَبِظَاهِرِهِ ظُهُورُ الْوَدُودِ

عرائس الأفكار في مدائح المختار لأبي العباس أحمد بن عبد الحي الحلبي

Al-Dārimī's "Chapter on the Beauty of the Prophet"

Al-Dārimī related the hadith of al-Rubayyiʿ in the introduction to his *Sunan* in the chapter he entitled "Chapter on the Beauty of the Prophet" (*Bāb fī ḥusn al-Nabiyyi ṣallā Allāhu ʿalayh wa-sallam*). In that chapter he also mentioned the following reports, all of which related to the Prophetic light:

37. [From Jābir b. Samura:] I saw the Messenger of Allah on a moonlit moon, wearing a red tunic. I began to look at him and at the moon alternately. I swear that he was more beautiful in my eyes than the moon.[62]

عَنْ جَابِرِ بْنِ سَمُرَةَ رَضِيَ اللهُ عَنْهُ قَالَ رَأَيْتُ رَسُولَ اللهِ ﷺ فِي لَيْلَةٍ إِضْحِيَانٍ وَعَلَيْهِ حُلَّةٌ حَمْرَاءُ فَجَعَلْتُ أَنْظُرُ إِلَيْهِ وَإِلَى الْقَمَرِ فَلَهُوَ كَانَ أَحْسَنَ فِي عَيْنِي مِنَ الْقَمَرِ سنن الدارمي باب حُسْن النبي ﷺ.

38. [Ibn ʿAbbās:] He was gap-toothed and whenever he spoke, you could see something like light coming out from between his two front teeth.[63]

61 In al-Kattānī's *Maṭāliʿ al-Saʿāda* (p. 268).
62 al-Dārimī, *Sunan* (*Muqaddima*, 10: *fī ḥusn al-Nabī*).
63 *Ibid.*

عَنِ ابْنِ عَبَّاسٍ رَضِيَ اللهُ عَنْهُمَا قَالَ كَانَ رَسُولُ اللهِ ﷺ أَفْلَجَ الثَّنِيَّتَيْنِ إِذَا تَكَلَّمَ رُئِيَ كَالنُّورِ يَخْرُجُ مِنْ بَيْنِ ثَنَايَاهُ. الدارمي باب حُسْن النبي ﷺ.

39. [Ibn ʿUmar:] I never saw anyone more helpful or more generous or more courageous or more luminous (*aḍwaʾa*) and lustrous (*awḍaʾa*) than the Messenger of Allah.[64]

قَالَ ابْنُ عُمَرَ رَضِيَ اللهُ عَنْهُمَا مَا رَأَيْتُ أَحَداً أَنْجَدَ وَلاَ أَجْوَدَ وَلاَ أَشْجَعَ وَلاَ أَضْوَأَ وَلَا أَوْضَأَ مِنْ رَسُولِ اللهِ ﷺ. الدارمي باب حُسْن النبي ﷺ.

40. [al-Barāʾ b. ʿĀzib:] A man asked: "Was his face like the sword?" al-Barāʾ said: "No, like the moon."[65]

عَنِ الْبَرَاءِ رَضِيَ اللهُ عَنْهُ قَالَ سَأَلَهُ رَجُلٌ قَالَ أَرَأَيْتَ كَانَ وَجْهُ رَسُولِ اللهِ ﷺ مِثْلَ السَّيْفِ قَالَ لاَ مِثْلَ الْقَمَرِ. الدارمي باب حُسْن النبي ﷺ.

ʿAzza bint ʿIyāḍ said she heard Abū Qirṣāfa narrate:

41. When I, my mother and my aunt pledged our loyalty to the Messenger of Allah and were on our way back from meeting him, my mother and my aunt said to me: "Son, we have never seen the like of this man or anyone with a more handsome face, or purer clothes, or softer speech. We saw as if light was coming out of his mouth."[66]

[64] *Ibid.*
[65] *Ibid.*
[66] al-Ṭabarānī, *al-Muʿjam al-Kabīr* (3:3 §2518).

عَنْ عَزَّةَ بِنْتِ عِيَاضٍ قَالَتْ سَمِعْتُ أَبَا قِرْصَافَةَ يَقُولُ لَمَّا بَايَعْنَا رَسُولَ اللهِ ﷺ أَنَا وَأُمِّي وَخَالَتِي وَرَجَعْنَا مِنْ عِنْدِهِ مُنْصَرِفِينَ قَالَتْ لِي أُمِّي وَخَالَتِي: يَا بُنَيَّ مَا رَأَيْنَا مِثْلَ هٰذَا الرَّجُلِ أَحْسَنَ مِنْهُ وَجْهًا وَلا أَنْقَى ثَوْبًا وَلا أَلْيَنَ كَلَامًا وَرَأَيْنَا كَأَنَّ النُّورَ يَخْرُجُ مِنْ فِيهِ. الطبراني

42. [Jābir b. Samura:] A man said: "Was his face like the sword?" Jābir replied: "No. Rather, it was like the sun and the moon, and it was round."[67]

عَنْ جَابِرِ بْنِ سَمُرَةَ رَضِيَ اللهُ عَنْهُ قَالَ رَجُلٌ وَجْهُهُ ﷺ مِثْلُ السَّيْفِ؟ قَالَ لَا بَلْ كَانَ مِثْلَ الشَّمْسِ وَالْقَمَرِ وَكَانَ مُسْتَدِيراً رواه مسلم. قال العبد الضعيف: كأن البراء وجابر يخطِّئان قول حسان وكعب بن زهير بتشبيه نور وجهه ﷺ بالسيف، وأنما الصحيح تشبيهه بنور القمرين، ومثل هذا التصحيح في جمع من أحاديث الصفات النبوية المأثورة عنهم رضي الله عنهم. كما يأتي.

Like the Sun and the Moon, not Like the Sword

Both Jābir b. Samura and al-Barā' b. ʿĀzib's correctives appear to take issue with the comparison of the Prophet's light to a burnished sword devised by poets such as Ḥassān b. Thābit and Kaʿb b. Zuhayr respectively:

43. *He came as an illuminating and guiding light*
shining bright just like the burnished Indian sword.[68]

[67] Muslim, *Ṣaḥīḥ* (*Faḍā'il, bāb shaybih ṣallā Allāh ʿalayhi wa-sallam*).
[68] Ḥassān, *Dīwān* (p. 101 §88).

فَأَمْسَى سِرَاجاً مُسْتَنِيراً وَهَادِياً * يَلُوحُ كَمَا لَاحَ الصَّقِيلُ الْمُهَنَّدُ

من ديوان حسان بن ثابت.

44. *Truly the Messenger is a light whose illumination is sought*
—a drawn Indian sword, one of the swords of Allah![69]

إِنَّ الرَّسُولَ لَنُورٌ يُسْتَضَاءُ بِهِ * مُهَنَّدٌ مِنْ سُيُوفِ اللهِ مَسْلُولُ

رواه ابن هشام في السيرة من قصيدة بانت سُعاد لكعب بن زهير.

This corrective is confirmed by the wording preferred by many other Companions:

45. [Kaʿb b. Mālik:] I greeted the Prophet as his face beamed with joy (*yabruqu wajhuhu*).... Whenever the Prophet was happy, his face was illuminated (*istanāra wajhuh*) as if it were a piece of the moon (*qiṭʿatu qamar*). We could tell.[70]

Another version from Kaʿb has: "as if it were the halo of the moon (*dāratu qamar*)."[71]

قَالَ كَعْبُ بْنُ مَالِكٍ رَضِيَ اللهُ عَنْهُ: سَلَّمْتُ عَلَى رَسُولِ اللهِ ﷺ وَهُوَ يَبْرُقُ وَجْهُهُ مِنَ السُّرُورِ .... وَكَانَ رَسُولُ اللهِ ﷺ إِذَا سُرَّ اسْتَنَارَ وَجْهُهُ كَأَنَّ وَجْهَهُ قِطْعَةُ قَمَرٍ. قَالَ: وَكُنَّا نَعْرِفُ ذٰلِكَ. رواه الشيخان. وعند الطبراني: إِسْتَنَارَ وَجْهُهُ كَأَنَّ وَجْهَهُ دَارَةُ قَمَرٍ.

[69] Ibn Hishām, *Sīra* (3/4: 510-512 lines 39-51).
[70] al-Bukhārī, *Ṣaḥīḥ* (*Manāqib, Bāb ṣifat al-Nabī*) and Muslim (*Ṣaḥīḥ, Tawba, Qiṣṣat ṭawbat Kaʿb b. Mālik*).
[71] al-Ṭabarānī, *al-Muʿjam al-Kabīr* (19:69-70 §136).

46. [Jubayr b. Muṭʿim:] The Prophet was at the arak-tree pass giving away [spoils] after he finished with Ḥunayn and he turned towards us, his face like the crescent moon (*shuqqat al-qamar*).[72]

عَنْ جُبَيرِ بْنِ مُطْعِمٍ رَضِيَ اللهُ عَنْهُ عَنِ النَّبِيِّ ﷺ قَالَ وَهُوَ عِنْدَ ثَنِيَّةِ الأَرَاكَةِ وَهُوَ يُعْطِي حِينَ فَرَغَ مِنْ حُنَيْنٍ إِلْتَفَتَ إِلَيْنَا وَوَجْهُهُ مِثْلُ شُقَّةِ الْقَمَرِ. الطبراني.

47. [Ṭāriq b. Shihāb al-Muḥāribī:] I saw the Prophet in Madina and he asked us: "Do you have anything with you to sell?" We replied: "This camel." The Prophet said: "How much?" We said: "So many *wasq* [about 240 double-handed scoops] of dates." He took its rein and went. I and my companion said: "We have just sold [on credit] to a man and we do not even know who he is!" One of the women that were with us said: "I guarantee the price of the camel. I saw the face of a man like the full moon. He will not cheat you." In the morning, a man brought us the dates and said: "I am the messenger of the Messenger of Allah. He bids you eat of these dates until sated, and weigh them until you have full weight." We did so. Then we entered Madina.[73]

عَنْ طَارِقِ بْنِ شِهَابٍ الْمُحَارِبِي رَضِيَ اللهُ عَنْهُ: نَزَلْنَا الْمَدِينَةَ ، فَخَرَجَ عَلَيْنَا رَجُلٌ ، فَقَالَ : مِنْ أَيْنَ أَقْبَلْتُمْ ؟ قَالَ : قُلْنَا : مِنَ الرَّبَذَةِ ، أَوْ مِنْ حَوَالَيْهَا ، قَالَ : مَعَكُمْ شَيْءٌ تَبِيعُونَهُ ؟ قَالَ : قُلْنَا : نَعَمْ ، هٰذَا الْبَعِيرُ ، قَالَ : بِكَمْ ؟ قُلْنَا : بِكَذَا وَكَذَا ، وَسْقًا مِنْ تَمْرٍ ، فَأَخَذَ بِخُطَامِهِ يَجُرُّهُ ، ثُمَّ دَخَلَ بِهِ الْمَدِينَةَ ،

[72] al-Ṭabarānī, *al-Muʿjam al-Kabīr* (2:136 §1575).

[73] Ibn al-Mubārak, *Zuhd* (p. 410-411 §1164); Dāraquṭnī, *Sunan* (3:44-45); Abū Yaʿlā, *Mafārīd* (p. 109-109 §109) cf. al-Būṣīrī, *Itḥāf* (5:197-198 §4522), Ibn Ḥajar, *Maṭālib* (7:284-286 §1393 *ḥadīth ṣaḥīḥ*); al-Ṭabarānī, *Kabīr* (8:376-377 §8175) cf. Haythamī, *Majmaʿ* (6:23); Ibn Ḥibbān, *Ṣaḥīḥ* (14:517-519 §6562 *isnād ṣaḥīḥ*) cf. al-Haythamī, *Mawārid* (5:293-295 §1683 *isnād ṣaḥīḥ*); al-Ḥākim, *Mustadrak* (2:611-612); Abū Nuʿaym, *Maʿrifa* (3:1555-1556 §3938); al-Bayhaqī, *Sunan* (1:76) and *Dalāʾil* (5:380).

فَقُلْتُ : أَيُّ شَيْءٍ صَنَعْنَا ؟ بِعْنَا بَعِيرًا مِنْ رَجُلٍ لاَ نَعْرِفُهُ ، قَالَ : وَمَعَنَا ظَعِينَةٌ فِي جَانِبِ الْخِبَاءِ ، فَقَالَتْ : أَنَا ضَامِنَةٌ ثَمَنَ الْبَعِيرِ ، لَقَدْ رَأَيْتُ وَجْهَ رَجُلٍ مِثْلَ الْقَمَرِ لَيْلَةَ الْبَدْرِ ، لاَ يَخِيسُ بِكُمْ ، فَلَمَّا أَصْبَحْنَا أَتَى رَجُلٌ وَمَعَهُ تَمْرٌ ، فَقَالَ : أَنَا رَسُولُ رَسُولِ اللهِ ﷺ إِلَيْكُمْ أَنْ تَأْكُلُوا مِنَ التَّمْرِ حَتَّى تَشْبَعُوا ، وَأَنْ تَكْتَالُوا حَتَّى تَسْتَوْفُوا ، قَالَ : فَفَعَلْنَا ، ثُمَّ دَخَلْنَا الْمَدِينَةَ. رواه ابن المبارك والدارقطني وأبو يعلى والطبراني وابن حبان والحاكم وأبو نعيم والبيهقي.

This comparison of the Prophet to the full moon recurs time and again on the lips of the Companions. Its effect and significance were self-evident to desert Arabs who knew the meaning of God-given light in pitch-dark night and appreciated the connection between it and dear guidance for survival. Thus did the grateful Madinan women and children express their joy when they saw the Prophet's convoy emerge from the outlying mountain trail at the time of his emigration and/or on his return from Tabūk, in what was to become the most famous couplet of *mawlid* celebrations everywhere, as narrated from ʿUbayd Allah b. Muḥammad b. ʿĀ'isha:

48. When the Messenger of Allah came to Madina the women, boys, and girls recited:

The full moon has risen over us
from the pass of al-Wadāʿ!
We must give thanks
as long as there remains one who calls to Allah![74]

[74] Abū al-Ḥasan al-Khilaʿī at the very end of his *Fawā'id* (Shāmila ed. §1020) and al-Bayhaqī, *Dalā'il* (2:506-507, 5:265-266); cf. Ibn Kathīr, *Bidāya* (4:488, 7:191); Ibn Ḥajar, *Fatḥ* (7:261).

قَالَ الحَافِظُ أَبُو الحَسَنِ عَلِيُّ بْنُ الحَسَنِ الخِلَعِيُّ المُتَوَفَّى سَنَةَ 492 في آخر الفَوَائِد المُنْتَقَاة الحِسَان الصِّحَاح وَالْغَرَائِب المعروف بِالخِلَعِيَّات: أَخْبَرَنَا أَبُو مُحَمَّدٍ عَبْدُ الرَّحْمٰنِ بْنُ عُمَرَ بْنِ مُحَمَّدٍ الشَّاهِدُ قَالَ حَدَّثَنَا مُحَمَّدُ بْنُ جَعْفَرِ بْنِ دُرَّانَ غُنْدَرٌ قَالَ حَدَّثَنَا الْفَضْلُ بْنُ الحَمَّانِي قَالَ:

سَمِعْتُ عُبَيْدَ اللهِ بْنَ مُحَمَّدِ بْنِ عَائِشَةَ يَقُولُ لَمَّا قَدِمَ رَسُولُ اللهِ ﷺ المَدِينَةَ جَعَلَ النِّسَاءُ وَالصِّبْيَانُ وَالْوَلَائِدُ يَقُلْنَ:

طَلَعَ الْبَدْرُ عَلَيْنَــــا * مِنْ ثَنِيَّــاتِ الْوَدَاعْ
وَجَبَ الشُّكْرُ عَلَيْنَا * مَــا دَعَــا لِلهِ دَاعْ

ورواه أيضاً الحافظ البيهقي في دلائل النبوة.

Ḥassān declaimed:

49. *Whenever his forehead emerged in pitch-black darkness*
it would shine like the blazing luminary of dark night.[75]

مَتَى يَبْدُ فِي الدَّاجِي الْبَهِيمِ جَبِينُهُ * يَلُحْ مِثْلَ مِصْبَاحِ الدُّجَى المُتَوَقِّدِ

البيهقي في الدلائل من ديوان حسان بن ثابت

ʿĀʾisha recalled the above verse when she observed:

50. He had a broad forehead. Whenever his forehead showed from beneath his hair, or in the early morning or at dusk, and whenever he emerged facing the people, they saw his forehead as if it were the light of the burning torch [i.e. the moon].[76]

[75] Ḥassān, *Dīwān* (p. 67 §52); al-Bayhaqī, *Dalāʾil* (1:302); cf. al-Zurqānī, *Sharḥ al-Mawāhib* (4:104-105 *Shamāʾil: wa-ammā jabīnuhu al-karīm*).
[76] al-Bayhaqī, *Dalāʾil* (1:302) and Ibn ʿAsākir, *Tārīkh* (3:359).

عَنْ عَائِشَةَ رَضِيَ اللهُ عَنْهَا قَالَتْ كَانَ ﷺ أَجْلَى الجَبِينِ إِذَا طَلَعَ جَبِينُهُ مِنْ بَيْنِ الشَّعْرِ أَوْ طَلَعَ فِي فَلَقِ الصُّبْحِ أَوْ عِنْدَ طَفَلِ اللَّيْلِ أَوْ طَلَعَ بِوَجْهِهِ عَلَى النَّاسِ تَرَاءَوْا جَبِينَهُ كَأَنَّهُ ضَوْءُ السِّرَاجِ المُتَوَقِّدِ يَتَلَأْلَأُ. رواه البيهقي في دلائل النبوة وابن عساكر.

Her father Abū Bakr al-Ṣiddīq declaimed in similar terms:

51. *Veracious, purified and elect, calling to goodness*
Like the light of the full moon dispelling darkness.[77]

أَمِينٌ مُصْطَفًى لِلْخَيْرِ يَدْعُو * كَضَوْءِ البَدْرِ زَايَلَهُ الظَّلَامُ

البيهقي وابن عساكر من ديوان أبي بكر الصديق رضي الله عنه

52. *Truly he is a beacon pointing to Allah and a mercy*
Immortal in those everlasting gardens.[78]

فَكَانَ سِرَاجاً لِلْإِلَهِ وَرَحْمَةً * يُخَلَّدُ فِي تِلْكَ الجِنَانِ المَوَاكِثِ

روى الأول ابن عساكر وكلاهما في ديوان الصّدّيق

Umar b. al-Khaṭṭāb habitually applied to the Prophet the famous verse of Zuhayr b. Abī Salmā:

53. *If you were anything other than a human being*
you would be light on the night of a full moon.[79]

[77] al-Bayhaqī, *Dalā'il* (1:301) and Ibn ʿAsākir, *Tārīkh* (3:358), cf. Abū Bakr al-Ṣiddīq, *Dīwān* (p. 162).
[78] Abū Bakr al-Ṣiddīq, *Dīwān* (p. 71).
[79] al-Bayhaqī, *Dalā'il* (1:301) and Ibn ʿAsākir, *Tārīkh* (3:358).

وكان يتمثل عمر الفاروق رضي الله عنه وأرضاه بقول زهير بن أبي سلمى:

لَوْ كُنْتَ مِنْ شَيْءٍ سِوَى بَشَرٍ * كُنْتَ المُضِيءَ لِلَيْلَةِ الْبَدْرِ

رواه البيهقي وابن عساكر

When the Prophet left Mecca and emigrated to Madina his paternal aunt, ʿĀtika bint ʿAbd al-Muṭṭalib, recited something similar—although, al-Bayhaqī said, she still followed the religion of Quraysh:

54. *My eyes! Overflow with streaming tears shed*
for the acclaimed one, the full moon of Hāshim's House![80]

وأنشدت عاتكة بنت عبد المطلب عند الهجرة:

عَيْنَيَّ جُودَا بِالدُّمُوعِ السَّوَاجِمِ * عَلَى المُرْتَضَى كَالْبَدْرِ مِنْ آلِ هَاشِمِ

رواه أبو نعيم والبيهقي وابن عساكر

Thus the Prophet evokes the light of the sun for its brilliance and the light of the moon for its beauty, themes which Ḥassān reunited and to which he added a third, the sparkle of stars, in the lines already quoted above (*When I beheld his lights shining out, I placed in awe my hand before my eyes…*).

The Prophet's uncle al-ʿAbbās b. ʿAbd al-Muṭṭalib said:

55. *You are a light from the Almighty, the Giver of Mercy*
subduing paganism and idol-worshippers.[81]

وقال أخوها العبّاس رضي الله عنه:

[80] Abū Nuʿaym, *Dalāʾil* (p. 639 §566), al-Bayhaqī, *Dalāʾil* (1:301), and Ibn ʿAsākir, *Tārīkh* (3:359).
[81] Abū Zayd al-Qurashī, *Jamharat Ashʿār al-ʿArab* (p. 29).

أَنْتَ نُورٌ مِنْ عَزِيزٍ رَاحِمٍ * تَقْمَعُ الشِّرْكَ وَعُبَّادَ الْوَثَنْ

حكاه عنه أبو زيد القرشي في جمهرة أشعار العرب.

[ʿAbd al-Raḥmān b. ʿAwf:]

56. *A Prophet who came when people sulked in haughtiness*
and in the pitch-black darkness of the night of disbelief,
Whereupon he dispelled this darkness with abundant light
and he was shouldered by all those who submitted.[82]

وقال عبد الرحمٰن بن عوف رضي الله عنه:

نَبِيٌّ أَتَى وَالنَّاسُ فِي عُنْجُهِيَّةٍ * وَفِي سَدَفٍ مِنْ ظُلْمَةِ الْكُفْرِ مُعْتِمِ

فَأَقْشَعَ بِالنُّورِ الْمُضِيءِ ظَلَامَهُ * وَسَاعَدَهُ فِي أَمْرِهِ كُلُّ مُسْلِمِ

رواه التيمي الأصفهاني وأورده الزمخشري في ربيع الأبرار

The first and foremost of those who shouldered him are the guarantee of religion for the common believers and thus deserve special honor:

[Abū al-Ṭufayl ʿĀmir b. Wāthila:]

57. *Truly the Prophet is the light that has dispelled*
the blindness of our past and future;
And his close friends are the protection of our religion,
and they have rights over us and we are obligated to them.[83]

وقال أبو الطفيل عامر بن واثلة رضي الله عنه:

[82] al-Taymī, *Dalā'il* (p. 185-187 §239) and al-Zamakhsharī, *Rabīʿ al-Abrār* (2:260 §88) cf. Ibn Sayyid al-Nās, *Minaḥ al-Madḥ* (p. 176).

[83] al-Kharā'iṭī, *Makārim* (3:1339-1341 §127); Abū al-Faraj al-Aṣfahānī, *Aghānī* (13:161 *Akhbār Abī al-Ṭufayl wa-Nasabuh*); Ibn ʿAsākir, *Tārīkh* (26:130); al-Jurrāwī, *Ḥamāsa Maghribiyya* (1:62-63 §15).

إِنَّ النَّبِيَّ هُوَ النُّورُ الَّذِي كُشِفَتْ * بِهِ عَمَايَاتُ مَاضِينَا وَبَاقِينَا

وَرَهْطُهُ عِصْمَةٌ فِي دِينِنَا وَلَهُمْ * فَضْلٌ عَلَيْنَا وَحَقٌّ وَاجِبٌ فِينَا

رواه الخرائطي وأبو الفرج الأصفهاني وابن عساكر والجُرّاوي في الحماسة المغربية

His Knowledge of the Unseen

[Ḥassān b. Thābit:]

58. *He left a people who preferred their minds over him*
and dawned on a people with a light renewed. ...
A Prophet who sees what those around him cannot see
reciting the Book of Allah in every place of prayer.
If he says something unseen one day
It is confirmed the same day or the next morning.[84]

وقال حسان رضي الله عنه:

تَرَحَّلَ عَنْ قَوْمٍ فَضَلَّتْ عُقُولُهُمْ * وَحَلَّ عَلَى قَومٍ بِنُورٍ مُجَدَّدِ

نَبِيٌّ يَرَى مَا لَا يَرَى النَّاسُ حَوْلَهُ * وَيَتْلُو كِتَابَ اللهِ فِي كُلِّ مَسْجِدِ

....

وَإِنْ قَالَ فِي يَوْمٍ مَقَالَةَ غَائِبٍ * فَتَصْدِيقُهَا فِي اليَوْمِ أَوْ فِي ضُحَى الْغَدِ

رواه الطبراني والبيهقي.

The Prophet's God-given knowledge of the unseen was indisputable to the believers in accordance with his title of *Nabī* by definition. When the unbelievers were routed at Ḥunayn their leader Mālik b.

[84] Ḥassān, *Dīwān* (p. 58-59 §47); al-Ṭabarānī, *al-Muʿjam al-Kabīr* (25: 256); al-Bayhaqī, *Dalāʾil* (1:280).

ʿAwf fled to Ṭā'if. The Prophet said: "If he came to me as a Muslim I would return to him all his relatives and property." When news of this reached Mālik, he went to the Prophet and accepted Islam. The Prophet then returned to him all his relatives and property, and gave him an additional hundred camels.[85] Mālik b. ʿAwf later declaimed:

59. *I have never seen nor heard of anyone*
among all people the like of Muḥammad.
True to his promise, he lavishly fulfills the seeker of a gift
and at your wish he foretells you the morrow.[86]

قال الإمام النووي رحمه الله في تهذيب الأسماء واللغات: مَالِكُ بْنُ عَوْفٍ هُوَ الَّذِي كَانَ رَئِيسَ الْمُشْرِكِينَ يَوْمَ حُنَين، فَلَمَّا انْهَزَمُوا لَحِقَ مَالِكٌ بِالطَّائِفِ، فَقَالَ رَسُولُ اللهِ ﷺ لَوْ أَتَانِي مَالِكٌ مُسْلِماً لَرَدَدْتُ عَلَيْهِ أَهْلَهُ وَمَالَهُ فَبلَغَهُ ذَلِكَ فَلَحِقَ بِرَسُولِ اللهِ ﷺ وَقَدْ خَرَجَ مِنَ الجَعْرَانَةِ فَأَسْلَمَ، فَأَعْطَاهُ أَهْلَهُ وَمَالَهُ وَأَعْطَاهُ مِائَةً مِنَ الإِبِلِ كَمَا أَعْطَى سَائِرَ الْمُؤَلَّفَةِ. فَأَنْشَدَ مَالِكُ:

مَا إِنْ رَأَيْتُ وَلَا سَمِعْتُ بِوَاحِدٍ * فِي النَّاسِ كُلِّهِمْ كَمِثْلِ مُحَمَّدِ

أَوْفَى وَأَعْطَى الجَزِيلَ لِمُجْتَدٍ * وَمَتَى تَشَأْ يُخْبِرْكَ عَمَّا فِي غَدِ

رواه ابن عساكر وابن عبد البر في الإصابة

The Prophet indicated that his knowledge of the unseen (*ʿilm al-ghayb*) was formerly partial then became complete at a later point. This completion took place first in dream as expressed in the hadith "everything became manifest to me" cited at the end of Part I; then while he was awake when he said in the famous hadith of the eclipse, "Nothing whatsoever that I had not been shown before is left but I was shown it while I stood right here." This was stated by the great

[85] al-Nawawī, *Tahdhīb al-Asmā' wal-Lughāt* (*sub* Mālik b. ʿAwf).
[86] Ibn ʿAsākir, *Tārīkh* (58:488); al-Jurrāwī, *Ḥamāsa Maghribiyya* (1:74 §23).

Andalusian scholar Ibn Abī Jamra (d. 699/1300) – whom Ibn ʿAṭā' Allāh in dream saw the Prophet call "the Sultan of East and West"[87] – in his commentary on his abridgment of *Ṣaḥīḥ al-Bukhārī*:

60. Asmā' bint Abī Bakr came to ʿĀ'isha while the latter was in prayer and said: "What are they doing?" She pointed to the sky – the people were all standing in prayer – and said "*Subḥān Allāh.*" Asmā' said: "A [cosmic] sign?" She nodded yes. Asmā' then stood in prayer until she became faint, whereupon she poured water on her head. The Prophet then glorified Allah Most High and said: "<u>Nothing whatsoever that I had not been shown before is left but I was shown it</u> while I stood right here, even Paradise and Hell. It was revealed to me that you will be tested in your graves just like the test of the Anti-Christ. It will be said 'What do you know about this man?' The believer will say: 'This is Muḥammad, he brought us clear proofs and guidance so we responded and followed him. This is Muḥammad!' three times. He will be told: 'Sleep the sleep of the righteous, we can tell that you were firm and sure about him.' But as for the hypocrite, he will say: 'I do not know; I heard people say something so I said it.'"[88]

عَنْ فَاطِمَةَ بِنْتِ المُنْذِرِ بْنِ الزُّبَيْرِ عَنْ أَسْمَاءَ بِنْتِ أَبِي بَكْرٍ الصِّدِّيقِ قَالَتْ أَتَيْتُ عَائِشَةَ وَهِيَ تُصَلِّي فَقُلْتُ: مَا شَأْنُ النَّاسِ؟ فَأَشَارَتْ إِلَى السَّمَاءِ، فَإِذَا النَّاسُ قِيَامٌ فَقَالَتْ: سُبْحَانَ اللهِ. قُلْتُ: آيَةٌ؟ فَأَشَارَتْ بِرَأْسِهَا أَيْ نَعَمْ. فَقُمْتُ حَتَّى تَجَلَّانِي الْغَشْيُ فَجَعَلْتُ أَصُبُّ عَلَى رَأْسِي المَاءَ فَحَمِدَ اللهَ عَزَّ وَجَلَّ النَّبِيُّ ﷺ وَأَثْنَى عَلَيْهِ ثُمَّ قَالَ: <u>مَا مِنْ شَيْءٍ لَمْ أَكُنْ أُرِيتُهُ إِلَّا رَأَيْتُهُ فِي مَقَامِي حَتَّى الجَنَّةُ وَالنَّارُ</u> فَأُوحِيَ إِلَيَّ أَنَّكُمْ تُفْتَنُونَ فِي قُبُورِكُمْ مِثْلَ – أَوْ

[87] Dream 70 of *al-Marā'ī al-Ḥisān* printed at the end of the 1997 edition of *Bahjat al-Nufūs*. Ibn Abī Jamra said that while he was writing *Bahjat al-Nufūs* he saw the Prophet visit him with the *Anbiyā'* and *Ṣaḥāba* seventy times and recorded all of it.

[88] al-Bukhārī, *Ṣaḥīḥ* (*ʿIlm, man ajāb al-futyā bi-ishārat al-yad wal-ra's*); Muslim, *Ṣaḥīḥ* (*Kusūf, mā ʿuriḍa ʿalā al-Nabī fī ṣalāt al-kusūf*).

قَرِيبَ، لَا أَدْرِي أَيَّ ذَٰلِكَ قَالَتْ أَسْمَاءُ – مِنْ فِتْنَةِ المَسِيحِ الدَّجَّالِ. يُقَالُ: مَا عِلْمُكَ بِهَٰذَا الرَّجُلِ؟ فَأَمَّا المُؤْمِنُ – أَوِ المُوقِنُ، لَا أَدْرِي بِأَيِّهِمَا قَالَتْ أَسْمَاءُ – فَيَقُولُ هُوَ مُحَمَّدٌ رَسُولُ الله، جَاءَنَا بِالْبَيِّنَاتِ وَالهُدَى فَأَجَبْنَا وَاتَّبَعْنَا، هُوَ مُحَمَّدٌ! ثَلَاثًا. فَيُقَالُ: نَمْ صَالِحًا، قَدْ عَلِمْنَا إِنْ كُنْتَ لَمُوقِنًا بِهِ. وَأَمَّا المُنَافِقُ – أَوِ المُرْتَابُ، لَا أَدْرِي أَيَّ ذَٰلِكَ قَالَتْ أَسْمَاءُ – فَيَقُولُ: لَا أَدْرِي، سَمِعْتُ النَّاسَ يَقُولُونَ شَيْئًا فَقُلْتُهُ. متفق عليه.

Ibn Abī Jamra said:

61. It contains a proof that he did not see all of the unseen before but only part of it, and that in that place his vision of all those things became complete… The question is: is what is meant here, *all* unseen matters in absolute terms, or only whatever he needed to tell his Community and what concerned him exclusively in his noble person? The wording can be understood either way; but the preponderant meaning is the latter one … and the first is precluded… since it is tantamount to making the Creator and the created equal, which is impossible.[89]

قال الإمام ابن أبي جمرة الأندلسي رحمه الله في بهجة النفوس شرح مختصر صحيح البخاري:

فِيهِ دَلِيلٌ عَلَى أَنَّهُ ﷺ لَمْ يَكُنْ يَرَى مِنَ الْغَيْبِ جَمِيعَهُ فِي الزَّمَانِ الْمُتَقَدِّمِ عَلَى هَٰذَا الْمَوْطِنِ إِلَّا الْبَعضَ، وَإِنَّهُ فِي هَٰذَا الْمَوْطِنِ تَكَمَّلَتْ لَهُ الرُّؤْيَةُ لِتِلْكَ الْأَشْيَاءِ كُلِّهَا. وَيَرِدُ عَلَى هَٰذَا سُؤَالٌ، وَهُوَ أَنْ يُقَالَ: هَلِ الْمُرَادُ بِهِ جَمِيعُ الْغُيُوبِ؟ أَوِ الْمُرَادُ بِهِ مَا يَحْتَاجُ بِهِ الإِخْبَارُ إِلَى أُمَّتِهِ وَمَا يَخُصُّهُ ﷺ فِي ذَاتِهِ

[89] Ibn Abī Jamra, *Bahjat al-Nufūs* (1:119-120).

الْمُكَرَّمَةِ؟ وَالْجَوَابُ: أَنَّ لَفْظَ الْحَدِيثِ مُحْتَمِلٌ لِلْوَجْهَيْنِ مَعاً، وَالظَّاهِرُ مِنْهُمَا: الْوَجْهُ الْأَخِيرُ؛ وَالْأَوَّلُ مَمْنُوعٌ... لِأَنَّ ذَلِكَ يُؤَدِّي إِلَى اسْتِوَاءِ الْخَالِقِ وَالْمَخْلُوقِ وَهُوَ مُسْتَحِيلٌ.

Ibn Abī Jamra continued:

> **62.** As for his words "What do you know about this man?" what is meant here by the man is the Prophet himself, and seeing him with one's own eyes. In this there is a proof of the greatness of the power of Allah Most High, since people die at one and the same time in all four corners of the earth, in different places, some near and some far, yet they all see him near them; as the term *hādhā* is not used by the Arabs except to indicate someone who is near. There is also in this a rebuttal of those who claim that it is impossible to see the Prophet at one and the same time in different places and in different forms, since the Divine power is able to effect all that. In addition the Prophet said: "Whoever sees me in dream has certainly seen me in reality." So whoever says he cannot be seen has belied this hadith and has put limits on infinite, boundless, and incomparable Divine power.[90]

ثم قال ابن أبي جمرة:

قَوْلُهُ ﷺ (يُقَالُ مَا عِلْمُكَ بِهَذَا الرَّجُلِ؟) هَذَا الرَّجُلُ الْمُرَادُ بِهِ: ذَاتُ النَّبِيِّ ﷺ، وَرُؤْيَتُهَا بِالْعَيْنِ. وَفِي هَذَا دَلِيلٌ عَلَى عِظَمِ قُدْرَةِ اللهِ تَعَالَى، إِذِ النَّاسُ يَمُوتُونَ فِي الزَّمَانِ الْفَرْدِ فِي أَقْطَارِ الْأَرْضِ عَلَى اخْتِلَافِهَا وَبُعْدِهَا وَقُرْبِهَا، كُلُّهُمْ يَرَاهُ ﷺ قَرِيباً مِنْهُ، لِأَنَّ لَفْظَ (هَذَا) لَا تَسْتَعْمِلُهُ الْعَرَبُ إِلَّا فِي

[90] Ibn Abī Jamra, *Bahjat al-Nufūs* (1:123).

الْقَرِيبِ. وَفِي هٰذَا رَدٌّ عَلَى مَنْ يَقُولُ بِأَنَّ رُؤْيَةَ النَّبِيِّ ﷺ فِي الزَّمَنِ الْفَرْدِ فِي أَقْطَارٍ مُخْتَلِفَةٍ عَلَى صُوَرٍ مُخْتَلِفَةٍ لَا تُمْكِنُ؛ لِأَنَّ الْقُدْرَةَ صَالِحَةٌ بِمُقْتَضَى مَا نَحْنُ بِسَبِيلِهِ، وَقَدْ قَالَ ﷺ: مَنْ رَآنِي فِي الْمَنَامِ فَقَدْ رَآنِي. فَمَنْ يَقُولُ بِعَدَمِ الرُّؤْيَةِ فَقَدْ كَذَّبَ هٰذَا الْحَدِيثَ وَقَدْ حَصَرَ الْقُدْرَةَ الَّتِي لَا تَنْحَصِرُ وَلَا تَرْجِعُ إِلَى حَدٍّ وَلَا إِلَى قِيَاسٍ.

His perspiration was luminous and seemed like pearls

63. ['Ā'isha:] I was spinning while the Messenger of Allāh was mending his sandals and I was observing him. His forehead began to perspire and his perspiration gave off light. I gaped in astonishment. He looked at me and said: "What is the matter? Why are you gaping?" I said: "Messenger of Allāh! I looked at you and your forehead began to perspire and your perspiration gave off light. If Abū Kabīr al-Hudhalī had seen you he would have known that you are most deserving of his poetry." The Prophet asked: "And what does Abū Kabīr say?" She said: "He says:

And one exempt of any remain of menses,
born of hale nurse unsoiled,
Were you to look at his facial traits
– they beam like a white lightning-cloud!

Hearing this, the Prophet rose and kissed me between the eyes, saying: "Allāh grant you goodness on my behalf, 'Ā'isha, for as long as you are happy with me just as I am happy with you!"[91]

[91] Narrated through al-Bukhārī by Abū Nu'aym in *Ḥilyat al-Awliyā'* (2:45-46), al-Khaṭīb with two more chains in *Tārīkh Baghdād* (13:252-253), al-Bayhaqī in *al-Sunan al-Kubrā* (7:422-423), and Ibn 'Asākir in his *Tārīkh* (3:307-309). Al-Mizzī narrated this ḥadīth in *Tahdhīb al-Kamāl* (28:318) as an example of a rare, lone-narrated report that comes only through the reliable Khārijī Imām, genealogist, philologist, and centenarian historian Ma'mar b. al-Muthannā Abū 'Ubayda al-Taymī al-Baṣrī. The verses are cited in Abū Kabīr al-Hudhalī's chapter at the begin-

عَنْ عَائِشَةَ رَضِيَ اللهُ عَنْهَا قَالَتْ كُنْتُ قَاعِدَةً أَغْزِلُ وَالنَّبِيُّ ﷺ يَخْصِفُ نَعْلَهُ فَجَعَلَ جَبِينُهُ يَعْرَقُ وَجَعَلَ عَرَقُهُ يَتَوَلَّدُ نُورًا فَبُهِتُّ فَنَظَرَ إِلَيَّ رَسُولُ اللهِ ﷺ فَقَالَ مَا لَكِ يَا عَائِشَةُ بُهِتِّ؟ قُلْتُ جَعَلَ جَبِينُكَ يَعْرَقُ وَجَعَلَ عَرَقُكَ يَتَوَلَّدُ نُورًا وَلَوْ رَآكَ أَبُو كَبِيرٍ الْهُذَلِيُّ لَعَلِمَ أَنَّكَ أَحَقُّ بِشِعْرِهِ. قَالَ وَمَا يَقُولُ أَبُو كَبِيرٍ؟ قَالَتْ قُلْتُ يَقُولُ:

وَمُبَرَّءٍ مِنْ كُلِّ غُبَّرِ حَيْضَةٍ * وَفَسَادِ مُرْضِعَةٍ وَدَاءٍ مُغْيِلِ
وَإِذَا نَظَرْتَ إِلَى أَسِرَّةِ وَجْهِهِ * بَرَقَتْ كَبَرْقِ الْعَارِضِ الْمُتَهَلِّلِ

قَالَتْ فَقَامَ إِلَيَّ النَّبِيُّ ﷺ وَقَبَّلَ بَيْنَ عَيْنَيَّ وَقَالَ جَزَاكِ اللهُ يَا عَائِشَةُ عَنِّي خَيْرًا مَا سُرِرْتِ مِنِّي كَسُرُورِي مِنْكِ. رواه أبو نعيم في الدلائل والخطيب في التاريخ والبيهقي وهذا لفظه.

Ḥassān b. Thābit reiterated that theme of superlative beauty from the moment of birth in two verses that became archetypes for insurpassable praise:

64. *And fairer than you my eye never saw;*
and more beautiful than you no woman bore.
You were born exempt of any imperfection
as if you had been born exactly as you wished![92]

ning of al-Ṭā'ī's *Dīwān al-Ḥamāsa* (p. 17-18 §12). The line *one exempt of any remain of menses, born of hale nurse unsoiled* is a reference to the biological possibility of menses during pregnancy cf. al-Bayhaqī, *al-Sunan al-Kubrā* (*Kitāb al-ʿIdda, Bāb al-ḥayḍ ʿala al-ḥaml*) and *al-Sunan al-Ṣughrā* (*Kitāb al-ʿAdad, Bāb ʿiddat man tabāʿada ḥayḍuhā*).

[92] Ḥassān, *Dīwān* (p. 17 §2).

وقال حسان رضي الله عنه:

وَأَحْسَنُ مِنْكَ لَمْ تَرَ قَطُّ عَيْنِي * وَأَجْمَلُ مِنْكَ لَمْ تَلِدِ النِّسَاءُ
خُلِقْتَ مُبَرَّأً مِنْ كُلِّ عَيْبٍ * كَأَنَّكَ قَدْ خُلِقْتَ كَمَا تَشَاءُ

ديوان حسان بن ثابت

He also said:

65. *By Allah, no woman has conceived nor given birth*
to one like the Messenger, the Prophet and guide of his Nation!
Nor has Allah created among His creatures
one more faithful to his neighbor or to his promise.[93]

وقال حسان أيضاً:

تَاللهِ مَا حَمَلَتْ أُنْثَى وَلَا وَضَعَتْ * مِثْلَ الرَّسُولِ نَبِيِّ الْأُمَّةِ الهَادِي
وَلَا بَرَا اللهُ خَلْقًا مِنْ بَرِيَّتِهِ * أَوْفَى بِذِمَّةِ جَارٍ أَوْ بِمِيعَادِ

سيرة ابن هشام وديوان حسان بن ثابت

The Companion Abū Dahbal Wahb b. Zumʿa al-Asadī (d. 63/683), among the greatest poets of Quraysh, took up the same theme in his famous lines:

66. *Truly lineages are minerals; his forefathers, therefore,*
are gold, and all his origins are great.
Women are incapable of giving birth to his like.
Truly women are barren of a second Muḥammad!
Shining bright with "Yes" and keeping far from "No,"
Whether he has plenty or nothing at all.
Of little speech from modesty you might construe
an impediment whereas his body is hale.[94]

[93] End of Ibn Hishām's *Sīra* cf. Ḥassān b. Thābit, *Dīwān* (p. 66-67 §51; p. 102 §89).

وقال أبو دَهْبَلِ الجُمَحِيُّ رضي الله عنه يمدح النبي ﷺ:

إِنَّ الْبُيُوتَ مَعَادِنٌ فَنِجَارُهُ * ذَهَبٌ وَكُلُّ بُيُوتِهِ ضَخْمُ

عَقِمَ النِّسَاءُ فَمَا يَلِدْنَ شَبِيهَهُ * إِنَّ النِّسَاءَ بِمِثْلِهِ عُقْمُ

مُتَهَلِّلٌ بِـ(نَعَمْ) بِـ(لَا) مُتَبَاعِدٌ * سِيَّانِ مِنْهُ الْوَفْرُ وَالْعُدْمُ

نَزْرُ الْكَلَامِ مِنَ الحَيَاءِ تَخَالُهُ * ضَمِنًا وَلَيْسَ بِجِسْمِهِ سُقْمُ

رواه ابن قتيبة والطائي في الحماسة والجُرَّاوي في الحماسة المغربية

The above three rhetorical "proclamations of incapacity" are a recurring trope in *mawlid* texts and panegyric poetry:

67. *Such as your beauty we have never seen, O face of happiness!... No eyes have seen or will ever see a man such as Ṭaha in creation.*[95]

مِثْلَ حُسْنِكْ مَا رَأَيْنَا قَطُّ يَا وَجْهَ السُّرُورِ ...

مَا رَأَتْ عَيْنٌ وَلَيْسَ تَرَى مِثْلَ طٰهَ فِي الْوَرَى بَشَرَا

Another report from 'Ā'isha states:

> **68.** I borrowed a needle from Ḥafṣa bint Rawāḥa with which I was mending the garment of the Messenger of Allah. The needle dropped from my hand and I searched for it in vain until the Prophet entered the room, whereupon the needle showed due to the radiance of his face. I smiled and he said: "Fair little one, why did you smile?" She replied: "Because this and that happened." Then he said thrice at the top of his voice: "O 'Ā'isha, woe! Woe! Woe to whoever is deprived of looking at this Face. On the Day

94 Ibn Qutayba, *'Uyūn al-Akhbār* (1:278-279 *Kitāb al-su'dud, bāb al-ḥayā'*); al-Ṭā'ī, *Ḥamāsa* (p. 329 §713); al-Jurrāwī, *Ḥamāsa Maghribiyya* (1:72-73 §22).
95 See also "The unfathomability of the Prophet's rank" I and II in Part VII.

of Resurrection, there is not a single believer or disbeliever but will want to see me."[96]

عَنْ عَائِشَةَ رَضِيَ اللهُ عَنْهَا قَالَت اِسْتَعَرْتُ مِنْ حَفْصَةَ بِنْتِ رَوَاحَةَ إِبْرَةً كُنْتُ أُخَيِّطُ بِهَا ثَوْبَ رَسُولِ اللهِ ﷺ فَسَقَطَتْ عَنِّي الإِبْرَةُ فَطَلَبْتُهَا فَلَمْ أَقْدِرْ عَلَيهَا فَدَخَلَ رَسُولُ اللهِ ﷺ فَتبَيَّنَت الإِبْرَةُ لِشُعَاعِ نُورِ وَجْهِهِ فَضَحِكْتُ فَقَالَ يَا حُمَيْرَاءُ بِمَ ضَحِكْتِ قُلْتُ كَانَ كَيْتَ وَكَيْتَ فَنَادَى بِأَعْلَى صَوْتِهِ يَا عَائِشَةُ الوَيْلُ ثُمَّ الْوَيْلُ ثَلَاثاً لِمَنْ حُرِمَ النَّظَرُ إِلَى هٰذَا الْوَجْهِ. رواه قوّام السّنّة التيمي وابن عساكر بزيادة مَا مِنْ مُؤْمِنٍ وَلَا كَافِرٍ إِلَّا وَيَشْتَهِي أَنْ يَنْظُرَ إِلَى وَجْهِي. وعلّقه أبو سعد النيسابوري في شرف المصطفى بلفظ وَيْلٌ لِمَنْ لَا يَرَانِي يَوْمَ الْقِيَامَةِ. قَالَتْ عَائِشَةُ: وَمَنْ لَا يَرَاكَ يَا رَسُولَ اللهِ؟ قَالَ: الْبَخِيلُ. قَالَتْ: وَمَنِ الْبَخِيلُ؟ قَالَ: الَّذِي لَا يُصَلِّي عَلَيَّ إِذَا سَمِعَ إِسْمِي. ﷺ

That the perspiration-beads of the Prophet were luminous like pearls is confirmed by other hadiths:

69. [Anas:] He was rosy-colored (*azhar al-lawn*) and his perspiration seemed like pearls.[97]

عَنْ أَنَسٍ قَالَ كَانَ رَسُولُ اللهِ ﷺ أَزْهَرَ اللَّوْنِ كَأَنَّ عَرَقَهُ اللُّؤْلُؤُ. رواه مسلم.

[96] al-Taymī, *Dalā'il* (p. 113 §117) and Ibn ʿAsākir, *Tārīkh* (3:310). Al-Laknawī erroneously dismissed it as chainless in *al-Āthār al-Marfūʿa* (p. 45), perhaps on the basis of its chainless citation in Abū Saʿd al-Naysābūrī's *Sharaf al-Muṣṭafā* (2:103 §314); however, it is narrated with a continuous chain through Ibn Isḥāq in the above two sources and furthermore supported by the other reports in this chapter.
[97] Narrated by Muslim, *Ṣaḥīḥ* (*Faḍā'il, ṭīb rā'iḥat al-Nabī*).

70. [ʿAlī b. Abī Ṭālib:] "His perspiration was pearls, as if perspiration in his face were pearls."[98]

عَنْ عَلِيٍّ فِي نَعْتِ النَّبِيِّ ﷺ قَالَ وَكَانَ عَرَقُهُ لُؤْلُؤاً كَأَنَّ الْعَرَقَ فِي وَجْهِهِ اللُّؤْلُؤُ. رواه البيهقي.

The lexicographers define *al-azhar* thus:

71. [Ibn al-Athīr:] *Azhar* means fair and filled with light (*al-abyaḍ al-mustanīr*). *Zahr* and *zahra* denote luminous whiteness (*al-bayāḍ al-nayyir*). [Ibn Manẓūr:] *Zuhra* is whiteness. Yaʿqūb [Ibn al-Sikkīt (d. 244/858)] said: "One says *azhar*, its *zuhra* shows, which denotes whiteness as beauty (*bayāḍ ʿitq*)." Shimr [b. Ḥamdawayh al-Harawī (d. 255/869)] said: "The *azhar* among men is the white, fair one, filled with light and handsome. It is the best of whiteness, as if flashing with light. It shines the way stars and torchlights shine." It was mentioned in the hadith: "Sūrat al-Baqara and Āl ʿImrān are the *Zahrāwān*," singular *zahrā'*, meaning the two light-giving, illuminated ones. [al-Fayrūzābādī:] *Azhar* denotes the moon, the day of Jumuʿa, the buffalo, the white lion, the light-filled face, the bursting camel that reaches to the top of the tree-leaves, and milk fresh from the udder. The two *azhar*s are the sun and moon.[99]

قال ابن الأثير في النهاية: الأَزْهَر: الأبيضُ المُسْتَنِير: والزَّهْر والزَّهْرة: البياضُ النيِّر، وهو أحسنُ الألوان. وفي لسان العرب: الزُّهْرَةُ: البياض؛ عن يعقوب: يقال أَزْهَرُ بَيِّنُ الزُّهْرَةِ، وهو بياضُ عِتْقٍ [العِتْقُ: الكَرَمُ والجَمالُ والنَّجابَةُ والشَّرَفُ والحُرِّيَّةُ. قاموس]. قال شمر: الأَزْهَرُ من الرجال: الأَبيض العتيقُ البياضِ النَّيِّرُ الحَسَنُ، وهو أَحسن البياض، كأَنَّ له بَرِيقاً ونُوراً، يُزْهِرُ كما يُزْهِرُ النجم والسراج وفي الحديث **سُورَةُ الْبَقَرَةِ**

[98] al-Bayhaqī, *Dalā'il* (1:252).
[99] Ibn al-Athīr, *Nihāya*; Ibn Manẓūr, *Lisān*; al-Fayrūzābādī, *Qāmūs* (all *sub z-h-r*).

وَآلِ عِمْرَانَ: الزَّهْرَاوَانِ. أَيِ المُنِيرَتَانِ المُضِيئَتَانِ، وَاحِدَتُهُمَا زَهْرَاءُ. وقال صاحب القاموس: الأَزْهَرُ: القمرُ، ويومُ الجُمُعَةِ، والثَّوْرُ الوحشيُّ، والأَسَدُ الأبيضُ اللَّوْنِ، والنَّيِّرُ، والمُشْرِقُ الوجهِ، والجَمَلُ المُتَفاجُّ، واللبنُ ساعةَ يُحْلَبُ. والأَزْهَرَانِ: القَمَرَانِ.

Additional hadiths confirm the above definitions:

72. [Abū Hurayra:] A man from the desert came and asked "Which one of you is the son of ʿAbd al-Muṭṭalib?" They said: "That tawny man (*amghar*) leaning on the arm-rest." Ḥamza [al-Nasā'ī's great-grandshaykh Ḥamza b. al-Ḥārith b. ʿUmayr] said: "By 'tawny' he meant white with some redness in his skin."[100] [al-Azharī:] al-Layth [b. al-Muẓaffar, co-author of *al-ʿAyn*] said the *amghar* is the one in whose face there is redness on top of unalloyed fairness (*bayāḍ ṣāfin*). By "tawny" they meant fair-faced, just as they called the fair-skinned person "red."[101]

عَنْ أَبِي هُرَيْرَةَ رَضِيَ اللهُ عَنْهُ: جَاءَ رَجُلٌ مِنْ أَهْلِ الْبَادِيَةِ - وَهُوَ ضِمَامُ بْنُ ثَعْلَبَةَ - فَقَالَ: أَيُّكُمُ ابْنُ عَبْدِ المُطَّلِبِ؟ فَقَالُوا: هَذَا الْأَمْغَرُ المُرْتَفِقُ. قَالَ حَمْزَةُ الْأَمْغَرُ الْأَبْيَضُ مُشْرَبٌ حُمْرَةً. رواه النسائي. وحمزة بن الحارث بن عُمَير شيخ شيخ النسائي. أَيْ: المُتَّكِىءُ على المِرْفَقَةِ وهي كالوِسَادة، وأَصلُه من المِرْفَقِ، كأنه استعمل مِرْفَقَه واتَّكَأَ عليه. نهاية. وقال الأزهري: قَالَ اللَّيْثُ: الْأَمْغَرُ: الَّذِي فِي وَجْهِهِ حُمْرَةٌ فِي بَيَاضٍ صَافٍ. وَأَرَادُوا بِالْأَمْغَرِ: الْأَبْيَضَ الْوَجْهِ، وَكَذَلِكَ الْأَحْمَرُ هُوَ الْأَبْيَضُ.

---

[100] al-Nasā'ī, *Sunan* (Ṣiyām, wujūb al-ṣiyām).
[101] al-Azharī, *Tahdhīb al-Lugha* (8:127-128 *sub* m-gh-r).

73. [Abū Hurayra, Ibn ʿAbbās, Abū Bakr and ʿĀʾisha:] Invoke abundant blessings on me on the radiant night (*al-laylat al-gharrāʾ*) and the rosy day (*al-yawm al-azhar*) – the night before Jumuʿa and the day of Jumuʿa – as your invocation is shown to me.[102]

وعَنْ أَبِي هُرَيْرَةَ وَابْنِ عَبَّاسٍ وَعَائِشَةَ وَأَبِي بَكْرٍ رَضِيَ اللهُ عَنْهُمْ مَرْفُوعاً:
أَكْثِرُوا الصَّلَاةَ عَلَيَّ فِي اللَّيْلَةِ الغَرَّاءِ واليَوْمِ الأَزْهَرِ لَيْلَةِ الجُمُعَةِ ويَوْمِ الجُمُعَةِ
فَإِنَّ صَلَاتَكُمْ تُعْرَضُ عَلَيَّ. البيهقي وابن عساكر.

The Long Hadiths of Hind b. Abī Hāla and ʿĀʾisha

Among the intimate descriptions of the Prophet mentioned in the narrations of personal attributes *(shamāʾil)* is *anwar al-mutajarrad/ mutajarrid* (both spellings are correct) or "radiating light upon disrobing" at the end of a list of descriptives all conveying luminosity, including, once again, *azhar*:

74. [al-Ḥasan b. ʿAlī:] I asked my maternal uncle Hind b. Abī Hāla al-Tamīmī, who was good at descriptions, to describe the Prophet—upon him blessings and peace—as I longed for him to describe for me something to which I might cling. He said: "The Messenger of Allah was awe-inspiring. His face shone like the full moon.... His complexion was rosy (*kāna azhar al-lawn*)[103]... with light shining over him.... His neck seemed that of a statue made of pure silver. ... He was luminous when disrobing.... Generally his laughter consisted of a smile showing [his teeth which were as white as] something like hailstones."[104]

[102] al-Bayhaqī, *Shuʿab* (4:434-435 §2772); Ibn ʿAsākir, *Tārīkh* (53:309, 58:374).
[103] This is a clear affirmation that *azhar* is a term denoting a color (*lawn*) contrary to the claim of some later scholars that it denotes only brightness or applies to any color.
[104] al-Tirmidhī, *Shamāʾil* (p. 51-66 §8 and p. 362-370 §225); al-Ṭabarānī, *al-Muʿjam al-Kabīr* (22:155-159 §414) and *al-Aḥādīth al-Ṭiwāl* (p. 64-68 §29), through him, Abū Nuʿaym, *Maʿrifa* (chapter on Hind) and *Dalāʾil* (p. 606-609 §552, first sentence only); Ibn Saʿd, *Ṭabaqāt* (1:362-366); al-Bayhaqī, *Shuʿab* (Branch 15; 3:24f. §1362) and *Dalāʾil* (1:285-292).

عَنِ الحَسَنِ بْنِ عَلِيٍّ قَالَ سَأَلْتُ خَالِي هِنْدَ بْنَ أَبِي هَالَةَ التَّمِيمِيَّ – هُوَ رَبِيبُ رَسُولِ اللهِ ﷺ أُمُّهُ خَدِيجَةُ بِنْتُ خُوَيْلِدٍ وَأَبُوهُ أَبُو هَالَةَ – وَكَانَ وَصَّافاً عَنْ حِلْيَةِ النَّبِيِّ ﷺ وَأَنَا أَشْتَهِي أَنْ يَصِفَ لِي مِنْهَا شَيْئاً أَتَعَلَّقُ بِهِ فَقَالَ كَانَ رَسُولُ اللهِ ﷺ فَخْماً مُفَخَّماً يَتَلَأْلَأُ وَجْهُهُ تَلَأْلُؤَ الْقَمَرِ لَيْلَةَ الْبَدْرِ ... أَزْهَرَ اللَّوْنِ ... لَهُ نُورٌ يَعْلُوهُ ... كَأَنَّ عُنُقَهُ جِيدُ دُمْيَةٍ فِي صَفَاءِ الْفِضَّةِ ... أَنْوَرَ الْمُتَجَرَّدِ... جُلُّ ضَحِكِهِ التَّبَسُّمُ، يَفْتَرُّ عَنْ مِثْلِ حَبِّ الْغَمَامِ. رواه الترمذي والطبراني وابن سعد وأبو نعيم والبيهقي. قال ابن الأثير في النهاية أَنْوَرَ الْمُتَجَرَّدِ أي: نَيِّرَ لَوْنِ الجِسْمِ مُشْرِقَ الجَسَدِ.

Al-Bayhaqī narrates another hadith from ʿĀ'isha – through "Ṣubayḥ b. ʿAbd Allāh al-Farghānī who is not well-known... except that it generally agrees with what we have narrated in the sound and well-known hadiths hence we narrated it, but we rely on the previous ones" – in which the images of bright light and lightning, pearls, and the moon recur once again:

75. A times he wore his hair in four long braids (*ghadā'ir*)... from behind which his ears emerged in their whiteness like diamond stars (*al-kawākib al-durriyya*) against his jet-black hair... He was gap-toothed and when he smiled it seemed like hailstones falling from clouds. When he laughed it seemed like a flash of lightning. ... His dimples around his lower lip were as white as pearls. Of all of Allah's servants his neck was the the most handsome, neither described as too long nor too short. The part of his neck exposed to the sun and wind [shone] like a silver ewer speckled with gold, the white of the silver shining through as did the red of the gold.

Whatever part of his neck was covered by clothing seemed like the full moon at night.[105]

كَانَ ﷺ رُبَّمَا جَعَلَ شَعْرَهُ غَدَائِرَ أَرْبَعاً ... وَتَخْرُجُ الْأُذُنَانِ بِبَيَاضِهِمَا مِنْ بَيْنِ تِلْكَ الْغَدَائِرِ كَأَنَّهَا تُوقَدُ الْكَوَاكِبُ الدُّرِّيَّةُ مِنْ سَوَادِ شَعْرِهِ ... كَانَ أَفْلَجَ الْأَسْنَانِ أَشْنَبَهَا وَكَانَ يَتَبَسَّمُ عَنْ مِثْلِ الْبَرَدِ الْمُنْحَدِرِ مِنْ مُتُونِ الْغَمَامِ فَإِذَا افْتَرَّ ضَاحِكاً اِفْتَرَّ عَنْ مِثْلِ سَنَاءِ الْبَرْقِ إِذَا تَلَأْلَأَ ... فَنِيكَاهُ حَولَ الْعَنْفَقَةِ كَأَنَّهَا بَيَاضُ اللُّؤْلُؤِ وَكَانَ أَحْسَنَ عِبَادِ اللهِ عُنُقاً لَا يُنْسَبُ إِلَى الطُّولِ وَلَا إِلَى الْقِصَرِ مَا ظَهَرَ مِنْ عُنُقِهِ لِلشَّمْسِ وَالرِّيَاحِ فَكَأَنَّهُ إِبْرِيقُ فِضَّةٍ يَشُوبُ ذَهَباً يَتَلَأْلَأُ فِي بَيَاضِ الْفِضَّةِ وَحُمْرَةِ الذَّهَبِ وَمَا غَيَّبَ الثِّيَابُ مِنْ عُنُقِهِ مَا تَحْتَهَا فَكَأَنَّهُ الْقَمَرُ لَيْلَةَ الْبَدْرِ رواه البيهقي وابن عساكر من حديث طويل قال البيهقي: رواه صُبَيح بن عبد الله الفرغاني - وليس بالمعروف - إلا أنه يوافق جملة ما روينا في الأحاديث الصحيحة والمشهورة فرويناه والاعتماد على ما مضى.

105 al-Bayhaqī, *Dalā'il* (1:298-304) and through him Ibn ʿAsākir, *Tārīkh* (3:356-363).

III

The Intercessory Status of the Prophet's Face and Grave

76. Ibn ʿUmar would frequently recite in the Prophet's mosque a famous verse by Abū Ṭālib describing his nephew's complexion, and anyone that heard it would instantly recognize the reference to the Prophet:

And a fair one by whose face the rain-prayer is raised to the clouds,
a nourisher of orphans and defender of widows.[106]

كَانَ ابْنُ عُمَرَ كَثِيراً مَا يُنْشِدُ فِي مَسْجِدِ رَسُولِ الله ﷺ نَعْتَ عَمِّهِ أَبِي طَالِبٍ لَهُ ﷺ فِي لَوْنِهِ وَوَسِيطِيَّتِهِ وَنَجْدَتِهِ حَيْثُ يَقُولُ:

وَأَبْيَضَ يُسْتَسْقَى الْغَمَامُ بِوَجْهِهِ * ثِمَالُ الْيَتَامَى عِصْمَةٌ لِلْأَرَامِلِ

وَيَقُولُ كُلُّ مَنْ سَمِعَهُ هٰكَذَا كَانَ النَّبِيُّ ﷺ. رواه البخاري والبيهقي وابن عساكر وهذا لفظها. وفي بعض الروايات رَبِيعُ الْيَتَامَى.

77. ʿĀ'isha recited the above verse to her father on his deathbed, whereupon he said: "That, by Allah, is the Messenger of Allah!"[107]

عَنْ عَائِشَةَ أَنَّهَا تَمَثَّلَتْ بِهٰذَا الْبَيْتِ وَأَبُو بَكْرٍ رَضِيَ اللهُ عَنْهُمَا يَقْضِي:

[106] al-Bukhārī, *Ṣaḥīḥ* (*Istisqā', su'āl al-nās al-imām al-istisqā' idhā quḥiṭū*); al-Bayhaqī, *Dalā'il* (1:298-299); Ibn ʿAsākir, *Tārīkh* (3:356). Also narrated as "the spring (*rabīʿ*) of the orphans": Ibn Saʿd, *Ṭabaqāt* (3:181); al-Bazzār, see next note; Ibn al-Aʿrābī, *Muʿjam* (2:541 §1054); and Ibn Abī al-Dunyā in *al-Muḥtaḍarīn* (p. 51-52 §37).

[107] Aḥmad, *Musnad* (1:205-206 §26) and others. Al-Bazzār declared its chain fair in his *Musnad* (1:128-129 §58).

وَأَبْيَضَ يُسْتَسْقَى الْغَمَامُ بِوَجْهِهِ * رَبِيعُ الْيَتَامَى عِصْمَةٌ لِلْأَرَامِلِ

فَقَالَ أَبُو بَكْرٍ رَضِيَ اللهُ عَنْهُ: ذَاكَ وَاللهِ رَسُولُ اللهِ ﷺ رواه أحمد والبزار وابن أبي شيبة وغيرهم.

Abū Ṭālib's verse comes from a long poem he declaimed at the time he feared the alliance of Arab tribes with Quraysh in persecution of the Prophet and Banū Hāshim in Mecca, in which he describes the Prophet as a blazing torchlight or star (*shihāb*):

78. *We swear by Allah that if matters worsen*
our swords will decimate even the best of men
Through a youth's hands, a blazing light of a leader,
a trustworthy brother who boldly stands for truth![108]

أنشد أبو طالب قصيدة طويلة لمّا خشي تحالف العرب وقريش على قومه قال فيها:

وَإِنَّا لَعَمْرُ اللهِ إِنْ جَدَّ مَا أَرَى * لَتَلْتَبِسَنْ أَسْيَافُنَا بِالْأَمَاثِلِ

بِكَفَّيْ فَتىً مِثْلِ الشِّهَابِ سَمَيْدَعٍ * أَخِي ثِقَةٍ حَامِي الحَقِيقَةِ بَاسِلِ

سيرة ابن هشام

The verse *And a fair one by whose face...* was much appreciated by the Prophet who famously alluded to it during one of his prayers for rain. The literate Companions expanded on his reference on the spot:

79. [Anas:] A Bedouin came to the Prophet and declaimed:

We have come to you as our virgins' milk has turned to blood,
and the mother worries for her own life over her child's.
The child lets down his arms sitting still
from hunger that brings weakness beyond bitter or sweet.

[108] Ibn Hishām, *Sīra* (1/2:275).

We have nothing left of what our people eat
but yearly colocynth and camel-wool mixed with tick-blood.
And we have none but you to flee to,
for where can people flee except to the Messengers?

Hearing this the Prophet stood up, dragging his garment, climbed up the pulpit and said: "O Allah, send rain down on us, life-giving, salubrious, quenching, abundant, widespread rain, swift and not delayed, beneficial and not harmful, by which You will fill the udders, sprout vegetation, and revive dead earth!" whereupon I swear by Allah that rain fell abundantly even before he brought down his hands to his chest. Later, the people of Biṭāḥ came crying out, "Messenger of Allāh, we are drowning, we are drowning!" Then the Messenger of Allah said: "O Allah, around us and not over us!" whereupon the rainclouds parted until they surrounded Madina like a diadem. The Prophet smiled until his molars showed and said: "If Abū Ṭālib were alive he would have liked to see this. Who will recite for us what he said?" ʿAlī stood up and said: "Messenger of Allah, I think you mean his saying:

And a fair one by whose face the rain-prayer rises to the clouds,
a caretaker for the orphans and protector of widows.
Through him the clan of Hāshim seek refuge from calamities,
*for they have in him immense favor [*var. *mercy] and grace.*
You lie, by the Kaʿba! Muḥammad will never be taken from us!
We will ever fight with sword and arrow to protect him
Never surrendering him until we are all slain around him,
and leave our sons and wives bereaved of us.

The Prophet said yes. A man then stood and declaimed:

To You belongs glory and thanks from those with gratitude!
We have received rain through the face of the Prophet.
He supplicated Allah, His Creator, with a prayer
that was answered, as his gaze searched the skies.
It was but the turning of coats
or faster, until we saw the rain
Bursting the dams, a heavy downpour
with which Allah rescued the crests of Muḍar.

It was just as his uncle Abū Ṭālib said:
a fair one with a shining forelock
Through whom Allah waters us with rainclouds:
This is our eyewitness of that report.
Whoever gives thanks to Allah shall find more
and whoever is ungrateful shall find other than that.

The Prophet said: "If any poet excelled, it is you!"[109]

عَنْ أَنَسِ بْنِ مَالِكٍ قَالَ: جَاءَ أَعْرَابِيٌّ إِلَى النَّبِيِّ ﷺ فَقَالَ يَا رَسُولَ اللهِ لَقَدْ أَتَيْنَاكَ وَمَا لَنَا بَعِيرٌ يَئِطُ وَلَا صَبِيٌّ يَغِطُ ثُمَّ أَنْشَدَ:

أَتَيْنَاكَ وَالْعَذْرَاءُ يَدْمَى لَبَانُهَا * وَقَدْ شُغِلَتْ أُمُّ الصَّبِيِّ عَنِ الطِّفْلِ
وَأَلْقَى بِكَفَّيْهِ الْفَتَى اسْتِكَانَةً * عَنِ الْجُوعِ ضَعْفاً مَا يُمِرُّ وَمَا يُحْلِي
وَلَا شَيْءَ مِمَّا يَأْكُلُ النَّاسُ عِنْدَنَا * سِوَى الْحَنْظَلَ الْعَامِيَّ وَالْعِلْهِزِ الْفَسْلِ
وَلَيْسَ لَنَا إِلَّا إِلَيْكَ فِرَارُنَا * وَأَيْنَ فِرَارُ النَّاسِ إِلَّا إِلَى الرُّسْلِ

فَقَامَ رَسُولُ اللهِ ﷺ يَجُرُّ رِدَاءَهُ حَتَّى صَعِدَ الْمِنْبَرَ ثُمَّ رَفَعَ يَدَيْهِ إِلَى السَّمَاءِ فَقَالَ اللّٰهُمَّ اسْقِنَا غَيْثاً مُغِيثاً مَرِيئاً مَرِيعاً غَدَقاً طَبَقاً عَاجِلاً غَيْرَ رَائِثٍ نَافِعاً غَيْرَ ضَارٍّ تَمْلَأُ بِهِ الضَّرْعَ وَتُنْبِتُ بِهِ الزَّرْعَ وَتُحْيِي الْأَرْضَ بَعْدَ مَوْتِهَا فَوَاللهِ مَا رَدَّ يَدَيْهِ إِلَى نَحْرِهِ حَتَّى أَلْقَتِ السَّمَاءُ بِأَوْرَامِهَا وَجَاءَ أَهْلُ الْبِطَاحِ يَعُجُّونَ يَصِيحُونَ يَا رَسُولَ اللهِ الْغَرَقُ الْغَرَقُ فَقَالَ رَسُولُ اللهِ ﷺ اللّٰهُمَّ حَوَالَيْنَا وَلَا عَلَيْنَا فَانْجَابَ السَّحَابُ حَتَّى أَحْدَقَ بِالْمَدِينَةِ كَالْإِكْلِيلِ فَضَحِكَ رَسُولُ اللهِ

[109] al-Ṭabarānī, *al-Aḥādīth al-Ṭiwāl* (p. 62-64 §28), *al-Du'ā'* (3:1775-1777 §2180), and *al-Mu'jam al-Kabīr* (25:243-245 §28); al-Taymī, *Dalā'il* (p. 184 §238); and al-Bayhaqī, *Dalā'il* (6:141); cf. Ibn 'Abd al-Barr, *Tamhīd* (22:63-67); Ibn Ḥajar, *Fatḥ* (2:495 *isnād ṣāliḥ*).

ﷺ حَتَّى بَدَتْ نَوَاجِذُهُ ثُمَّ قَالَ لَوْ كَانَ أَبُو طَالِبٍ حَيّاً لَقَرَّتْ عَيْنَاهُ مَن يُنْشِدُنَا قَوْلَهُ؟ فَقَامَ عَلِيُّ بْنُ أَبِي طَالِبٍ فَقَالَ يَا رَسُولَ اللهِ كَأَنَّكَ أَرَدْتَ قَوْلَهُ

وَأَبْيَضَ يُسْتَسْقَى الْغَمَامُ بِوَجْهِهِ * ثِمَالُ الْيَتَامَى عِصْمَةٌ لِلْأَرَامِلِ
يَلُوذُ بِهِ الْهُلَّاكُ مِنْ آلِ هَاشِمٍ * فَهُمْ عِنْدَهُ فِي نِعْمَةٍ وَفَوَاضِلِ
كَذَبْتُمْ وَبَيْتِ اللهِ نُبْزَى مُحَمَّداً * وَلَمَّا نُقَاتِلْ دُونَهُ وَنُنَاضِلِ
وَنُسْلِمْهُ حَتَّى نُصَرَعَ حَوْلَهُ * وَنُذْهَلَ عَنْ أَبْنَائِنَا وَالْحَلَائِلِ

فَقَالَ رَسُولُ اللهِ ﷺ أَجَلْ. وَقَامَ رَجُلٌ مِنْ كِنَانَةَ فَقَالَ:

لَكَ الْحَمْدُ وَالْحَمْدُ مِمَّنْ شَكَرْ * سُقِينَا بِوَجْهِ النَّبِيِّ الْمَطَرْ
دَعَى اللهَ خَالِقَهُ دَعْوَةً * أُجِيبَتْ وَأَشْخَصَ مِنْهُ الْبَصَرْ
وَلَمْ يَكُ إِلَّا كَلَفِّ الرِّدَاءِ * وَأَسْرَعَ حَتَّى رَأَيْنَا الْمَطَرْ
دُفَاقُ الْعَزَالِي (العزائل) وَجَمُّ الْبُعَاقِ * أَغَاثَ بِهِ اللهُ عَلْيَا مُضَرْ
وَكَانَ كَمَا قَالَهُ عَمُّهُ * أَبُو طَالِبٍ أَبْيَضَ ذَا غَرَرْ
وَيَسْقِي بِهِ اللهُ صَوْبَ الْغَمَامِ * وَهَذَا الْعِيَانُ لِذَاكَ الْخَبَرْ
فَمَنْ يَشْكُرِ اللهَ يَلْقَ الْمَزِيدَ * وَمَنْ يَكْفُرِ اللهَ يَلْقَ الْغِيَرْ

فَقَالَ رَسُولُ اللهِ ﷺ إِنْ يَكُ شَاعِرٌ يُحْسِنُ فَقَدْ أَحْسَنْتَ. رواه الطبراني والبيهقي. وعند ابن هشام:

يَلُوذُ بِهِ الْهُلَّافُ مِنْ آلِ هَاشِمٍ * فَهُمْ عِنْدَهُ فِي رَحْمَةٍ وَفَوَاضِلِ.

ويروى مختصراً عن كعب بن مُرّة وابن عباس وعائشة ويزيد بن رومان رضي الله عنهم.

The Verse of *qibla* change confirms the intercessory status of the face of the Prophet highlighted by Abū Ṭālib (and his father ʿAbd al-Muṭṭalib before him, see Part V): *We have seen the turning of your face to heaven. And now verily We shall make you turn toward a qibla which is dear to you* (2:144), since one of the meanings of the turning of the Prophet's face to heaven is supplication (al-Rāzī). The supplication was silent, as the innermost wish of the Prophet was that Allah command him to take the Kaʿba for *qibla*, but it was a mark of his perfect character that he waited without asking (al-Bayḍāwī).[110]

قال الفخر الرازي: الوجه الرابع من القول الأول في قوله: ﴿ قَدْ نَرَىٰ تَقَلُّبَ وَجْهِكَ فِي ٱلسَّمَآءِ فَلَنُوَلِّيَنَّكَ قِبْلَةً تَرْضَىٰهَا ﴾ الآية: أَنَّ تَقَلُّبَ وَجْهِهِ ﷺ فِي السَّمَاءِ هُوَ الدُّعَاءُ. وقال البيضاوي: وَكَانَ رَسُولُ الله ﷺ يَقَعُ فِي رُوعِهِ وَيَتَوَقَّعُ مِنْ رَبِّهِ أَنْ يُحَوِّلَهُ إِلَى الْكَعْبَةِ ... وَذٰلِكَ يَدُلُّ عَلَى كَمَالِ أَدَبِهِ حَيْثُ انْتَظَرَ وَلَمْ يَسْأَلْ.

As the Successor al-Aswad b. Masʿūd al-Thaqafī declaimed:

80. *The Prophet is he whose gifts are sought*
when drought holds up the rain.[111]

وللتابعي أسود بن مسعود الثقفي:

إِنَّ الرَّسُولَ الَّذِي تُرْجَى نَوَافِلُهُ * عِنْدَ الْقُحُوطِ إِذَا مَا أَقْحَطَ الْمَطَرُ

Hence it came as no surprise to the Madinan Companions and Successors that in a time of drought ʿĀ'isha commanded for a window to be opened up in the ceiling above his grave, "so that there will be no ceiling between him and the sky," whereupon abundant rain came down, as related from Aws b. ʿAbd Allah:

110 al-Rāzī, *Mafātīḥ al-Ghayb*; al-Bayḍāwī, *Anwār al-Tanzīl* (*sub* 2:144).
111 In Kayyāl, *Yawm wa-Layla* (p. 100).

81. The people of Madina complained to ʿĀ'isha of the severe drought they were suffering. She said: "Go to the Prophet's grave and open a window towards the sky so that there will be no roof between him and the sky." They did so, after which they were watered with such rain that vegetation grew and the camels burst with fat. That year was named the Year of Bursting.[112]

Al-Qārī commented:

82. ʿĀ'isha commanded for the grave to be uncovered as a hyperbolic request for his intercession (*mubālaghatan fīl-istishfāʿ bih*)… like a metaphor (*kināya*) for the exposition of one's petition merely through his turning to the sky, which is the *qibla* of supplication and the place of sustenance.[113]

أَبُو الجَوْزَاءِ أَوْسُ بْنُ عَبْدِ الله قَالَ قُحِطَ أَهْلُ المَدِينَةِ قَحْطاً شَدِيداً فَشَكَوْا إِلَى عَائِشَةَ رَضِيَ اللهُ عَنْهَا فَقَالَتْ انْظُرُوا قَبْرَ النَّبِيِّ ﷺ فَاجْعَلُوا مِنْهُ كِوًى إِلَى السَّمَاءِ حَتَّى لاَ يَكُونَ بَيْنَهُ وَبَيْنَ السَّمَاءِ سَقْفٌ قَالَ فَفَعَلُوا فَمُطِرْنَا مَطَراً حَتَّى نَبَتَ الْعُشْبُ وَسَمِنَتِ الإِبِلُ حَتَّى تَفَتَّقَتْ مِنَ الشَّحْمِ فَسُمِّيَ عَامَ الْفَتْقِ رواه الدارمي في سننه بسند حسن. قال الملا علي القاري في المرقاة: قَدْ قِيلَ فِي سَبَبِ كَشْفِ قَبْرِ النَّبِيِّ ﷺ أَنَّ السَّمَاءَ لَمَّا رَأَتْ قَبْرَ النَّبِيِّ ﷺ سَالَ الْوَادِي مِنْ بُكَائِهَا قَالَ تَعَالَى ﴿ فَمَا بَكَتْ عَلَيْهِمُ ٱلسَّمَآءُ وَٱلْأَرْضُ وَمَا كَانُوا۟ مُنظَرِينَ ﴾ الدخان ٢٩ حِكَايَةً عَنْ حَالِ الْكُفَّارِ فَيَكُونُ أَمْرُهَا عَلَى خِلَافِ ذَٰلِكَ بِالنِّسْبَةِ إِلَى الْأَبْرَارِ وَقِيلَ إِنَّهُ كَانَ يُسْتَشْفَعُ بِهِ عِنْدَ الْجَدْبِ فَتُمْطِرُ السَّمَاءُ

[112] al-Dārimī, *Sunan* (*Muqaddima, bāb mā akrama Allāhu taʿālā Nabiyyahu baʿda mawtih*).

[113] al-Qārī, *Mirqāt* (*al-Faḍā'il wal-shamā'il, bāb fīl-karāmāt*).

فَأَمَرَتْ عَائِشَةُ رَضِيَ اللهُ عَنْهَا بِكَشْفِ قَبْرِهِ مُبَالَغَةً فِي الإِسْتِشْفَاعِ بِهِ فَلَا يَبْقَى بَيْنَهُ وَبَيْنَ السَّمَاءِ حِجَابٌ. أَقُولُ: وَكَأَنَّهُ كِنَايَةٌ عَنْ عَرْضِ الْغَرَضِ الْمَطْلُوبِ بِتَوَجُّهِهِ إِلَى السَّمَاءِ وَهِيَ قِبْلَةُ الدُّعَاءِ وَمَحَلُّ رِزْقِ الضُّعَفَاءِ كَمَا قَالَ تَعَالَى ﴿وَفِي السَّمَاءِ رِزْقُكُمْ وَمَا تُوعَدُونَ ﴿٢٢﴾﴾ الذاريات.

When Kaʿb al-Aḥbār visited ʿĀ'isha, Kaʿb said:

83. Not one day rises except 70,000 angels descend until they closely surround the grave of the Prophet, striking their wings and invoking blessings upon the Messenger of Allah. When night comes, they ascend and their like come down replacing them, and thus until the earth cleaves open for him, at which time he shall come out in the midst of seventy thousand angels carrying him in procession.[114]

عَنْ نُبَيْهِ بْنِ وَهْبٍ أَنَّ كَعْباً دَخَلَ عَلَى عَائِشَةَ فَذَكَرُوا رَسُولَ اللهِ ﷺ فَقَالَ كَعْبٌ مَا مِنْ يَوْمٍ يَطْلُعُ إِلاَّ نَزَلَ سَبْعُونَ أَلْفاً مِنَ الْمَلَائِكَةِ حَتَّى يَحُفُّوا بِقَبْرِ النَّبِيِّ ﷺ يَضْرِبُونَ بِأَجْنِحَتِهِمْ وَيُصَلُّونَ عَلَى رَسُولِ اللهِ ﷺ حَتَّى إِذَا أَمْسَوْا عَرَجُوا وَهَبَطَ مِثْلُهُمْ فَصَنَعُوا مِثْلَ ذَلِكَ حَتَّى إِذَا انْشَقَّتْ عَنْهُ الأَرْضُ خَرَجَ فِي سَبْعِينَ أَلْفاً مِنَ الْمَلَائِكَةِ يَزِفُّونَهُ رواه الدارمي من طريق رجال الصحيحين.

In echo of the bedouin's petition of the Prophet in the long hadith of Anas cited above, the Omani Companion Māzin b. al-Ghaḍūba al-Ṭā'ī al-Khaṭāmī declaimed:

[114] al-Dārimī, *Sunan* (*Muqaddima, bāb mā akrama Allāhu taʿālā Nabiyyahu baʿda mawtih*), through al-Bukhārī and Muslim's narrators.

84. *To you, Messenger of Allah, my mount has jogged*
crossing the deserts from Oman to ʿArj [near Madīna]
So you will intercede for me, O best of those who trod the earth
then my Lord will forgive me and I shall return with victory.[115]

عَنْ مَازِنِ بن الْغَضُوبَةِ رَضِيَ اللهُ عَنْهُ قَالَ بَعْدَ إِسْلَامِهِ:

إِلَيْكَ رَسُولَ اللهِ خَبَّـــتْ مَطِيَّتِي * تَجُوبُ الْفَيَافِي مِنْ عُمَانَ إِلَى الْعَرْجِ

لِتَشْفَعَ لِي يَا خَيْرَ مَنْ وَطِئَ الحَصَى * فَيَغْفِرَ لِي رَبِّي فَأَرْجِعَ بِالْفَلْـــجِ

رواه الطبراني وأبو نعيم والبيهقي

Such entreaties are the essence of intercessory requests (*tawassul*) as the Companions understood and practiced them with the Prophet's full approval and encouragement. They did so after his death as well, as shown by the above report from ʿĀ'isha and confirmed by additional reports.[116] This understanding is the backdrop of all their propitiations of the Prophet's light and is summarized by Ḥassān b. Thābit in his address to the grave of the Prophet (see below) and in the extemporaneous eulogy he declaimed on the Conquest of Mecca:

85. *Pillar relied upon, surety of refuge-seekers,*
resort of the parched and protecting neighbor!
You whom the One God chose for His creatures
then granted perfection and pure character—
You are The Prophet, you are the best of Adam's kind!
Open-handed, like the outpouring of a swelling sea—
Mīkāl is with you and Jabra'īl, both helping you to victory,
sent by One Mighty, Irresistible![117]

[115] al-Ṭabarānī, *al-Muʿjam al-Kabīr* (20:337-339 §799) and *al-Aḥādīth al-Ṭiwāl* (p. 145-147 §63); Abū Nuʿaym, *Dalā'il* (p. 114-117 §63); al-Bayhaqī, *Dalā'il* (2:34-37).

[116] Such as the report through Mālik al-Dār from the Companion Bilāl b. al-Ḥārith al-Muzanī which was declared sound by Ibn Ḥajar and Ibn Kathīr, cf. our article "*Tawassul* and *Tabarruk* of the *Salaf*" at http://mac.abc.se/~onesr/d/twss_e.pdf. Also the report of *istiṭʿām* (request for food) at the Prophetic grave performed by al-Ṭabarānī, Abū al-Shaykh, and Ibn al-Muqri' as narrated from the latter by Dhahabī in *Tadhkirat al-Ḥuffāẓ* (3:973 §913) and elsewhere. A similar "feeding miracle" took place with Abū al-Khayr al-Aqṭaʿ as narrated by Ibn al-Jawzī, *Muthīr* (p. 491).

[117] Ibn ʿAbd al-Barr, *Istīʿāb* (p. 133 §378) and Ibn Ḥajar, *Iṣāba* (*sub* Janāb al-Kalbī).

رَوَى جَنَابٌ الْكَلْبِيُّ رَضِيَ اللهُ عَنْهُ عَنِ النَّبِيِّ ﷺ أَنَّهُ سَمِعَهُ يَقُولُ لِرَجُلٍ رَبْعَةٍ يَوْمَ الْفَتْحِ إِنَّ جِبْرِيلَ عَنْ يَمِينِي وَمِيكَائِيلَ وَالْمَلَائِكَةَ قَدْ أَظَلَّتْ عَسْكَرِي فَخُذْ فِي بَعْضِ هَنَاتِكَ فَأَطْرَقَ الرَّجُلُ شَيْئاً ثُمَّ طَفِقَ يَقُولُ فَذَكَرَ الشِّعْرَ وَقَالَ وَالرَّجُلُ حَسَّانُ بْنُ ثَابِتٍ رَضِيَ اللهُ عَنْهُ قَالَ:

يَا رُكْنَ مُعْتَمِدٍ وَعِصْمَةَ لَائِذٍ * وَمَلَاذَ مُنْتَجِعٍ وَجَارَ مُجَاوِرِ
يَا مَنْ تَخَيَّرَهُ الْإِلَٰهُ لِخَلْقِهِ * وَحَبَاهُ بِالْخُلُقِ الزَّكِيِّ الطَّاهِرِ
أَنْتَ النَّبِيُّ وَخَيْرُ عُصْبَةِ آدَمٍ * يَا مَنْ يَجُودُ كَفَيْضِ بَحْرٍ زَاخِرِ
مِيكَالُ مَعْكَ وَجَبْرَئِيلُ كِلَاهُمَا * مَدَدٌ لِنَصْرِكَ مِنْ عَزِيزٍ قَاهِرِ

ذكره ابن عبد البر والحافظ في الإصابة كلاهما في ترجمة جَناب الكلبي ونسبه إلى ابن منده.

The Prophet as a Light in the Companions' Funeral Elegies

The physical disappearance of the Prophet brought darkness and was the sharpest reminder to the Companions of the palpable aspect of his light which was no longer daily before their eyes:

86. [Anas b. Mālik:] The day the Messenger of Allah—upon him blessings and peace—entered Madina, everything became illuminated in Madina; and the day the Messenger of Allah—upon him blessings and peace—died, everything became dark in Madina. We had hardly finished burying him when already we no longer recognized our own hearts.[118]

[118] Aḥmad (21:35 §13312 and 21:330 §13830), al-Tirmidhī, *Sunan* (*al-Manāqib ʿan Rasūl Allāh, ṣaḥīḥ gharīb*), Ibn Mājah, *Sunan* (*Janā'iz, Dhikr wafāt Rasūl Allāh*) etc.

Ibn Ḥajar explained the expression "we no longer recognized our own hearts" to mean that "they observed that their hearts had changed from the state they were in during his life of attraction, purity, and softness, due to their losing the teaching and training he was helping them with."[119]

عَنْ أَنَسٍ رَضِيَ اللهُ عَنْهُ قَالَ لَمَّا كَانَ الْيَوْمُ الَّذِي دَخَلَ فِيهِ رَسُولُ اللهِ ﷺ الْمَدِينَةَ أَضَاءَ مِنَ الْمَدِينَةِ كُلُّ شَيْءٍ فَلَمَّا كَانَ الْيَوْمُ الَّذِي مَاتَ فِيهِ رَسُولُ اللهِ ﷺ أَظْلَمَ مِنَ الْمَدِينَةِ كُلُّ شَيْءٍ وَمَا فَرَغْنَا مِنْ دَفْنِهِ حَتَّى أَنْكَرْنَا قُلُوبَنَا رواه أحمد والترمذي وقال صحيح غريب وابن ماجه وغيرهم. قال الحافظ في الفتح: يريد أنهم وجدوها تغيرت عما عهدوه في حياته من الأُلْف والصَّفاء والرِّقَّة، لفقدان ما كان يُمِدُّهم به من التعليم والتأديب.

Ḥassān b. Thābit did not fail to expound on this theme:

87. *He was illumination itself and the light for us to follow,*
second only to Allah; he was our sight and hearing. ...
By Allah, no woman has conceived nor given birth
to one like the Messenger, the Prophet and guide of his Nation!
Nor has Allah created among His creatures
one more faithful to his neighbor or to his promise
Than him who in our midst was the source of our light,
all-blessed, just and righteous.[120]

قال حسان رضي الله عنه يرثي النبي ﷺ:

كَانَ الضِّيَاءَ وَكَانَ النُّورَ نَتْبَعُهُ * بَعْدَ الْإِلَهِ وَكَانَ السَّمْعَ وَالْبَصَرَا

....

[119] Ibn Ḥajar, *Fatḥ al-Bārī* (8:149).
[120] Last lines of Ibn Hishām, *Sīra*; cf. Ḥassān b. Thābit, *Dīwān* (p. 66 §51; p. 102 §89).

تَاللهِ مَا حَمَلَتْ أُنْثَى وَلَا وَضَعَتْ * مِثْلَ الرَّسُولِ نَبِيِّ الْأُمَّةِ الهَادِي

وَلَا بَرَا اللهُ خَلْقًا مِنْ بَرِيَّتِهِ * أَوْفَى بِذِمَّةِ جَارٍ أَوْ بِمِيعَادِ

مِنَ الَّذِي كَانَ فِينَا يُسْتَضَاءُ بِهِ * مُبَارَكَ الْأَمْرِ ذَا عَدْلٍ وَإِرْشَادِ

سيرة ابن هشام وديوان حسان بن ثابت

88. *In Ṭayba is a vestige of the Messenger and a memorial*
radiant, even if vestiges can fade and disappear. ...
In it are chambers in the midst of which descended
from Allah a light [cf. Q 5:15] *shining and burning bright. ...*
I remained there weeping the Messenger, and was helped
by my eyes, for such are quick to help,
Remembering the bounties of the Messenger, nor do I think
I can reckon them all, for I remain bewildered,
In shock, consumed by the loss of Aḥmad.
As my soul kept recounting the bounties of the Messenger,
It never reached one tenth of any single matter!
but my soul can at least glorify some of it.
Long does she stand, eyes pouring out tears,
over the remaining grave that contains Aḥmad.
May you be blessed, Grave of the Messenger, and may
the lands in which the Supported Guide died be blessed!
And may the Grave-niche that enfolds the Pure One be blessed,
topped with a structure of unequal stones.[121]

وقال حسان رضي الله عنه:

بِطَيْبَةَ رَسْمٌ لِلرّسُولِ وَمَعْهَدُ * مُنِيرٌ وَقَدْ تَعْفُو الرُّسُومُ وَتَهْمُدُ

وَلَا تَمْتَحِي الْآيَاتُ مِنْ دَارِ حُرْمَةٍ * بِهَا مِنْبَرُ الهَادِي الَّذِي كَانَ يَصْعَدُ

وَوَاضِحُ آثَارٍ وَبَاقِي مَعَالِمَ * وَرَبْعٌ لَهُ فِيهِ مُصَلًّى وَمَسْجِدُ

[121] Ibn Hishām, *Sīra* (3/4:666-669) cf. Ḥassān, *Dīwān* (p. 60-64 §49).

بِهَا حُجُرَاتٌ كَانَ يَنْزِلُ وُسْطَهَـــــا * مِـــــنَ اللهِ نُـــورٌ يُسْتَضَاءُ وَيُوقَدُ

مَعَارِفُ لَمْ تُطْمَسْ عَلَى الْعَهْدِ آيُهَـــا * أَتَاهَـــا الْبِلَـى فَالْآيُ مِنْهَـــا تَجَدَّدُ

عَرَفْتُ بِهَا رَسْمَ الرَّسُولِ وَعَهْـــــدَهُ * وَقَبْـــرًا بِهَا وَارَاهُ فِي التُّرْبِ مُلْحِـدُ

ظَلِلْتُ بِهَا أَبْكِي الرَّسُولَ فَأَسْعَـدَتْ * عُيُـــونٌ وَمِثْلَاهَا مِنَ الْجَفْنِ تُسْعَدُ

يُذَكِّرْنَ آلَاءَ الرَّسُولِ وَمَـــــا أَرَى * لَهَا مُحْصِيًا نَفْسِي فَنَفْسِي تَبَلَّدُ (تتحيَّر)

مُفَجَّعَةً قَدْ شَفَّـــهَا (أضعفها) فَقْدُ أَحْمَدَ * فَظَلَّتْ لِآلَاءِ الرَّسُولِ تُعَدِّدُ

وَمَا بَلَغَـــتْ مِنْ كُلِّ أَمْرٍ عَشِـــيرَهُ * وَلَكِنْ نَفْسِي بَعْضَ مَا فِيهِ تَحْمَدُ

أَطَالَتْ وُقُوفًا تَذْرِفُ الْعَيْنُ جُهْدَهَـــا * عَلَى طَلَلِ الْقَبْرِ الَّذِي فِيهِ أَحْمَدُ

فَبُورِكْتَ يَا قَبْرَ الرَّسُولِ وَبُورِكَـــتْ * بِلَادٌ ثَوَى فِيهَا الرَّشِيدُ الْمُسَدَّدُ

وَبُورِكَ لَحْدٌ مِنْكَ ضُمِّنَ طَيِّبًـــــا * عَلَيْهِ بِنَاءٌ مِنْ صَفِيحٍ مُنَضَّدُ

سيرة ابن هشام وديوان حسان بن ثابت

How the Early Muslims Acted at the Prophet's Grave

Similar addresses were spoken by other pious visitors to the Noble Grave among the early Muslims.

ʿAlī narrated:

89. When the Prophet was buried, his daughter Fāṭima came to his grave, took a handful of earth from it and, placing it over her eyes, wept and said:

What loss does one who smells the scent of Aḥmad's grave
suffer if he never smelled the sweetest ghawālī perfumes?

Troubles were poured on me, had days
endured them they would have turned to night.[122]

عَنْ عَلِيٍّ كَرَّمَ اللهُ وَجْهَهُ قَالَ:

لَمَّا دُفِنَ رَسُولُ اللهِ ﷺ جَاءَتْ فَاطِمَةُ فَوَقَفَتْ عَلَى قَبْرِهِ، وَأَخَذَتْ قَبْضَةً مِنْ تُرَابِ الْقَبْرِ، وَأَنْشَأَتْ تَقُولُ:

مَا عَلَى مَنْ شَمَّ تُرْبَةَ أَحْمَـــدٍ * أَلَّا يَشُمْ مَّدَى الزَّمَانِ غَوَالِيَا
صُبَّتْ عَلَيَّ مَصَائِبٌ لَوْ أَنَّهَا * صُبَّتْ عَلَى الْأَيَّامِ عُدْنَ لَيَالِيَا

رواه ابن الجوزي وابن النجار

90. The Umayyad governor of Madīna Marwān b. al-Ḥakam acted scandalized one day when he saw a man placing his face on top of the grave of the Prophet. He said: "Do you know what you are doing?" When the man turned around, he realized it was Abū Ayyūb al-Anṣārī. In another version Marwān grabbed him by the neck and said: "Do you know what you are doing?" Abū Ayyūb said: "Yes, I know! I have come to the Prophet, not to a stone or a room. I heard the Messenger of Allah say: 'Do not weep over the Religion when its rightful people are in charge of it; but weep over it when those who are unqualified take it over!'"[123]

عَنْ دَاوُدَ بْنِ أَبِي صَالِحٍ قَالَ أَقْبَلَ مَرْوَانُ يَوْمًا فَوَجَدَ رَجُلًا وَاضِعًا وَجْهَهُ عَلَى الْقَبْرِ فَقَالَ أَتَدْرِي مَا تَصْنَعُ فَأَقْبَلَ عَلَيْهِ فَإِذَا هُوَ أَبُو أَيُّوبَ فَقَالَ نَعَمْ جِئْتُ رَسُولَ اللهِ ﷺ وَلَمْ آتِ الحَجَرَ سَمِعْتُ رَسُولَ اللهِ ﷺ يَقُولُ لَا تَبْكُوا

[122] Ibn al-Jawzī, *Wafā* (p. 819 §1538), *Muthīr* (p. 489); Ibn al-Najjar, *Durra* (p. 205).
[123] Aḥmad, *Musnad* (38:558 §23585) and al-Ḥākim, *Mustadrak* (4:515) through identical chains confirmed with parallel chains by al-Ṭabarānī in *al-Muʿjam al-Kabīr* (4:158 §3999) and Ibn ʿAsākir, *Tārīkh* (57:249-250) although al-Ṭabarānī's narrative mentions only the Prophetic hadith without the encounter.

عَلَى الدِّينِ إِذَا وَلِيَهُ أَهْلُهُ وَلَكِنْ إِبْكُوا عَلَيْهِ إِذَا وَلِيَهُ غَيْرُ أَهْلِهِ رواه أحمد والحاكم وله ومتابع عند الطبراني وابن عساكر وجاء عند الأخير بلفظ جَاءَ أَبُو أَيُّوبَ الْأَنْصَارِيُّ يُرِيدُ أَنْ يُسَلِّمَ عَلَى رَسُولِ اللهِ ﷺ فَجَاءَ مَرْوَانُ وَهُوَ كَذَلِكَ فَأَخَذَ بِرَقَبَتِهِ فَقَالَ هَلْ تَدْرِي مَا تَصْنَعُ فَقَالَ قَدْ دَرَيْتُ إِنِّي لَمْ آتِ الحَجَرَ وَلَا الخِدْرَ وَلَكِنِّي جِئْتُ رَسُولَ اللهِ.

Al-Bayhaqī narrates with his chain from Abū Isḥāq al-Qurashī:

91. There was with us a man in Madina who, any time he saw something wrong which he could not change himself, would come to the Grave and say:

O Grave of the Prophet and his two Companions!
will you not help us when you are well aware of our state?[124]

أخبرنا أبو عبد الله الحافظ أخبرني أبو محمد بن زياد نا محمد بن إسحاق الثقفي قال سمعت أبا إسحاق القرشي يقول كَانَ عِنْدَنَا رَجُلٌ بِالْمَدِينَةِ إِذَا رَأَى مُنْكَراً لَا يُمْكِنُهُ أَنْ يُغَيِّرَهُ أَتَى الْقَبْرَ فَقَالَ:

أَيَا قَبْرَ النَّبِيِّ وَصَاحِبَيهِ * أَلَا يَا غَوْثَنَا لَوْ تَعْلَمُونَا

رواه البيهقي والرجل هو الصحابي: النابغةُ قيس بن عبد الله الجَعدي رضي الله عنه

The man in question was the centenarian poet-Companion al-Nābigha, whom the Prophet addressed as Abū Laylā and whose full name was Qays b. ʿAbd Allāh b. ʿAmr al-Jaʿdī. He once said:

92. *We came to the Prophet when he brought guidance*

[124] al-Bayhaqī, *Shuʿab al-Īmān* (6:60 §3879).

reciting a Book as luminous as the constellations.
We have reached the sky through our glory and fame
but we desire a higher summit yet.

The Prophet asked him, "And what summit is that, Abū Laylā?" He replied, "Paradise." The Prophet said: "Yes, if Allah wills."[125]

في لُبَاب الآداب للثعالبي ومِنَح المَدْح لابن سيّد الناس: أَنْشَدَ النَّابِغَةُ الجَعْدِيُّ:

أَتَيْتُ رَسولَ اللهِ إِذْ جَاءَ بِالهُدَى * وَيَتْلُو كِتَاباً كَالمَجَرَّةِ نَيِّرا

بَلَغْنَا السَّمَاءَ مَجْدُنَا وَسَنَاؤُنَا * وَإِنَّا لَنَرْجُوا فَوْقَ ذَلِكَ مَظْهَرَا

وروي أنه ﷺ قَالَ: أَيْنَ المَظْهَرُ يَا أَبَا لَيْلَى؟ قُلْتُ: الجَنَّةُ يَا رَسُولَ اللهِ. قَالَ: أَجَلْ إِنْ شَاءَ اللهُ. رواه أبو نعيم وتمام الرازي والحارث والبيهقي

Abū Ḥarb al-Hilālī narrated that a bedouin visited the grave of the Prophet and addressed it in similar terms:

93. A Bedouin went on pilgrimage. When he reached the door of the Prophet's Mosque he tied his mount, entered, walked up to the Grave, stood opposite the face of the Messenger of Allah, and said: "Peace be upon you, Messenger of Allah!" Then he greeted Abū Bakr and ʿUmar and returned to face the Prophet, saying: "My father and mother be sacrificed for you, Messenger of Allah! I have come to you burdened with sins and offenses, seeking you as my intercessor before your Lord Who said in His inabrogable Book: *Had they but come to you when they wronged themselves, and asked forgiveness of Allah, and the Messenger had asked forgiveness for them, they would have found Allah Oft-Forgiving, Most Merciful* (4:64). And I have come to you – My father and

---

[125] Narrated by Abū Nuʿaym, *Dalāʾil* (§385) and *Maʿrifat al-Ṣaḥāba* (*sub* Qays b. ʿAbd Allāh); al-Ḥārith in his *Musnad*, cf. al-Haythamī, *Bughya* (2:844 §894); Tammām, *Fawāʾid* (4:334-335 §1513); al-Bayhaqī, *Dalāʾil* (6:232); and Ibn ʿAsākir, *Tārīkh* (36:202, 50:132); cf. Ibn Sayyid al-Nās, *Minaḥ* (p. 235-237).

mother be sacrificed for you! – I have come to you burdened with sins and offenses, seeking you as my intercessor before your Lord, asking Him to forgive me for my sins and that you intercede for me." Then he turned again amid the people and declaimed:

O Best of those whose bones are buried in the earth,
and whose soil and mound are fragrant with their scent!
My soul be sacrificed for a grave you inhabit,
in which are found virtue, generosity and honor![126]

Another version adds between the two verses:

You are the Prophet whose intercession is hoped
at the Bridge when feet will slip.[127]

عَنْ أَبِي حَرْبٍ الهِلَالِيِّ قَالَ: حَجَّ أَعْرَابِيٌّ فَلَمَّا جَاءَ إِلَى بَابِ مَسْجِدِ رَسُولِ اللهِ ﷺ أَنَاخَ رَاحِلَتَهُ فَعَلَّقَهَا ثُمَّ دَخَلَ المَسْجِدَ حَتَّى أَتَى القَبْرَ وَوَقَفَ بِحِذَاءِ وَجْهِ رَسُولِ اللهِ ﷺ فَقَالَ: السَّلَامُ عَلَيْكَ يَا رَسُولَ اللهِ ثُمَّ سَلَّمَ عَلَى أَبِي بَكْرٍ وَعُمَرَ ثُمَّ أَقْبَلَ عَلَى رَسُولِ اللهِ ﷺ فَقَالَ بِأَبِي أَنْتَ وَأُمِّي يَا رَسُولَ اللهِ جِئْتُكَ مُثْقَلاً بِالذُّنُوبِ وَالخَطَايَا مُسْتَشْفِعاً بِكَ عَلَى رَبِّكَ لِأَنَّهُ قَالَ فِي مُحْكَمِ كِتَابِهِ ﴿وَلَوْ أَنَّهُمْ إِذ ظَّلَمُوٓاْ أَنفُسَهُمْ جَآءُوكَ فَٱسْتَغْفَرُواْ ٱللَّهَ وَٱسْتَغْفَرَ لَهُمُ ٱلرَّسُولُ لَوَجَدُواْ ٱللَّهَ تَوَّابًا رَّحِيمًا ﴿٦٤﴾﴾ وَقَدْ جِئْتُكَ بِأَبِي أَنْتَ وَأُمِّي

[126] Narrated from Muḥammad b. Ḥarb al-Hilālī by al-Bayhaqī, *Shu'ab al-Īmān* (6:60 §3880); Ibn al-Najjār, *Durra* (p. 224); Ibn al-Jawzī, *Muthīr* (p. 490); and Ibn 'Asākir, *Mu'jam* (1:600 §738, 2:601). It is mentioned in al-Nawawī's *Adhkār*, the *Tafsīr*s of Abū Ḥayyān, Ibn Kathīr, and others, and countless books of *fiqh* toward the end of the chapters on *Ḥajj*. This report is also attributed to Ibn 'Uyayna's student the historian and poet al-'Utbī – Abū 'Abd al-Raḥmān Muḥammad b. 'Abd Allāh b. 'Amr b. Mu'āwiya b. 'Amr b. 'Utba b. Abī Sufyān (d. 228/843) – but there is no known chain to that effect.
[127] al-Jurrāwī, *Ḥamāsa Maghribiyya* (2:799 §430).

جِئْتُكَ مُثْقَلاً بِالذُّنُوبِ وَالخَطَايَا أَسْتَشْفِعُ بِكَ عَلَى رَبِّكَ أَنْ يَغْفِرَ لِي ذُنُوبِي وَأَنْ تَشْفَعَ فِيَّ ثُمَّ أَقْبَلَ فِي عَرْضِ النَّاسِ وَهُوَ يَقُولُ:

يَـا خَيْرَ مَنْ دُفِنَتْ فِي الْأَرْضِ أَعْظُمُهُ * فَطَابَ مِنْ طِيبِهِنَّ الْقَاعُ وَالْأَكَمُ
نَفْسِي الْفِدَاءُ لِقَبْرٍ أَنْتَ سَاكِنُــــهُ * فِيهِ الْعَفَافُ وَفِيهِ الْجُودُ وَالْكَرَمُ

قَالَ الْبَيْهَقِيُّ: وَفِي غَيْرِ هَذِهِ الرِّوَايَةِ:

فَطَابَ مِنْ طِيبِهِ الْقِيعَانُ وَالْأَكَمُ

رواه البيهقي وابن النجار وابن الجوزي وابن عساكر. وذكره النووي في الأذكار وابن كثير في التفسير والفقهاء في كتبهم إثر أبواب الحج. وفي ديوان الحماسة المغربية للجراوي:

يَا خَيْرَ مَنْ دُفِنَتْ فِي التُّرْبِ أَعْظُمُهُ * فَطَابَ مِنْ طِيبِهِنَّ الْقَاعُ وَالْأَكَمُ
أَنْتَ النَّبِيُّ الَّذِي تُرْجَى شَفَاعَتُهُ * عِنْدَ الصِّرَاطِ إِذَا مَا زَلَّتِ الْقَدَمُ
نَفْسِي الْفِدَاءُ لِقَبْرٍ أَنْتَ سَاكِنُــــهُ * فِيهِ الْعَفَافُ وَفِيهِ الْجُودُ وَالْكَرَمُ

Ibn Abī Fudayk (d. 200/815) narrated from those before him:

94. Whoever stands at the grave of the Prophet—upon him blessings and peace—and recites this verse: *Truly Allah and the angels bless the Prophet* (33:56), then says: "Allah bless you O Muḥammad!" (*ṣallā Allāhu ʿalayka yā Muḥammad*), and says so seventy times, an angel will call him and say to him: "Allah bless you O So-and-so! None of your needs has gone unfulfilled."[128]

[128] ʿIyāḍ, *Shifā* II.iv.8 (p. 585 §1471 *fī ḥukmi ziyārati qabrih*) and Ibn al-Jawzī, *Wafā* (p. 817 §1533).

عَنِ ابْنِ أَبِي فُدَيْكٍ قَالَ سَمِعْتُ بَعْضَ مَنْ أَدْرَكْتُ يَقُولُ بَلَغَنَا أَنَّهُ مَنْ وَقَفَ عِنْدَ قَبْرِ النَّبِيِّ ﷺ فَتَلَا هَذِهِ الْآيَةَ: ﴿ إِنَّ ٱللَّهَ وَمَلَٰٓئِكَتَهُۥ يُصَلُّونَ عَلَى ٱلنَّبِيِّۚ يَٰٓأَيُّهَا ٱلَّذِينَ ءَامَنُواْ صَلُّواْ عَلَيْهِ وَسَلِّمُواْ تَسْلِيمًا ﴿٥٦﴾ ﴾ الأحزاب فَقَالَ: صَلَّى اللهُ عَلَيْكَ يَا مُحَمَّدُ يَقُولُهَا سَبْعِينَ مَرَّةً، نَادَاهُ مَلَكٌ: صَلَّى اللهُ عَلَيْكَ يَا فُلَانُ لَمْ تَسْقُطْ لَكَ حَاجَةٌ. رواه عياض وابن الجوزي

Ibn al-Jawzī (510-597/ca.1116-1201) said after adducing the above report that one of the visitors to the Grave said – namely, the pious fourth-century grammarian and lexicographer Ismāʿīl al-Dahhān:

95. *I have come to you on foot and I wish that I*
were able to turn the apple of my eyes into my mount;
Why should I not travel on top of my pupils
to a Grave that contains the Messenger of Allah?[129]

زاد ابن الجوزي بعد سياق خبر ابن أبي فُدَيك: وَقَالَ بَعْضُ زُوَّارِ قَبْرِهِ:

أَتَيْتُكَ رَاجِلاً وَوَدِدْتُ أَنِّي * مَلَكْتُ سَوَادَ عَيْنِي أَمْتَطِيهِ
وَمَا لِيَ لَا أَسِيرُ عَلَى الْمَآقِي * إِلَى قَبْرٍ رَسُولُ اللهِ فِيهِ

والقائل هو النحوي الزاهد تلميذ الجوهري (ت 393) أبو محمد إسماعيل بن محمد بن عبدوس الدهّان كما في يتيمة الدهر للثعالبي والوافي بالوفيات ومعجم الأدباء.

[129] Ibn al-Jawzī, *Wafā* (p. 817 §1533) cf. his *Muthīr* (p. 492). The poet was al-Jawharī's (d. 393/1003) student the ascetic linguist Abū Muḥammad Ismāʿīl b. Muḥammad al-Dahhān as narrated by al-Thaʿālibī in his anthology of pre-fifth century poets entitled *Yatīmat al-Dahr* (4:498).

The Yemeni hadith master Ibn al-Dayba' (866-944/1461-1537) built on this image in his famous *mawlid*:

96. *Even if we rode [to him] every moment*
on top of our eyeballs, not on top of camels;
And even if we celebrated every day
a mawlid for Aḥmad, that would still be our duty.[130]

قال الحافظ ابن الدَّيبَع الزَّبِيدي في مولده المشهور:

فَلَوْ أَنَّا سَعَيْنَا كُلَّ حِينٍ عَلَى الْأَحْدَاقِ لَا فَوْقَ النَّجَائِبِ
وَلَوْ أَنَّا عَمِلْنَا كُلَّ يَوْمٍ لِأَحْمَدَ مَوْلِداً قَدْ كَانَ وَاجِب

The hadith master Abū Ṭāhir al-Silafī (475-576/1082-1180) narrated the above verses as he heard them from "Abū 'Alī 'Ubayd Allāh b. Ibrāhīm b. 'Abd al-Wahhāb al-Ḥusaynī the orator of Madīna, the Grave, and the Pulpit" then followed them up with two more verses from another Madinan teacher of his:

97. *And when we reach on our camels Muḥammad*
their backs become forbidden to all riders.
We are approaching the Best of those who trod the stones,
hence they demand of us his high respect and awe.[131]

وروى البيتين الحافظ أبو طاهر السِّلَفي في مُعجم السَّفَر قال: أنشدنا أبو علي عبيد الله بن إبراهيم بن عبد الوهاب الحسيني خطيب المدينة والقبر والمنبر لبعض المتقدمين، أَتَيْتُكَ رَاجِلاً الخ. ثم قال السِلفي: ثم أنشدنا أبو محمد الحسن بن عبد الله بن مولاه الكاتب الأصبهاني بالمدينة فكتبناه أيضا تبركا بها والشعر مشهور قديم:

130 *Mawlid al-Dayba'ī* in *Majmū' Mushtamil* (p. 49).
131 al-Silafī, *Mu'jam al-Safar* (p. 224 §727).

وَإِذَا الْمَطِيُّ بِنَا بَلَغْــــنَ مُحَمَّدًا ❋ فَظُهُورُهُنَّ عَلَى الرِّحَالِ حَرَامُ

قَرَّبْنَا مِنْ خَيْرِ مَنْ وَطِئَ الْحَصَا ❋ فَلَهَا عَلَيْنَا حُرْمَةٌ وَذِمَــــامُ

The major Imam of *fiqh* Isḥāq b. Rāhūyah (d. 238/852) said:

98. It has been from the very beginning the practice of whoever went on pilgrimage to pass by Madina and be sure to perform prayer in the Mosque of the Messenger of Allah and obtain blessing by beholding his *Rawḍa*, his Pulpit and his Grave, as well as where he sat, where his hands touched, where his feet walked, the pillar against which he leaned, and where Jibrīl descended on him with revelation, and obtain blessing through whoever frequented it and made sure to visit it among the Companions and the Imams of the Muslims, and to reflect upon all that and follow its example.[132]

في الشفا للقاضي عياض: قَالَ إِسْحَاقُ بْنُ إِبْرَاهِيمَ الْفَقِيهُ – يَعْنِي إِسْحَاقَ بْنَ رَاهُوْيَهْ مِنْ كِبَارِ أَئِمَّةِ الْحَدِيثِ الْمُجْتَهِدِينَ: وَمِمَّا لَمْ يَزَلْ مِنْ شَأْنِ مَنْ حَجَّ الْمُرُورُ بِالْمَدِينَةِ وَالْقَصْدُ إِلَى الصَّلَاةِ فِي مَسْجِدِ رَسُولِ اللهِ ﷺ وَالتَّبَرُّكُ بِرُؤْيَةِ رَوْضَتِهِ وَمِنْبَرِهِ وَقَبْرِهِ وَمَجْلِسِهِ وَمَلَامِسِ يَدَيْهِ وَمَوَاطِئِ قَدَمَيْهِ وَالْعَمُودِ الَّذِي كَانَ يَسْتَنِدُ إِلَيْهِ وَيَنْزِلُ جِبْرِيلُ بِالْوَحْيِ فِيهِ عَلَيهِ وَبِمَنْ عَمَرَهُ وَقَصَدَهُ مِنَ الصَّحَابَةِ وَأَئِمَّةِ الْمُسْلِمِينَ وَالاِعْتِبَارُ بِذَٰلِكَ كُلِّهِ.

What Ibn Rāhūyah describes as the ethics of the *Salaf al-Ṣāliḥ* in visitation (*ziyāra*) and seeking blessings through relics (*tabarruk bil-āthār*) is confirmed by the practice of the Companions and Succes-

[132] In ʿIyāḍ, *Shifā* II.iv.8 (p. 585 §1471 *fī ḥukmi ziyārati qabrih*).

sors and in the notable fatwas of his friend Aḥmad b. Ḥanbal and Imām Mālik among others.[133]

Ḥassān lists the places which Muslims assiduously visit to commemorate the Prophet in one of his funeral elegies:

99. *Has Man seen any mortal grief ever match*
the grief of the day in which Muḥammad died?
He—the alighting-place of revelation—was severed from them,
and he was full of light that plunged deep and soared high,
Pointing whoever followed his guidance to the All-Beneficent
and saving them from disasters, and showing them the way.
Their leader, guiding them to truth with utmost striving
and a teacher of truthfulness: to obey him spells bliss.
He always forgave slips, accepting their excuses;
and if they did their best, Allah is Most Generous with bounty.
If something was too difficult for them to carry
they found him lenient and leaving aside strictness.
As they basked in that light, behold, one morning
death's arrow smote their light.
Praised and beloved, he returned to Allah,
mourned by the angels and glorified.
And the sanctified country has become desolate
after the disappearance of prophecy which descended on it—
Wild caves, except for the oft-visited side-niche dwelt
by the one they lost, wept by Balāṭ and the gharqad-tree,
And also by his Mosque, filled with sad reminders of his loss:
the empty spots where he stood praying and where he sat,
And at the Major Stoning Station, there also he is missed
by houses and plains and living quarters and birthplace.
So weep the Messenger of Allah, my eyes, with copious tears,
and let me never catch you refraining for the rest of my life!
And why should you not weep the owner of favor
that bestowed it on the people who then basked in it?
So weep him and weep with profuse tears and sobs
for the loss of the one like whom none will ever exist.

[133] Cf. Haddad, *Four Imams* (pp. 177, 321-322, 390-392).

The ancients never lost the like of Muḥammad,
nor will his like until the Resurrection ever be lost again.[134]

قال حسان:

وَهَلْ عَدَلَتْ يَوْمًا رَزِيَّةُ هَالِكٍ * رَزِيَّةَ يَوْمٍ مَاتَ فِيهِ مُحَمَّدُ؟
تَقَطَّعَ فِيهِ مَنْزِلُ الْوَحْيِ عَنْهُمْ * وَقَدْ كَانَ ذَا نُورٍ يَغُورُ وَيُنْجِدُ
يَدُلُّ عَلَى الرَّحْمٰنِ مَنْ يَقْتَدِي بِهِ * وَيُنْقِذُ مِنْ هَوْلِ الْخَزَايَا وَيُرْشِدُ
إِمَامٌ لَهُمْ يَهْدِيهِمُ الحَقَّ جَاهِدًا * مُعَلِّمُ صِدْقٍ إِنْ يُطِيعُوهُ يُسْعَدُوا
عَفُوٌّ عَنِ الزَّلَّاتِ يَقْبَلُ عُذْرَهُمْ * وَإِنْ يُحْسِنُوا فَاللهُ بِالْخَيْرِ أَجْوَدُ
وَإِنْ نَابَ أَمْرٌ لَمْ يَقُومُوا بِحَمْلِهِ * فَمِنْ عِنْدِهِ تَيْسِيرُ مَا يُتَشَدَّدُ
فَبَيْنَا هُمْ فِي ذٰلِكَ النُّورِ إِذْ غَدَا * إِلَى نُورِهِمْ سَهْمٌ مِنَ الْمَوْتِ مُقْصِدُ
فَأَصْبَحَ مَحْمُوداً إِلَى اللهِ رَاجِعاً * يَبْكِيهِ جَفْنُ الْمُرْسَلَاتِ وَيُحْمَدُ
وَأَمْسَتْ بِلَادُ الْحُرْمِ وَحْشًا بِقَاعُهَا * لِغَيْبَةِ مَا كَانَتْ مِنَ الْوَحْيِ تُعْهَدُ
قِفَارًا سِوَى مَعْمُورَةِ اللَّحْدِ ضَافَهَا * فَقِيدٌ يُبَكِّيْنَهُ بَلَاطٌ وَغَرْقَدُ
وَمَسْجِدُهُ فَالْمُوحِشَاتُ لِفَقْدِهِ * خَلَاءٌ لَهُ فِيهِ مَقَامٌ وَمَقْعَدُ
وَبِالْجَمْرَةِ الْكُبْرَى لَهُ ثَمَّ أَوْحَشَتْ * دِيَارٌ وَعَرَصَاتٌ وَرَبْعٌ وَمَوْلِدُ
فَبَكِّي رَسُولَ اللهِ يَا عَيْنُ عَبْرَةً * وَلَا أَعْرِفَنَّكِ الدَّهْرَ دَمْعُكِ يَجْمُدُ
وَمَا لَكِ لَا تَبْكِينَ ذَا النَّعْمَةِ الَّتِي * عَلَى النَّاسِ مِنْهَا سَابِغٌ يُتَغَمَّدُ
فَجُودِي عَلَيْهِ بِالدُّمُوعِ وَأَعْوِلِي * لِفَقْدِ الَّذِي لَا مِثْلُهُ الدَّهْرَ يُوجَدُ

[134] Ibn Hishām, *Sīra* (3/4:666-669) cf. Ḥassān, *Dīwān* (p. 60-64 §49).

سيرة ابن هشام وديوان حسان بن ثابت

Both Abū Bakr al-Ṣiddīq and ʿAlī b. Abī Ṭālib echoed the same feeling of insurmountable loss with utterances that celebrated the perfections of the Prophet even in death. Abū Bakr said:

100. *He was the quintessence of characters and they knew this,*
[variant: He was exempt of defects and they knew this well,]
and virtue, therefore we compare none to him.
*[*var.*: and virtue, therefore you cannot compare anyone to him.]*
My soul be sacrificed for you who lay dead, and for your body!
How pure your mention, how pure your character and frame![135]

قال أبو بكر الصدّيق رضي الله عنه:

كَانَ الْمُصَفَّاءَ فِي الْأَخْلَاقِ قَدْ عَلِمُوا * وَفِي الْعَفَافِ فَلَمْ نَعْدِلْ بِهِ أَحَدَا
نَفْسِي فِدَاؤُكَ مِنْ مَيْتٍ وَمِنْ بَدَنٍ * مَا أَطْيَبَ الذِّكْرَ وَالْأَخْلَاقَ وَالْجَسَدَا

رواه ابن سعد في الطبقات وجاء بلفظ:

كَانَ الْمُصَفَّى مِنَ الآفَاتِ قَدْ عَلِمُوا * وَفِي الْعَفَافِ فَلَا تَعْدِلْ بِهِ أَحَدَا

كذا في كتاب المُتَمَنِّين لابن أبي الدنيا وديوان الصّدّيق المطبوع

101. [From ʿĀ'isha] Abū Bakr came and uncovered the Prophet—upon him blessings and peace. He kissed him and said: "By my father and my mother! Truly you are pure in life and you are pure in death."[136]

[135] Ibn Saʿd, *Ṭabaqāt* (2:278) cf. Abū Bakr al-Ṣiddīq, *Dīwān* (p. 83) and Ibn Abī al-Dunyā, *Mutamannīn* (p. 45 §56).
[136] al-Bukhārī, *Ṣaḥīḥ* (*Manāqib, qawl al-Nabī law kuntu muttakhidhan khalīlā*).

عَنْ عَائِشَةَ فَجَاءَ أَبُو بَكْرٍ فَكَشَفَ عَنْ رَسُولِ اللهِ ﷺ فَقَبَّلَهُ قَالَ بِأَبِي أَنْتَ وَأُمِّي طِبْتَ حَيًّا وَمَيِّتًا رواه البخاري

102. [From ʿAlī:] When he washed the Prophet he expected to experience whatever the washers of the dead experience but he did not. Then he said: "By my father, how pure he is! You are pure in life and you are pure in death."[137]

عَنْ عَلِيِّ بْنِ أَبِي طَالِبٍ كَرَّمَ اللهُ وَجْهَهُ قَالَ لَـمَّا غَسَلَ النَّبِيَّ ﷺ ذَهَبَ يَلْتَمِسُ مِنْهُ مَا يُلْتَمَسُ مِنَ الْمَيِّتِ فَلَمْ يَجِدْهُ فَقَالَ: بِأَبِي الطَّيِّبُ طِبْتَ حَيّاً وَطِبْتَ مَيِّتاً

رواه ابن ماجه وفي الزوائد: هذا إسناد صحيح ورجاله ثقات

[137] Ibn Mājah, *Sunan* (*Janāʾiz, mā jāʾ fī ghasl al-Nabī*) with a sound chain according to al-Būṣīrī in his *Miṣbāḥ al-Zujāja*.

IV

The Prophet as a Light from the Light of Allah

Two other Qur'anic passages go further than 33:45-46 in identifying the Prophet as a light not only *by means of* which but also *to* which Allah guides, the first one addressing Christians and Jews at the forefront of humankind at large (5:15-16), the second treating them as outsiders between the two poles—Ibrāhīm and Muḥammad—of pure monotheism (24:35); what is more, both passages cite that attribute of light as literally "from God" (*min Allāh*) and "of God" (*nūrihi*).

There has come to you from Allah a Light

The first passage is nearly explicit:

> *O People of the Book, Our Messenger has come to you, making clear to you much of what you used to conceal from the Book, and forgiving much. There has come to you from Allah a Light (nūrun) and a Book most lucid; With it Allah guides him who conforms to His good pleasure to the paths of tranquillity; He shall lead them from the folds of darkness to the light, by His leave; and He shall guide them to a straight path* (*ṣirāṭ mustaqīm*) (5:15-16).

﴿ يَٰٓأَهۡلَ ٱلۡكِتَٰبِ قَدۡ جَآءَكُمۡ رَسُولُنَا يُبَيِّنُ لَكُمۡ كَثِيرٗا مِّمَّا
كُنتُمۡ تُخۡفُونَ مِنَ ٱلۡكِتَٰبِ وَيَعۡفُواْ عَن كَثِيرٖۚ قَدۡ جَآءَكُم
مِّنَ ٱللَّهِ نُورٞ وَكِتَٰبٞ مُّبِينٞ ﴿١٥﴾ يَهۡدِي بِهِ ٱللَّهُ مَنِ ٱتَّبَعَ
رِضۡوَٰنَهُۥ سُبُلَ ٱلسَّلَٰمِ وَيُخۡرِجُهُم مِّنَ ٱلظُّلُمَٰتِ إِلَى ٱلنُّورِ بِإِذۡنِهِۦ
وَيَهۡدِيهِمۡ إِلَىٰ صِرَٰطٖ مُّسۡتَقِيمٖ ﴿١٦﴾ ﴾ المائدة.

103. Qatāda (d. 117/735), al-Zajjāj (241-311/ca. 855-923) and two dozen others gloss *nūrun* here as Muḥammad, "with whom Allah has illuminated truth, brought out Islam, and eradicated polytheism; he is a light for whoever uses his light, which makes truth (*al-ḥaqq*) manifest" according to Ṭabarī (224-310/839-ca.922).[138] The *ṣirāṭ mustaqīm* itself has also been glossed as the Prophet Muḥammad.[139]

قال الطبري: يَعْنِي بِالنُّورِ: مُحَمَّداً ﷺ الَّذِي أَنَارَ اللهُ بِهِ الحَقَّ وَأَظْهَرَ بِهِ الإِسْلَامَ وَمَحَقَ بِهِ الشِّرْكَ فَهُوَ نُورٌ لِمَنِ اسْتَنَارَ بِهِ يُبَيِّنُ الحَقَّ. وقال به قتادة والزَّجَّاج والواحدي والماوردي والثعلبي ومكي والثعالبي والبغوي وابن الجوزي وابن عطية والرازي والعز ابن عبد السلام والخازن وابن جُزَي وابن عادل والجلالين والبقاعي والأعقم الآنسي الزيدي والشربيني والقاري والآلوسي وابن عاشور والنووي الجاوي وأطفيش الإباضي ومحمد أبو زهرة وغيرهم وقال مكي ﴿ٱلصِّرَٰطَ ٱلْمُسْتَقِيمَ﴾: مُحَمَّدٌ ﷺ. كما سبق ذكر قول كعب بن زهير:

إِنَّ الرَّسولَ لَنُورٌ يُسْتَضَاءُ بِهِ

وقول أبي الطفيل عامر بن واثلة:

إِنَّ النَّبِيَّ هُوَ النُّورُ الَّذِي كُشِفَتْ * بِهِ عِمَايَةُ مَاضِينَا وَبَاقِينَا

وقول حسّان:

[138] *Tafsīrs* of al-Ṭabarī (8:264 *sub* 5:15), al-Zajjāj, al-Wāḥidī, al-Māwardī, al-Tha'labī, Makkī al-Qaysī, al-Tha'ālibī, al-Baghawī, Ibn al-Jawzī, Ibn 'Aṭiyya, al-Rāzī ("as for the interpretation of the Light and the Book as both meaning the Qur'ān, it is a weak interpretation" and a Mu'tazilī exegesis promoted by al-Jubbā'ī and al-Zamakhsharī), Ibn 'Abd al-Salām, al-Khāzin, Ibn Juzay, Ibn 'Ādil, al-Jalālayn, al-Biqā'ī, al-A'qam al-Ānisī (Zaydī), al-Shirbīnī, al-Qārī, al-Ālūsī, Ibn 'Āshūr, Nawawī al-Jāwī, Aṭfīsh (Ibāḍī), Muḥammad Abū Zahra, and others.
[139] Makkī, *Hidāya* (*sub* 1:6).

الَّذِي كَانَ فِينَا يُسْتَضَاءُ بِهِ * مُبَارَكَ الْأَمْرِ ذَا عَدْلٍ وَإِرْشَادِ

وقوله أيضاً:

بِهَا حُجُرَاتٌ كَانَ يَنْزِلُ وَسْطَهَا * مِنَ اللهِ نُورٌ يُسْتَضَاءُ وَيُوقَدُ

ونحوه قول الناظم:

وَاسْتَضِيئُوا بِجَمَالٍ * فَاقَ فِي الْحُسْنِ تَفَرَّدْ

The above gloss echoes the Companions Ka'b b. Zuhayr, Abū al-Ṭufayl, and Ḥassān b. Thābit's verses already cited, "*Truly the Messenger of Allah is a light whose illumination is sought*" (*inna al-Rasūla la-nūrun yustaḍā'u bihi*), "*Truly the Prophet is the light that has dispelled the blindness of our past and future,*" "*he who in our midst was the source of our light*" (*yustaḍā'u bihi*), and "*In it are chambers in the midst of which descended from Allah a light illuminating and burning bright (min Allāhi nūrun yustaḍā'u wa-yūqadu)*. Similarly the *mawlid* poem *Yā Nabī, Salām 'alayka* states:

104. *And seek the light of a beauty exceedingly superior and unique.*

Al-Biqā'ī (809-885/1406-1480) stated:

> **105.** *There has come to you* – and He magnified it by using the Greatest Name and saying *from Allah*, that is, the One to Whom belongs the all-encompassing attributes of perfection – *a Light*, that is the one whose luminosity is abundantly clear, namely Muḥammad.[140]

قال البِقاعي في نظم الدرر ﴿ قَدْ جَآءَكُم ﴾ وَعَظَّمَهُ بِقَوْلِهِ مُعَبِّراً بِالْإِسْمِ الْأَعْظَمِ: ﴿ مِّنَ ٱللَّهِ ﴾ أَيِ الَّذِي لَهُ الْإِحَاطَةُ بِأَوْصَافِ الْكَمَالِ ﴿ نُورٌ ﴾

[140] al-Biqā'ī, *Naẓm al-Durar* (6:63, *sub* 5 :15).

أَيْ وَاضِحُ النُّورِيَّةِ وَهُوَ مُحَمَّدٌ ﷺ. وقال الآلوسي: ﴿قَدْ جَآءَكُم مِّنَ ٱللَّهِ نُورٌ﴾ عَظِيمٌ وَهُوَ نُورُ الْأَنْوَارِ وَالنَّبِيُّ الْمُخْتَارُ ﷺ.

106. Al-Ālūsī and Muḥammad Abū Zahra (1315-1394/1898-1974) respectively stated: "*There has come to you from Allah a Light* most tremendous, and he is the Light of lights and the elect Prophet."[141] "Indeed the noble Prophet is the Light of all lights as al-Ālūsī phrased it."[142]

Al-Qārī said:

> **107.** It has also been said that both the Light and the Book refer to Muḥammad, because just as he is a tremendous Light and the source of all lights, he is also a Book that gathers up and makes clear all the secrets.[143]

قال الملا علي القاري في شرح الشفا: وَقِيلَ الْمُرَادُ بِهِمَا أَيْ فِي قَوْلِهِ تَعَالَى ﴿نُورٌ وَكِتَٰبٌ مُّبِينٌ﴾: مُحَمَّدٌ ﷺ لِأَنَّهُ كَمَا هُوَ نُورٌ عَظِيمٌ وَمَنْشَأٌ لِسَائِرِ الْأَنْوَارِ، فَهُوَ كِتَابٌ جَامِعٌ مُبَيِّنٌ لِجَمِيعِ الْأَسْرَارِ.

Al-Ālūsī also said:

> **108.** I do not consider it far-fetched that what is meant by both the Light and the Manifest Book is the Prophet.... There is no doubt that all can be said to refer to the Prophet. Perhaps you will be reluctant to accept this from the viewpoint of expression *(ʿibāra)*; then let it be from that of allusion *(ishāra)*!"[144]

[141] Ālūsī, *Rūḥ al-Maʿānī* (*sub* 5:15).
[142] Abū Zahra, *Zahrat al-Tafāsīr* (*sub* 5:15).
[143] al-Qārī, *Sharḥ al-Shifā* I.iii.14 (1:505).
[144] al-Ālūsī, *Rūḥ al-Maʿānī* (6:97).

قال الآلوسي وَلَا يَبْعُدُ عِنْدِي أَنْ يُرَادَ بِالنُّورِ وَالْكِتَابِ الْمُبِينِ النَّبِيُّ ﷺ ... وَلَا شَكَّ فِي صِحَّةِ إِطْلَاقِ كُلٍّ عَلَيْهِ ﷺ، وَلَعَلَّكَ تَتَوَقَّفُ فِي قَبُولِهِ مِنْ بَابِ الْعِبَارَةِ فَلْيَكُنْ ذَلِكَ مِنْ بَابِ الْإِشَارَةِ

The allusion is based on the description of the Prophet as a living, walking Qur'ān as mentioned in the saying of ʿĀ'isha to Anas b. Mālik's paternal cousin Saʿd b. Hishām al-Anṣārī:

109. Do you not read the Qur'ān? Truly his character was the Qur'ān.[145]

The exegetes adduced the above hadith in commentary of the verse *And truly you are of a magnificent character* (68:4).[146]

عَنْ عَائِشَةَ رَضِيَ اللهُ عَنْهَا قَالَتْ لِسَعْدِ بْنِ عَامِرٍ: أَلَيْسَ تَقْرَأُ الْقُرْآنَ؟ فَإِنَّ خُلُقَ نَبِيِّ اللهِ ﷺ كَانَ الْقُرْآنَ رواه مسلم وأبو داود وجاء بلفظ كَانَ خُلُقُهُ الْقُرْآنَ رواه أحمد وبلفظ فَإِنَّ خُلُقَ نَبِيِّ اللهِ ﷺ الْقُرْآنُ النسائي. ذكره المفسرون في تفسير آية ﴿وَإِنَّكَ لَعَلَىٰ خُلُقٍ عَظِيمٍ ۝٤﴾. القلم.

"I.e. his character was the character of Allah" (Suhrawardī)

The Shāfiʿī grandmaster and Shaykh al-Islām Shihāb al-Dīn al-Suhrawardī (539-632/ca.1145-1235) said in commentary of the above hadith in *ʿAwārif al-Maʿārif*, one of the founding texts of *taṣawwuf*:

[145] Muslim, *Ṣaḥīḥ* (*Ṣalāt al-musāfirīn, jāmiʿ ṣalāt al-layl*); al-Nasā'ī, *Sunan* (*Qiyām al-layl wa-taṭawwuʿ al-nahār*; *bāb qiyām al-layl*); Aḥmad, *Musnad* (41:314-317 §24269, 42:183 §25302, 43:15 §25813); Abū Dāwūd, *Sunan* (*Ṭahāra, ṣalāt al-layl*; *Ṣalāt, abwāb qiyām al-layl*).

[146] *Tafsīrs* of ʿAbd al-Razzāq, al-Ṭabarī, al-Qurṭubī, and others (*sub* 68:4).

110. Know that in the statement of ʿĀ'isha "his character was the Qur'ān" there is a hidden sign and a subtle hint pointing to the Divine Traits (*al-akhlāq al-rabbāniyya*). She was too shy before Allah to say: "His character was the character of Allah," so she expressed the same meaning by saying "his character was the Qur'ān" out of modesty before the glories of Divine Majesty and as a cover for the actual state of affairs through fine language. This is from her superior intelligence and her accomplished manners. There is also, between the saying of Allah *We have given you Seven of the Oft-repeated and the great Qur'ān* (15:87) and His saying *And truly you are of a magnificent character* (68:4) a congruence (*munāsaba*) that proclaims [the same thing as] the saying of ʿĀ'isha: "his character was the Qur'ān."[147]

قال السهروردي رحمه الله في باب أخلاق الصوفية وشرح الخُلُق من عوارف المعارف:

إِعْلَمْ أَنَّ قَوْلَ عَائِشَةَ رَضِيَ اللهُ عَنْهَا: كَانَ خُلُقُهُ الْقُرْآنَ فِيهِ رَمْزٌ غَامِضٌ وَإِيمَاءٌ خَفِيٌّ إِلَى الْأَخْلَاقِ الرَّبَّانِيَّةِ، فَاحْتَشَمَتْ مِنَ الْحَضْرَةِ الْإِلٰهِيَّةِ أَنْ تَقُولَ: كَانَ ﷺ مُتَخَلِّقاً بِأَخْلَاقِ اللهِ تَعَالَى، فَعَبَّرَتْ عَنِ الْمَعْنَى بِقَوْلِهَا كَانَ خُلُقُهُ الْقُرْآنَ اسْتِحْيَاءً مِنْ سُبُحَاتِ الْجَلَالِ، وَسَتْراً لِلْحَالِ بِلُطْفِ الْمَقَالِ، وَهٰذَا مِنْ وُفُورِ عَقْلِهَا وَكَمَالِ أَدَبِهَا. وَبَيْنَ قَوْلِهِ تَعَالَى ﴿وَلَقَدْ ءَاتَيْنَٰكَ سَبْعًا مِّنَ ٱلْمَثَانِى وَٱلْقُرْءَانَ ٱلْعَظِيمَ ﴿٨٧﴾﴾ الحجر وبَيْنَ قَوْلِهِ ﴿وَإِنَّكَ لَعَلَىٰ خُلُقٍ عَظِيمٍ ﴿٤﴾﴾ القلم مُنَاسَبَةٌ مُشْعِرَةٌ بِقَوْلِ عَائِشَةَ رَضِيَ اللهُ عَنْهَا: كَانَ خُلُقُهُ الْقُرْآنَ.

147 al-Suhrawardī, *ʿAwārif* (p. 166 *Bāb 29: fī akhlāq al-ṣūfiyya wa-sharḥ al-khuluq*).

"He is the mirror of the Essence and Attributes" (al-Wartujabī)

The erudite linguist and Sufi scholar Ibn Kīrān (1172-1227/1759-1812) in his commentary on the *Ṣalāt Mashīshiyya* cited some of the above explanation then said:

> al-Wartujabī[148] said: in His saying *Truly those who swear allegiance unto you swear allegiance only unto Allah* (48:10) He made His Prophet a mirror for the appearance of His Essence and Attributes. This is how some understood the hadith "Whoever sees me sees Truth (*man ra'ānī fa-qad ra'ā al-Ḥaqq*)."[149] It is also the meaning of their statement that the Prophet is the Perfect Human Being (*al-insān al-kāmil*), and that He is created "in the image of Allah," and "in the image of the All-Beneficent," as narrated.[150] Hence he was named after many of the Divine Names, such as the Kindly (al-Ra'ūf), the Merciful (al-Raḥīm), and the Light (al-Nūr). The Prophet alluded to that meaning for other than him as well when he said: "The best of my Community are those who, when you see them, you remember Allah."[151]

قال ابن كيران رحمه الله في شرح الصلاة المشيشية:

قَالَ الوَرْتُجُبِيُّ فِي قَولِهِ تَعَالَى: ﴿ إِنَّ ٱلَّذِينَ يُبَايِعُونَكَ إِنَّمَا يُبَايِعُونَ ٱللَّهَ ﴾ الآية. الفتح: جَعَلَ نَبِيَّهُ ﷺ مِرْآةً لِظُهُورِ ذَاتِهِ وَصِفَاتِهِ، وَعَلَى هٰذَا حَمَلَ بَعْضُهُمْ قَوْلَهُ ﷺ: مَنْ رَآنِي فَقَدْ رَأَى الحَقَّ متفق عليه. وَهُوَ أَيضاً مَعْنَى قَوْلِهِمْ إِنَّ النَّبِيَّ ﷺ هُوَ الإِنْسَانُ الْكَامِلُ، وَأَنَّهُ مَخْلُوقٌ عَلَى صُورَةِ الله، وَعَلَى صُورَةِ الرَّحْمٰنِ. [متفق عليه بلفظ خَلَقَ اللهُ عَزَّ وَجَلَّ آدَمَ عَلَى صُورَتِهِ]. وَقَدْ وَرَدَ الْخَبَرُ

[148] One of Ibn 'Ajība's sources in his *Tafsīr al-Baḥr al-Madīd.*
[149] al-Bukhārī and Muslim.
[150] "Allah created Adam in his/His image" in al-Bukhārī and Muslim.
[151] See Part VIII on this hadith. Ibn Kīrān, *Sharḥ al-Ṣalāt al-Mashīshiyya* (p. 47).

بِذٰلِكَ. وَمِنْ هُنَا سُمِّيَ ﷺ بِكَثِيرٍ مِنْ أَسْمَائِهِ تَعَالَى كَالرَّؤُوفِ، وَالرَّحِيمِ، وَالنُّورِ. وَقَدْ أَشَارَ ﷺ إِلَى هٰذَا المَعْنَى فِي حَقِّ غَيْرِهِ بِقَولِهِ خِيَارُ أُمَّتِي الَّذِينَ إِذَا رُؤُوا ذُكِرَ اللهُ. أحمد والطبراني والبزار.

His Face Resembled the Qur'ān

Indeed, not only did the Prophet's character reflect the Holy Qur'ān and "the Traits of Allah" but so did his face, as witnessed by the hadith of Anas (10BH-93/613-712):

111. Abū Bakr led the prayer for them during the Prophet's final illness. On Monday, as they were all in the rows of prayer, the Prophet opened the curtain of his room and looked at us, standing, his face looking like a page from the volume of the Qur'ān.[152] Then he smiled broadly. We almost broke up our prayer from the joy we felt at seeing the Prophet. Abū Bakr retreated backwards to join up with the first row, thinking that the Prophet was coming out to pray. But the Prophet motioned to us to continue our prayer as we were and he closed the curtain. He died on that day.[153]

عَنْ أَنَسٍ رَضِيَ اللهُ عَنْهُ أَنَّ أَبَا بَكْرٍ كَانَ يُصَلِّي لَهُمْ فِي وَجَعِ النَّبِيِّ ﷺ الَّذِي تُوُفِّيَ فِيهِ حَتَّى إِذَا كَانَ يَوْمُ الإِثْنَيْنِ وَهُمْ صُفُوفٌ فِي الصَّلَاةِ فَكَشَفَ النَّبِيُّ ﷺ سِتْرَ الْحُجْرَةِ يَنْظُرُ إِلَيْنَا وَهُوَ قَائِمٌ كَأَنَّ وَجْهَهُ وَرَقَةُ مُصْحَفٍ ثُمَّ تَبَسَّمَ يَضْحَكُ فَهَمَمْنَا أَنْ نَفْتَتِنَ مِنْ الْفَرَحِ بِرُؤْيَةِ النَّبِيِّ ﷺ فَنَكَصَ أَبُو بَكْرٍ عَلَى

[152] By the time Anas died the ʿUthmanic *muṣḥaf* had been in circulation for over half a century.

[153] al-Bukhārī, *Ṣaḥīḥ* (*al-Jamāʿa wal-Jumuʿa, ahl al-ʿilm wal-faḍl aḥaqq bil-imāma*); Muslim, *Ṣaḥīḥ* (*Ṣalāt, istikhlāf al-imām idhā ʿaraḍa lahu ʿudhr*).

عَقِبَيْهِ لِيَصِلَ الصَّفَّ وَظَنَّ أَنَّ النَّبِيَّ ﷺ خَارِجٌ إِلَى الصَّلَاةِ فَأَشَارَ إِلَيْنَا النَّبِيُّ ﷺ أَنْ أَتِمُّوا صَلَاتَكُمْ وَأَرْخَى السِّتْرَ فَتُوُفِّيَ مِنْ يَوْمِهِ. متفق عليه.

Such reflection, moreover, was reciprocal, since the Qur'ān itself reflects the character and even the body of the Prophet as shown at the end of the next section.

***The Similitude of the Divine Light* is the Prophet**

The second passage is allusive and allegorical:

> *Allah is the Light of the heavens and the earth. The similitude of His light is like a niche in which is a lamp, the lamp is in a crystal, the crystal resembles a star of diamond kindled from a blessed tree, an olive neither of the East nor of the West, its oil almost aglow though untouched by fire; Light upon Light! Allah guides to His Light whomever He wills and strikes parables for mankind. Allah has knowledge of all things* (24:35).

﴿ ۞ ٱللَّهُ نُورُ ٱلسَّمَٰوَٰتِ وَٱلْأَرْضِ ۚ مَثَلُ نُورِهِۦ كَمِشْكَوٰةٍ فِيهَا مِصْبَاحٌ ۖ ٱلْمِصْبَاحُ فِى زُجَاجَةٍ ۖ ٱلزُّجَاجَةُ كَأَنَّهَا كَوْكَبٌ دُرِّىٌّ يُوقَدُ مِن شَجَرَةٍ مُّبَٰرَكَةٍ زَيْتُونَةٍ لَّا شَرْقِيَّةٍ وَلَا غَرْبِيَّةٍ يَكَادُ زَيْتُهَا يُضِىٓءُ وَلَوْ لَمْ تَمْسَسْهُ نَارٌ ۚ نُّورٌ عَلَىٰ نُورٍ ۗ يَهْدِى ٱللَّهُ لِنُورِهِۦ مَن يَشَآءُ ۚ وَيَضْرِبُ ٱللَّهُ ٱلْأَمْثَٰلَ لِلنَّاسِ ۗ وَٱللَّهُ بِكُلِّ شَىْءٍ عَلِيمٌ ٣٥ ﴾

Among the earliest glosses Muqātil b. Sulaymān (d. 150/767) explained the expression *the similitude of His light* as referring to the Prophet Muḥammad to the end of the verse:

112. *Allah is the Light of the heavens and the earth* means He is the Guide of the dwellers of the heavens and the earth. After that the discourse ends and the description of His Prophet begins, with whatever similitude He coined for him. So He said *the likeness of his light*: the likeness of Muḥammad's light when it was deposited in the loins of ʿAbd Allāh b. ʿAbd al-Muṭṭalib, *is like a niche* which is the aperture (*kuwwa*) that has no back opening; *in which is a lamp* meaning a torchlight (*sirāj*); *the lamp is in a crystal* pure and completely transparent. What is meant by the niche is the loins of ʿAbd Allah the father of Muḥammad, and what is meant by the crystal is the body of Muḥammad, and what is meant by the torchlight is faith inside the body of Muḥammad. ... Then He made the crystal an allegory for Muḥammad in the Books of the Prophets which is self-evident, like the light of the *star of diamond* which is al-Zuhara (Venus) among the planets, or al-Mushtarī (Jupiter), which is al-Birjīs in Syriac. *The crystal resembles a star of diamond kindled from a blessed tree*: the blessed tree means Ibrāhīm the Friend of the Merciful. Allah is saying that Muḥammad is kindled by Ibrāhīm as he is his descendent. Then follows the descriptive mention of Ibrāhīm as *an olive*, that is, perfect obedience, *neither of the East nor of the West*, because Ibrāhīm prayed neither toward the east like Christians, nor toward the west like Jews, but toward the Kaʿba... *Its oil is almost aglow* because—according to Abū Ṣāliḥ al-Hudhayl b. Ḥabīb al-Zaydānī, the narrator from Muqātil—Muḥammad would almost utter words of prophecy even before he received revelation, *though untouched by fire*, that is, even if prophethood had not yet come to him, his obedience would have matched that of Prophets. *Light upon Light*, meaning that Muḥammad was a Prophet that issued forth from the loins of another Prophet, Ibrāhīm. *Allah guides to His Light whomever He wills*: Allah guides to His Religion whomever He wills among His servants.[154]

[154] Muqātil, *Tafsīr* (*sub* 24:35). Cf. al-Qasṭallānī, *Mawāhib* (2:452 *fī waṣfihi taʿālā lahu bil-nūr*).

جاء في تفسير مقاتل بن سليمان ﴿ ٱللَّهُ نُورُ ٱلسَّمَٰوَٰتِ وَٱلْأَرْضِ ﴾ يَقُولُ: اللهُ هَادِي أَهْلِ السَّمٰوَاتِ وَالْأَرْضِ، ثُمَّ انْقَطَعَ الْكَلَامُ، وَأَخَذَ فِي نَعْتِ نَبِيِّهِ ﷺ وَمَا ضَرَبَ لَهُ مِنَ الْمَثَلِ، فَقَالَ سُبْحَانَهُ ﴿ مَثَلُ نُورِهِۦ ﴾ مَثَلُ نُورِ مُحَمَّدٍ ﷺ إِذَا كَانَ مَسْتَودَعاً فِي صُلْبِ أَبِيهِ عَبْدِ اللهِ بْنِ عَبْدِ الْمُطَّلِبِ ﴿ كَمِشْكَوٰةٍ ﴾ يَعْنِي بِالْمِشْكَاةِ الْكُوَّةَ لَيْسَتْ بِالنَّافِذَةِ ﴿ فِيهَا مِصْبَاحٌ ﴾ يَعْنِي السِّرَاجَ ﴿ ٱلْمِصْبَاحُ فِى زُجَاجَةٍ ﴾ الصَّافِيَةِ تَامَّةِ الصَّفَاءِ يَعْنِي بِالْمِشْكَاةِ صُلْبَ عَبْدِ اللهِ أَبِي مُحَمَّدٍ ﷺ وَيَعْنِي بِالزُّجَاجَةِ جَسَدَ مُحَمَّدٍ ﷺ وَيَعْنِي بِالسِّرَاجِ الإِيمَانَ فِي جَسَدِ مُحَمَّدٍ ﷺ ... ثُمَّ شَبَّهَ الزُّجَاجَةَ بِمُحَمَّدٍ ﷺ فِي كُتُبِ الْأَنْبِيَاءِ عَلَيْهِمُ السَّلَامُ، لَا خَفَاءَ فِيهِ، كَضَوْءِ الْكَوْكَبِ الدُّرِّيِّ وَهُوَ الزُّهَرَةُ فِي الْكَوَاكِبِ، وَيُقَالُ: الْمُشْتَرِي وَهُوَ الْبِرْجِيسُ بِالسِّرْيَانِيَّةِ. ﴿ ٱلزُّجَاجَةُ كَأَنَّهَا كَوْكَبٌ دُرِّىٌّ يُوقَدُ مِن شَجَرَةٍ مُّبَٰرَكَةٍ ﴾ يَعْنِي بِالشَّجَرَةِ الْمُبَارَكَةِ إِبْرَاهِيمَ خَلِيلَ الرَّحْمٰنِ ﷺ يَقُولُ: يُوقَدُ مُحَمَّدٌ مِنْ إِبْرَاهِيمَ، عَلَيْهِمَا السَّلَامُ، وَهُوَ مِنْ ذُرِّيَّتِهِ، ثُمَّ ذَكَرَ إِبْرَاهِيمَ عَلَيْهِ السَّلَامُ، فَقَالَ سُبْحَانَهُ: ﴿ زَيْتُونَةٍ ﴾ قَالَ: طَاعَةٌ حَسَنَةٌ ﴿ لَّا شَرْقِيَّةٍ وَلَا غَرْبِيَّةٍ ﴾ يَقُولُ: لَمْ يَكُنْ إِبْرَاهِيمُ عَلَيْهِ السَّلَامُ يُصَلِّي قِبَلَ الْمَشْرِقِ كَفِعْلِ النَّصَارَى وَلَا قِبَلَ الْمَغْرِبِ كَفِعْلِ الْيَهُودِ، وَلَكِنَّهُ كَانَ يُصَلِّي قِبَلَ الْكَعْبَةِ... وَعَنْ أَبِي صَالِحٍ – وهو الهُذَيْلُ بْنُ حَبِيبٍ

الزَّيدَانِي الرَّاوِي عَنْ مُقَاتِلٍ – فِي قَوْلِهِ تَعَالَى ﴿ يَكَادُ زَيْتُهَا يُضِيٓءُ ﴾ قَالَ يَكَادُ مُحَمَّدٌ ﷺ أَنْ يَتَكَلَّمَ بِالنُّبُوَّةِ قَبْلَ أَنْ يُوحَى إِلَيْهِ، يَقُولُ ﴿ وَلَوْ لَمْ تَمْسَسْهُ نَارٌ ﴾ وَلَوْ لَمْ تَأْتِهِ النُّبُوَّةُ لَكَانَتْ طَاعَتُهُ مَعَ طَاعَةِ الْأَنْبِيَاءِ عَلَيْهِمُ السَّلَامُ، ثُمَّ قَالَ عَزَّ وَجَلَّ ﴿ نُّورٌ عَلَىٰ نُورٍ ﴾ قَالَ مُحَمَّدٌ ﷺ نَبِيٌّ خَرَجَ مِنْ صُلْبِ نَبِيٍّ، يَعْنِي إِبْرَاهِيمَ عَلَيْهِمَا السَّلَامُ ﴿ يَهْدِى ٱللَّهُ لِنُورِهِۦ مَن يَشَآءُ ﴾ قَالَ: يَهْدِي اللهُ لِدِينِهِ مَنْ يَشَاءُ مِنْ عِبَادِهِ.

Qadi ʿIyāḍ cited the following exegesis of the Ẓāhirī jurist, *ḥāfiẓ*, and grammarian Nafṭawayh (244-323/858-935)

113. The *oil almost aglow though untouched by fire* is the likeness that Allah has coined of His Prophet, by which He is saying that his external appearance virtually revealed his Prophethood even before he was reciting the Qur'ān, as [the Companion] Ibn Rawāḥa said:

Even if there had not been clear signs among us,
his face would have told you the news.[155]

قَالَ نَفْطَوَيْهُ فِي قَولِهِ تَعَالَى ﴿ يَكَادُ زَيْتُهَا يُضِيٓءُ وَلَوْ لَمْ تَمْسَسْهُ نَارٌ ﴾ هَٰذَا مَثَلٌ ضَرَبَهُ اللهُ تَعَالَى لِنَبِيِّهِ ﷺ يَقُولُ يَكَادُ مَنْظَرُهُ يَدُلُّ عَلَى نُبُوَّتِهِ وَإِنْ لَمْ يَتْلُ قُرْآنًا كَمَا قَالَ ابْنُ رَوَاحَةَ رَضِيَ اللهُ عَنْهُ:

[155] ʿIyāḍ, *Shifā* I.iv (p. 309); Ibn Ḥajar, *Iṣāba* (4:66-67, *sub* ʿAbd Allāh b. Rawāḥa).

لَوْ لَمْ تَكُنْ فِيهِ آيَاتٌ مُبَيِّنَةٌ * كَانَتْ بُدَاهَتُهُ تُنْبِيكَ بِالْخَبَرِ

حكاه عياض في الشِّفا وذكر البيت الحافظ ابن حجر في الإصابة

In other words, the Prophet Muḥammad is luminous in his very person because that is how he was created, and the light of Prophethood in him is a *Light upon Light*, a revealed light on top of a native light. Furthermore, the expression refers to the witnessing of Divine Oneness immediately followed by the witnessing of Muḥammadan Messengership: لا إله إلّا الله محمّد رسول الله.[156]

The meanings expounded above are the gist of the exegeses narrated from the Successors Sa'īd b. Jubayr and Ka'b al-Aḥbār by al-Ṭabarī:

> **114.** "Sa'īd b. Jubayr said of *the likeness of his light*: '[It is] Muḥammad.'... Some said the *mishkāt* is any aperture that has no back opening (*kullu kuwwatin lā manfadha lahā*). They said it is a comparison Allāh made for the heart of Muḥammad – upon him blessings and peace." Al-Ṭabarī then mentions Ibn 'Abbās's report from Ka'b that the niche (*mishkāt*) is Muḥammad, the lamp (*miṣbāḥ*) his heart, the crystal *(zujāja)* his chest, and the lighting *neither of the East nor of the West* in the sense that it is untouched by the sun of the East or the sun of the West or, as al-Ḥasan al-Baṣrī glossed, that "it is not a tree of this world." *Its oil is almost aglow though untouched by fire* because Muḥammad was almost evident to people even before he had revealed to them that he was a Prophet.[157]

قال الطبري رحمه الله في التفسير: إِخْتَلَفَ أَهْلُ التَّأْوِيلِ فِي مَعْنَى المِشْكَاةِ وَالمِصْبَاحِ وَمَا المُرَادُ بِذٰلِكَ، وَبِالزُّجَاجَةِ، فَقَالَ بَعْضُهُمْ: المِشْكَاةُ كُلُّ كُوَّةٍ لَا

[156] Shaykh Hisham Kabbani, *suḥba* of 15 May 2012, Jakarta, Indonesia.
[157] al-Ṭabarī, Ibn Abī Ḥātim, and others (*sub* 24:35). Cf. also Yūsuf Muḥammad al-'Āmirī, *Ka'b al-Aḥbār: Marwiyyātuh wa-Aqwāluh fil-Tafsīr bil-Ma'thūr Jam'an wa-Dirāsa*, unpublished Master's thesis, Mecca: Jāmi'at Umm al-Qurā, 1412/1992, pp. 489-492. A similar explanation was given by Abū Sa'īd al-Kharrāz (d. 286/899) cf. al-Qasṭallānī, *Mawāhib* (2:452 *fī waṣfihi ta'ālā lahu bil-nūr*).

مَنفَذَ لَهَا، وَقَالُوا: هَٰذَا مَثَلُ ضَرَبَهُ اللهُ لِقَلْبِ مُحَمَّدٍ ﷺ. جَاءَ ابْنُ عَبَّاسٍ رَضِيَ اللهُ عَنْهُمَا إِلَى كَعْبِ الْأَحْبَارِ، فَقَالَ لَهُ: حَدِّثْنِي عَنْ قَوْلِ اللهِ ﴿ مَثَلُ نُورِهِۦ كَمِشْكَوٰةٍ ﴾ قَالَ: الْمِشْكَاةُ هِيَ الْكُوَّةُ، ضَرَبَهَا اللهُ مَثَلاً لِمُحَمَّدٍ ﷺ، ﴿ فِيهَا مِصْبَاحٌ ۖ ٱلْمِصْبَاحُ ﴾ قَلْبُهُ ﴿ فِى زُجَاجَةٍ ﴾ صَدْرِهِ ﴿ ٱلزُّجَاجَةُ كَأَنَّهَا كَوْكَبٌ دُرِّىٌّ ﴾ شَبَّهَ صَدْرَ النَّبِيِّ ﷺ بِالْكَوْكَبِ الدُّرِّيِّ، ثُمَّ رَجَعَ الْمِصْبَاحَ إِلَى قَلْبِهِ فَقَالَ ﴿ يُوقَدُ مِن شَجَرَةٍ مُّبَٰرَكَةٍ زَيْتُونَةٍ لَّا شَرْقِيَّةٍ وَلَا غَرْبِيَّةٍ ﴾ لَمْ تَمَسَّهَا شَمْسُ الْمَشْرِقِ وَلَا شَمْسُ الْمَغْرِبِ، ﴿ يَكَادُ زَيْتُهَا يُضِىٓءُ وَلَوْ لَمْ تَمْسَسْهُ نَارٌ ﴾ يَكَادُ مُحَمَّدٌ يُبَيِّنُ لِلنَّاسِ وَإِنْ لَمْ يَتَكَلَّمْ أَنَّهُ نَبِيٌّ... وَقَالَ آخَرُونَ: لَيْسَتْ هَذِهِ الشَّجَرَةُ مِنْ شَجَرِ الدُّنْيَا. عَنِ الْحَسَنِ فِي قَوْلِ اللهِ ﴿ لَّا شَرْقِيَّةٍ وَلَا غَرْبِيَّةٍ ﴾ قَالَ وَاللهِ لَوْ كَانَتْ فِي الْأَرْضِ لَكَانَتْ شَرْقِيَّةً أَوْ غَرْبِيَّةً، وَلَكِنَّهَا هُوَ مَثَلٌ ضَرَبَهُ اللهُ لِنُورِهِ.

The definition of the *mishkāt* as "an aperture that has no back opening" is given in all the major lexicons in keeping with the earlier glosses by Ibn ʿAbbās, Ibn ʿUmar, and the Successors Saʿīd b. ʿIyāḍ and al-Ḥasan al-Baṣrī; however, a deeper meaning of "collective source" emerges from the statement reported by Umm Salama:

115. When the Negus of Abyssinia heard the beginning of Surat Maryam recited before him and his court he and his bishops wept until their beards and books were damp and he said: "Truly I swear that this and what Mūsā brought both come out from one and the same *mishkāt*!"[158]

عَنْ أُمِّ سَلَمَةَ رَضِيَ اللهُ عَنْهَا قَرَأَ عَلَيْهِ صَدْرًا مِنْ ﴿ كٓهيعٓصٓ ﴿١﴾ ﴾ مريم قَالَتْ: فَبَكَى وَاللهِ النَّجَاشِيُّ حَتَّى أَخْضَلَ لِحْيَتَهُ وَبَكَتْ أَسَاقِفَتُهُ حَتَّى أَخْضَلُوا مَصَاحِفَهُمْ حِينَ سَمِعُوا مَا تَلاَ عَلَيْهِمْ، ثُمَّ قَالَ النَّجَاشِيُّ: إِنَّ هٰذَا وَاللهِ وَالَّذِي جَاءَ بِهِ مُوسَى لَيَخْرُجُ مِنْ مِشْكَاةٍ وَاحِدَةٍ رواه أحمد

The two meanings of *mishkāt* as "backless aperture" and "source" convey a sense of accumulation and comprehensiveness so that it is possible to interpret *ka-mishkātin fīhā miṣbāḥ* as the original cluster of all created lights over which towers the archetypal *miṣbāḥ* of the Muḥammadan Light and that of the elite of the believers. This understanding is strengthened by three canonical variants related from Ubay b. Kaʿb and others:

116. *Allah has enlightened the heavens and the earth* (*Allāhu nawwara al-samāwāti wal-arḍ*), *the similitude of the light of the believer(s)* (*mathalu nūri al-mu'min/īn*) *is like a niche*, and *the similitude of the light of him who believes in Him* (*mathalu nūri man āmana bih*).[159]

القراءات في ﴿ ٱللَّهُ نُورُ ٱلسَّمَـٰوَٰتِ وَٱلْأَرْضِ ۚ مَثَلُ نُورِهِۦ ﴾: قرأ علي بن أبي طالب وأبو جعفر وعبد العزيز المكي وزيد بن علي ومَسلَمة بن عبد الملك وثابت بن أبي حفصة والقَورصي وأبو عبد الرحمٰن السُلَمي وابن أبي عَبْلَة وعبد الله بن عياش وأُبيّ بن كعب وأبو المتوكّل وابن السَّمَيْفَع اللهُ نَوَّرَ

[158] Aḥmad, *Musnad* (3:263-270 §1740) and others, all through Ibn Isḥāq.
[159] al-Khaṭīb, *Muʿjam al-Qirā'āt* (6:264-265).

السَّمَاوَاتِ والأَرْضَ وقرأ أُبيّ مَثَلُ نُورِ المُؤْمِنِينَ. وقرأ أيضاً مَثَلُ نُورِ المُؤْمِنِ.

وروي عنه قراءة ثالثة وهي: مَثَلُ نُورِ مَنْ آمَنَ بِهِ. معجم القراءات للخطيب.

Allah Cast His Light on All Creation

The Prophet himself described this cluster of the light of everything created as issued, at the time of its creation, "from" (*min*) the Divine Light in a momentous sound-chained hadith narrated from ʿAbd Allāh b. ʿAmr b. al-ʿĀṣ:

> **117.** Truly Allah Most High created His creation in a darkness then cast upon them from His light on that day. Whoever He touched out of His light on that day has been guided, and whoever He left out has gone astray.[160]

عَنْ عَبْدِ اللهِ بْنِ عَمْرِو بْنِ الْعَاصِ رَضِيَ اللهُ عَنْهُمَا إِنَّ اللهَ عَزَّ وَجَلَّ خَلَقَ خَلْقَهُ فِي ظُلْمَةٍ ثُمَّ أَلْقَى عَلَيْهِم مِنْ نُورِهِ يَوْمَئِذٍ فَمَنْ أَصَابَهُ مِنْ نُورِهِ يَوْمَئِذٍ اِهْتَدَى وَمَنْ أَخْطَأَهُ ضَلَّ رواه أحمد والترمذي وقال حديث حسن.

118. Mughulṭāy (689-762/1290-1361) in his commentary on Ibn Mājah's *Sunan* mentioned that the above narration was seen as a proof that "souls are a light from the Light of Allah and life from His life."[161]

قال الحافظ مُغُلْطَاي في شرح سنن ابن ماجه المسمى الإعلام بسنّته عليه الصلاة والسلام: وَقَالَ بَعْضُهُمْ: الأَرْوَاحُ نُورٌ مِنْ نُورِ اللهِ تَعَالَى وَحَيَاةٌ مِنْ حَيَاتِهِ

[160] Aḥmad, *Musnad* 11:219- §6644; al-Tirmidhī, *Sunan*, *Īmān*, *mā jā' fī iftirāq hādhih al-umma*, *ḥasan*).
[161] Mughulṭāy, *Iʿlām* (3:1061: *bāb man nām ʿan al-ṣalāt aw nasiyahā*).

وَاحْتَجُّوا بِقَوْلِهِ ﷺ: إِنَّ اللهَ عَزَّ وَجَلَّ خَلَقَ خَلْقَهُ فِي ظُلْمَةٍ ثُمَّ أَلْقَى عَلَيْهِمْ نُورًا مِنْ نُورِهِ.

Ibn al-ʿArabī al-Mālikī (468-543/1075-1148) said in commentary of that narration:

119. It is clear from it that each individual receives a share of that light to the extent he has been granted, generally and specifically, wholly and in detail, in the heart and in the limbs.[162]

قال ابن العربي المالكي في عارضة الأحوذي: تَبَيَّنَ بِهٰذَا أَنَّ كُلَّ أَحَدٍ يَلْقَى مِنْ ذٰلِكَ النُّورِ بِقَدَرِ مَا وُهِبَ لَهُ مِنَ الْعُمُومِ وَالْخُصُوصِ وَالْجُمْلَةِ وَالتَّفْصِيلِ وَفِي الْقَلْبِ وَالْجَوَارِحِ.

One of the *Awliyā* among the Successors, Ṭalq b. Ḥabīb (d. before 100/719) – he narrated from Ibn ʿAbbās, Anas, and Jābir b. ʿAbd Allāh among others – used the expression "a light from the light of Allah" in the following advice:

120. Protect yourself from dissensions (*fitna*) with righteousness (*taqwā*) which consists in putting into practice obedience of Allah on the basis of a Light from the Light of Allah, hoping for reward from Allah, and to abandon disobedience to Allah on the basis of a Light from the Light of Allah, fearing His punishment.[163]

لَمَّا وَقَعَتِ الْفِتْنَةُ قَالَ طَلْقُ بْنُ حَبِيبٍ إِتَّقُوهَا بِالتَّقْوَى قَالُوا وَمَا التَّقْوَى؟ قَالَ: أَنْ تَعْمَلَ بِطَاعَةِ اللهِ عَلَى نُورٍ مِنْ نُورِ اللهِ رَجَاءَ ثَوَابِ اللهِ، وَالتَّقْوَى

[162] Ibn al-ʿArabī, *ʿĀriḍat al- Aḥwadhī* (10:108).
[163] Ibn Baṭṭa, *Ibāna* (*Īmān* 2:598 §766).

تَرْكُ مَعَاصِي اللهِ عَلَى نُورٍ مِنْ نُورِ اللهِ خَوْفَ عِقَابِ اللهِ. رواه ابن بطة في الإبانة الكبرى.

The term "that day" (*yawma'idhin*) in the phrase "then He cast upon them from His light on that day" refers to the absolute beginning of the creation of humankind known as the Day of Promises (*yawm al-mīthāq*) described in the verse *And when your Lord brought forth from the Children of Adam, from their reins, their progeny, and made them testify of themselves: Am I not your Lord? They said: Yes, truly. We testify. That was lest you should say on the Day of Resurrection: Truly of this we were unaware* (7:172).

﴿ وَإِذْ أَخَذَ رَبُّكَ مِنۢ بَنِىٓ ءَادَمَ مِن ظُهُورِهِمْ ذُرِّيَّتَهُمْ وَأَشْهَدَهُمْ عَلَىٰٓ أَنفُسِهِمْ أَلَسْتُ بِرَبِّكُمْ ۖ قَالُوا۟ بَلَىٰ ۛ شَهِدْنَآ ۛ أَن تَقُولُوا۟ يَوْمَ ٱلْقِيَـٰمَةِ إِنَّا كُنَّا عَنْ هَـٰذَا غَـٰفِلِينَ ﴿١٧٢﴾ ﴾

The reference is explicit another, similarly-worded Prophetic hadith from Abū Umāma:

121. When Allah created creation and decreed the whole matter and took the Covenant from the Prophets as His Throne was over the water, He took the People of the Right in His Right Hand and the People of the Left in his Other Hand—and both Hands of the All-Beneficent are Right—then He said: "O People of the Right!" They replied: "At Your obedient service, O our Lord!" He said: "Am I not your Lord?" They said yes. Then He said: "O People of the Left!" They replied: "At Your obedient service, O our Lord!" He said: "Am I not your Lord?" They said yes. Then He mixed them together.[164]

[164] Part of a longer hadith narrated by al-Ṭabarānī, *al-Mu'jam al-Kabīr* (8:288 §7942) and others cf. al-Būṣīrī, *Itḥāf* (1:167-168 §190) and Ibn Ḥajar, *Maṭālib* (12:478-480 §2966).

عَنْ أَبِي أُمَامَةَ مَرفُوعاً قَالَ: لَـمَّا خَلَقَ اللهُ الخَلْقَ وَقَضَى الْقَضِيَّةَ وَأَخَذَ مِيثَاقَ النَّبِيِّينَ وَعَرْشُهُ عَلَى المَاءِ فَأَخَذَ أَهْلَ الْيَمِينِ بِيَمِينِهِ وَأَهْلَ الشِّمَالِ بِيَدِهِ الأُخْرَى وَكِلْتَا يَدَي الرَّحْمَٰنِ يَمِينٌ ثُمَّ قَالَ يَا أَصْحَابَ الْيَمِينِ فَقَالُوا لَبَّيْكَ رَبَّنَا وَسَعْدَيْكَ قَالَ أَلَسْتُ بِرَبِّكُمْ؟ قَالُوا بَلَى ثُمَّ قَالَ يَا أَصْحَابَ الشِّمَالِ فَقَالُوا لَبَّيْكَ رَبَّنَا وَسَعْدَيْكَ قَالَ أَلَسْتُ بِرَبِّكُمْ؟ قَالُوا بَلَى فَخَلَطَ بَعْضَهُمْ بِبَعْضٍ

الحديث. رواه الطبراني وغيره.

The Meaning of *min nūrih* ("from His Light")

The expression "from His light" or "out of His light" (*min nūrih*)—which occurs twice in Aḥmad's version of the hadith of ʿAbd Allāh b. ʿAmr—is the same one used in the "hadith of Jābir." Shaykh ʿAbd Allāh Sirāj al-Dīn (1343-1422/1924-2002) said:

> **122.** The preposition *min* (from) in *min nūrih* (from His Light) is not partitive (*laysat lil-tabʿīḍ*) by consensus of the gnostics, for the Light of Allah Most High and all His Attributes cannot be divided; rather, it denotes Divine origination (*ibtidā'*), as in His saying: *It is all from Him* (*jamīʿan minhu*) in the verse *And He has subjected to you whatever is in the heavens and whatever is on the earth. It is all from Him* (45:13). The gnostics said the upshot is that the first of the light-made realities created is the Muḥammadan Reality (*al-ḥaqīqat al-muḥammadiyya*) as indicated in the hadith of Jābir and the like, and the first spirit created is the Greatest Spirit, the spirit of our liegelord Muḥammad—upon him blessings and peace. Allah Most High made him a Prophet in that spiritual world before all the other Prophets, as shown by the hadith "When were you made a Prophet?" and another wording has "When was Prophethood made incumbent for you?" That is, when was Prophethood definitely established as yours? He replied: "When Adam was still between the soul and the body." Abū

Nuʿaym's version has: "I was the first of the Prophets in creation and the last one to be sent."[165]

قَالَ الشَّيْخُ الْحَافِظُ عَبْدُ اللهِ سِرَاجُ الدِّينِ رَحِمَهُ اللهُ تَعَالَى آخِرَ كِتَابِهِ (شَهَادَةُ لَا إِلَهَ إِلَّا اللهُ مُحَمَّدٌ رَسُولُ اللهِ) فِي شَرْحِ عِبَارَةِ (نُورَ نَبِيِّكَ مِنْ نُورِهِ):

وَ(مِنْ) هَهُنَا لَيْسَتْ لِلتَّبْعِيضِ قَطْعاً بِإِجْمَاعِ الْعَارِفِينَ، فَإِنَّ نُورَ اللهِ تَعَالَى وَجَمِيعَ صِفَاتِهِ لَا تَتَجَزَّأُ، وَإِنَّمَا هِيَ لِلإِبْتِدَاءِ، نَظِيرَ قَوْلِهِ تَعَالَى: ﴿وَسَخَّرَ لَكُم مَّا فِي ٱلسَّمَـٰوَٰتِ وَمَا فِي ٱلْأَرْضِ جَمِيعًا مِّنْهُ﴾ الآية. وَخُلَاصَةُ الْقَوْلِ عِنْدَ الْعَارِفِينَ: أَنَّ أَوَّلَ الحَقَائِقِ النُّورَانِيَّةِ خَلْقاً هِيَ الحَقِيقَةُ الْمُحَمَّدِيَّةُ ﷺ وَآلِهِ كَمَا دَلَّ عَلَيْهِ حَدِيثُ جَابِرٍ وَنَحْوُهُ، وَأَنَّ أَوَّلَ الْأَرْوَاحِ خَلْقاً هُوَ الرُّوحُ الْأَعْظَمُ رُوحُ سَيِّدِنَا مُحَمَّدٍ ﷺ، وَنَبَّأَهُ اللهُ تَعَالَى فِي ذَٰلِكَ الْعَالَمِ الرُّوحِيِّ قَبْلَ الْأَنْبِيَاءِ كُلِّهِمْ كَمَا دَلَّ عَلَيْهِ حَدِيثُ (مَتَى اسْتُنْبِئْتَ)، وَفِي رِوَايَةٍ: (مَتَى وَجَبَتْ لَكَ النُّبُوَّةُ)، أَيْ: مَتَى ثَبَتَتْ لَكَ النُّبُوَّةُ؟ قَالَ: كُنْتُ نَبِيّاً وَآدَمُ بَيْنَ الرُّوحِ وَالجَسَدِ. وَفِي رِوَايَةِ أَبِي نُعَيمٍ: كُنْتُ أَوَّلَ النَّبِيِّينَ فِي الخَلْقِ وَآخِرَهُمْ فِي الْبَعْثِ. اهـ. ويتميز هذا الكتاب لسيدي الشيخ عبد الله سراج الدين بباب أسماه (ذكر الدليل التفصيلي على أنه ﷺ قد رأى ربه بعيني رأسه ليلة الإسراء والمعراج) فليراجع.

The Egyptian Shāfiʿī jurist al-Shabrāmallasī (997-1087/1589-1676) said in his commentary on the *Mawāhib*:

123. It is possible that the construct (*iḍāfa*) [in the phrase "the light of your Prophet"] is explicative (*bayāniyya*), meaning He

[165] Sirāj al-Dīn, *Shahādatu Lā Ilāha Illā Allāh Muḥammadun Rasūl Allāh* (p. 151).

created the light of His Prophet from a Light which is His own Essence, but not in the sense that it is a substance out of which the light of His Prophet was created; rather, in the sense that His Divine Will applied itself to bringing into existence a light without any intermediary in its existence. This is the most appropriate reply and corresponds to what al-Bayḍāwī said in explanation of the saying of Allah Most High *Then He fashioned him and breathed into him of His spirit* (32:9) where he said: "He annexed it to Himself to honor it and as a proclamation that it is a wonderful creation and that it is connected to the Divine Presence."[166]

في كشف الخفاء مادة (أول ما خلق اللهُ نورُ نبيكِ يا جابر): قَالَ الشَّبْرَامَلِّسِيُّ يَحْتَمِلُ أَنَّ الإِضَافَةَ بَيَانِيَّةٌ، أَيْ خَلَقَ نُورَ نَبِيِّهِ مِنْ نُورٍ هُوَ ذَاتُهُ تَعَالَى، لَكِنْ لَا بِمَعْنَى أَنَّهَا مَادَّةٌ خَلَقَ نُورَ نَبِيِّهِ مِنْهَا، بَلْ بِمَعْنَى أَنَّهُ تَعَالَى تَعَلَّقَتْ إِرَادَتُهُ بِإِيجَادِ نُورٍ بِلَا تَوَسُّطِ شَيْءٍ فِي وُجُودِهِ. قَالَ: وَهٰذَا أَوْلَى الْأَجْوِبَةِ، نَظِيرَ مَا ذَكَرَهُ الْبَيْضَاوِيُّ فِي قَوْلِهِ تَعَالَى ﴿ ثُمَّ سَوَّىٰهُ وَنَفَخَ فِيهِ مِن رُّوحِهِۦ ﴾ الآية. السجدة. حَيْثُ قَالَ: أَضَافَهُ إِلَى نَفْسِهِ تَشْرِيفاً وَإِشْعَاراً بِأَنَّهُ خَلْقٌ عَجِيبٌ وَأَنَّ لَهُ مُنَاسَبَةٌ إِلَى حَضْرَةِ الرُّبُوبِيَّةِ.

The above commentaries all show that the "light of Allah" which He cast on creation in the hadith of ʿAbd Allah b. ʿAmr b. al-ʿĀṣ is the Muḥammadan Light, through which, the Masters said, Allah brought everything into existence, and without which nothing exists:

124. *Sayyidūnā* ʿAbd al-Khāliq [Ghujduwānī] continued: "Everyone's real essence is embedded in the Prophet's essence." Grandshaykh [ʿAbd Allāh al-Dāghistānī] says in his notes: *Know that the Prophet is in you* (49:7) means if he is not within you you cannot exist. Allah made every person to have to appear because of

[166] In al-ʿAjlūnī, *Kashf al-Khafā* (1:304 §827).

the existence of *Sayyidinā* Muḥammad in the Divine Presence, or else you cannot appear; then you are not created. If you see yourself here, created, that is an indication you are in the reality of the Prophet and that you are in the Divine Presence.... They translate that verse: Know that the Prophet is *among* you; but it must be known that Muḥammad is *in* you, the trace of his Light in your forehead is in you! So he cannot be far. Everyone, if he looks well into his heart, will find the Light of *Sayyidinā* Muḥammad!"[167]

How All Lights Are Extracted from the Muḥammadan Light

The erudite Tijani scholar Aḥmad Sukayrij (1294-1363/1877-1944) wrote on the same issue:

125. The hadith of Jābir, "'My father and mother be sacrificed for you, tell me the first thing Allah created before anything else,' he replied: 'O Jābir, truly the first thing Allah created before anything else was my light, from His light,'" is mentioned by those who celebrate *mawlid*. Al-Qasṭallānī cited it in *al-Mawāhib al-Ladunniyya* and said it was narrated by ʿAbd al-Razzāq and this is how we know of it. Likewise those who celebrate *mawlid* mention the report that "Allah grasped a handful of His Light and said to it 'Be Muḥammad,'"[168] etc. The meaning is that Allah grasped a handful of the light that is related to Him (*uḍīfat ilayh*), and *min* (from) in the phrase *min nūrih* (from his light) is explicative (*lil-bayān*). It is as if he were saying: "the light of His Prophet that is His own light," and "a Divine Handful (*qabḍa*) that is His own light," by defining *min* as explicative the way grammarians do. The Light of our liegelord Muḥammad is the origin of all lights, from which all of them are extracted in all their stages; so the light is created. One of the gnostics said the possessive adjective "his" in "his light" goes back to "your Prophet" in the phrase "the light

[167] Shaykh Hisham Kabbani, *Ṣuḥba*s of 11 September 2009, Fenton, Michigan (USA) and 5 May 2012, Singapore. See also Shaykh ʿAbd al-Hādī Kharsa, *Sharḥ al-Qaṣīdat al-Muḥammadiyya* (Damascus: Dār Fajr al-ʿUrūba, 1996) p. 64-65 on al-Būṣīrī's line 22: "Muḥammad—everything in creation is his appearance."

[168] It is nowhere to be found in the hadith sources. Al-Ṣufūrī mentions it in *Nuzhat al-Majālis*, chapter of the Prophet's birth.

of your Prophet" so it is a kind of double usage (*istikhdām*),[169] as if he were saying: the light of your Prophet was created from the light of your Prophet, in the sense that out of that light the essence of the Prophet, his spirit, and all his states were created. So from his light he came into existence, and from it all created things came into existence.

As for the Light of the Divine Essence it is pre-eternal and unoriginated in time, and the Light of Allah Most High cannot be described with a modality nor is it divisible. Moreover, *nūr* (light) with respect to Him is in the sense of *munawwir* (enlightener), as mentioned in the exegeses for *Allah is the Light of the heavens and the earth* (24:35), meaning the giver of light to the heavens and the earth. So it is impossible to take something from the Essence – exalted is our Lord from any divisibility in His Essence, His Attributes, or His Acts! In other words: Allah has created the light of your Prophet from the light of His creation, and that very light was the light of your Prophet. So there is nothing before it in all creation, rather, everything created and all creatures were formed out of it. Everything that belongs to the realm of possibilities is from it; and the extraction of every existent thing in creation is from it no matter what.

I saw myself discussing this with one of our gnostic masters, Shaykh Abu al-Qāsim Muḥammad Fatḥā b. Qāsim al-Qādirī. I asked him of the modality of the formation of creation out of the Muḥammadan Light and the extraction of lights from his Light, according to the various stages, phases, and evolutions of creation, from coming into being to physical demise to everlasting bliss and other aspects whether glorious or ignoble, blessedness and damnation, life and death, animals, inanimate objects, plants, and other than that. He said to me in that vision:

> "Truly Allah Most High when He created the universes, all the worlds and creatures that had been decreed to exist were

[169] "*Istikhdām* is to mention a term that has two meanings, whereby the first meaning is meant by the term itself, then the second meaning is meant through its pronoun, as in *And let any of you that witness the month fast it* (2:185), where *the month* means the new moon, and *it* means the duration of time." Karam al-Bustānī, *al-Bayān* (Beirut: Maktabat Ṣādir, n.d.) pp. 86-87.

> folded up, in the order of their creation and extinction, within an all-encompassing sphere (*taḥta dā'irat al-falak al-muḥīṭ bil-kull*) that contains other spherical layers and so to the last existent thing, like a globe or an onion. In it there are holes that pierce through all the layers so that light passes through each hole and out of the globe on all sides. The layers of the globe are to the number of centuries, years, months, days, weeks, and minutes, down to a fraction of the glimpse of an eye. When Allah desired to supply everything with the Muḥammadan Light and bring it all into existence as He wished, He created the Muḥammadan Light. That globe – the all-encompassing sphere – faced its shadow, and without that Light it would not have appeared. The light spread within the globe and pierced out through all the holes. Then Allah Most High commanded the sphere to turn, and He commanded every layer under it to turn, in a wondrous arrangement devised by the All-Wise and Incomparable Originator. The holes now hit one another and so did the light that circulated through them; either that light found an exit through the hole that coincides with whatever is above it, or, on the contrary, the hole is blocked from what comes next to it when the latter is not pierced. In the latter scenario, light is blocked from exiting through that hole. Whoever light shines upon is in bliss and light, and whoever is blocked from light is in misery and darkness. This is how faith and unbelief appear, as well as everything that leads to either of them secretly or openly, in every period of time until whenever Allah wishes. All take from that light to the extent decreed for them; so all is from him and deriving its light from him as you can see." …

By the grace of Allah it is clear, then, that the possessive adjective "his" in "his light" refers to the Muḥammadan Light as a figure of double usage (*istikhdām*), a rhetorical trope used by its experts. It should not, however, be said that the light here is the same as the first light in the phrase "the light of your Prophet," which would result in the creation of a thing out of itself. What we say is that in the phrase *min nūrih* (from his Light), *min* (from) is explicative (*bayāniyya*) and thus means: "the light of your Prophet of which he himself is the light" (*nūru Nabiyyika al-ladhī huwa nūruh*). It is certainly not partitive (*tabʿīḍiyya*). You can also say that the possessive adjective "his" refers to Allah Most High, the light being created but related to Allah in the same way as in the verse *This is the Creation of Allah* (31:11). So it is annexed (*muḍāf*) to Allah, and that created light is the light of your Prophet and nothing else.

If it is asked: anything being created must have a time and a place, which presupposes that those are either with it or before it, although in this case he is the first thing created; how can that be? We say: time and place are part and parcel of his shadow, without which they would not have been formed. The Prophet witnessed that being formed of him, and saw it in motion through the motion of the revolving all-encompassing sphere in that vision. In this way do we understand his being addressed in the Station of Divine Munificence: *Have you not seen how your Lord has stretched the shadow, and if He willed He could have made it still, then We have made the sun its pilot?* (25:45). Allah addressed His Prophet in that verse through what is familiar to him in the Station of the joining of the spirit with the body, as a reminder for him of what he had witnessed when he was all spirit. **For the Muḥammadan Light, as soon as it existed, possessed reason and understood whatever Allah showed it**. He was certainly made a Prophet in that Chamber where he was absolutely alone with his Lord before the creation of anything whatsoever, whether Adam or other than him, as he alluded in his hadith: "I was a Prophet when Adam was still between spirit and body,"[170] when he had witnessed His Lord with the manifestation that He bestowed upon his noble shadow, then He stretched it, so that everything came out of it. It is as if Allah is saying "Have you not seen, O Muḥammad, how your Lord stretched the shadow?" as a confirmation for what he had seen. For he had witnessed his Lord and he had witnessed the modality in which He stretched the shadow that consists in all creatures. So the Prophet gathered up both kinds [of witnessing], namely, the sight of Allah and the sight of creatures, according to what was apportioned to him in that view which no one witnessed beside him. **He came to know his own reality in a way none**

[170] See above (p. 30).

other than him has ever been able to know, hence he said: "None knows me truly but my Lord" (*lā yaʿrifunī ḥaqīqatan ghayru Rabbī*).[171] Thus he is the Greatest Veil alluded to in the saying of Ibn Mashīsh, "and make the Greatest Veil the very life of my soul."[172]

قال العلّامة أبو العباس أحمد سُكَيرِج رحمه الله في شرح النور المحمدي آخر كتاب (الشَطَحَات السُكَيْرِجِيَّة):

حَدِيثُ بِأَبِي أَنْتَ وَأُمِّي أَخْبِرْنِي عَنْ أَيِّ شَيْءٍ خَلَقَهُ اللهُ تَعَالَى قَبْلَ الأَشْيَاءِ، قَالَ يَا جَابِرُ إِنَّ اللهَ خَلَقَ قَبْلَ الأَشْيَاءِ نُورَ نَبِيِّكَ مِنْ نُورِهِ يَذْكُرُهُ أَصْحَابُ المَوَالِيدِ وَقَدْ ذَكَرَهُ الْقَسْطَلَّانِيُّ فِي المَوَاهِبِ اللَّدُنِّيَّةِ وَرَاوِيهِ عَبْدَ الرَّزَّاقِ، وَمِنْ طَرِيقِهِ عُرِفَتْ رِوَايَتُهُ؛ كَمَا يَذْكُرُ أَصْحَابُ المَوالِيدِ **حَدِيثَ أَنَّ اللهَ قَبَضَ قَبْضَةً مِنْ نُورِهِ فَقَالَ لَهَا كُونِي مُحَمَّداً فَكَانَتْ** إلخ [لا يوجد، وذكره صاحب نزهة المجالس في باب مولد المصطفى ﷺ]، وَالمَعْنَى أَنَّ اللهَ قَبَضَ قَبْضَةً مِنَ النُّورِ المُضَافِ لَهُ. وَ(مِنْ) فِي قَوِلِهِ (مِنْ نُورِهِ) لِلْبَيَانِ، فَكَأَنَّهُ يَقُولُ: نُورُ نَبِيِّهِ الَّذِي هُوَ نُورُهُ وَقَبْضَةٌ هِيَ نُورُهُ عَلَى قَاعِدَةِ تَفْسِيرِ (مِنْ البَيَانِيَّةِ عِنْدَ النُّحَاةِ. وَنُورُ سَيِّدِنَا مُحَمَّدٍ ﷺ هُوَ أَصْلُ الْأَنْوَارِ، وَهُوَ الَّذِي تُقْتَبَسُ مِنْهُ فِي سَائِرِ الْأَنْوَارِ وَالْأَطْوَارِ. فَالنُّورُ مَخْلُوقٌ. وَبَعْضُ الْعَارِفِينَ جَعَلَ الضَّمِيرَ مِنْ (نُورِهِ) يَعُودُ عَلَى (نَبِيِّكَ) مِنْ قَوْلِهِ (نُورِ نَبِيِّكَ) فَفِيهِ نَوْعُ اسْتِخْدَامٍ[173] فَكَأَنَّهُ يَقُولُ: خُلِقَ

[171] I could not find it.

[172] Sukayrij, *al-Shaṭaḥāt al-Sukayrijiyya* (p. 55-57). See also al-Ṣāwī's explanation given a hundred years before Sukayrij, which we quote further down (Part VII).

[173] الإستخدام: هو أن يُذكر لفظٌ له معنيان، فيُراد به أحدهما، وبضميره المعنى الآخر؛ نحو: ﴿فَمَن شَهِدَ مِنكُمُ ٱلشَّهْرَ فَلْيَصُمْهُ﴾: أراد بالشهر الهلالَ، وبضميره الزمانَ المعلوم. اهـ كرم البستاني (البيان) ص ٨٦-٨٧.

نُورُ نَبِيِّكَ مِنْ نُورِ نَبِيِّكَ، بِمَعْنَى أَنَّ نُورَ النَّبِيِّ ﷺ خُلِقَتْ مِنْهُ ذَاتُ النَّبِيِّ ﷺ وَرُوحُهُ وَجَمِيعُ أَحْوَالِهِ، فَنُورُهُ ﷺ مِنْهُ وُجِدَ ﷺ وَوُجِدَ مِنْهُ كُلُّ مَخْلُوقٍ.

أَمَّا نُورُ الذَّاتِ الْعَلِيَّةِ فَهُوَ قَدِيمٌ غَيْرُ حَادِثٍ، وَنُورُهُ تَعَالَى غَيْرُ مُتَكَيِّفٍ وَلَا مُتَجَزِّئٍ، وَالنُّورُ فِي حَقِّهِ تَعَالَى بِمَعْنَى مُنَوِّرٌ كَمَا فُسِّرَ بِهِ قَوْلُهُ تَعَالَى ﴿ ٱللَّهُ نُورُ ٱلسَّمَـٰوَٰتِ وَٱلْأَرْضِ ﴾ أَيْ مُنَوِّرُهُمَا فَلَا يُمْكِنُ الْأَخْذُ مِنَ الذَّاتِ – تَعَالَى مَوْلَانَا عَنِ التَّجَزُّئِ فِي الذَّاتِ وَالصِّفَاتِ وَالْأَفْعَالِ! وَبِعِبَارَةٍ أخرى: إِنَّ اللهَ خَلَقَ نُورَ نَبِيِّكَ مِنْ نُورِ خَلْقِهِ، فَكَانَ ذٰلِكَ النُّورُ هُوَ نُورُ نَبِيِّكَ، فَلَا شَيْءَ قَبْلَهُ مِنَ الْمَخْلُوقَاتِ، بَلْ مِنْهُ تَكَوَّنَتِ الْمُكَوَّنَاتُ وَالْكَائِنَاتُ، وَكُلُّ مَا دَخَلَ فِي دَائِرَةِ الْإِمْكَانِ فَمِنْهُ، وَاقْتِبَاسُ كُلِّ مُتَكَوِّنٍ مِنْهُ كَيْفَ مَا كَانَ.

وَرَأَيْتُ نَفْسِي أَتَذَاكَرُ مَعَ بَعْضِ أَشْيَاخِنَا الْعَارِفِينَ بِاللهِ، وَهُوَ الشَّيْخُ أَبُو الْقَاسِمِ سَيِّدِي مُحَمَّدُ فَتْحَا بْنُ قَاسِمٍ الْقَادِرِيُّ، إِلَى أَنْ سَأَلْتُهُ عَنْ كَيْفِيَّةِ تَكْوِينِ الْخَلْقِ مِنَ النُّورِ الْمُحَمَّدِيِّ وَاقْتِبَاسِ الْأَنْوَارِ مِنْ نُورِهِ ﷺ عَلَى اخْتِلَافِ أَطْوَارِ الْخَلْقِ وَأَدْوَارِهِمْ وَتَقَلُّبَاتِهِمْ مِنْ نَشْأَةِ الْخَلْقِ إِلَى الْفَنَاءِ الْجِسْمَانِيِّ إِلَى النَّعِيمِ الْمُقِيمِ وَغَيْرِهِ مِنْ مَحْمُودٍ وَمَذْمُومٍ وَسَعَادَةٍ وَشَقَاوَةٍ وَمَوْتٍ وَحَيَاةٍ وَحَيَوَانٍ وَجَمَادٍ وَنَبَاتٍ وَغَيْرِ ذٰلِكَ، فَقَالَ لِي فِي ذٰلِكَ الْمَشْهَدِ: إِنَّ اللهَ سُبْحَانَهُ وَتَعَالَى لَمَّا خَلَقَ سَائِرَ الْعَوَالِمِ كَانَتِ الْأَكْوَانُ وَالْمُكَوَّنَاتُ مِمَّا قُدِّرَ أَنْ يَكُونَ عَلَى تَرْتِيبِ وُجُودِهَا وَفَنَائِهَا مُنْطَوِيَةً تَحْتَ دَائِرَةِ الْفَلَكِ الْمُحِيطِ بِالْكُلِّ، وَالْفَلَكُ تَحْتَهُ دَوَائِرُ إِلَى آخِرِ مَوْجُودٍ كَالْكُرَةِ، بَلْ كَدَوَائِرِ

الْبَصَلَةِ، دَائِرَةٌ تَحْتَ دَائِرَةٍ، وَفِيهَا ثُقُبٌ خَرَقَتْ جَمِيعَ الدَّوَائِرِ، بِحَيْثُ يَنْفُذُ النُّورُ مِنَ الثَّقْبَةِ لِخَارِجِ الْكُرَةِ مِنْ سَائِرِ الْجِهَاتِ، وَطَبَقَاتُ الْكُرَةِ بِعَدَدِ الْقُرُونِ وَالسِّنِينَ وَالشُّهُورِ وَالْأَيَّامِ وَالسَّوَابِعِ وَالدَّقَائِقِ إِلَى أَقَلِّ مِنْ طَرْفَةِ عَيْنٍ، فَلَمَّا أَرَادَ اللهُ إِمْدَادَ الْكُلِّ مِنَ النُّورِ الْمُحَمَّدِيِّ وَإِيجَادَهُ عَلَى وَفْقِ مُرَادِهِ، خَلَقَ النُّورَ الْمُحَمَّدِيَّ، فَقَابَلَتْهُ مِنْ ظِلِّهِ: تِلْكَ الْكُرَةُ – دَائِرَةُ الْفَلَكِ الْمُحِيطِ – وَلَوْلَاهُ مَا ظَهَرَتْ. فَانْتَشَرَ النُّورُ عَلَى الْكُرَةِ، وَنَفَذَ مِنْ سَائِرِ الثُّقُبِ لِلْخَارِجِ، ثُمَّ أَمَرَ الْحَقُّ الْفَلَكَ بِالدَّوَرَانِ وَبِدَوَرَانِ كُلِّ دَائِرَةٍ تَحْتَهُ بِتَرْتِيبٍ بَدِيعٍ بِتَدْبِيرِ الْبَدِيعِ الْحَكِيمِ، فَصَارَتِ الثُّقُبُ يُصَادِمُ بَعْضُهَا بَعْضاً، وَالنُّورُ مُنْبَسِطٌ عَلَيْهَا، فَتَارَةً يَجِدُ مَنْفَذاً لِلْخَارِجِ مِنَ الثَّقْبِ الْمُصَادِفِ لِمَا هُوَ أَعْلَى، وَتَارَةً يُحْجَبُ الثَّقْبُ مَا وَالَاهُ مِمَّا لَيْسَ بِمَثْقُوبٍ، فَيُحْجَبُ النُّورُ عَمَّا تَحْتَ الثَّقْبِ. فَمَنْ أَشْرَقَ النُّورُ عَلَيْهِ فَهُوَ فِي سَعَادَةٍ وَنُورٍ، وَمَا حُجِبَ عَنِ النُّورِ فَهُوَ فِي شَقَاوَةٍ وَظَلَامٍ. وَبِذَٰلِكَ ظَهَرَ الْإِيمَانُ وَالْكُفْرُ وَمَا يُؤَدِّي إِلَيْهِمَا فِي السِّرِّ وَالْعَلَنِ فِي كُلِّ زَمَنٍ إِلَى مَا شَاءَ اللهُ. وَالْكُلُّ آخِذٌ مِنْهُ عَلَى قَدْرِ مَا قُدِّرَ لَهُ، فَكَانَ الْجَمِيعُ مِنْهُ وَمُقْتَبِساً مِنْهُ طِبْقَ مَا تَرَى....

وَاتَّضَحَ بِحَمْدِ اللهِ أَنَّ ضَمِيرَ **(نُورِهِ)** رَاجِعٌ لِلنُّورِ الْمُحَمَّدِيِّ مِنْ بَابِ الْإِسْتِخْدَامِ، وَهُوَ نَوْعٌ مِنْ أَنْوَاعِ الْبَدِيعِ عِنْدَ عُلَمَاءِ الْفَنِّ، لَا يُقَالُ أَنَّ النُّورَ هُنَا نَفْسُ النُّورِ الْأَوَّلِ مِنْ قَوْلِهِ **(نُورُ نَبِيِّكَ)** فَيَقْتَضِي تَكْوِينُ الشَّيْءِ مِنْ نَفْسِهِ، لِأَنَّا نَقُولُ **(مِنْ)** مِنْ قَوْلِهِ **(مِنْ نُورِهِ)** بَيَانِيَّةٌ، وَالْمَعْنَى: عَلَيْهَا نُورُ نَبِيِّكَ

الَّذِي هُوَ نُورُهُ، وَلَيْسَتْ بِتَبْعِيضِيَّةٍ. وَلَكَ أَنْ تَجْعَلَ الضَّمِيرَ عَائِداً إِلَى الحَقِّ سُبْحَانَهُ، وَالنُّورُ مَخْلُوقٌ، مَنْسُوبٌ لِلْحَقِّ عَلَى حَدِّ ﴿ هَٰذَا خَلْقُ ٱللَّهِ ﴾ الآية. لقمان. فَهُوَ مُضَافٌ لِلْحَقِّ، وَذَٰلِكَ النُّورُ المَخْلُوقُ هُوَ نُورُ نَبِيِّكَ لَا غَيْرُ.

فَإِنْ قِيلَ: المَخْلُوقُ لَا بُدَّ لَهُ مِنْ زَمَانٍ وَمَكَانٍ، فَيَقْتَضِي كَوْنُهُمَا مَعَهُ أَوْ قَبْلَهُ، مَعَ أَنَّهُ هُوَ أَوَّلُ الْأَشْيَاءِ، فَكَيْفَ الحَالُ؟ فَنَقُولُ: الزَّمَانُ وَالمَكَانُ هُمَا مِنْ جُمْلَةِ ظِلِّهِ، وَلَوْلَاهُ مَا تَكَوَّنَا، وَقَدْ شَاهَدَ ﷺ ذَٰلِكَ مِنْهُ مُتَكَوِّناً، وَرَآهُ مُتَحَرِّكاً بِتَحَرُّكِ دَوَرَانِ الْفَلَكِ المُحِيطِ فِي ذَٰلِكَ المَشْهَدِ. وَبِهِ تُفْهَمُ مُخَاطَبَتُهُ بِقَوْلِهِ تَعَالَى فِي مَقَامِ المِنَّةِ: ﴿ أَلَمْ تَرَ إِلَىٰ رَبِّكَ كَيْفَ مَدَّ ٱلظِّلَّ وَلَوْ شَآءَ لَجَعَلَهُۥ سَاكِنًا ثُمَّ جَعَلْنَا ٱلشَّمْسَ عَلَيْهِ دَلِيلًا ﴿٤٥﴾ ﴾ الفرقان. فَقَدْ خَاطَبَ الحَقُّ سُبْحَانَهُ نَبِيَّهُ فِي هَذِهِ الآيَةِ بِمَا آنَسَهُ بِهِ فِي مَقَامِ جَمْعِ الرُّوحِ بِالْجِسْمِ، كَالذِّكْرِ لَهُ لِمَا شَاهَدَهُ حَالَ تَجَرُّدِ الرُّوحِ الْكَرِيمِ، فَإِنَّ النُّورَ المُحَمَّدِيَّ عِنْدَ وُجُودِهِ كَانَ يَعْقِلُ وَيَفْهَمُ عَنِ الْحَقِّ، وَقَدْ نُبِّئَ فِي ذَٰلِكَ المِخْدَعِ الَّذِي انْفَرَدَ فِيهِ بِرَبِّهِ قَبْلَ خَلْقِ شَيْءٍ مِنَ الْأَشْيَاءِ لَا آدَمَ وَلَا غَيْرِهِ، وَقَدْ رَمَزَ لِذَٰلِكَ فِي حَدِيثِ: **كُنْتُ نَبِيّاً وَآدَمُ بَيْنَ الرُّوحِ وَالجَسَدِ**، وَقَدْ شَاهَدَ ﷺ رَبَّهُ بِالتَّجَلِّي الَّذِي تَجَلَّى بِهِ عَلَى ظِلِّهِ الْكَرِيمِ، فَمَدَّهُ، فَكَانَ مِنْهُ كُلُّ شَيْءٍ فَكَأَنَّهُ تَعَالَى يَقُولُ: أَلَمْ تَنْظُرْ يَا مُحَمَّدُ إِلَى رَبِّكَ كَيْفَ مَدَّ الظِّلَّ، فَهُوَ تَقْرِيرٌ لِمَا رَآهُ، فَقَدْ شَاهَدَ رَبَّهُ وَشَاهَدَ كَيْفِيَّةَ مَدِّهِ لِلظِّلِّ الَّذِي هُوَ كُلُّ الخَلَائِقِ فَجَمَعَ ﷺ مِنَ الجِنْسَيْنِ وَهُمَا رُؤْيَةُ الحَقِّ وَرُؤْيَةُ الخَلْقِ عَلَى وَفْقِ مَا قُدِّرَ لَهُ فِي ذَٰلِكَ المَشْهَدِ الَّذِي لَمْ يُشَاهِدْهُ غَيْرُهُ

فَعَرَفَ حَقِيقَتَهُ بِمَا لَمْ يَعْرِفْهَا بِهِ غَيْرُهُ فَقَالَ لَا يَعْرِفُنِي حَقِيقَةً غَيْرُ رَبِّي [لم أجده]
فَهُوَ الْحِجَابُ الْأَعْظَمُ الْمُشَارُ لَهُ بِقَوْلِ ابْنِ مَشِيشٍ: وَاجْعَلِ الْحِجَابَ
الْأَعْظَمَ حَيَاةَ رُوحِي الخ. اهـ. بتصرّف يسير.

Allah Derived the Prophet's Name from His Own Name

Ḥassān b. Thābit and others used the preposition *min* ("from," "out of") to convey a sense of that sublime derivation in their poetry. Originally conceived by Abū Ṭālib in praise of his nephew, the third verse in the following poem uses expressions and images that remain unmatched in their effect to this day:

126. *Blazing white over him and signifying prophecy is a seal*
from Allah, made of light that glows and testifies.
And the God has joined the name of the Prophet to His
when the caller to the five prayers says: "I bear witness,"
And He derived for him [a name] out of His own Name to exalt him,
for the Owner of the Throne is the All-Glorious (maḥmūd),
and here is the Glorified One (muḥammad).
A Prophet who came to us after despair and a period
without Prophets, as idols were worshipped on earth.
He came as an illuminating and guiding light
shining bright just like the burnished Indian sword.[174]

قال حسّان رضي الله عنه:

[174] The third verse is narrated from Abū Ṭālib by al-Bukhārī in *al-Tārīkh al-Awsaṭ* (1:82 §29) cf. Ibn Ḥajar, *Iṣāba* (7:112 *sub* "Abū Ṭālib") and *Fatḥ* (6:555, *Manāqib, asmā' al-Nabī*); Abū Nu'aym, *Dalā'il* (p. 41), and others (see next note). It is also attributed to 'Abd al-Muṭṭalib as mentioned by Ibn 'Abd al-Barr, *Tamhīd* (9:154) and *Istidhkār* (27:444-445 §41811). It was incorporated by Ḥassān b. Thābit into his own poetry cf. Ḥassān, *Dīwān* (p. 101 §88); 'Iyāḍ, *Shifā* I.iii.14 (p. 295); al-Suyūṭī, *al-Riyāḍ al-Anīqa* (p. 41); Ibn Kathīr, *Sīra* (1:211), *Bidāya* (3:390 *Ṣifat mawlidihi al-sharīf*; 9:374 *al-qawl fī-mā ūtiya Idrīs 'alayh al-salām*) and *Tafsīr* for the verse *Did we not exalt your fame?* (94:4).

أَغَرُّ عَلَيْهِ لِلنُّبُوَّةِ خَاتَمٌ * مِنَ اللهِ مِنْ نُورٍ يَلُوحُ وَيَشْهَدُ
وَضَمَّ الإِلَهُ اسْمَ النَّبِيِّ إِلَى اسْمِهِ * إِذَا قَالَ فِي الخَمْسِ المُؤَذِّنُ أَشْهَدُ
وَشَقَّ لَهُ مِنْ إِسْمِهِ لِيُجِلَّهُ * فَذُو الْعَرْشِ مَحْمُودٌ وَهٰذَا مُحَمَّدُ
نَبِيٌّ أَتَانَا بَعْدَ يَأْسٍ وَفَتْرَةٍ * مِنَ الرُّسْلِ وَالأَوْثَانُ فِي الأَرْضِ تُعْبَدُ
فَأَمْسَى سِرَاجاً مُسْتَنِيراً وَهَادِياً * يَلُوحُ كَمَا لاحَ الصَّقِيلُ المُهَنَّدُ

من ديوان حسان بن ثابت والبيت الثالث لأبي طالب كما رواه البخاري في التاريخ الأوسط الذي يعرف أيضاً بالتاريخ الصغير وأحمد في العلل والبيهقي وغيرهم.

The generation of the Successors considered the underlined verse the best ever declaimed.[175] It is rivalled by the second verse of the following couplet by the son of the Jāhiliyya poetess al-Khansā', the desert warlord Companion al-ʿAbbās b. Mirdās al-Sulamī:

127. *Seal of the Prophets, you were indeed sent*
with truth, and all of true guidance is your guidance!
Truly the God has based all love on you
from His creatures, by naming you Glorified.[176]

قال العبَّاس بنُ مِرداس السُلَمي رضي الله عنه من رواية ابن إسحاق في السيرة:

يَا خَاتَمَ النُّبَآءِ إِنَّكَ مُرْسَلٌ * بِالحَقِّ كُلُّ هُدَى السَّبِيلِ هُدَاكَا
إِنَّ الإِلَهَ بَنَى عَلَيْكَ مَحَبَّةً * فِي خَلْقِهِ وَمُحَمَّداً سَمَّاكَا

Shaykh Yūsuf al-Nabhānī (1265-1350/1849-1932) in his book *Saʿādat al-Dārayn* cited many explanations of the *Awliyā* on the perfection of the name *Muḥammad*, among them the Antiochene Ḥanafī scholar

[175] Aḥmad, *ʿIlal* (1:454 §1032); al-Khallāl, *Sunna* (1:193 §209); al-Bayhaqī, *Dalā'il* (1:160-161); Ibn ʿAsākir, *Tārīkh* (3:32-33); Ibn ʿAbd al-Barr (previous note).
[176] Ibn Hishām, *Sīra* (Battle of Ḥunayn); Ibn Diḥya, *Nihāyat al-Sūl* (p. 12).

ʿAbd al-Raḥmān b. ʿAlī al-Bisṭāmī al-Anṭākī (d. 858/1454) who said in his book *Durrat al-Ẓunūn fī Ruʾyat Qurrat al-ʿUyūn*:

128. No one has ever been named in reality by that holiest name – Muḥammad – whether before or after the Prophet. People only shared various nominal aspects (*mushārakāt fī jihāt min jihāt lafẓih*) but never essential aspects. For there is no creature other than him who is not marred by imperfection in some way. The impossibility of reaching absolute perfection on his level makes them other than glorified (*muḥammad*) in absolute and real terms, and therefore **there is no *muḥammad* except Muḥammad**. ... If someone asks: If the name *Muḥammad* was derived from *Maḥmūd* which is the Name of the Almighty as Ḥassān said:

And He derived for him [a name] out of His own Name to exalt him,
for the Owner of the Throne is the All-Glorious (maḥmūd),
and here is the Glorified One (muḥammad).

then why does the hyperbole apply here [i.e. to the Prophet] but not there [i.e. not to others thus named]? The answer is that since he is a human being, and human beings are not typically described as possessing attributes of perfection nor utmost perfection, hyperbole was needed in his name as a proclamation that he is not like them in his being human; rather, his mirror is capable of reflecting all the realities of the Divine Names and Attributes.[177]

قال الشيخ عبد الرحمن بن علي البسطامي رحمه الله تعالى في كتاب (درة الظنون في رؤية قرة العيون) في الفصل الثاني منه:

ثُمَّ إِنَّ هٰذَا الإِسْمَ الْأَقْدَسَ لَمْ يَتَسَمَّ بِهِ عَلَى الحَقِيقَةِ أَحَدٌ قَبْلَهُ وَلَا بَعْدَهُ ﷺ وَإِنَّمَا وَقَعَ لِلنَّاسِ مُشَارَكَاتٌ فِي جِهَاتٍ مِنْ جِهَاتِ لَفْظِهِ لَا مِنْ جِهَاتِ مَعْنَاهُ إِذْ مَا مِنْ مَخْلُوقٍ سِوَاهُ إِلَّا وَيَلْحَقُهُ نَقْصٌ مَا. وَلَوْ عُدِمَ التَّنَاهِي فِي

[177] In al-Nabhānī, *Saʿādat al-Dārayn* (p. 390-391).

الْكَمَالِ إِلَى رُتْبَتِهِ ﷺ فَلَا يَكُونُ مُحَمَّداً عَلَى الإِطْلَاقِ فَإِنَّ الْوَصْفَ بِعَدَمِ بُلُوغِ الْغَايَةِ فِي الْكَمَالِ نَوْعٌ مِنَ الذَّمِّ، وَمَنْ يَلْحَقُهُ الذَّمُّ بِوَجْهٍ مَا فَلَيْسَ مُحَمَّداً عَلَى الحَقِيقَةِ. **فَلَا مُحَمَّداً إِلَّا مُحَمَّدٌ** ﷺ. ... فَإِنْ قِيلَ إِذَا كَانَ اشْتِقَاقُ إِسْمِ (مُحَمَّدٍ) مِنْ إِسْمِهِ عَزَّ وَجَلَّ (مَحْمُودٌ) كَمَا قَالَ حَسَّانُ رَضِيَ اللهُ تَعَالَى عَنْهُ أَيْ فِي قَوْلِهِ

وَشَقَّ لَهُ مِنْ إِسْمِهِ لِيُجِلَّهُ * فَذُو الْعَرْشِ مَحْمُودٌ وَهٰذَا مُحَمَّدُ

فَلِمَ بُولِغَ فِي هٰذَا دُونَ ذٰلِكَ؟ فَالجَوَابُ أَنَّهُ ﷺ لَمَّا كَانَ بَشَراً، وَلَيْسَ مِنْ شَأْنِ الْبَشَرِ الْكَمَالُ فِي الْأَوْصَافِ وَلَا بُلُوغُ الْغَايَةِ فِيهَا، أُحْتِيجَ إِلَى الْمُبَالَغَةِ فِي إِسْمِهِ ﷺ لِلْإِعْلَامِ بِأَنَّهُ لَيْسَ مِثْلَهُمْ فِي هٰذَا الْوَصْفِ، بَلْ مِرْآتُهُ قَابِلَةٌ لِجَمِيعِ حَقَائِقِ الْأَسْمَاءِ وَالصِّفَاتِ.

The hadith master Ibn Bukayr (d. 388/998) compiled all of the reports on the blessing of being named Muḥammad and Aḥmad, which al-Nabhānī reproduced in full.[178]

Ḥassān's comparison of the Prophet's light to a burnished sword—of which, as mentioned, other Companions disapproved—was taken up by another great poet, Kaʿb b. Zuhayr (d. 26/647) in his poem *Bānat Suʿād* (Suʿād Has Left) in which he recited to the Prophet in his Mosque, his hand in the Prophet's hand, this entreaty for forgiveness:

129. *The son of woman, as long as he may safely live,*
one day is borne upon a raised bier.
I was told the Messenger of Allah threatened me with death,
but with the Messenger of Allah I hope to find pardon.
Gently! Be guided by Him Who gave you the gift of Qur'ān,
wherein are admonitions and detailed exposition.

[178] al-Nabhānī, *Saʿādat al-Dārayn* (p. 394-400).

Do not punish me for what informers said, when I have not
sinned, even should the false sayings about me be many.
Truly I stand in such a place that if an elephant stood there,
seeing and hearing what I see and hear,
It would shake with terror unless it might expect
a reprieve from the Messenger of Allah.
I did not cease to cross the desert under cover
of darkness when the mantle of night unfurled,
Until I laid my right hand, not to withdraw it,
in the hand of the avenger who has the final word.
For truly he is more feared by me when I speak to him
—even if they tell me I have lineage and fame—
Than a lion in the jungle, whose lair
is mid dense thickets in the lowland of ʿAththar....
Truly the Messenger of Allah is a light whose illumination is sought
—a drawn Indian sword, one of the swords of Allah![179]

Another version states: *Truly the Messenger of Allah is a sword whose illumination is sought*. This was explained thus:

> When the Arabs wanted to summon the people that surrounded their region they would draw a burnished sword and let it flash and draw attention from afar, so the others would come to it, guided by its lights and following its direction. Likewise when the Prophet brought manifest Light and overwhelming miracles and he summoned the people to himself, they came guided by his all-encompassing light and following its shining radiance.[180]

وقال كعب بن زهير رضي الله عنه:

كُلُّ ابْنِ أُنْثَى وَإِنْ طَالَتْ سَلَامَتُهُ * يَوْمًا عَلَى آلَةٍ حَدْبَاءَ مَحْمُـــــولُ

نُبِّئْتُ أَنَّ رَسُولَ اللهِ أَوْعَــــــدَنِي * وَالْعَفْوُ عِنْدَ رَسُولِ اللهِ مَأْمُــــولُ

[179] Ibn Hishām, *Sīra* (3/4: 510-512 lines 39-51).
[180] al-Bājūrī, *Ḥāshiyat al-Isʿād ʿalā Bānat Suʿād* (p. 91).

مَهْلًا هَدَاكَ الَّذِي أَعْطَاكَ نَافِلَةَ الْـ * ـقُرْآنِ فِيهَا مَوَاعِيظٌ وَتَفْصِيلُ
لَا تَأْخُذَنِّي بِأَقْوَالِ الْوُشَاةِ وَلَمْ * أُذْنِبْ وَلَوْ كَثُرَتْ فِيَّ الْأَقَاوِيلُ
لَقَدْ أَقُومُ مَقَاماً لَوْ يَقُومُ بِهِ * أَرَى وَأَسْمَعُ مَا لَوْ يَسْمَعُ الْفِيلُ
لَظَلَّ يَرْعَدُ إِلَّا أَنْ يَكُونَ لَهُ * مِنَ الرَّسُولِ بِإِذْنِ اللهِ تَنْوِيلُ
مَا زِلْتُ أَقْتَطِعُ الْبَيْدَاءَ مُدَّرِعاً * جُنْحَ الظَّلَامِ وَثَوْبُ اللَّيْلِ مَسْبُولُ
حَتَّى وَضَعْتُ يَمِينِي مَا أُنَازِعُهُ * فِي كَفِّ ذِي نَقِمَاتٍ قِيلُهُ الْقِيلُ
فَلَهْوَ أَخْوَفُ عِنْدِي إِذْ أُكَلِّمُهُ * وَقِيلَ إِنَّكَ مَنْسُوبٌ وَمَسْئُولُ
مِنْ ضَيْغَمٍ بِضَرَاءِ الْأَرْضِ مُخْدَرُهُ * فِي بَطْنِ عَثَّرَ غِيلٌ دُونَهُ غِيلُ

إلى أن قال:

إِنَّ الرَّسُولَ لَنُورٌ يُسْتَضَاءُ بِهِ * مُهَنَّدٌ مِنْ سُيُوفِ اللهِ مَسْلُولُ

رواه ابن هشام في السيرة من قصيدة بانت سُعاد لكعب بن زهير. وفي رواية:

إِنَّ الرَّسُولَ لَسَيفٌ يُسْتَضَاءُ بِهِ * مُهَنَّدٌ مِنْ سُيُوفِ اللهِ مَسْلُولُ

كذا في شرحَي الإمام جمال الدين الأنصاري والشيخ إبراهيم الباجوري وقال: قَدْ كَانَتْ عَادَةُ الْعَرَبِ أَنَّهُمْ إِذَا أَرَادُوا اسْتِدْعَاءَ مَنْ حَوْلَهُمْ مِنَ الْقَوْمِ شَهَرُوا السَّيْفَ الصَّقِيلَ فَيَبْرُقُ فَيَظْهَرُ لَمَعَانُهُ مِنْ بُعْدٍ فَيَأْتُونَ إِلَيْهِ مُهْتَدِينَ بِنُورِهِ وَمُؤْتَمِّينَ بِهَدْيِهِ، وَكَذٰلِكَ النَّبِيُّ ﷺ لَمَّا جَاءَ بِالنُّورِ الْمُبِينِ وَالْمُعْجِزَاتِ الظَّاهِرَةِ وَدَعَا النَّاسَ إِلَيْهِ، أَتَوْا مُهْتَدِينَ بِنُورِهِ السَّاطِعِ وَمُؤْتَمِّينَ بِضِيَائِهِ اللَّامِعِ.

V

The Progression of the Prophet's Light in Time

Thus not only do the texts show that the Prophet is at the forefront of the sequence of creation—his creation and appointment taking place even before the Day of Promises according to the hadith "I was the first of the Prophets to be created and the last one to be sent"—but also that he is created as a primal light. This nature-specific firstness is made clear in Abū Hurayra's *ḥadīth qudsī* of Adam sighting the light of the Prophet already mentioned in the first section (§16):

> "This is your son Aḥmad, he is the first and the last."

Apart from the aforementioned proofs from Qur'ān and Hadith on the Prophet as the first creation and on his being created as a light, **the latter narration is the most authentic explicit proof reuniting both aspects**.

More Reports on the Prophet as the First Light Created

Among the famous but unverified similar narrations are the three bulleted reports mentioned below:

- The report of ʿAlī b. al-Ḥusayn, from his father, from his grandfather, that the Prophet said:

130. I was a light in front of my Lord for 14,000 years before He created Adam.[181]

[181] al-Qasṭallānī, *Mawāhib* (1:39) sources it to Ibn al-Qaṭṭān's critique of ʿAbd al-Ḥaqq al-Ishbīlī's *Aḥkām* "as mentioned in Ibn Marzūq" but it is more likely found only in the latter's commentary on Ibn al-Qaṭṭān and is not mentioned by Ibn al-Qaṭṭān himself. Ibn Marzūq is Muḥammad b. Aḥmad b. Muḥammad b. Muḥammad b. Abī Bakr b. Marzūq al-Tilimsānī al-Khaṭīb (710-781/1310-1379), author of commentaries on the *Shifā*, the *Burda*, ʿAbd al-Ḥaqq al-Ishbīlī's *al-Aḥkām al-Ṣughrā* and Ibn al-Qaṭṭān's book on the latter, and other books. A similar report adds the men-

قال القسطلاني في المواهب: وفي كتاب الأحكام للحافظ الناقد أبي الحسن ابن القطان **رَوَى عَلِيُّ بْنُ الحُسَيْنِ عَنْ أَبِيهِ عَنْ جَدِّهِ رَضِيَ اللهُ عَنْهُمْ مَرْفُوعاً: كُنْتُ نُوراً بَيْنَ يَدَيْ رَبِّي عَزَّ وَجَلَّ قَبْلَ أَنْ يُخْلَقَ آدَمُ بِأَرْبَعَةَ عَشَرَ أَلْفِ عَامٍ** انتهى وهو ليس عند ابن القطان فيبدو أنه عند شارحه ابن مرزوق فقط. وليس كتاب الأحكام لابن القطان بل للحافظ الفقيه عبد الحق الإشبيلي صنّف الأحكام الكبرى والوسطى والصغرى وإنما ابن القطان نقد الوسطى بكتابه (بيان الوهم والإيهام الواقعين في كتاب الأحكام). ونحوه في فضائل الصحابة للإمام أحمد وابن عساكر في التاريخ بلفظ **كُنْتُ أَنَا وَعَلِيٌّ نُوراً.** قيل هو من وضع الحسن بن علي بن زكريا العَدَوي كما في موضوعات ابن الجوزي والميزان. والله أعلم.

Also related is the report of ʿAmr b. ʿAbasa that the Prophet said:

> **131.** Truly Allah created the spirits of His servants 2,000 years before He created His servants. Then whichever among them recognized each other came together, and whichever did not, stayed apart.[182]

عَنْ عَمْرِو بْنِ عَبَسَةَ رَضِيَ اللهُ عَنْهُ مَرْفُوعاً إِنَّ اللهَ خَلَقَ أَرْوَاحَ الْعِبَادِ قَبْلَ الْعِبَادِ بِأَلْفَيْ عَامٍ فَمَا تَعَارَفَ مِنْهَا ائْتَلَفَ وَمَا تَنَافَرَ مِنْهَا اخْتَلَفَ رواه ابن منده وأورد إسناده ابن القيم في كتاب الروح فصل تقدّم خلق الأرواح على الأجساد وهو ضعيف جداً

tion of ʿAlī as narrated by Aḥmad, *Faḍāʾil al-Ṣaḥāba* (2:662-663 §1130) and Ibn ʿAsākir, *Tārīkh* (42:67), apparently forged by al-Ḥasan b. ʿAlī b. Zakariyyā al-ʿAdawī cf. al-Dhahabī, *Mīzān al-Iʿtidāl* (*sub* al-Ḥasan b. ʿAlī b. Zakariyyā) and others.

[182] Ibn Mandah with a very weak chain adduced by Ibn al-Qayyim, *al-Rūḥ* (p. 384-385 *Masʾala 18*).

Also related is the more general report on *qadar* in *Saḥīḥ Muslim* from ʿAbd Allāh b. ʿAmr b. al-ʿĀṣ that the Prophet said:

132. Truly Allah wrote the apportionments of all creatures before creating the heavens and the earth by 50,000 years, while His Throne was over the water."[183]

عَنْ عَبْدِ اللهِ بْنِ عَمْرِو بْنِ الْعَاصِ رَضِيَ اللهُ عَنْهُمَا قَالَ سَمِعْتُ رَسُولَ اللهِ ﷺ يَقُولُ: كَتَبَ اللهُ مَقَادِيرَ الخَلَائِقِ قَبْلَ أَنْ يَخْلُقَ السَّمَاوَاتِ وَالْأَرْضَ بِخَمْسِينَ أَلْفِ سَنَةٍ قَالَ وَعَرْشُهُ عَلَى المَاءِ رواه مسلم.

A scholar commented: "and part of what He wrote in that *dhikr*, which is *Umm al-Kitāb*, is that Muḥammad is the Seal of Prophets"[184] —an explanatory comment which some later readers mistook for the continuation of the above hadith.

Also related is the report from Ibn ʿUmar that the Prophet said:

133. Truly the first thing Allah created is the Pen, which is made of light for a distance of 500 years. He commanded it and it coursed through what is to take place until the Day of Resurrection. Therefore believe everything that reaches you concerning the Divine Power.[185]

عَنِ ابْنِ عُمَرَ رَضِيَ اللهُ عَنْهُمَا مَرْفُوعاً: إِنَّ اللهَ تَبَارَكَ وَتَعَالَى أَوَّلُ شَيْءٍ خَلَقَ، خَلَقَ الْقَلَمَ وَهُوَ مِنْ نُورٍ مَسِيرَةَ خَمْسِمِئَةِ عَامٍ، فَأَمَرَ اللهُ عَزَّ وَجَلَّ الْقَلَمَ،

[183] Muslim, *Ṣaḥīḥ* (*Qadar, Ḥijāj Ādama Mūsā*).
[184] Ibn Rajab, *Laṭāʾif al-Maʿārif* (beginning of the chapter on the month of Rabīʿ al-Awwal).
[185] Abū al-Shaykh, *al-ʿAẓama* (2:590 §222).

فَجَرَى بِمَا هُوَ كَائِنٌ إِلَى يَوْمِ الْقِيَامَةِ، فَصَدِّقُوا كَمَا بُلِّغْتُمْ عَنِ اللهِ تَبَارَكَ وَتَعَالَى مِنْ قُدْرَتِهِ. رواه أبو الشيخ في العظمة.

• The report forwarded by Abū Saʿd al-Naysābūrī (d. 406/1015) and Ibn Bābūyah (d. 381/991) as narrated from Jaʿfar b. Muḥammad al-Ṣādiq, from his father, from his grandfather, from ʿAlī b. Abī Ṭālib:

134. Truly Allah Most High created the light of Muḥammad—upon him blessings and peace—424,000 years before He created the heavens and the earth and the Throne and the Footstool and the Pen and Paradise and Hellfire; and before He created Adam, Nūḥ, Ibrāhīm, Ismāʿīl, Isḥāq, Yaʿqūb, Mūsā, ʿĪsā, Sulaymān, and Dāwūd; and everyone He has named when He said *And We bestowed upon him Isḥāq and Yaʿqūb* until He said *and We chose them and guided them unto a straight path* (6:84-87); and before He created all the Prophets.

Together with him He created twelve veils: (i) the veil of Power (*ḥijāb al-qudra*); (ii) the veil of Magnificence (*ʿaẓama*); (iii) the veil of Bestowal (*minna*); (iv) the veil of Mercy (*raḥma*); (v) the veil of Bliss (*saʿāda*); (vi) the veil of Munificence (*karāma*); (vii) the veil of Eminence (*makāna*); (viii) the veil of Guidance (*hidāya*); (ix) the veil of Prophethood (*nubuwwa*); (x) the veil of Loftiness (*rifʿa*); (xi) the veil of Dignity (*hayba*); and (xii) the veil of Intercession (*shafāʿa*).

Then He confined the Light of Muḥammad—upon him blessings and peace—within the veil of Power for 12,000 years while it said: "Glory to my Lord the Most High!" (*subḥāna Rabbiya al-Aʿlā*); within the veil of Magnificence for 11,000 years while it said: "Glory to the Knower of the secret and what is more secret!" (*subḥān ʿĀlim al-sirr wa-akhfā*);[186] within the veil

[186] In Sūrat Ṭaha: *And if you speak aloud, then truly He knows the secret (thought) and (that which is yet) more hidden* (20:7, Pickthall). "*Sirr* is what you keep secret from people and *akhfā* is whispering (*al-waswasa*)" (Mujāhid); "*Sirr* is what you keep secret in yourself and *akhfā* is what you did not even tell yourself" (Saʿīd b. Jubayr). Mujāhid, *Tafsīr* (p. 460 *sub* 20:7).

of Bestowal for 10,000 years while it said: "Glory to the Supreme and Highest!" (*subḥān al-Rafīʿ al-Aʿlā*); within the veil of Mercy for 9,000 years while it said: "Glory to the Compassionate, the Great!" (*subḥān al-Raʾūf al-Kabīr*); within the veil of Bliss for 8,000 years while it said: "Glory to Him Who is Everlasting and never heedless!" (*subḥān al-Dāʾim lā yas-hū*); within the veil of Munificence for 7,000 years while it said: "Glory to the Self-Sufficient Who is never in need!" (*subḥāna man huwa Ghanī lā yaftaqir*); within the veil of Eminence for 6,000 years while it said: "Glory to the All-Knowing, the Most Forbearing!" (*subḥān al-ʿAlīm al-Ḥalīm*); within the veil of Guidance for 5,000 years while it said: "Glory to the Owner of the Throne, the Almighty!" (*subḥāna Dhīl-ʿarsh, al-ʿAẓīm*); within the veil of Prophethood for 4,000 years while it said: "Glory to the Lord of Might beyond what they claim!" (*subḥāna Rabb al-ʿizza ʿammā yaṣifūn*); within the veil of Loftiness for 3,000 years while it said: "Glory to the Owner of Sovereignty and Dominion!" (*subḥān Dhīl-Mulk wal-Malakūt*); within the veil of Dignity for 2,000 years while it said: "Glory to Allah and Praise to Him!" (*subḥān Allāh wa-bi-ḥamdih*); within the veil of Intercession for 1,000 years while it said: "Glory to My Magnificent Lord and Praise to Him!" (*subḥāna Rabbiya al-ʿAẓīm wa-bi-ḥamdih*).

Then He made his name manifest on the Tablet—whereupon the Tablet became illumined—for 4,000 years. Then He made it manifest on the Throne, whereupon it was affirmed on the pillar of the Throne for 7,000 years, until Allah Most High placed it in the loins of Adam. Then He moved it from the loins of Adam to the loins of Nūḥ, and so forth from loin to loin until Allah brought him out from the loins of ʿAbd Allāh b. ʿAbd al-Muṭṭalib.[187]

قال أبو سعد النيسابوري في كتاب شرف المصطفى: عن عبد الله بن المبارك، عن سفيان الثوري، (ح) وفي معاني الأخبار لابن بابويه أبي جعفر القُمّي الشيعي المعروف عندهم بالشيخ الصدوق (ت 381/991م): حدثنا الحاكم أحمد بن محمد بن عبد الرحمٰن

[187] Abū Saʿd al-Naysābūrī, *Sharaf al-Muṣṭafā* (1:305-311 §79) and Ibn Bābūyah, *Maʿānī al-Akhbār* (p. 306-308).

المروزي، قال: حدثنا أبو بكر محمد ابن إبراهيم الجرجاني، قال: حدثنا أبو بكر عبد الصمد بن يحيى الواسطي، قال: حدثنا الحسن بن علي المدني، عن عبد الله بن المبارك، عن سفيان الثوري، عَنْ جَعْفَرِ بْنِ مُحَمَّدٍ الصَّادِقِ، عَنْ أَبِيهِ، عَنْ جَدِّهِ، عَنْ أَبِيهِ، عَنْ عَلِيِّ بْنِ أَبِي طَالِبٍ عَلَيْهِمُ السَّلَامُ أَنَّهُ قَالَ:

إِنَّ اللهَ تَبَارَكَ وَتَعَالَى خَلَقَ نُورَ مُحَمَّدٍ ﷺ وَآلِهِ قَبْلَ أَنْ يَخْلُقَ السَّمَاوَاتِ وَالْأَرْضَ وَالْعَرْشَ وَالْكُرْسِيَّ وَاللَّوْحَ وَالْقَلَمَ وَالْجَنَّةَ وَالنَّارَ وَقَبْلَ أَنْ يَخْلُقَ آدَمَ وَنُوحاً وَإِبْرَاهِيمَ وَإِسْمَاعِيلَ وَإِسْحَاقَ وَيَعْقُوبَ وَمُوسَى وَعِيسَى وَدَاوُدَ وَسُلَيْمَانَ وَكُلَّ مَنْ قَالَ اللهُ عَزَّ وَجَلَّ فِي قَوْلِهِ ﴿وَوَهَبْنَا لَهُۥٓ إِسْحَٰقَ وَيَعْقُوبَ﴾ الأنعام إِلَى قَوْلِهِ ﴿وَهَدَيْنَٰهُمْ إِلَىٰ صِرَٰطٍ مُّسْتَقِيمٍ﴾ وَقَبْلَ أَنْ يَخْلُقَ الْأَنْبِيَاءَ كُلَّهُمْ بِأَرْبَعِمِائَةِ أَلْفِ سَنَةٍ وَأَرْبَعٍ وَعِشْرِينَ أَلْفِ سَنَةٍ وَخَلَقَ عَزَّ وَجَلَّ مَعَهُ إِثْنَى عَشَرَ حِجَاباً: حِجَابُ الْقُدْرَةِ، وَحِجَابُ الْعَظَمَةِ، وَحِجَابُ الْمِنَّةِ، وَحِجَابُ الرَّحْمَةِ، وَحِجَابُ السَّعَادَةِ، وَحِجَابُ الْكَرَامَةِ، وَحِجَابُ الْمَنْزِلَةِ، وَحِجَابُ الْهِدَايَةِ، وَحِجَابُ النُّبُوَّةِ، وَحِجَابُ الرِّفْعَةِ، وَحِجَابُ الْهَيْبَةِ، وَحِجَابُ الشَّفَاعَةِ.

ثُمَّ حَبَسَ نُورَ مُحَمَّدٍ ﷺ وَآلِهِ فِي حِجَابِ الْقُدْرَةِ اثْنَى عَشَرَ أَلْفِ سَنَةٍ وَهُوَ يَقُولُ سُبْحَانَ رَبِّيَ الْأَعْلَى. وَفِي حِجَابِ الْعَظَمَةِ إِحْدَى عَشَرَ أَلْفِ سَنَةٍ وَهُوَ يَقُولُ سُبْحَانَ عَالِمِ السِّرِّ وَأَخْفَى وَفِي حِجَابِ الْمِنَّةِ عَشْرَةَ آلَافِ سَنَةٍ وَهُوَ يَقُولُ سُبْحَانَ الرَّفِيعِ الْأَعْلَى وَفِي حِجَابِ الرَّحْمَةِ تِسْعَةَ آلَافِ سَنَةٍ وَهُوَ يَقُولُ

سُبْحَانَ الرَّؤُوفِ الْكَبِيرِ وَفِي حِجَابِ السَّعَادَةِ ثَمَانِيَةَ آلَافِ سَنَةٍ وَهُوَ يَقُولُ سُبْحَانَ مَنْ هُوَ دَائِمٌ لَا يَسْهُو وَفِي حِجَابِ الْكَرَامَةِ سَبْعَةَ آلَافِ سَنَةٍ وَهُوَ يَقُولُ سُبْحَانَ مَنْ هُوَ غَنِيٌّ لَا يَفْتَقِرُ وَفِي حِجَابِ الْمَنْزِلَةِ سِتَّةَ آلَافِ سَنَةٍ وَهُوَ يَقُولُ سُبْحَانَ الْعَلِيمِ الْكَرِيمِ وَفِي حِجَابِ الْهِدَايَةِ خَمْسَةَ آلَافِ سَنَةٍ وَهُوَ يَقُولُ سُبْحَانَ ذِي الْعَرْشِ الْعَظِيمِ وَفِي حِجَابِ النُّبُوَّةِ أَرْبَعَةَ آلَافِ سَنَةٍ وَهُوَ يَقُولُ سُبْحَانَ رَبِّ الْعِزَّةِ عَمَّا يَصِفُونَ وَفِي حِجَابِ الرِّفْعَةِ ثَلَاثَةَ آلَافِ سَنَةٍ وَهُوَ يَقُولُ سُبْحَانَ ذِي الْمُلْكِ وَالْمَلَكُوتِ وَفِي حِجَابِ الْهَيْبَةِ أَلْفَي سَنَةٍ وَهُوَ يَقُولُ سُبْحَانَ اللهِ وَبِحَمْدِهِ وَفِي حِجَابِ الشَّفَاعَةِ أَلْفَ سَنَةٍ وَهُوَ يَقُولُ سُبْحَانَ رَبِّيَ الْعَظِيمِ وَبِحَمْدِهِ.

ثُمَّ أَظْهَرَ اسْمَهُ عَلَى اللَّوْحِ – فَكَانَ اللَّوْحُ مُنَوَّراً – أَرْبَعَةَ آلَافِ سَنَةٍ، ثُمَّ أَظْهَرَهُ عَلَى الْعَرْشِ فَكَانَ عَلَى سَاقِ الْعَرْشِ مُثْبَتاً سَبْعَةَ آلَافِ سَنَةٍ، إِلَى أَنْ وَضَعَهُ اللهُ عَزَّ وَجَلَّ فِي صُلْبِ آدَمَ عَلَيْهِ السَّلَامُ، ثُمَّ نَقَلَهُ مِنْ صُلْبِ آدَمَ إِلَى صُلْبِ نُوحٍ عَلَيْهِ السَّلَامُ، ثُمَّ مِنْ صُلْبٍ إِلَى صُلْبٍ حَتَّى أَخْرَجَهُ اللهُ تَعَالَى مِنْ صُلْبِ عَبْدِ اللهِ بْنِ عَبْدِ الْمُطَّلِبِ.

- The "light of Quraysh" hadith of Ibn ʿAbbās in Ibn Abī ʿUmar al-ʿAdanī's *Musnad*:

135. Truly Quraysh was a light standing before Allāh Most High for 2,000 years before He created Adam, glorifying Allah, so that the angels would glorify Him in the same terms. When Allah created Adam He placed that light in his loins. The Messenger of Allah said: "Then Allah made me alight on earth in the loins of

Adam and He placed me in the loins of Nūḥ in the ship and He cast me into the fire in the loins of Ibrāhīm, and He never stopped transporting me from the noble loins into the pure wombs until He brought me out from my two parents. None of my foreparents ever met in fornication."[188]

عَنِ ابْنِ عَبَّاسٍ رَضِيَ اللهُ عَنْهُمَا قَالَ إِنَّ قُرَيْشًا كَانَتْ نُورًا بَيْنَ يَدَيِ اللهِ عَزَّ وَجَلَّ قَبْلَ أَنْ يَخْلُقَ آدَمَ عَلَيْهِ السَّلَامُ بِأَلْفَيْ عَامٍ يُسَبِّحُ ذٰلِكَ النُّورُ فَتُسَبِّحُ الْمَلَائِكَةُ بِتَسْبِيحِهِ فَلَمَّا خَلَقَ اللهُ آدَمَ جَعَلَ ذٰلِكَ النُّورَ فِي صُلْبِهِ فَقَالَ رَسُولُ اللهِ ﷺ فَأَهْبَطَنِيَ اللهُ الْأَرْضَ فِي صُلْبِ آدَمَ وَجَعَلَنِي فِي صُلْبِ نُوحٍ فِي السَّفِينَةِ وَقَذَفَ بِي فِي النَّارِ فِي صُلْبِ إِبْرَاهِيمَ عَلَيْهِ السَّلَامُ وَلَمْ يَزَلْ يَنْقُلُنِي مِنَ الْأَصْلَابِ الْكَرِيمَةِ إِلَى الْأَرْحَامِ الطَّاهِرَةِ حَتَّى أَخْرَجَنِي مِنْ بَيْنِ أَبَوَيَّ، لَمْ يَلْتَقِيَا عَلَى سِفَاحٍ قَطُّ. رواه الآجري في الشريعة من طريق ابن أبي عمر العَدَني كما في المطالب العالية، كتاب السيرة والمغازي، باب أوّليّة النبيّ ﷺ وشرف أصله بإسناد ضعيف جداً. وروى ابن عساكر نحوه في التاريخ.

Al-ʿAbbās b. ʿAbd al-Muṭṭalib's "Light of *Mawlid*" Poem

Qāḍī ʿIyāḍ cites the above report then says: "al-ʿAbbās's panegyric of the Prophet bears witness to the veracity of that report"[189] in reference to the "Light of *Mawlid*" narration from the newly converted emigrant Khuraym b. Aws b. Jāriya in which he witnesses the paternal uncle of the Prophet, al-ʿAbbās b. ʿAbd al-Muṭṭalib, saying:

[188] al-Ājurrī [through al-ʿAdanī], *al-Sharīʿa* (3:1418-1420 §960) with a very weak chain cf. Ibn Ḥajar, *al-Maṭālib al-ʿĀliya* (17:195 §4209, *Kitāb al-sīra wal-maghāzī, Bāb awwaliyyat al-Nabiyyi ṣallā Allāhu ʿalayh wa-sallam wa-sharaf aṣlih*). Ibn ʿAsākir narrates something very similar in his *Tarikh* (3:408).

[189] ʿIyāḍ, *Shifā* I.ii.6 (p. 127 §131 *sharaf nasabih wa-karam baladih wa-mansha'ih*).

"Messenger of Allāh, I wish to praise you." The Prophet replied: "Go ahead, Allāh bless your mouth!" *(lā yufaḍḍiḍi Allāhu fāk)*. Al-ʿAbbās then eulogized the Prophet's Adamic creation and compared him to a light:

136. *Beforetime you were blessed in the shades [of Paradise]*
and the Repository where leaves were used for garments.
Then you alighted upon earth, neither a human being
nor a piece of flesh nor clot,
But as a drop that boarded the Ark
when the flood destroyed Nasr and the rest of the idols,
Transported from loins to wombs
in the succession of worlds and centuries.
You came upon the fire of Allah's Friend, concealed
in his loins—how could he possibly burn?
[Variant: O coolness of the Friend's furnace, O reason
for protection from the fire despite its burning!]
Until your noble House, proclaiming [your merit], took hold
of the highest summit of the line of Khindif.
And you, when you were born, the earth was illumined
and the firmament became filled with your light.
So we – in that radiance and that light
and paths of guidance – can pierce through.[190]

مِنْ قَبْلِهَا طِبْتَ فِي الظِّلَالِ وَفِي * مُسْتَوْدَعٍ حَيْثُ يُخْصَفُ الْوَرَقُ

ثُمَّ هَبَطْتَ الْبِلَادَ لَا بَشَرٌ * أَنْتَ وَلَا مُضْغَةٌ وَلَا عَلَقُ

بَلْ نُطْفَةٌ تَرْكَبُ السَّفِينَ وَقَدْ * أَلْجَمَ نَسْراً وَأَهْلَهُ الْغَرَقُ

[190] al-Ḥākim, *Mustadrak* (3:326-327); al-Ṭabarānī, *al-Muʿjam al-Kabīr* (4:213 §4167); Abū Bakr al-Shāfiʿī, *Ghaylāniyyāt* (1:282-284 §285); al-Bayhaqī, *Dalāʾil* (5:268); ʿIyāḍ, *Shifā* I.iii.1 (p. 216 §393); and Ibn al-Jawzī, *Wafā* (p. 28 §9); cf. Abū Nuʿaym, *Ḥilya* (1:364) and Ibn Sayyid al-Nās in *Minaḥ al-Madḥ* (p. 192-193). Al-Suyūṭī in *al-Laʾāliʾ al-Maṣnūʿa* (1:244) said: "There is no question that these verses are by al-ʿAbbās." The variant is cited in al-Thaʿālibī, *al-Tamthīl wal-Muḥāḍara* and al-Nuwayrī, *Nihāyat al-Arab*. Khindif is the nickname of Laylā the wife of Ilyās b. Muḍar: al-Ṣāliḥī, *Subul* (1:93).

تُنْقَلُ مِنْ صَالِبٍ إِلَى رَحِمٍ * إِذَا مَضَى عَالَمٌ بَدَا طَبَقُ
وَرَدْتَ نَارَ الخَلِيلِ مُسْتَتِراً * فِي صُلْبِهِ أَنْتَ كَيْفَ يَحْتَرِقُ
حَتَّى احْتَوَى بَيْتُكَ الْمُهَيْمِنُ مِنْ * خِنْدِفٍ عَلْيَاءَ تَحْتَهَا النُّطُقُ
وَأَنْتَ لَمَّا وُلِدْتَ أَشْرَقَتِ الْأَرْضُ * وَضَاءَتْ بِنُورِكَ الْأُفُقُ
فَنَحْنُ فِي ذٰلِكَ الضِّيَاءِ وَفِي * النُّورِ وَسُبُلِ الرَّشَادِ نَخْتَرِقُ

رواه الطبراني وأبو بكر الشافعي والحاكم والبيهقي ويروى أيضاً بلفظ

يَا بَرْدَ نَارِ الخَلِيلِ يَا سَبَباً * لِعِصْمَةِ النَّارِ وَهْيَ تَحْتَرِقُ

كذا في الشفا والتمثيل والمحاضرة للثعالبي ونهاية الأَرَب للنويري

The Qur'ān alludes to the Prophet's antediluvian origin in both universal and specific terms:

137. *Truly when the waters rose We carried you upon the ship* (69:11): "During the Flood, that is, your ancestors as you were in their loins, on board the ark of Nūḥ, upon him peace" (Bayḍāwī);[191]

138. *And a token unto them is that We bore their offspring in the laden ship* (36:41), "that is, their ancestors on the ship of Nūḥ, as the term 'offspring' (*dhurriyya*) is used for forefathers just as it is used for descendants" (al-Wāḥidī);[192]

139. *And your translation (taqallubaka) among the worshippers* (26:219) in the sense of "your descent from the loins of a Prophet to those of another Prophet" as related from Ibn ʿAbbās.[193]

[191] al-Bayḍāwī, *Anwār al-Tanzīl* (*sub* 69:11).
[192] al-Wāḥidī, *Wasīṭ* (*sub* 36:41).
[193] *Tafsīr*s of Ibn Abī Ḥātim and al-Naḥḥās (*sub* 26:219); al-Ājurrī, *al-Sharīʿa* (3:1418-1419 §959); al-Bazzār, al-Ṭabarānī, and al-Ḥākim with a sound chain according to al-Haythamī, *Majmaʿ* (7:86 and 8:214).

﴿إِنَّا لَمَّا طَغَا ٱلۡمَآءُ حَمَلۡنَٰكُمۡ فِي ٱلۡجَارِيَةِ ۝١١﴾ قال البيضاوي في أنوار التنزيل: وَذَلِكَ فِي الطُّوفَانِ... حَمَلْنَاكُمْ أَيْ آبَاءَكُمْ وَأَنْتُمْ فِي أَصْلَابِهِمْ فِي الجَارِيَةِ فِي سَفِينَةِ نُوحٍ عَلَيْهِ الصَّلَاةُ وَالسَّلَامُ. ﴿وَءَايَةٞ لَّهُمۡ أَنَّا حَمَلۡنَا ذُرِّيَّتَهُمۡ فِي ٱلۡفُلۡكِ ٱلۡمَشۡحُونِ ۝٤١﴾ قال الواحدي في الوسيط: يَعْنِي آبَاءَهُمْ وَأَجْدَادَهُمْ الَّذِينَ هَؤُلَاءِ مِنْ نَسْلِهِمْ فِي الفُلْكِ المَشْحُونِ، يَعْنِي سَفِينَةَ نُوحٍ لِأَنَّ مَنْ حُمِلَ مَعَ نُوحٍ كَانَ هَؤُلَاءِ مِنْ نَسْلِهِمْ، وَالذُّرِّيَّةُ تَقَعُ عَلَى الآبَاءِ كَمَا تَقَعُ عَلَى الأَوْلَادِ، وَالمَشْحُونِ: المَمْلُوءِ. ﴿وَتَقَلُّبَكَ فِي ٱلسَّٰجِدِينَ ۝٢١٩﴾ عَنِ ابْنِ عَبَّاسٍ قَالَ مِنْ نَبِيٍّ إِلَى نَبِيٍّ حَتَّى أَخْرَجَكَ نَبِيّاً. رواه ابن أبي حاتم في التفسير وأبو جعفر النحاس في معاني القرآن. وفي رواية الآجري في الشريعة: قَالَ ابْنُ عَبَّاسٍ مَا زَالَ رَسُولُ اللهِ ﷺ يَتَقَلَّبُ فِي أَصْلَابِ الأَنْبِيَاءِ حَتَّى وَلَدَتْهُ أُمُّهُ.

Al-Suyūṭī adduced some of the above evidence as proof that the father and mother of the Prophet were among the people of Paradise, a topic on which he wrote seven treatises. In one of them, *Masālik al-Ḥunafā fī Wāliday al-Muṣṭafā* (The Paths of Pure Muslims Regarding the Prophet's Parents), he cites the poetry of the hadith master of Damascus, Ibn Nāṣir al-Dīn al-Dimashqī (777-842/1375-1438):

140. *Aḥmad progressed as a great light*
which shone in the foreheads of those who made prostration.
He took turns in them century after century
until he appeared as the Best of Messengers. ...
Allah preserved as an honor to Muḥammad
his lofty fathers to protect his name
They avoided fornication, its shame never touched them,

from Adam down to his father and mother.[194]

Al-Suyūṭī then cites the beginning of al-Būṣīrī's *Hamziyya* at length (see next section).

قال الجلال السيوطي في كتابه (مَسَالِك الحُنَفَا فِي وَالِدَيِّ الْمُصْطَفَى ﷺ):

وَمَا أَحْسَنَ قَوْلُ الحَافِظِ شَمْسِ الدِّينِ ابْنِ نَاصِرِ الدِّينِ الدِّمَشْقِيِّ رَحِمَهُ اللهُ:

تَنَقَّلَ أَحْمَدُ نُوراً عَظِيماً ❋ تَلأْلَأَ فِي جِبَاهِ السَّاجِدِينَا

تَقَلَّبَ فِيهِمْ قَرْناً فَقَرْناً ❋ إِلَى أَنْ جَاءَ خَيْرُ الْمُرْسَلِينَا

وقال أيضا:

حَفِظَ الإِلَهُ كَرَامَةً لِمُحَمَّدٍ ❋ آبَاءَهُ الْأَمْجَادَ صَوْناً لِإِسْمِهِ

تَرَكُوا السِّفَاحَ فَلَمْ يُصِبْهُمْ عَارُهُ ❋ مِنْ آدَمَ وَإِلَى أَبِيهِ وَأُمِّهِ

His Visible Light in the Foreheads of His Ancestors

Another long report on the translation of the Prophetic light through the loins and wombs of his progenitors adds a description of the Prophet's original earthly material as luminous. It was narrated through a major Successor and one of those reputed to be *awliyā'*, ʿAmr b. Shuraḥbīl al-Anṣārī, who said: "I never saw someone who had never actually seen the Prophet more brilliant at describing him than Kaʿb al-Aḥbār." He then relates that the latter said:

141. When Allah Most High desired to create Muḥammad—upon him blessings and peace—He ordered Jibrīl to bring Him the soil that is the heart of the earth, its beauty and its light. Jibrīl alighted among the angels of Firdaws and the angels of the Highest As-

[194] In al-Suyūṭī, *Masālik al-Ḥunafā'* (p. 68-69).

sembly. He took the soil that was to be the Messenger of Allah from the spot of his noble grave. It was white and luminous. It was kneaded with water from Tasnīm in the wellsprings of the rivers of Paradise until it turned into a white pearl with great radiance. The angels carried it and circumambulated the Throne, the Footstool, the heavens and the earth, so the angels knew Muḥammad before they knew Ādam the father of mankind. Then the light of Muḥammad could be seen in the brightness of the forehead of Ādam. It was said to him: "O Adam, this is the master of your offspring among the Messengers." When Ḥawwā' carried Shīth the light moved from Adam to Ḥawwā'. Every time she delivered she would give birth to twins except when she gave birth to Shīth alone, in honor of Muḥammad—upon him blessings and peace. Thereafter the light did not stop moving on from pure parent to pure parent until he was born.[195]

عَنْ كَعْبِ الأَحْبَارِ رَضِيَ اللهُ عَنْهُ: لَمَّا أَرَادَ اللهُ سُبْحَانَهُ وَتَعَالَى أَنْ يَخْلُقَ مُحَمَّداً أَمَرَ جِبْرِيلَ أَنْ يَأْتِيَهُ بِالطِّينَةِ الَّتِي هِيَ قَلْبُ الأَرْضِ وَبَهَاؤُهَا وَنُورُهَا فَهَبَطَ جِبْرِيلُ فِي مَلَائِكَةِ الْفِرْدَوسِ وَمَلَائِكَةِ الرَّفِيقِ الْأَعْلَى فَقَبَضَ قَبْضَةَ رَسُولِ اللهِ ﷺ مِنْ مَوْضِعِ قَبْرِهِ الشَّرِيفِ وَهِيَ بَيْضَاءُ نَيِّرَةٌ فَعُجِنَتْ بِمَاءِ التَّسْنِيمِ فِي مَعِينِ أَنْهَارِ الجَنَّةِ حَتَّى صَارَتْ كَالدُّرَّةِ البَيْضَاءِ لَهَا شُعَاعٌ عَظِيمٌ ثُمَّ طَافَتْ بِهَا المَلَائِكَةُ حَوْلَ الْعَرْشِ وَالْكُرْسِيِّ وَالسَّمَاوَاتِ وَالْأَرْضِ فَعَرَفَتِ المَلَائِكَةُ مُحَمَّداً ﷺ قَبْلَ أَنْ تَعْرِفَ آدَمَ أَبَا الْبَشَرِ ثُمَّ كَانَ نُورُ مُحَمَّدٍ ﷺ يُرَى فِي غُرَّةِ جَبْهَةِ آدَمَ وَقِيلَ لَهُ يَا آدَمُ هٰذَا سَيِّدُ وَلَدِكَ مِنَ الْمُرْسَلِينَ فَلَمَّا حَمَلَتْ حَوَّاءُ

[195] Abū Sa'd al-Naysābūrī, *Sharaf al-Muṣṭafā* (1:294-303 §77); Ibn al-Jawzī, *Wafā* (1:27 without chain); al-Qasṭallānī in the *Mawāhib* (1:34, 1:52, 1:65) sources it to Ibn Abī Jamra in *Bahjat al-Nufūs*, Ibn Sab' in *Shifā' al-Ṣudūr*, and Abū Sa'd; al-Qārī also cites it in his *Mirqāt* (beginning of the book of *Faḍā'il wal-Shamā'il*).

بِشِيثٍ اِنْتَقَلَ النُّورُ عَنْ آدَمَ إِلَى حَوَّاءَ وَكَانَتْ تَلِدُ فِي كُلِّ بَطْنٍ وَلَدَيْنِ إِلَّا شِيثاً فَإِنَّهَا وَلَدَتْهُ وَحْدَهُ كَرَامَةً لِمُحَمَّدٍ ﷺ ثُمَّ لَمْ يَزَلِ النُّورُ يَنْتَقِلُ مِنْ طَاهِرٍ إِلَى طَاهِرٍ إِلَى أَنْ وُلِدَ ﷺ رواه أبو سعد النيسابوري في شرف المصطفى ﷺ وابن الجوزي معلّقاً في الوفا وهذا لفظه. وعزاه القسطلاني في المواهب إلى ابن أبي جمرة في بهجة النفوس وابن سَبع في شفاء الصدور.

Sīra and other accounts report the progression of that light in the years immediately preceding the Prophet's birth, first in the forehead of ʿAbd al-Muṭṭalib[196] then in that of ʿAbd Allāh b. ʿAbd al-Muṭṭalib, then in that of his wife Āmina bint Wahb, respectively the Prophet's grandfather and parents.[197] Shahrastānī (469-548/1076-1153) wrote:

142. The Arabs in Jāhiliyya excelled in three types of knowledge: one of them was knowledge of genealogy, dates and doxography. They counted it an especially noble science to know the lineages of the forefathers of the Prophet and investigate that light that emerged from the loins of Ibrāhīm to be passed to Ismāʿīl. Then that light passed through all his children, until a glimpse of it was seen in the facial traits of ʿAbd al-Muṭṭalib – Shaybat al-Ḥamd, the master of the valley. The chief elephant prostrated to him, as mentioned in the story of the army of the elephants.[198] With the blessing of that light Allah repelled Abraha's harm and sent against them *birds in flocks* (105:4). With the blessing of that light he pinpointed the spot of Zamzam and where to find the [golden]

[196] Abū Saʿd al-Naysābūrī, *Sharaf al-Muṣṭafā* (1:334-336) cf. al-Qasṭallānī, *Mawāhib* (1:52-53).
[197] Ibn Hisham, *Sīra* (1/2:155-156); Ibn Saʿd, *Ṭabaqāt* (1:58); al-Bayhaqī, *Dalāʾil* (1:87); cf. al-Qasṭallānī, *Mawāhib* (1:59-60); al-Ṭabarī, *Tārīkh* (2:174, 2:243); al-Nuwayrī, *Nihāyat al-Arab* (16:58-61, 16:77).
[198] al-Qasṭallānī, *Mawāhib* (1:52-53) cites a report that Abraha's huge white elephant Sāyis—which alone did not prostrate to Abraha the way his other elephants did—when he saw the face of ʿAbd al-Muṭṭalib kneeled the way camels kneel then prostrated, whereupon Allah caused him to speak in plain Arabic and say: "Peace upon the Light that is in your progeny, O ʿAbd al-Muṭṭalib! (*al-salāmu ʿalā al-nūr al-ladhī fī ẓahrika yā ʿAbd al-Muṭṭalib*)." The rest of the sources name it Maḥmūd.

gazelle and swords which Jurhum had buried. With the blessing of that light ʿAbd al-Muṭṭalib was inspired to make the vow that he made, to slaughter the tenth of his boys. That is what the Prophet proudly implied when he said: "I am the son of the Two Sacrificed Ones" (*anā ibnu al-dhabīḥayn*).[199] He meant by the first one Ismāʿīl—and he is the first one who received that light which then became invisible—and by the second one ʿAbd Allāh b. ʿAbd al-Muṭṭalib,[200] the last one to whom the light arrived, at which time it appeared in full. ... And what shows that ʿAbd al-Muṭṭalib knew of the status of the Mission and the honor of Prophethood is that when the people of Mecca were afflicted with that great drought and had no rain for two years, he ordered Abū Ṭālib to bring him the Elect One, Muḥammad. He brought him wrapped in his swathes. ʿAbd al-Muṭṭalib took him in his hands and, facing the Kaʿba, threw him up in the air and said: "O our Lord! By the right of this child!" Then he threw him up a second time, and a third time, saying: "By the right of this child, give us abundant, continuous rain and quench our thirst!" Not long passed before clouds covered the sky and it rained until they feared for the Mosque. Abū Ṭālib later said his *lām*-rhymed poetry in which is the line *And a fair one by whose face the rain-prayer rises to the clouds, / nourisher of orphans and defender of widows*.[201]

قال الشَّهْرَسْتَانِي في كتاب المِلَل والنِّحَل الجزء الثالث من القسم الثاني: باب العلوم المحصَّلة من العرب:

[199] Baseless in that wording by agreement of the scholars. However, Muʿāwiya related that a Bedouin once addressed the Prophet: "O Son of the Two Sacrificed Ones!" (*yā ibna al-dhabīḥayn*) i.e. O descendant of both Ismāʿīl and ʿAbd Allāh b. ʿAbd al-Muṭṭalib, whereupon the Prophet smiled and did not disapprove of him: al-Ṭabarī, *Tafsīr* (19:598 *sub* 37:107) and *Tārīkh* (1:263); al-Ḥākim, *Mustadrak* (2:554); al-Khilaʿī, *Khilaʿiyyāt* (Shamila ed. §605) cf. Ibn Ḥajar, *Fatḥ al-Bārī* (12:378); Abū Nuʿaym, *Maʿrifa* (*sub* Muʿāwiya); Ibn ʿAsākir, *Tārīkh* (56:200-201); Ibn Mardūyah and al-Thaʿālibī per al-Suyūṭī in *al-Durr al-Manthūr*. Al-Zamakhsharī cites it in *al-Kashshāf* (5:224). The fact that Ibn Ḥajar cites it in *Fatḥ al-Bārī* suggests he considered it overall acceptable, and Allah knows best.

[200] His father had vowed to sacrifice him at the Kaʿba but then he was allowed to sacrifice 100 camels instead as mentioned in the books of *Sīra*.

[201] al-Shahrastānī, *al-Milal wal-Niḥal* II.iii.2 (3:275-287).

إِعْلَمْ أَنَّ الْعَرَبَ فِي الْجَاهِلِيَّةِ كَانَتْ عَلَى ثَلَاثَةِ أَنْوَاعٍ مِنَ الْعُلُومِ: أَحَدُهَا عِلْمُ الْأَنْسَابِ وَالتَّوَارِيخِ وَالْأَدْيَانِ، وَيَعُدُّونَهُ نوعاً شَرِيفاً؛ خُصُوصاً مَعْرِفَةَ أَنْسَابِ أَجْدَادِ النَّبِيِّ ﷺ وَالإِطِّلَاعَ عَلَى ذٰلِكَ النُّورِ الوَارِدِ مِنْ صُلْبِ إِبْرَاهِيمَ إِلَى إِسْمَاعِيلَ عَلَيهِمَا الصَّلَاةُ والسَّلَامُ، وَتَوَاصُلِهِ فِي ذُرِّيَّتِهِ إِلَى أَنْ ظَهَرَ بَعْضَ الظُّهُورِ فِي أَسَارِيرِ عَبْدِ الْمُطَّلِبِ: سَيِّدِ الوَادِي شَيْبَةَ الحَمْدِ؛ وَسَجَدَ لَهُ الْفِيلُ الْأَعْظَمُ؛ وَعَلَيْهِ قِصَّةُ أَصْحَابِ الْفِيلِ. وَبِبَرَكَةِ ذٰلِكَ النُّورِ: دَفَعَ اللهُ تَعَالَى شَرَّ أَبْرَهَةَ وَأَرْسَلَ عَلَيْهِمْ طَيراً أَبَابِيلَ. وَبِبَرَكَةِ ذٰلِكَ النُّورِ: رَأَى تِلْكَ الرُّؤْيَا فِي تَعْرِيفِ مَوْضِعِ زَمْزَمَ وَوُجْدَانِ الْغَزَالَةِ وَالسُّيُوفِ الَّتِي دَفَنَتْهَا جُرْهُمُ. وَبِبَرَكَةِ ذٰلِكَ النُّورِ: أُلْهِمَ عَبْدُ الْمُطَّلِبِ النَّذْرَ الَّذِي نَذَرَ فِي ذَبْحِ الْعَاشِرِ مِنْ أَوْلَادِهِ؛ وَبِهِ افْتَخَرَ النَّبِيُّ ﷺ حِينَ قَالَ: **أَنَا ابْنُ الذَّبِيحَيْنِ** [والصواب أنه قول الأعرابي فيه ﷺ من حديث معاوية رضي الله عنه: **أَنَّ أَعْرَابِيّاً قَالَ لِلنَّبِيِّ ﷺ يَا ابْنَ الذَّبِيحَيْنِ، فَتَبَسَّمَ وَلَمْ يُنْكِرْ عَلَيْهِ** رواه الطبري والحاكم والخلعي وأبو نعيم وابن عساكر وأورده الحافظ في الفتح] أَرَادَ بِالذَّبِيحِ الْأَوَّلِ إِسْمَاعِيلَ عَلَيْهِ السَّلَامُ؛ وَهُوَ أَوَّلُ مَنِ انْحَدَرَ إِلَيْهِ النُّورُ فَاخْتَفَى، وَبِالذَّبِيحِ الثَّانِي عَبْدَ اللهِ بْنَ عَبْدِ الْمُطَّلِبِ؛ وَهُوَ آخِرُ مَنِ انْحَدَرَ إِلَيْهِ النُّورُ فَظَهَرَ كُلَّ الظُّهُورِ.... وَمِمَّا يَدُلُّ عَلَى مَعْرِفَةِ عَبْدِ الْمُطَّلِبِ بِحَالِ الرِّسَالَةِ وَشَرَفِ النُّبُوَّةِ: أَنَّ أَهْلَ مَكَّةَ لَمَّا أَصَابَهُمْ ذٰلِكَ الْجَدْبُ الْعَظِيمُ وَأَمْسَكَ السَّحَابُ عَنْهُمْ سَنَتَيْنِ أَمَرَ أَبَا طَالِبٍ إِبْنَهِ أَنْ يُحْضِرَ الْمُصْطَفَى مُحَمَّداً ﷺ فَأَحْضَرَهُ وَهُوَ

رَضِيعٌ فِي قِمَاطٍ فَوَضَعَهُ عَلَى يَدَيْهِ، وَاسْتَقْبَلَ الْكَعْبَةَ وَرَمَاهُ إِلَى السَّمَاءِ، وَقَالَ: يَا رَبِّ! بِحَقِّ هٰذَا الْغُلَامِ وَرَمَاهُ ثَانِياً، وَثَالِثاً. وَكَانَ يَقُولُ: بِحَقِّ هٰذَا الْغُلَامِ اسْقِنَا غَيْثاً مُغِيثاً دَائِماً هَطِلاً! فَلَمْ يَلْبَثْ سَاعَةً أَنْ طَبَقَ السَّحَابُ وَجْهَ السَّمَاءِ وَأَمْطَرَ؛ حَتَّى خَافُوا عَلَى الْمَسْجِدِ. وَأَنْشَدَ أَبُو طَالِبٍ ذٰلِكَ الشِّعْرَ اللَّامِيَّ الَّذِي مِنْهُ:

وَأَبْيَضَ يُسْتَسْقَى الْغَمَامُ بِوَجْهِهِ * ثِمَالُ الْيَتَامَى عِصْمَةٌ لِلْأَرَامِلِ

Al-Zuhrī (52?-124/672-742) narrated:

143. ʿAbd Allah b. ʿAbd al-Muṭṭalib was the most handsome man ever seen among the Quraysh. One day he went out and was seen by an assembly of the women of Quraysh. One of them said: "Women of Quraysh, who among you will marry this youth and catch thereby the light that beams between his eyes?" For verily there was a light between his eyes. Thereafter Āmina bint Wahb b. ʿAbd Manāf b. Zuhra married him, and after he joined her she bore the Messenger of Allah.[202]

عَنِ الزُّهْرِيِّ قَالَ كَانَ عَبْدُ اللهِ بْنُ عَبْدِ الْمُطَّلِبِ أَحْسَنَ مَنْ رُؤِيَ فِي قُرَيْشٍ قَطُّ فَخَرَجَ يَوْماً عَلَى نِسَاءٍ مِنْ قُرَيْشٍ مُجْتَمِعَاتٍ فَقَالَتِ امْرَأَةٌ مِنْهُنَّ يَا نِسَاءَ قُرَيْشٍ أَيَّتُكُنَّ تَتَزَوَّجُ هٰذَا الْفَتَى فَتَصْطَادُ النُّورَ الَّذِي بَيْنَ عَيْنَيْهِ وَإِنَّ بَيْنَ عَيْنَيْهِ نُوراً قَالَ فَتَزَوَّجَتْهُ آمِنَةُ بِنْتُ وَهْبِ بْنِ عَبْدِ مَنَافِ بْنِ زُهْرَةَ فَجَامَعَهَا فَحَمَلَتْ بِرَسُولِ اللهِ ﷺ. رواه البيهقي.

[202] al-Bayhaqī, *Dalā'il* (1:87).

Another version in Ibn Hishām (d. 218?/833) states:

> **144.** It is said a woman of Banū Asad who was the sister of Waraqa b. Nawfal proposed to ʿAbd Allah, but he married Āmina bint Wahb instead and consummated the marriage. Then he left her presence and met the woman who had proposed to him. He asked her why she did not reiterate the proposal she had made to him the day before; she replied that the light that was in him the day before had left him, and she no longer had need of him... She said: "When you passed me there was a white blaze between your eyes and when I invited you you refused me and went to Āmina, and she has taken it away."[203]

في سيرة ابن هشام: قَالَ ابْنُ إِسْحَاقَ : ثُمَّ انْصَرَفَ عَبْدُ الْمُطَّلِبِ آخِذًا بِيَدِ عَبْدِ اللهِ فَمَرَّ بِهِ – فِيمَا يَزْعُمُونَ – عَلَى امْرَأَةٍ مِنْ بَنِي أَسَدِ بْنِ عَبْدِ الْعُزَّى، وَهِيَ أُخْتُ وَرَقَةَ بْنِ نَوْفَلِ بْنِ أَسَدِ بْنِ عَبْدِ الْعُزَّى، وَهِيَ عِنْدَ الْكَعْبَةِ؛ فَقَالَتْ لَهُ حِينَ نَظَرَتْ إِلَى وَجْهِهِ: أَيْنَ تَذْهَبُ يَا عَبْدَ اللهِ؟ قَالَ مَعَ أَبِي، قَالَتْ: لَكَ مِثْلُ الْإِبِلِ الَّتِي نُحِرَتْ عَنْكَ، وَقَعْ عَلَيَّ الْآنَ، قَالَ أَنَا مَعَ أَبِي وَلَا أَسْتَطِيعُ خِلَافَهُ وَلَا فِرَاقَهُ. فَخَرَجَ بِهِ عَبْدُ الْمُطَّلِبِ حَتَّى أَتَى بِهِ وَهْبَ بْنَ عَبْدِ مَنَافِ بْنِ زُهْرَةَ وَهُوَ يَوْمَئِذٍ سَيِّدُ بَنِي زُهْرَةَ نَسَبًا وَشَرَفًا، فَزَوَّجَهُ ابْنَتَهُ آمِنَةَ بِنْتَ وَهْبٍ، وَهِيَ يَوْمَئِذٍ أَفْضَلُ امْرَأَةٍ فِي قُرَيْشٍ نَسَبًا وَمَوْضِعًا. فَزَعَمُوا أَنَّهُ دَخَلَ عَلَيْهَا حِينَ أُمْلِكَهَا مَكَانَهُ فَوَقَعَ عَلَيْهَا فَحَمَلَتْ بِرَسُولِ اللهِ ﷺ ثُمَّ خَرَجَ مِنْ عِنْدِهَا فَأَتَى الْمَرْأَةَ الَّتِي عَرَضَتْ عَلَيْهِ مَا عَرَضَتْ فَقَالَ لَهَا : مَا لَكِ لَا تَعْرِضِينَ عَلَيَّ الْيَوْمَ مَا كُنْتِ عَرَضْتِ عَلَيَّ بِالْأَمْسِ؟ قَالَتْ لَهُ فَارَقَكَ النُّورُ الَّذِي كَانَ

[203] Ṭabarī, *Tārīkh* (2:243), Ibn al-Jawzī in *al-Wafā* (p. 82-83, ch. 16 of *Abwāb Bidāyati Nabiyyinā*), and Ibn Hishām, *Sīra* (1/2:156-157).

مَعَك بِالْأَمْسِ فَلَيْسَ لِي بِكَ الْيَوْمَ حَاجَةٌ وفي رواية عنده مَرَرْتَ بِي وَبَيْنَ عَيْنَيْكَ غُرَّةٌ بَيْضَاءُ فَدَعَوْتُك فَأَبَيْتَ عَلَيَّ وَدَخَلْتَ عَلَى آمِنَةَ فَذَهَبْتَ بِهَا.

The Prophetic Light as a Marker of Selection and Refinement

Other sound Prophetic hadiths show that the "light of Quraysh" mentioned in the hadith of Ibn ʿAbbās stands for the selection and refinement of the Prophet himself within the larger scheme of creation and, by extension, of whatever human subset he was part of. Although outwardly attributed to the Prophet's tribe, in reality that light is but one of several links all teleologically pointing to his own light both as the source and the end:

145. [From Abū Hurayra:] I was sent out of the best of each generation of human beings, century after century, until I was from the century in which I found myself.[204]

عَنْ أَبِي هُرَيرَةَ رَضِيَ اللهُ عَنْهُ مَرْفُوعاً: بُعِثْتُ مِنْ خَيْرِ قُرُونِ بَنِي آدَمَ قَرْنًا فَقَرْنًا حَتَّى كُنْتُ مِنَ الْقَرْنِ الَّذِي كُنْتُ فِيهِ. رواه البخاري.

146. [From Wāthila b. al-Asqaʿ:] Verily Allah has purified and elected Kināna out of Banū Ismāʿīl; and He purified and elected, out of Banū Kināna, Quraysh; and He purified and elected, out of Quraysh, Banū Hāshim; and He purified and elected me out of Banū Hāshim.[205]

عَنْ وَاثِلَةَ بْنِ الأسقَعِ رَضِيَ اللهُ عَنْهُ مَرْفُوعاً: إِنَّ اللهَ اصْطَفَىٰ كِنَانَةَ مِنْ وَلَدِ إِسْمَاعِيلَ وَاصْطَفَىٰ قُرَيْشاً مِنْ كِنَانَةَ وَاصْطَفَىٰ مِنْ قُرَيْشٍ بَنِي هَاشِمٍ وَاصْطَفَانِي مِنْ بَنِي هَاشِمٍ. رواه مسلم.

[204] al-Bukhārī, *Ṣaḥīḥ* (*Manāqib, Bāb ṣifat al-Nabī*).
[205] Muslim, *Ṣaḥīḥ* (*Faḍāʾil, Faḍl Nasab al-Nabī*).

147. [From Ibn ʿUmar:] Verily Allah created the seven heavens… then He created creatures and elected human beings among all creatures; then He elected, out of human beings, the Arabs; then He elected, out of the Arabs, Muḍar; then He created, out of Muḍar, Quraysh; then He elected, out of Quraysh, Banū Hāshim; then He elected me out of Banū Hāshim. Thus, I come from the elect of the elect. So whoever loves the Arabs, it is by loving me that he loves them; and whoever hates the Arabs, it is by hating me that he hates them.[206]

عَنِ ابْنِ عُمَرَ رَضِيَ اللهُ عَنْهُمَا مَرْفُوعاً: إِنَّ اللهَ عَزَّ وَجَلَّ خَلَقَ السَّمَاوَاتِ وَالأَرْضَ سَبْعًا فَاخْتَارَ الْعُلْيَا مِنْهَا فَسَكَنَهَا وَأَسْكَنَ سَمَاوَاتِهِ مَنْ شَاءَ مِنْ خَلْقِهِ وَخَلَقَ الأَرْضَ سَبْعًا فَاخْتَارَ الْعُلْيَا مِنْهَا فَأَسْكَنَهَا مَنْ شَاءَ مِنْ خَلْقِهِ وَخَلَقَ الْخَلْقَ فَاخْتَارَ مِنَ الْخَلْقِ بَنِي آدَمَ وَاخْتَارَ مِنْ بَنِي آدَمَ الْعَرَبَ وَاخْتَارَ مِنَ الْعَرَبِ مُضَرَ وَاخْتَارَ مِنْ مُضَرَ قُرَيْشاً وَاخْتَارَ مِنْ قُرَيْشٍ بَنِي هَاشِمٍ وَاخْتَارَنِي مِنْ بَنِي هَاشِمٍ فَأَنَا مِنْ خِيَارٍ إِلَى خِيَارٍ فَمَنْ أَحَبَّ الْعَرَبَ فَبِحُبِّي أَحَبَّهُمْ وَمَنْ أَبْغَضَ الْعَرَبَ فَبِبُغْضِي أَبْغَضَهُمْ. رواه الطبراني والحكيم الترمذي وأبو نعيم وهذا لفظهم ورواه الحاكم والبيهقي دون لفظ فَاخْتَارَ الْعُلْيَا مِنْهَا فَسَكَنَهَا وَأَسْكَنَ سَمَاوَاتِهِ مَنْ شَاءَ مِنْ خَلْقِهِ وَخَلَقَ الأَرْضَ سَبْعًا فَاخْتَارَ الْعُلْيَا مِنْهَا فَأَسْكَنَهَا مَنْ شَاءَ مِنْ خَلْقِهِ وإنما لفظهما خَلَقَ السَّمَاوَاتِ سَبْعًا فَاخْتَارَ الْعُلْيَا مِنْهَا فَأَسْكَنَهَا مَنْ شَاءَ مِنْ خَلْقِهِ ثُمَّ خَلَقَ الْخَلْقَ حسّنه الحافظ في الأمالي المطلقة.

[206] al-Ṭabarānī, *Kabīr* (12:455-456 §13650) and *al-Muʿjam al-Awsaṭ* (6:199-200 §6182); al-Ḥākim, *Mustadrak* (4:73, *Maʿrifat al-Ṣaḥāba, Faḍā'il Quraysh*, and 4:86, *Faḍā'il Kāffat al-ʿArab*) and *Maʿrifat ʿUlūm al-Ḥadīth* (p. 483 §425); Abū Nuʿaym, *Dalā'il* (p. 58-59 §18); al-Bayhaqī, *Shuʿab* (2:520-521 §1330) and *Dalā'il* (1:171-172); a fair hadith according to Ibn Ḥajar, *al-Amālī al-Muṭlaqa* (p. 68-69).

148. [al-ʿAbbās b. ʿAbd al-Muṭṭalib:] Truly Allah created creatures and He made me come from the best of them, from the best of their subsets (*firaqihim*) and the best of each two subsets; then He selected the tribes and He made me come from the best tribe; then He selected the houses and He made me come from the best of their houses. I am truly the best of them in myself (*khayruhum nafsan*) and the best of them in my house.[207]

The above hadith shows that the Family of the Prophet is the best house of all humankind.

عَنِ الْعَبَّاسِ بْنِ عَبْدِ الْمُطَّلِبِ مَرفُوعاً: إِنَّ اللهَ خَلَقَ الخَلْقَ فَجَعَلَنِي مِنْ خَيْرِهِمْ مِنْ خَيْرِ فِرَقِهِمْ وَخَيْرِ الفَرِيقَيْنِ ثُمَّ تَخَيَّرَ الْقَبَائِلَ فَجَعَلَنِي مِنْ خَيْرِ الْقَبِيلَةِ ثُمَّ تَخَيَّرَ الْبُيُوتَ فَجَعَلَنِي مِنْ خَيْرِ بُيُوتِهِمْ فَأَنَا خَيْرُهُمْ نَفْساً وَخَيْرُهُمْ بَيْتاً. رواه الترمذي وقال حديث حسن. وتحقق به أن أهل بيته ﷺ خير بيوتات بني آدم.

The bedouin Companion ʿAbbās b. Mirdās al-Sulamī echoes al-ʿAbbās b. ʿAbd al-Muṭṭalib's panegyric in the light of such narrations when he says, toward the end of the poem in which he mentions his conversion and praises the Prophet:

149. *I speak of you, O best of all creation, always*
found in the best of two branches and reaping glory.
And you are the quintessence of Quraysh as it soared
despite penury, and kept its generations blessed.[208]

قال العبَّاس بنُ مِرداس السُلَمي من رواية أبي نعيم في دلائل النبوّة:

عَنَيْتُكَ يَا خَيْرَ البَرِيَّةِ كُلِّهَا * تَوَسَّطْتَ فِي الْفَرْعَيْنِ وَالمَجْدِ مَالِكاً

[207] al-Tirmidhī, *Sunan* (*Manāqib, faḍl al-Nabī, ḥasan*).
[208] Abū Nuʿaym, *Dalāʾil* (p. 119 §66).

وَأَنْتَ الْمُصَفَّى مِنْ قُرَيْشٍ إِذَا سَمَتْ * عَلَى ضُمْرِهَا تُبْقِي الْقُرُونَ الْمُبَارَكَا

These narrations collectively highlight a Divine refinement of creation leading from the Arabs as the better subset of humankind, through narrower subsets, up to the Prophet as the quintessential human being:

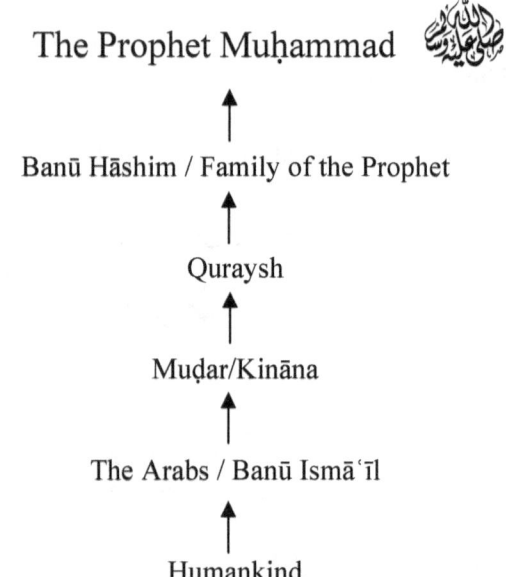

The Prophet Muḥammad ﷺ

↑

Banū Hāshim / Family of the Prophet

↑

Quraysh

↑

Muḍar/Kināna

↑

The Arabs / Banū Ismāʿīl

↑

Humankind

ʿAlī al-Ḥabshī's Necklace of Pearls (*Simṭ al-Durar*)

The erudite Knower of Allah al-Ḥabīb ʿAlī b. Muḥammad b. Ḥusayn al-Ḥabshī (1259-1333/1843-1915) summarized this theme in the opening of his *Simṭ al-Durar*, a work he dictated in three brief sittings, perhaps the most moving and beautiful *Mawlid* text of all and nowadays the most frequently recited in Indonesia:

> **150.** When the Divine Will attached itself in pre-existent Knowledge to the appearance of the secrets of exclusive bestowal of precedence and bounty for the noble Human Person [of the Prophet], the astonishing [Divine] Power brought to pass vast favor and en-

compassing munificence, whereupon the core of fashioning in the absolute macrocosm was sundered and brought forth a beauty visible to the naked eye and containing all the attributes of absolute beauty and perfect grace and comeliness. This propitious beauty then moved through the noble loins and wombs. No loins carried it except complete Divine favor was bestowed on them. Truly he is the full moon that moves through its mansions, ennobling the stations where it settles and the place where it comes out. The foreordained destinies took effect and showed whatever they showed of the secret of that Light, singling out whoever was specified to be singled out with it. Thus he settled in the lofty loins and the noble wombs until he emerged in the world of witnessing – a human being unlike human beings and a dazzling light that shone and left minds astonished.[209]

روينا عن العلَّامة الحبيب عبد القادر بن محمد بن أحمد الحداد الإندونيسي عن الحبيب عبد القادر بن أحمد بَلْفَقِيه عالم جاوة الشرقية عن الحبيب عَلِيِّ بْنِ مُحَمَّدِ بْنِ حُسَينِ الحَبْشِيِّ قَالَ فِي سِمْطِ الدُّرَر:

لَمَّا تَعَلَّقَتْ إِرَادَةُ اللهِ فِي الْعِلْمِ الْقَدِيمِ بِظُهُورِ أَسْرَارِ التَّخْصِيصِ لِلْبَشَرِ الْكَرِيمِ بِالتَّقْدِيمِ وَالتَّكْرِيمِ نَفَذَتِ الْقُدْرَةُ الْبَاهِرَةُ بِالنِّعْمَةِ الْوَاسِعَةِ وَالْمِنَّةِ الْغَامِرَةِ، فَانْفَلَقَتْ بَيْضَةُ التَّصْوِيرِ فِي الْعَالَمِ الْمُطْلَقِ الْكَبِيرِ عَنْ جَمَالٍ مَشْهُودٍ بِالْعَيْنِ حَاوٍ لِوَصْفِ الْكَمَالِ الْمُطْلَقِ وَالْحُسْنِ التَّامِّ وَالزَّيْنِ. فَتَنَقَّلَ ذٰلِكَ الْجَمَالُ الْمَيْمُونُ فِي الْأَصْلَابِ الْكَرِيمَةِ وَالْبُطُونِ. فَمَا مِنْ صُلْبٍ ضَمَّهُ إِلَّا وَتَمَّتْ عَلَيْهِ مِنَ اللهِ النِّعْمَةُ. فَهُوَ الْقَمَرُ التَّامُّ الَّذِي يَتَنَقَّلُ فِي بُرُوجِهِ لِيَتَشَرَّفَ بِهِ مَوَاطِنُ اسْتِقْرَارِهِ وَمَوْضِعُ خُرُوجِهِ. وَقَدْ قَضَتِ الْأَقْدَارُ الْأَزَلِيَّةُ بِمَا قَضَتْ وَأَظْهَرَتْ

[209] al-Ḥabshī, *Simṭ al-Durar* (p. 18-19). Cf. al-Haytamī, *Tuḥfat al-Akhyār bi-Mawlid al-Mukhtār*, ed. ʿAbd al-Salām Shaṭṭī al-Ḥanbalī (1283/1867 Damascus ed. p. 8-9).

مِنْ سِرِّ هٰذَا النُّورِ مَا أَظْهَرَتْ وَخَصَّصَتْ بِهِ مَنْ خَصَّصَتْ. فَكَانَ مُسْتَقَرُّهُ
فِي الْأَصْلَابِ الْفَاخِرَةِ وَالْأَرْحَامِ الشَّرِيفَةِ الطَّاهِرَةِ حَتَّى بَرَزَ فِي عَالَمِ الشَّهَادَةِ،
بَشَراً لَا كَالْبَشَرِ وَنُوراً حَيَّرَ الْأَفْكَارَ ظُهُورُهُ وَبَهَرَ.

The Light of His *Mawlid* as Witnessed by His Mother

The *mawlid* light eulogized by al-ʿAbbās and his son was confirmed by the Prophet himself in the famous narration from several Companions describing his own birth in reply to the question: "Messenger of Allāh, when was the beginning of your status?" He replied:

> **151.** Truly I was [already], in the sight of Allāh, the Seal of Prophets when Adam was still kneaded in his clay. I shall inform you of the meaning *(ta'wīl)* [or: "beginning" *(awwal)*] of this status: It is the supplication of my father Ibrāhīm [Q 2:129] and the glad tidings of my brother ʿĪsā to his people [Q 61:6]; and the vision my mother saw the night I was delivered, she saw a light that lit the castles of Syro-Palestine (al-Shām) so that she could see them. Thus do the mothers of Prophets see visions.[210]

[210] Narrated from **(1)** al-ʿIrbāḍ b. Sāriya by Aḥmad (28:382 §17151, 28:395 §17163); al-Bukhārī, *al-Tārīkh al-Kabīr* (*sub* ʿAbd al-Aʿlā b. Hilāl al-Sulamī); al-Bazzār (10: 135-136 §4199, its best chain to his knowledge); al-Ṭabarānī, *al-Kabīr* (18:252-253 §629-631) and *Musnad al-Shāmiyyīn* (2:340-341 §1455); Ibn Saʿd, *Ṭabaqāt* (1:148-149); al-Ṭabarī, *Tafsīr* (*sub* 2:129); al-Ḥākim, *Mustadrak* (2:600); Abū Nuʿaym, *Ḥilya* (6:89-90); and al-Bayhaqī, *Dalā'il* (1:83); **(2)** ʿUtba b. ʿAbdin al-Sulamī in Aḥmad, *Musnad* (29:194-196 §17648); al-Dārimī, *Sunan* (*Muqaddima, kayfa kāna awwalu sha'n al-Nabī ṣallā Allāhu ʿalayhi wa-sallam*); al-Ṭabarānī, *Musnad al-Shāmiyyīn* (2:197-199 §1181), al-Ḥākim (2:616-617), al-Bayhaqī, *Dalā'il* (1:110, 2:7-8) and others; al-Haythamī, *Majmaʿ* (8:221-222) declared its chain fair *(ḥasan)*; **(3)** Abū Umāma al-Bāhilī by Aḥmad (36:595-596 §22261) with a fair chain cf. al-Haythamī, *Majmaʿ* (8:407), al-Ṭabarānī, *al-Kabīr* (8:253) and al-Bayhaqī, *Dalā'il* (1:69); **(4)** Shaddād b. Aws by Abū Yaʿlā in his *Musnad* cf. al-Būṣīrī, *Itḥāf* (7:16-19 §6319), Ibn Ḥajar, *Maṭālib* (17:185-191 §4207); al-Zaylaʿī and Ibn Ḥajar in their respective *Takhrīj Aḥādīth al-Kashshāf*, and ʿIyāḍ in the *Shifā Shifā* I.3.1 (p. 222); also by al-Ṭabarī, *Tārīkh* (2:160-165); al-Ājurrī, *Sharīʿa* (3:1422-1426 §962); and Ibn ʿAsākir, *Tārīkh* (3:469-473); **(5)** Ḥalīma bint al-Ḥārith al-Saʿdiyya by Abū Yaʿlā, *Musnad* (13:93-99 §7163); al-Ṭabarānī, *Kabīr* (24:212-215 §545); al-Ṭabarī, *Tārīkh* (2:158-160); al-Ājurrī, *Sharīʿa* (3:1427-1431 §964); *Dalā'il* of Abū Nuʿaym (p. 193-196

عَنِ الْعِرْبَاضِ بْنِ سَارِيَةَ مَرْفُوعاً إِنِّي عِنْدَ اللهِ فِي أُمِّ الكِتَابِ لَخَاتَمُ النَّبِيِّينَ وَإِنَّ آدَمَ لَمُنْجَدِلٌ فِي طِينَتِهِ وَسَأُخْبِرُكُمْ بِتَأْوِيلِ ذٰلِكَ أَنَا دَعْوَةُ أَبِي إِبْرَاهِيمَ وَبِشَارَةُ عِيسَى بِي وَرُؤْيَا أُمِّي الَّتِي رَأَتْ حِينَ وَضَعَتْ أَنَّهُ خَرَجَ مِنْهَا نُورٌ أَضَاءَتْ لَهُ قُصُورُ الشَّامِ رواه الحاكم والبيهقي وجاء عند أحمد والبزار والطبراني بزيادة وَكَذٰلِكَ أُمَّهَاتُ النَّبِيِّينَ يَرَيْنَ. وهو مستفاض عن الصحابة رضي الله عنهم.

ودعوة إبراهيم عليه السلام قوله ﴿ رَبَّنَا وَٱبْعَثْ فِيهِمْ رَسُولًا مِّنْهُمْ يَتْلُوا۟ عَلَيْهِمْ ءَايَـٰتِكَ وَيُعَلِّمُهُمُ ٱلْكِتَـٰبَ وَٱلْحِكْمَةَ وَيُزَكِّيهِمْ ۚ إِنَّكَ أَنتَ ٱلْعَزِيزُ ٱلْحَكِيمُ ﴿١٢٩﴾ ﴾ البقرة. وبشارة عيسى عليه السلام قوله ﴿ وَإِذْ قَالَ عِيسَى ٱبْنُ مَرْيَمَ يَـٰبَنِىٓ إِسْرَٰٓءِيلَ إِنِّى رَسُولُ ٱللَّهِ إِلَيْكُم مُّصَدِّقًا لِّمَا بَيْنَ يَدَىَّ مِنَ ٱلتَّوْرَىٰةِ وَمُبَشِّرًۢا بِرَسُولٍ يَأْتِى مِنۢ بَعْدِى ٱسْمُهُۥٓ أَحْمَدُ ۖ فَلَمَّا جَآءَهُم بِٱلْبَيِّنَـٰتِ قَالُوا۟ هَـٰذَا سِحْرٌ مُّبِينٌ ﴿٦﴾ ﴾. الصف.

The scholars pointed out that the illumination of Syro-Palestine with the light of the Prophet is an allusion to its foremost status as the Holy Land of Prophets and *Awliyā* from the time of Adam and Ibrāhīm to the time of al-Mahdī—a Prophetic descendant—and ʿĪsā just before Resurrection, as well as its historical centrality in representing true Islamic belief in the end of times.[211]

§94) and Bayhaqī (1:132-136); and Ibn Ḥibbān, *Ṣaḥīḥ* (14:243-249 §6335); **(6)** ʿAbd al-Raḥmān b. ʿAwf's mother by al-Ājurrī, *Sharīʿa* (3:1426-1427 §963); **(7)** Khālid b. Maʿdān from an unnamed group of Companions by al-Ḥākim (2:600), al-Bayhaqī, *Dalāʾil* (1:83-84), Ibn Hishām, *Sīra* (1/2:166) al-Ṭabarī, *Tārīkh* with a chain Ibn Kathīr deems good *(jayyid al-isnād)*, *Sira* (1:51) and *Bidāya* (2:275).

211 Cf. Ibn Kathīr, *Tafsīr* (*sub* 2:129) and Haddad, *The Excellence of Syro-Palestine – al-Shām – and Its People: Forty Hadiths*.

The long variant wording from the Companion Shaddād b. Aws contains a similar account:

152. Truly the reality of my message and the start of my affair is the supplication of my father Ibrāhīm and the glad tidings of my brother ʿĪsā b. Maryam. I was the firstborn of my mother and she bore me as heavily as any woman bears a child, until she complained to her friends about the heaviness she was experiencing. Then she saw in her dream that she was carrying light in her womb. She said: "My gaze followed that light and the light ran faster than it until it lit the easternmost parts of the earth and the westernmost parts." Then she gave birth to me.[212]

عَنْ شَدَّادِ بْنِ أَوسٍ رَضِيَ اللهُ عَنْهُ قَالَ قَالَ النَّبِيُّ ﷺ إِنَّ حَقِيقَةَ قَولِي وَبَدْءَ شَأْنِي دَعْوَةُ أَبِي إِبْرَاهِيمَ وَبُشْرَى أَخِي عِيسَى بْنِ مَرْيَمَ وَإِنِّي كُنْتُ بِكْرًا لِأُمِّي وَإِنَّهَا حَمَلَتْنِي كَأَثْقَلِ مَا تَحْمِلُ النِّسَاءُ حَتَّى جَعَلَتْ تَشْتَكِي إِلَى صَوَاحِبِهَا ثِقَلَ مَا تَجِدُ. وَإِنَّ أُمِّي رَأَتْ فِي المَنَامِ أَنَّ الَّذِي فِي بَطْنِهَا نُورٌ؛ قَالَتْ: فَجَعَلْتُ أُتْبِعُ بَصَرِي النُّورَ فَجَعَلَ النُّورُ يَسْبِقُ بَصَرِي حَتَّى أَضَاءَ لِي مَشَارِقَ الأَرْضِ وَمَغَارِبَهَا. ثُمَّ إِنَّهَا وَلَدَتْنِي. أبو يعلى والطبري والآجُرّي وابن عساكر

ʿUthmān b. Abī al-ʿĀṣ said:

153. My mother related to me: "I was there the night Āmina bint Wahb gave birth to the Messenger of Allah. Everything I laid eyes on inside the house was filled with light. Truly I was looking at the stars approaching me and I was saying surely they are going to fall on me!"[213]

[212] See next to previous note, no. 4.
[213] al-Bayhaqī, *Dalā'il* (1:111); Ibn ʿAsākir, *Tārīkh* (3:78-79).

عَنْ عُثْمَانَ بْنِ أَبِي الْعَاصِ قَالَ حَدَّثَتْنِي أُمِّي أَنَّهَا شَهِدَتْ وِلَادَةَ آمِنَةَ بِنْتِ وَهْبٍ رَسُولَ الله ﷺ لَيْلَةَ وَلَدَتْهُ قَالَتْ فَمَا شَيْءٌ أَنْظُرُ إِلَيْهِ فِي الْبَيْتِ إِلَّا نُورٌ وَإِنِّي لَأَنْظُرُ إِلَى النُّجُومِ تَدْنُو حَتَّى إِنِّي لَأَقُولُ لَيَقَعْنَ عَلَيَّ. رواه البيهقي وابن عساكر.

Ḥassān b. Thābit referred to the above event in the following lines in which he repeats the verb "give birth" (*walada*) but gives it two different subjects of praise—first Āmina who gave birth to him, then the Anṣār as a whole, who also "gave birth to him" through her since she hailed from Banū Zuhra and raised him among Banū Sa'd, both of them Madīnan tribes:

154. *O Āmina's firstborn of blessed memory,*
to whom she gave birth, married, in Sa'd of the stars,
As a light that lit up the entire universe!
Whoever is guided to that blessed light is guided. ...
And we gave birth to him, and among us is his grave,
and the surfeit of his bounty to us is undeniable. ...
And we have given birth to the greatest of the Quraysh:
we gave birth to the Prophet of goodness from Hāshim.[214]

قال حسان:

يَا بِكْرَ آمِنَةَ الْمُبَارَكَ بِكْرُهَا * وَلَدَتْهُ مُحْصَنَةٌ بِسَعْدِ الْأَسْعُدِ
نُورًا أَضَاءَ عَلَى الْبَرِيَّةِ كُلِّهَا * مَنْ يُهْدَ لِلنُّورِ الْمُبَارَكِ يَهْتَدِ ...
وَلَقَدْ وَلَدْنَاهُ وَفِينَا قَبْرُهُ * وَفُضُولُ نِعْمَتِهِ فِينَا لَمْ تُجْحَدِ

وقال:

وَنَحْنُ وَلَدْنَا مِنْ قُرَيْشٍ عَظِيمَهَا * وَلَدْنَا نَبِيَّ الْخَيْرِ مِنْ آلِ هَاشِمِ

ابن هشام وابن سعد وديوان حسان بن ثابت

[214] Ibn Hishām, *Sīra* (3/4:670); Ibn Sa'd, *Ṭabaqāt* (2:280); cf. Ḥassān, *Dīwān* (p. 65 §50, p. 249 §218).

The Splittings of the Chest and His Immersion in Light

The "splitting of the chest" hadiths in which the Prophet's heart and innermost were filled with light inform us that his *nūr* kept being refined after his earthly creation as well, as shown by the continuation of Shaddād b. Aws's report already quoted:

> **155.** When I was raised, idols were loathsome to me, as was poetry. I was nursed among the Banū Jusham b. Bakr. One day, as I was in some valley playing with boys my age, all of a sudden there were three men standing in front of me. One of them was carrying a basin of gold full of light and snow. They took me from my friends who fled. … One of them made me lie down on the ground gently, then he split open my chest down to my pelvis, as I looked on without feeling any pain. He brought out my entrails and washed them with that snow, then he put them back in their place. The second one came and said to his friend to move over. Then he inserted his hand into my chest and brought out my heart as I looked on. He split it open and extracted from it a black piece of flesh which he threw away. Then he gestured with his hand as if he were taking something. I saw in his hand a seal of light, the light of Prophethood and wisdom, so dazzling it would blind anyone that looked on. He sealed my heart with it and it became filled with light and wisdom.[215]

فَلَمَّا نَشَأْتُ بُغِّضَتْ إِلَيَّ الأَوثَانُ ، وَبُغِّضَ إِلَيَّ الشِّعْرُ ، وَاسْتُرْضِعَ لِي فِي بَنِي جُشَمَ بْنِ بَكرٍ ، فَبَينَمَا أَنَا ذَاتَ يَومٍ فِي بَطْنِ وَادٍ مَعَ أَتْرَابٍ لِي مِنَ الصِّبْيَانِ ، إِذَا أَنَا بِرَهْطٍ ثَلاَثٍ مَعَهُمْ طَسْتٌ مِنْ ذَهَبٍ مَلآنُ نُورًا وَثَلْجًا ، فَأَخَذُونِي مِنْ بَيْنِ أَصْحَابِي ، وَانطَلَقَ أَصْحَابِي هَرَبًا … فَعَمِدَ إِلَيَّ أَحَدُهُمْ فَأَضْجَعَنِي إِلَى الأَرْضِ إِضْجَاعًا لَطِيفًا ، ثُمَّ شَقَّ مَا بَيْنَ صَدْرِي إِلَى مُنْتَهَى عَانَتِي ، وَأَنَا

[215] See note 210 no. 4.

أَنْظُرُ لَمْ أَجِدْ لِذٰلِكَ مَسًّا ، ثُمَّ أَخْرَجَ أَحشَاءَ بَطْنِي فَغَسَلَهُ بِذٰلِكَ الثَّلْجِ فَأَنْهَى غَسْلَهُ ، ثُمَّ أَعَادَهَا فِي مَكَانِهَا ، ثُمَّ قَامَ الثَّانِي ، فَقَالَ لِصَاحِبِهِ : تَنَحَّ ، ثُمَّ أَدْخَلَ يَدَهُ فِي جَوْفِي فَأَخْرَجَ قَلْبِي وَأَنَا أَنظُرُ، فَصَدَعَهُ ، فَأَخْرَجَ مِنْهُ مُضْغَةً سَوْدَاءَ رَمَى بِهَا ، ثُمَّ قَالَ بِيَدِهِ : يَمْنَةً مِنْهُ ، كَأَنَّهُ يَتَنَاوَلُ شَيْئًا ، ثُمَّ إِذَا بِالْخَاتَمِ فِي يَدِهِ مِنْ نُورِ نُورِ النُّبُوَّةِ وَالْحِكْمَةِ تُخْطَفُ أَبْصَارُ النَّاظِرِينَ دُوْنَهُ ، فَخَتَمَ قَلْبِي فَامْتَلَأَ نُورًا وَحِكْمَةً. رواه أبو يعلى والطبري في التاريخ والآجري وابن عساكر، وهو تتمة حديث شداد بن أوس المذكور أعلاه.

The splitting of the chest and its filling with light took place three more times: at puberty, before the beginning of the Prophetic mission, and just before the Night Journey and Heavenly ascent (*al-isrā' wal-mi'rāj*), as narrated from Anas, Abū Dharr, Mālik b. Ṣa'ṣa'a and 'Utba b. 'Abdin.[216]

The Prophet framed his self-image as light in a famous Madinan night supplication that begins with self-immersion in light from all six directions and ends with the complete self-identification of his person with light, inwardly and outwardly, as related from Ibn 'Abbās:

> **156.** I spent the night in my maternal aunt Maymūna's house and observed how the Messenger of Allah prayed. [...] He said in his prayer—or his prostration: *O Allah, place light in my heart, light in my hearing, light in my sight, light to my right, light to my left, light before me, light behind me, light above me, and light under me—and make me light!*[217]

[216] Cf. 'Iyāḍ, *Shifā* I.3.1-3 (p. 221-222, 230-231, 241); Ibn Ḥajar, *Fatḥ* (7:204-205); and al-Zurqānī, *Sharḥ al-Mawāhib* (4:217-223 *Shamā'il*: *wa-ammā qalbuhu al-sharīf*, esp. 4:222) but al-Dabbāgh in *al-Ibrīz* numbers the splittings as three only.
[217] Aḥmad, *Musnad* (4:343-344 §2567); Muslim, *Ṣaḥīḥ* (*Ṣalāt al-musāfirīn, al-du'ā' fī ṣalāt al-layl wa-qiyāmih*).

O Allah, put light in my heart, light in my grave, light before me, light behind me, light to my right, light to my left, light above me, light below me, light in my hearing, light in my eyesight, light in my hair, light in my skin, light in my flesh, light in my blood, light in my bones! O Allah, enhance light for me, give me light and grant me light.[218] [In Ibn Abī ʿĀṣim's *Kitāb al-Duʿāʾ*:] *And grant me Light upon Light (wa-hab lī nūran ʿalā nūr).*[219]

عَنِ ابْنِ عَبَّاسٍ مَرْفُوعاً اللّٰهُمَّ اجْعَلْ فِي قَلْبِي نُوراً وَفِي سَمْعِي نُوراً وَفِي بَصَرِي نُوراً وَعَنْ يَمِينِي نُوراً وَعَنْ يَسَارِي نُوراً وَأَمَامِي نُوراً وَخَلْفِي نُوراً وَفَوْقِي نُوراً وَتَحْتِي نُوراً وَاجْعَلْنِي نُوراً رواه مسلم وأحمد وجاء عند الترمذي بلفظ اللّٰهُمَّ اجْعَلْ لِي نُوراً فِي قَلْبِي وَنُوراً فِي قَبْرِي وَنُوراً مِنْ بَيْنِ يَدَيَّ وَنُوراً مِنْ خَلْفِي وَنُوراً عَنْ يَمِينِي وَنُوراً عَنْ شِمَالِي وَنُوراً مِنْ فَوْقِي وَنُوراً مِنْ تَحْتِي وَنُوراً فِي سَمْعِي وَنُوراً فِي بَصَرِي وَنُوراً فِي شَعْرِي وَنُوراً فِي بَشَرِي وَنُوراً فِي لَحْمِي وَنُوراً فِي دَمِي وَنُوراً فِي عِظَامِي. اللّٰهُمَّ أَعْظِمْ لِي نُوراً وَأَعْطِنِي نُوراً وَاجْعَلْ لِي نُوراً. وفي كتاب الدعاء لابن أبي عاصم: وَهَبْ لِي نُوراً عَلَى نُورٍ ذكره الحافظ ابن حجر في الفتح.

The Body of the Prophet in the Holy Qur'ān

That remarkable hadith is a Sunna counterpart of the Quranic high-lighting of the Prophet's physical body, including not only his limbs but also his senses and his entire person, in which the scholars saw yet another kind of Divine emphasis of the greatness of the Prophet:[220]

[218] al-Tirmidhī, *Sunan* (*Daʿawāt*, chapter 30).
[219] Cited by Ibn Ḥajar, *Fatḥ* (11:142).
[220] Cf. Abū Saʿd al-Naysābūrī, *Sharaf* (4:186-188 §1455).

قال أبو سعد النَّيسابوري رحمه الله في كتاب (شرف المصطفى ﷺ) وغيره من الأئمة وأصحاب كتب الشمائل ودلائل النبوّة:

إِنَّ اللهَ عَزَّ وَجَلَّ ذَكَرَ أَعْضَاءَ رَسُولِ اللهِ ﷺ فِي الْقُرْآنِ مَحَبَّةً لَهُ وَمَدْحاً فَذَكَرَ نَفْسَهُ الشَّرِيفَةَ وَوَجْهَهُ وَعَيْنَيْهِ وَبَصَرَهُ وَأُذُنَهُ وَقَلْبَهُ وَفُؤَادَهُ وَنُطْقَهُ وَصَدْرَهُ وَلِسَانَهُ وَظَهْرَهُ وَيَدَهُ وَيَمِينَهُ وَرِجْلَهُ وَقَدَمَهُ وَصُورَتَهُ أي عند ذكر ﴿أَحْسَنِ تَقْوِيمٍ﴾ وَخُلُقَهُ وَعُمْرَهُ ﷺ تسليماً.

1. **His Person** (*nafs*): *Let not your soul (nafsak) waste away with grief for them* (35:8); *Yet it may be that you will let your soul waste away following after them* (18:6); *And do remember your Lord within your soul* (7:205).

ذِكْرُ نَفْسِهِ الشَّرِيفَةِ ﷺ: ﴿فَلَا تَذْهَبْ نَفْسُكَ عَلَيْهِمْ حَسَرَٰتٍ﴾ الآية. فاطر. ﴿فَلَعَلَّكَ بَٰخِعٌ نَّفْسَكَ عَلَىٰٓ ءَاثَٰرِهِمْ﴾ الآية. الكهف. ﴿وَٱذْكُر رَّبَّكَ فِى نَفْسِكَ﴾ الآية. الأعراف.

2. **His Face** (*wajh*): *We have seen the turning of your face to heaven; and now truly We shall make you turn toward a direction of prayer which is dear to you. So turn your face toward the Inviolable Place of Worship* (2:144).

ذِكْرُ وَجْهِهِ الشَّرِيفِ ﷺ: ﴿قَدْ نَرَىٰ تَقَلُّبَ وَجْهِكَ فِى ٱلسَّمَآءِ ۖ فَلَنُوَلِّيَنَّكَ قِبْلَةً تَرْضَىٰهَا ۚ فَوَلِّ وَجْهَكَ شَطْرَ ٱلْمَسْجِدِ ٱلْحَرَامِ ۚ﴾ الآية. البقرة.

3. **His Eyes** (*ʿaynayn*): *Stretch not your eyes toward that which We cause some wedded pairs among them to enjoy* (15:88).

ذِكْرُ عَيْنَيهِ الشَّرِيفَتَينِ ﷺ: ﴿ لَا تَمُدَّنَّ عَيْنَيْكَ إِلَىٰ مَا مَتَّعْنَا بِهِۦٓ أَزْوَٰجًا مِّنْهُمْ ﴾ الآية. الحِجْر.

4. **His Sight** (*baṣar*): *The sight turned not aside nor yet was overbold* (53:17).

ذِكْرُ بَصَرِهِ الشَّرِيفِ ﷺ: ﴿ مَا زَاغَ ٱلْبَصَرُ وَمَا طَغَىٰ ﴿١٧﴾ ﴾ النجم.

5. **His Ear** (*udhun*): *and of them are those who speak ill of the Prophet and say, "He is all ear." Say, "An ear of good for you!"* (9:61).

ذِكْرُ أُذُنِهِ الشَّرِيفَةِ ﷺ: ﴿ وَمِنْهُمُ ٱلَّذِينَ يُؤْذُونَ ٱلنَّبِيَّ وَيَقُولُونَ هُوَ أُذُنٌ قُلْ أُذُنُ خَيْرٍ لَّكُمْ ﴾ الآية. التوبة

6. **His Heart** (*qalb*): *He has revealed it to your heart* (2:97); *the trustworthy Spirit brought it down upon your heart* (26:193-194).

ذِكْرُ قَلْبِهِ الشَّرِيفِ ﷺ: ﴿ نَزَّلَهُۥ عَلَىٰ قَلْبِكَ ﴾ الآية. البقرة. ﴿ نَزَلَ بِهِ ٱلرُّوحُ ٱلْأَمِينُ ﴿١٩٣﴾ عَلَىٰ قَلْبِكَ لِتَكُونَ مِنَ ٱلْمُنذِرِينَ ﴿١٩٤﴾ ﴾ الشعراء.

7. **His Heart** (*fuʾād*): *His heart lies not about what he saw* (53:11).

﴿ ذِكْرُ فُؤَادِهِ الشَّرِيفِ ﷺ: مَا كَذَبَ ٱلْفُؤَادُ مَا رَأَىٰ ﴿١١﴾ ﴾ النجم.

8. **His Speech** (*nuṭq*): *Nor does he speak out of his own desire* (53:3).

ذِكْرُ نُطْقِهِ الشَّرِيفِ ﷺ: ﴿ وَمَا يَنطِقُ عَنِ ٱلْهَوَىٰٓ ۝٣ ﴾ النجم.

9. **His Chest** (*ṣadr*): *so let there be no doubt in your breast therefrom* (7:2); *have We not expanded your breast?* (94:1).

ذِكْرُ صَدْرِهِ الشَّرِيفِ ﷺ: ﴿ فَلَا يَكُن فِي صَدْرِكَ حَرَجٌ مِّنْهُ ﴾ الآية.

الأعراف. ﴿ أَلَمْ نَشْرَحْ لَكَ صَدْرَكَ ۝١ ﴾ الشرح.

10. **His Tongue** (*lisān*): *And We have made it easy in your tongue only so that you may bear good tidings therewith unto those who ward off evil* (19:97); *And We have made it easy in your tongue only so that they may heed* (44:58); *Move not your tongue with it to hasten it* (75:16).

ذِكْرُ لِسَانِهِ الشَّرِيفِ ﷺ: ﴿ فَإِنَّمَا يَسَّرْنَٰهُ بِلِسَانِكَ لِتُبَشِّرَ بِهِ ٱلْمُتَّقِينَ وَتُنذِرَ بِهِۦ قَوْمًا لُّدًّا ۝٩٧ ﴾ مريم. ﴿ فَإِنَّمَا يَسَّرْنَٰهُ بِلِسَانِكَ لَعَلَّهُمْ يَتَذَكَّرُونَ ۝٥٨ ﴾ الدخان. ﴿ لَا تُحَرِّكْ بِهِۦ لِسَانَكَ لِتَعْجَلَ بِهِۦٓ ۝١٦ ﴾ القيامة.

11. **His Back** (*ẓahr*): *which burdened your back* (94:3).

ذِكْرُ ظَهْرِهِ الشَّرِيفِ ﷺ: ﴿ ٱلَّذِىٓ أَنقَضَ ظَهْرَكَ ۝٣ ﴾ الشرح.

12-13. **His Hand** (*yad*) and **Neck** (*ʿunuq*): *And keep not your hand chained to your neck, nor outspread it altogether* (17:29).

ذِكْرُ يَدِهِ الشَّرِيفَةِ وَعُنُقِهِ الشَّرِيفِ ﷺ: ﴿وَلَا تَجْعَلْ يَدَكَ مَغْلُولَةً إِلَىٰ عُنُقِكَ وَلَا تَبْسُطْهَا كُلَّ ٱلْبَسْطِ فَتَقْعُدَ مَلُومًا مَّحْسُورًا ﴿٢٩﴾﴾ الإسراء.

14. **His Right Hand** (*yamīn*): *And you did not recite before it any book or inscribe it with your right hand* (29:48); *and those whom your right hand possesses whom Allah has given you as spoils of war* (33:50); *except those your right hand possesses* (33:52); *We would certainly have seized him by the right hand* (69:45).[221]

ذِكْرُ يَمِينِهِ الشَّرِيفَةِ ﷺ: ﴿وَمَا كُنتَ تَتْلُواْ مِن قَبْلِهِۦ مِن كِتَٰبٍ وَلَا تَخُطُّهُۥ بِيَمِينِكَ﴾ الآية. العنكبوت. ﴿وَمَا مَلَكَتْ يَمِينُكَ مِمَّآ أَفَآءَ ٱللَّهُ عَلَيْكَ﴾ الآية. ﴿إِلَّا مَا مَلَكَتْ يَمِينُكَ﴾ الآية. كلتاهما من سورة الأحزاب. ﴿لَأَخَذْنَا مِنْهُ بِٱلْيَمِينِ ﴿٤٥﴾﴾ الحاقة.

15. **His Foot** (*rijl*): *Ṭaha. We have not revealed the Qur'ān to you to cause you difficulty* (20:1-2). Zamakhsharī (467-538/ca.1074-1143) said *ṭaha* stands for *ṭa'hā* ("tread it!" i.e. with both feet), the imperative of the verb *waṭi'a*. This is supported by the following reports:

157. [ʿAlī b. Abī Ṭālib:] The Prophet used to take turns between his two feet [in prayer], standing on one foot then the other, until the verse was revealed, *Ṭaha! We have not revealed the Qur'ān to you to cause you difficulty.*[222]

[221] The seizure by the right hand is when the executor holds the standing man's outstretched right hand and decapitates him with his sword from the front which is more dreadful than from the back because the executee sees the sword striking him. The mention of this mode of execution is a trope conveying extreme wrath, itself meant to highlight the utmost gravity of betrayal and thus the utmost reliability of the Prophet: *Tafsīrs* of al-Zamakhsharī, al-Rāzī, Abū Ḥayyān, and al-Ālūsī (*sub* 69:45).

[222] al-Bazzār, *Musnad* (3:136 §926), cf. al-Haythamī, *Majma*ʿ (7:56). Al-Suyūṭī graded its chain fair in the *Durr* (*sub* 20:7).

158. [Ibn ʿAbbās:] When revelation first descended on the Prophet he used to stand on tiptoes (*ʿalā ṣadri qadamayh*) whenever he prayed, whereupon Allah Most High revealed *Ṭaha! We have not revealed the Qur'ān to you to cause you difficulty.*[223]

ذِكْرُ رِجْلِهِ الشَّرِيفَةِ ﷺ: قال الزمخشري في الكشاف: رُوِيَ عَنِ النَّبِيِّ ﷺ أَنَّهُ كَانَ يَقُومُ فِي تهَجُّدِهِ عَلَى إِحْدَى رِجْلَيْهِ فَأَمَرَهُ أَنْ يَطَأَ الْأَرْضَ بِقَدَمَيْهِ مَعاً فَقِيلَ ﴿ طه ۝١ ﴾ وَأَصْلُهُ طَأْهَا. اهـ.

عَنْ عَلِيٍّ كَرَّمَ اللهُ وَجْهَهُ قَالَ كَانَ النَّبِيُّ ﷺ يُرَاوِحُ بَيْنَ قَدَمَيْهِ يَقُومُ عَلَى كُلِّ رِجْلٍ حَتَّى نَزَلَتْ ﴿ طه ۝١ مَآ أَنزَلْنَا عَلَيْكَ ٱلْقُرْءَانَ لِتَشْقَىٰٓ ۝٢ ﴾. رواه البزار وحسّن السيوطي إسناده.

عَنِ ابْنِ عَبَّاسٍ رَضِيَ اللهُ عَنْهُمَا أَنَّ النَّبِيَّ ﷺ أَوَّلَ مَا أُنْزِلَ عَلَيْهِ الْوَحْيُ كَانَ يَقُومُ عَلَى صُدُورِ قَدَمَيْهِ إِذَا صَلَّى فَأَنْزَلَ اللهُ تَعَالَى ﴿ طه ۝١ مَآ أَنزَلْنَا عَلَيْكَ ٱلْقُرْءَانَ لِتَشْقَىٰٓ ۝٢ ﴾. رواه البيهقي.

16. **His Foot** (*qadam*): *and bring unto those who believe the good tidings that they have a truthful foothold/forerunner (qadama ṣidqin) with their Lord* (10:2), that is, Muḥammad as their intercessor.[224]

[223] al-Bayhaqī, *Shuʿab* (3:83-84 §1416 *faṣl fī marātib Nabiyyinā fīl-Nubuwwa*) and Ibn ʿAsākir, *Tārīkh* (4:144).
[224] al-Bukhārī, *Ṣaḥīḥ* (*Tafsīr*, *Sūrat Yūnus*) and al-Ṭabarī, *Tafsīr* (*sub* 10:2) on the authority of Zayd b. Aslam, the latter also narrating it from al-Ḥasan and Qatāda.

ذِكْرُ قَدَمِهِ الشَّرِيفِ ﷺ: عَنْ زَيْدِ بْنِ أَسْلَمَ فِي قَوْلِهِ ﴿ وَبَشِّرِ ٱلَّذِينَ ءَامَنُوٓاْ أَنَّ لَهُمْ قَدَمَ صِدْقٍ عِندَ رَبِّهِمْ ﴾ الآية. يونس. قَالَ: مُحَمَّدٌ ﷺ. ورُوِي مثله عن الحسن وقتادة. البخاري وتفسير الطبري.

17. **His Frame** (*taqwīm*): *Truly We created man in the fairest stature* (95:4). It is related from Ibn ʿAbbās that this is a reference to the Prophet.[225]

ذِكْرُ صُورَتِهِ الشَّرِيفَةِ ﷺ: يُروَى عَنِ ابْنِ عَبَّاسٍ رَضِيَ اللهُ عَنْهُمَا أَنَّهُ قَالَ فِي تَفْسِيرِ قَوْلِهِ تَعَالَى فِي سُورَةِ التِّينِ ﴿ لَقَدْ خَلَقْنَا ٱلْإِنسَـٰنَ فِىٓ أَحْسَنِ تَقْوِيمٍ ﴿٤﴾ ﴾: مُحَمَّدٌ. رواه الخطيب وابن عساكر وهو عند أهل الحديث من وضع أبي العباس محمد بن بيان بن مسلم الثقفي المعروف بابن البختري والله تعالى أعلم. وأورد الآية الشريفة أبو سعد النيسابوري في عداد الآيات التي فيها ذكر أعضاء النبي ﷺ.

18. **His Character** (*khuluq*): *And truly you are upon a sublime character* (68:4).

ذِكْرُ خُلُقِهِ الشَّرِيفِ ﷺ: ﴿ وَإِنَّكَ لَعَلَىٰ خُلُقٍ عَظِيمٍ ﴿٤﴾ ﴾ القلم.

19. **His Life** (*ʿamr*): *By your life! They wandered blindly in their drunken lust* (15:72).

225 al-Khaṭīb, *Tārīkh* (2:97-98 §493) and Ibn ʿAsākir, *Tārīkh* (1:214). Forged by Muḥammad b. Bayān b. Muslim by agreement. Its meaning is true as the Prophet is the archetype and apex of human perfection, hence Abū Saʿd al-Naysābūrī included it among the verses that refer to the Prophet.

ذِكْرُ عَمْرِهِ الشَّرِيفِ ﷺ: ﴿ لَعَمْرُكَ إِنَّهُمْ لَفِى سَكْرَتِهِمْ يَعْمَهُونَ ﴿٧٢﴾ ﴾ الحِجْر.

The Light of the Prophet in Early Scriptures

159. *In Mūsā's Torah are his description and attributes*
and in ʿĪsā's Gospel and the chaptered Psalms.[226]

أنشد عبد الرحيم البرعي رحمه الله:

بِتَوْرَاةِ مُوسَى نَعتُهُ وَصِفَاتُهُ * وَإِنْجِيلِ عِيسَى وَالزَّبُورِ المُفَصَّلِ

As demonstrated by the several reports already cited from Kaʿb al-Aḥbār, the Prophetic light was often mentioned in previous heavenly Scriptures. Ibn al-Jawzī in his *Wafā* devoted an entire chapter of quotations to that effect, in which he says:

160. Ibn Qutayba quoted Habakkuk – a Prophet in the time of the Prophet Daniel – as saying: "God has come from Teman [Yemen]; the Holy One has come from the Mountain of Paran. The earth was filled with the glorification of the Glorified One (Aḥmad) and his sanctification. He has dominated the earth with his right hand and subdued the nations. The earth is illuminated with his light and his steeds are carried upon the sea." … Another one said in the same description: "He is the light of God that will not be put out nor opposed, until He firmly establishes My Proof on earth and removes all subterfuge; to His Book the jinn will be led. … Ibn Qutayba further quoted Isaiah's description of him: "I am God and I have empowered you with righteousness, and have made you a light for the nations and the covenant of the people, so that the eyes of the blind would be opened and the prisoners of darkness would be delivered unto light."[227]

[226] ʿAbd al-Raḥīm al-Barʿī in Kayyāl, *Yawm wa-Layla* (p. 104).
[227] Ibn al-Jawzī, *Wafā* (p. 58-59). Cf. Habakkuk 3:3-6 and 3:15, Isaiah 42:6-7.

قَالَ ابْنُ الْجَوْزِيِّ فِي كِتَابِ الْوَفَا (بَابُ ذِكْرِ النَّبِيِّ ﷺ فِي التَّوْرَاةِ): قَالَ ابْنُ قُتَيْبَةَ: وَمِنْ قَوْلِ حَبَقُوقَ الْمُتَنَبِّىءِ فِي زَمَانِ دَانِيَالَ قَالَ حَبَقُوقٌ: جَاءَ اللهُ مِنَ التَّيْمَنِ وَالْقِدِّيسُ مِنْ جِبَالِ فَارَانَ، فَامْتَلَأَتِ الْأَرْضُ مِنْ تَحْمِيدِ أَحْمَدَ وَتَقْدِيسِهِ، وَمَلَكَ الْأَرْضَ بِيَمِينِهِ وَرِقَابَ الْأُمَمِ. قَالَ: وَقَالَ أَيْضاً: تُضِيءُ لِنُورِهِ الْأَرْضُ وَتُحْمَلُ خَيْلُهُ فِي الْبَحْرِ. ... وَزَادَ آخَرُ فِي التَّرْجَمَةِ: ... وَهُوَ نُورُ اللهِ الَّذِي لَا يُطْفَأُ وَلَا يُخْصَمُ حَتَّى يُثْبَتَ فِي الْأَرْضِ حُجَّتِي وَيَنْقَطِعَ بِهِ الْعُذْرُ، وَإِلَى تَوْرَاتِهِ تَنْقَادُ الْجِنُّ. ... قَالَ ابْنُ قُتَيْبَةَ: وَمِنْ ذِكْرِ شَعْيَا لَهُ قَالَ: أَنَا اللهُ عَظَّمْتُكَ بِالْحَقِّ، وَجَعَلْتُكَ نُورَ الْأُمَمِ وَعَهْدَ الْعَامَّةِ، لِتُفْتَحَ أَعْيُنُ الْعُمْيَانِ، وَتُنْقَذَ الْأَسْرَى مِنَ الظُّلُمَاتِ إِلَى النُّورِ.

Ibn al-Qayyim (691-751/1292-1350) said in explanation of the phrase "He is the light of God that will not be put out nor opposed, until He firmly establishes My Proof on earth and removes all subterfuge:"

161. This description fits the Prophet perfectly and the Qur'ān witnesses to it in several places, such as the sayings of Allah Most High *They seek to extinguish the light of Allah with their mouths* (9:32); *O Prophet, truly We have sent you as a witness, a herald of glad tidings and a warner, one who calls to Allah by His permission, and a Luminous Lamp!* (33:45-46); *There has come to you from Allah a Light and a manifest Book whereby Allah guides whosoever follows His good pleasure in the ways of peace* (5:15); *O people! a clear proof has now come to you from your Lord; We have sent down to you a manifest light* (4:174); and *Those who believe in him, and honor him, and help him, and follow the light which was sent down with him: they are the successful* (7:157).[228]

---

[228] Ibn al-Qayyim, *Hidāyat al-Ḥayārā* (p. 128).

قَالَ ابْنُ قَيِّمِ الجَوْزِيَّةِ فِي شَرْحِ عِبَارَةِ (وَهُوَ نُورُ اللهِ الَّذِي لَا يُطْفَأُ وَلَا يُخْصَمُ حَتَّى يُثَبِّتَ فِي الْأَرْضِ حُجَّتِي وَيَنْقَطِعَ بِهِ الْعُذْرُ): وَهٰذَا مُطَابِقٌ لِحَالِهِ وَأَمْرِهِ ﷺ وَلِمَا شَهِدَ بِهِ الْقُرْآنُ فِي غَيْرِ مَوْضِعٍ كَقَوْلِهِ تَعَالَى ﴿ يُرِيدُونَ أَن يُطْفِـُٔواْ نُورَ ٱللَّهِ بِأَفْوَٰهِهِمْ وَيَأْبَى ٱللَّهُ إِلَّآ أَن يُتِمَّ نُورَهُۥ وَلَوْ كَرِهَ ٱلْكَـٰفِرُونَ ﴿٣٢﴾ ﴾ وَقَوْلِهِ ﴿ يَـٰٓأَيُّهَا ٱلنَّبِىُّ إِنَّآ أَرْسَلْنَـٰكَ شَـٰهِدًا وَمُبَشِّرًا وَنَذِيرًا ﴿٤٥﴾ وَدَاعِيًا إِلَى ٱللَّهِ بِإِذْنِهِۦ وَسِرَاجًا مُّنِيرًا ﴿٤٦﴾ ﴾ وَقَوْلِهِ ﴿ قَدْ جَآءَكُم مِّنَ ٱللَّهِ نُورٌ وَكِتَـٰبٌ مُّبِينٌ ﴿١٥﴾ يَهْدِى بِهِ ٱللَّهُ مَنِ ٱتَّبَعَ رِضْوَٰنَهُۥ سُبُلَ ٱلسَّلَـٰمِ ﴾ وَقَوْلِهِ ﴿ يَـٰٓأَيُّهَا ٱلنَّاسُ قَدْ جَآءَكُم بُرْهَـٰنٌ مِّن رَّبِّكُمْ وَأَنزَلْنَآ إِلَيْكُمْ نُورًا مُّبِينًا ﴿١٧٤﴾ ﴾ وَقَوْلِهِ ﴿ فَٱلَّذِينَ ءَامَنُواْ بِهِۦ وَعَزَّرُوهُ وَنَصَرُوهُ وَٱتَّبَعُواْ ٱلنُّورَ ٱلَّذِىٓ أُنزِلَ مَعَهُۥٓ أُوْلَـٰٓئِكَ هُمُ ٱلْمُفْلِحُونَ ﴿١٥٧﴾ ﴾ ونظائره في القرآن كثيرة. اهـ. من هداية الحيارى.

VI

His Pre-Existent Universal Intercession

"Prophets are intermediaries between Allah and creation" (ʿIyāḍ)

The hadith of ʿAbd Allāh b. ʿAmr ("Truly Allah Most High created His creation in a darkness…") and its explanation by Ibn al-ʿArabī cited in Part IV show that the characteristic of Believers is light. As the first of the Believers, the Prophet undoubtedly possesses that trait before anybody else and more than anybody else, including angels who are formed of light and the jinn who are formed of smokeless fire, since he outranks them both in the hierarchy of creation even if he was physically created from flesh and blood. Nevertheless one scholar took the latter aspect so literally that he claimed that "the Prophet could not possibly be a light since human beings are created from earth into which the spirit is blown, while angels alone are created from light."[229] To support his view, he cited the hadith from ʿĀ'isha whereby the Prophet said:

162. The angels were created from light, the jinn from smokeless fire, and Adam from what was described to you (i.e. in Qur'ān).[230]

عَنْ عَائِشَةَ قَالَتْ قَالَ رَسُولُ الله ﷺ خُلِقَتِ الْمَلاَئِكَةُ مِنْ نُورٍ وَخُلِقَ الْجَانُّ مِنْ مَارِجٍ مِنْ نَارٍ وَخُلِقَ آدَمُ مِمَّا وُصِفَ لَكُمْ. رواه مسلم.

To deduce from the above hadith that a human being can never be characterized as a light or become light is precisely what Iblīs presumed when he resorted to comparative reasoning and disobeyed Allah on the pretense that smokeless fire is a nobler element than humble earth. Further, it contradicts the above-mentioned hadith of

[229] Ibn Taymiyya, *Majmūʿ al-Fatāwā* (11:94, 18:366).
[230] Muslim, *Ṣaḥīḥ* (*Zuhd wal-raqā'iq, Aḥādīth mutafarriqa*).

ʿAbd Allah b. ʿAmr narrated by al-Tirmidhī ("Truly Allah Most High created His creation in a darkness then cast upon them from His light…") and the evidence from the Qur'ān and Sunna describing the Prophet as light instead of elucidating it as would be required for a correct and comprehensive understanding of the subject.

The correct view is that Prophets are a brand of human beings that match the angels with respect to light and the other gifts bestowed on human beings by Allah "universally and individually, generally and specifically, in the heart and in the limbs," to use Ibn al-ʿArabī al-Mālikī's language. This is shown by Qadi ʿIyāḍ in the *Shifā* with regard to the Prophets' angelic inward qualities:

> **163.** Prophets and Messengers are intermediaries (*wasā'iṭ*) between Allah and His creation. They convey to creation His commands and prohibitions, His promises and threats, and they acquaint them with things they did not know regarding His command, creation, majesty, authority, might, and dominion. Their outward forms, bodies, and native frames are characterized by the human condition such as accidents, illnesses, death and passing away, and being human. But their spirits and inward selves have superhuman qualities (*arwāḥuhum wa-bawāṭinuhum muttaṣifatun bi-aʿlā min awṣāf al-bashar*). They are connected to the Highest Assembly, possess what resembles the attributes of angels, and are free of change or defects. Generally speaking the incapacity and weakness typical of humanity does not affect them. For if their inward selves had been human in the same way as their outward persons, they would have been incapable of receiving [revelation] from the angels, seeing them, communicating with them, and mixing with them, just as other human beings are incapable of doing so. And if their bodies and outward persons had been marked by angelic attributes as opposed to human ones, people and whoever else they were sent to would not have been able to mix with them, as Allah said: *Say: If there were in the earth angels walking secure, We would have sent down for them from heaven an angel as messenger* (17:95). Thus they were made to be with men as far as their bodies and outward persons are

concerned, and they were made to be with angels in respect of their souls and inward selves.[231]

قال القاضي عياض في القسم الثالث من كتاب الشفا (فِيمَا يَجِبُ لِلنَّبِيِّ ﷺ وَمَا يَسْتَحِيلُ فِي حَقِّهِ أَوْ يَجُوزُ عَلَيْهِ وَمَا يَمْتَنِعُ أَوْ يَصِحُّ مِنَ الْأَحْوَالِ الْبَشَرِيَّةِ أَنْ يُضَافَ إِلَيْهِ): الْأَنْبِيَاءُ وَالرُّسُلُ عَلَيْهِمُ السَّلَامُ وَسَائِطُ بَيْنَ اللهِ تَعَالَى وَبَيْنَ خَلْقِهِ، يُبَلِّغُونَهُمْ أَوَامِرَهُ وَنَوَاهِيَهُ وَوَعْدَهُ وَوَعِيدَهُ، وَيُعَرِّفُونَهُمْ بِمَا لَمْ يَعْلَمُوهُ مِنْ أَمْرِهِ وَخَلْقِهِ وَجَلَالِهِ وَسُلْطَانِهِ وَجَبَرُوتِهِ وَمَلَكُوتِهِ. فَظَوَاهِرُهُمْ وَأَجْسَادُهُمْ وَبِنْيَتُهُمْ مُتَّصِفَةٌ بِأَوْصَافِ الْبَشَرِ، طَارِئٌ عَلَيْهَا مَا يَطْرَأُ عَلَى الْبَشَرِ مِنَ الْأَعْرَاضِ وَالْأَسْقَامِ وَالْمَوْتِ وَالْفَنَاءِ وَنُعُوتِ الْإِنْسَانِيَّةِ. وَأَرْوَاحُهُمْ وَبَوَاطِنُهُمْ مُتَّصِفَةٌ بِأَعْلَى مِنْ أَوْصَافِ الْبَشَرِ، مُتَعَلِّقَةٌ بِالْمَلَإِ الْأَعْلَى، مُتَشَبِّهَةٌ بِصِفَاتِ الْمَلَائِكَةِ، سَلِيمَةٌ مِنَ التَّغَيُّرِ وَالْآفَاتِ، لَا يَلْحَقُهَا غَالِباً عَجْزُ الْبَشَرِيَّةِ وَلَا ضَعْفُ الْإِنْسَانِيَّةِ. إِذْ لَوْ كَانَتْ بَوَاطِنُهُمْ خَالِصَةً لِلْبَشَرِيَّةِ كَظَوَاهِرِهِمْ، لَمَا أَطَاقُوا الْأَخْذَ عَنِ الْمَلَائِكَةِ وَرُؤْيَتَهُمْ وَمُخَاطَبَتَهُمْ وَمُخَالَطَتَهُمْ، كَمَا لَا يُطِيقُهُ غَيْرُهُمْ مِنَ الْبَشَرِ. وَلَوْ كَانَتْ أَجْسَادُهُمْ وَظَوَاهِرُهُمْ مُتَّسِمَةً بِنُعُوتِ الْمَلَائِكَةِ وَبِخِلَافِ صِفَاتِ الْبَشَرِ، لَمَا أَطَاقَ الْبَشَرُ وَمَنْ أُرْسِلُوا إِلَيْهِ مُخَالَطَتَهُمْ كَمَا تَقَدَّمَ مِنْ قَوْلِ اللهِ تَعَالَى ﴿ قُلْ لَوْ كَانَ فِي الْأَرْضِ مَلَائِكَةٌ يَمْشُونَ مُطْمَئِنِّينَ لَنَزَّلْنَا عَلَيْهِم مِّنَ

---

[231] ʿIyāḍ, *Shifā* III, introduction (p. 604).

ٱلسَّمَآءِ مَلَكًا رَّسُولًا ﴿٩٥﴾ الإسراء فَجُعِلُوا مِنْ جِهَةِ الْأَجْسَامِ
وَالظَّوَاهِرِ مَعَ الْبَشَرِ، وَمِنْ جِهَةِ الْأَرْوَاحِ وَالْبَوَاطِنِ مَعَ الْمَلَائِكَةِ.

"The Prophet is the ultimate purpose of creation" (Ibn Taymiyya)

Although Aḥmad b. Taymiyya (661-728/1263-1328), as mentioned, denied that Prophets were made of light because, in his view, only angels can be thus described, yet he went on to endorse the known position of *Ahl al-Sunna* that Prophets – chief among them the Seal of Prophets – possess a rank superior to angels:

> **164.** Allah manifests some of His Power and Wisdom through righteous human beings, saints and Prophets, which He does not manifest through the angels, for He combines in the former group qualities which are scattered among other creation. Thus He creates man's body from the earth and his spirit from the Highest Company, hence it is said that man is a microcosm and a copy of the greater universe. Muḥammad – upon him blessings and peace – is the leader of human beings, the Best of Creation and the noblest of them in the sight of Allah Most High. This is why some have said that Allah created the universe because of him, or that "Were it not for him, He would have neither created a Throne, nor a Footstool, nor a heaven, earth, sun or moon." .... Since the best of the righteous human beings is Muḥammad, creating him was a desirable end of deep-seated purposeful wisdom, more than for anyone else, and hence the completion of creation and the fulfillment of perfection was attained with Muḥammad.... Since man is the seal and last of all creation and its microcosm, and since the best of men is thus the best of all creation in absolute terms, then Muḥammad, being the Pupil of the Eye, the Axis of the Mill, and the Components of the Microcosm, is, as it were, the ultimate purpose of all the purposes of creation. Thus it cannot be denied

to say that "Due to him all of this was created," or that "Were it not for him, none of this would have been created."[232]

قال ابن تيمية في مجموع الفتاوى له (11/ 57-58): اللهُ تَعَالَى أَظْهَرَ مِنْ عَظِيمِ قُدْرَتِهِ وَعَجِيبِ حِكْمَتِهِ مِنْ صَالِحِي الآدَمِيِّينَ مِنَ الْأَنْبِيَاءِ وَالْأَوْلِيَاءِ مَا لَمْ يُظْهِرْ مِثْلَهُ مِنَ الْمَلَائِكَةِ، حَيْثُ جَمَعَ فِيهِمْ مَا تَفَرَّقَ فِي الْمَخْلُوقَاتِ، فَخَلَقَ بَدَنَهُ مِنَ الْأَرْضِ وَرُوحَهُ مِنَ الْمَلَإِ الْأَعْلَى، وَلِهَذَا يُقَالُ هُوَ الْعَالَمُ الصَّغِيرُ وَهُوَ نُسْخَةُ الْعَالَمِ الْكَبِيرِ. وَمُحَمَّدٌ ﷺ سَيِّدُ وَلَدِ آدَمَ وَأَفْضَلُ الْخَلْقِ وَأَكْرَمُهُمْ عَلَيْهِ، وَمِنْ هُنَا قَالَ مَنْ قَالَ: إِنَّ اللهَ مِنْ أَجْلِهِ خَلَقَ الْعَالَمَ، أَوْ إِنَّهُ لَوْلَا هُوَ لَمَا خَلَقَ عَرْشاً وَلَا كُرْسِيّاً وَلَا سَمَاءً وَلَا أَرْضاً وَلَا شَمْساً وَلَا قَمَراً. بَلْ يَقْتَضِي إِذَا كَانَ أَفْضَلَ صَالِحِي بَنِي آدَمَ مُحَمَّدٌ: كَانَتْ خِلْقَتُهُ غَايَةً مَطْلُوبَةً وَحِكْمَةً بَالِغَةً مَقْصُودَةً أَعْظَمَ مِنْ غَيْرِهِ، وَصَارَ تَمَامُ الْخَلْقِ وَنِهَايَةُ الْكَمَالِ حَصَلَ بِمُحَمَّدٍ ﷺ. فَإِذَا كَانَ الْإِنْسَانُ هُوَ خَاتَمَ الْمَخْلُوقَاتِ وَآخِرَهَا وَهُوَ الْجَامِعُ لِمَا فِيهَا، وَفَاضِلُهُ هُوَ فَاضِلُ الْمَخْلُوقَاتِ مُطْلَقاً، وَمُحَمَّدٌ ﷺ إِنْسَانُ هَذَا الْعَيْنِ وَقُطْبُ هَذِهِ الرَّحَى وَأَقْسَامُ هَذَا الْجَمْعِ: كَانَ كَأَنَّهُ ﷺ غَايَةُ الْغَايَاتِ فِي الْمَخْلُوقَاتِ، فَمَا يُنْكَرُ أَنْ يُقَالَ: إِنَّهُ لِأَجْلِهِ ﷺ خُلِقَتْ جَمِيعُهَا، وَإِنَّهُ لَوْلَاهُ لَمَا خُلِقَتْ.

[232] Ibn Taymiyya, *Majmū' al-Fatāwā* (11:57-58).

"Were it not for Muḥammad, I would not have created Adam"

Ibn Taymiyya's last sentence refers to a well-known narration from Ibn ʿAbbās which the generality of scholars, just like Ibn Taymiyya, deemed true in its meaning:

> **165.** Allāh Most High revealed to ʿĪsā: "O ʿĪsā! Believe in Muḥammad and command whoever reaches his time among your Community to believe in him. Were it not for Muḥammad, I would not have created Adam, and were it not for Muḥammad, I would not have created Paradise or Hellfire. Indeed, I created the Throne on top of water and it shook, so I inscribed upon it LĀ ILĀHA ILLĀ ALLĀH MUḤAMMADUN RASŪLULLĀH, then it stood still."[233]

في كتاب السنة لأبي بكر الخلال: عَنِ ابْنِ عَبَّاسٍ رَضِيَ اللهُ عَنْهُمَا قَالَ أَوْحَى اللهُ تَبَارَكَ وَتَعَالَى إِلَى عِيسَى عَلَيْهِ السَّلَامُ فِيمَا أَوْحَى: أَنْ صَدِّقْ مُحَمَّداً وَأْمُرْ أُمَّتَكَ مَنْ أَدْرَكَهُ مِنْهُمْ أَنْ يُؤْمِنُوا بِهِ، فَلَوْلَا مُحَمَّدٌ مَا خَلَقْتُ آدَمَ، وَلَوْلَا مُحَمَّدٌ مَا خَلَقْتُ النَّارِ، وَلَقَدْ خَلَقْتُ الْعَرْشَ عَلَى الْمَاءِ فَاضْطَرَبَ فَكَتَبْتُ عَلَيهِ لَا إِلٰهَ إِلَّا اللهُ مُحَمَّدٌ رَسُولُ اللهِ فَسَكَنَ. قال الخلال: فألقيته على أبي عبد الله محمد بن

[233] In al-Khallāl, *al-Sunna* (1:261 §316): al-Faḍl b. Muslim al-Muḥāribī [unknown] narrated to us: Muḥammad b. ʿIṣma [al-Karābīsī al-Balkhī, *mastūr* per *Miṣbāḥ al-Arīb* §24806] narrated to us: Jundul [b. Wāliq, *thiqa* per al-Haythamī] narrated to us: ʿAmr b. Aws al-Anṣārī [*mastūr* per al-Dhahabī] narrated to us: from Saʿīd b. Abī ʿArūba: from Qatāda: from Saʿīd b. Musayyab [all three trustworthy], from Ibn ʿAbbās. Also narrated through other chains by al-Ḥākim, *Mustadrak* (2:614-615), Abū al-Shaykh, *Ṭabaqāt al-Aṣbahāniyyīn* (3:287-288 §494), al-Thaʿlabī, *al-Kashf wal-Bayān* (7:61, *sub* 23:115), Ibn al-Jawzī, *Wafā* (p. 55 §52), and Abū Saʿd al-Naysābūrī, *Sharaf al-Muṣṭafā* (1:163-165 §15) where the editor rejects al-Dhahabī's verdict of fabrication in *Talkhīṣ al-Mustadrak* and *Mīzān al-Iʿtidāl* (*sub* ʿAmr b. Aws) who conjectures that the narration is forged without citing any proof, whereas its chain contains neither a liar nor a forger and is an acceptable chain by the *Salaf*'s criteria for *faḍāʾil* hadiths as evidenced by al-Khallāl's postscript, especially in light of other versions. Al-Ṣāliḥī in *Subul al-Hudā* (1:94 *al-bāb al-thānī fī khalqi Ādam*) stated that al-Ḥākim had declared it sound and that both al-Subkī in *Shifāʾ al-Siqām* and al-Bulqīnī in his *Fatāwā* had confirmed his verdict.

بشر بن شريك فأقر به. وله متابعات في المستدرك للحاكم وتفسير الثعلبي وطبقات الأصبهانيين لأبي الشيخ وشرف المصطفى لأبي سعد النيسابوري والوفا لابن الجوزي.

Al-Būṣīrī (608-694/1211-1295) took up that meaning in his *Burda*:

166. *I profaned the Sunna of him who enlivened the dark [of night with worship]*
until his feet complained of injury for being swollen.
And he straightened his stomach on account of hunger and folded
over his mid-section a stone atop delicate skin.
And lofty mountains of gold tried to tempt him
away from himself, but he showed them true loftiness.
His extreme need emphasized his abstinence.
Verily need never prevails over the infallible.
And how could need attract toward this world such a one
but for whom this world would not have come out of the void?[234]

The last line highlights the irony of the fact that the paragon and liegelord of creatures—for whom everything in existence was created (Q 2:29) and made subservient (Q 45:13)—stands in no need of any of it but only of Allah Most High, since he is *the* Servant of Allah par excellence (Q 17:1, 72:19) and represents the essence of worship, which is the reason for their creation (Q 51:56). Ibn al-Jawzī went so far as to extend this teleological role in the scheme of creation to all *awliyā* in his *Ṣifat al-Ṣafwa*, because they stand for true remembrance of Allah (see Part VIII).

As noted in Qāḍī 'Iyāḍ's statement, "Prophets and Messengers are intermediaries between Allah and His creation," and **Prophetic Intermediacy (*wasīṭiyya*) is the very definition of belief in the Prophetic Messengership** and its witnessing by every Muslim in the second half of the *shahāda*: "and I bear witness that Muḥammad is the Messenger of Allah."[235]

[234] al-Būṣīrī, *Burda* (lines 29-33, p. 201-220).
[235] On the central theme of the Prophet's intermediacy see al-Kattānī, *Maṭāli' al-Sa'āda* (p. 264-281: *al-Nabī huwa al-wāsiṭa bayna al-Ḥaqq wal-khalq fa-yajib adā'u*

Such intercessory status of the Prophet, moreover, covers all things. Sahl al-Tustarī said:

> **167.** Whoever does not acknowledge the authority (*wilāya*) of the Prophet over him in all situations without exception, and [instead] considers himself his own master, has not tasted the sweetness of his Sunna. For the Prophet said: "None of you believes until I am more beloved to him than his own soul."[236]

جاء في الشِفا فاتحة باب (في لزوم محبّته ﷺ): قَالَ سَهْلٌ: مَنْ لَمْ يَرَ وِلَايَةَ الرَّسُولِ ﷺ عَلَيْهِ فِي جَمِيعِ الْأَحْوَالِ، وَيَرَى نَفْسَهُ فِي مِلْكِهِ لَا يَذُوقُ حَلَاوَةَ سُنَّتِهِ، لِأَنَّ النَّبِيَّ ﷺ قَالَ: **لَا يُؤْمِنُ أَحَدُكُمْ حَتَّى أَكُونَ أَحَبَّ إِلَيْهِ مِنْ نَفْسِهِ.** وتتمته **وَأَهْلِي أَحَبَّ إِلَيْهِ مِنْ أَهْلِهِ وَعِتْرَتِي أَحَبَّ إِلَيْهِ مِنْ عِتْرَتِهِ وَذَاتِي أَحَبَّ إِلَيْهِ مِنْ ذَاتِهِ.** الطبرانى والبيهقى عن أبى ليلى الأنصاري بلفظ **لَا يُؤْمِنُ عَبْدٌ.**

Ibn Diḥya (544-633/1149-1236) listed the following verses and hadiths among further proofs of the above rule:

> **168.** Among his special attributes is that Allah Most High commanded that he has priority before all other souls…. He said: *The Prophet is nearer to the believers than themselves* (9:6), that is, more deserving. Allah Most High in the Qur'ān actually put him before fathers, sons, wives, tribes, and possessions when He said:

ḥaqqih), al-Nabhānī's *Shawāhid al-Ḥaqq*, al-Mazālī al-Murrākishī's (d. 683/1284) *Miṣbāḥ al-Ẓalām fil-Mustaghīthīn bi-Khayr al-Anām*, and Aḥmad Riḍā Khān's *al-Amnu wal-ʿUlā li-Nāʿitī al-Muṣṭafā bi-Dāfiʿ al-Balā* among many other works. This doctrine is of course denied by adherents of Wahhabism and their offshoot sects, cf. *al-Wala' wal-Bara' According to the 'Aqeedah of the Salaf* (London: Firdous Ltd., 1993) p. 99 by a certain Muhammad Saeed al-Qahtani who lists "relying on an intermediary between oneself and Allah when seeking intercession" among the "ten actions that negate Islam."

[236] In ʿIyāḍ, *Shifā* II.2 (p. 493) cf. al-Qārī, *Sharḥ al-Shifā* (2:35). It continues "and my spouses are more beloved to him than his and my close relatives are more beloved to him than his and my person is more beloved to him than himself." al-Ṭabarānī, *Kabīr* (7:86 §6416) and *Awsaṭ* (6:59 §5790) and al-Bayhaqī, *Shuʿab* (3:88 §1420).

Say: If your fathers, sons, brothers, wives, clan, possessions that you have gained, commerce you fear may slacken, dwellings you love – if these are dearer to you than Allah and His Messenger, and to struggle in His way, then wait till Allah brings His command to pass; Allah guides not the wrongdoing folk (9:24). … And in the authentic Sunna: "None of you truly believes until I am more beloved to him than his offspring, his parents, and all people;" and in another version "than his spouses, his possessions, and all people." That is why the Ṣiddīq brought him everything he owned and said: "I have left for my family Allah and His Messenger," and ʿAlī sacrificed his life for him the night he left for the cave, wearing the Prophet's cloak and lying down in his spot while a hundred conspirators of Quraysh kept watch at his door to kill him – or so they thought. But the Prophet came out and Allah had blinded their eyes so that they never saw him.[237]

قال أبو الخَطَّاب ابن دِحْيَة رحمه الله في كتابه نهاية السُّول في خصائص الرسول ﷺ:

وَمِنْ خَصَائِصِهِ ﷺ أَنَّ اللهَ تَعَالَى أَمَرَ بِتَقْدِيمِهِ عَلَ النُّفُوسِ، عَلَى مَا ثَبَتَ فِي الْكِتَابِ وَالسُّنَّةِ، فَقَالَ جَلَّ مِنْ قَائِلٍ: ﴿ ٱلنَّبِىُّ أَوْلَىٰ بِٱلْمُؤْمِنِينَ مِنْ أَنفُسِهِمْ ﴾ الآية. الأحزاب. وَقَدَّمَهُ عَلَى الْآبَاءِ وَالْأَبْنَاءِ وَالْأَزْوَاجِ وَالْعَشَائِرِ وَالْأَمْوَالِ فَقَالَ ﴿ قُلْ إِن كَانَ ءَابَآؤُكُمْ وَأَبْنَآؤُكُمْ وَإِخْوَٰنُكُمْ وَأَزْوَٰجُكُمْ وَعَشِيرَتُكُمْ وَأَمْوَٰلٌ ٱقْتَرَفْتُمُوهَا وَتِجَٰرَةٌ تَخْشَوْنَ كَسَادَهَا وَمَسَٰكِنُ تَرْضَوْنَهَآ أَحَبَّ إِلَيْكُم مِّنَ ٱللَّهِ وَرَسُولِهِۦ وَجِهَادٍ فِى سَبِيلِهِۦ فَتَرَبَّصُوا۟ حَتَّىٰ يَأْتِىَ ٱللَّهُ بِأَمْرِهِۦ ۗ وَٱللَّهُ لَا يَهْدِى ٱلْقَوْمَ ٱلْفَٰسِقِينَ ﴿٢٤﴾ ﴾

[237] Ibn Diḥya, *Nihāyat al-Sūl* (p. 31-32).

التوبة. وَأَمَّا السُّنَّةُ الثَّابِتَةُ فَفِي صَحِيحِ الْبُخَارِيِّ: لَا يُؤْمِنُ أَحَدُكُمْ حَتَّى أَكُونَ أَحَبَّ إِلَيْهِ مِنْ وَالِدِهِ وَوَلَدِهِ وَالنَّاسِ أَجْمَعِينَ. وَفِي رِوَايَةٍ: مِنْ أَهْلِهِ وَمَالِهِ وَالنَّاسِ أَجْمَعِينَ. وَلِذَلِكَ جَاءَهُ الصِّدِّيقُ بِمَالِهِ كُلِّهِ وَقَالَ: تَرَكْتُ لِأَهْلِي اللهَ وَرَسُولَهُ، وَفَدَاهُ عَلِيٌّ الْمُرْتَضَى بِنَفْسِهِ لَيْلَةَ خُرُوجِهِ إِلَى الْغَارِ، وَعَلَيْهِ بُرْدُ رَسُولِ اللهِ ﷺ وَجَلَسَ فِي مَكَانِهِ، وَعَلَى بَابِهِ مِئَةٌ مِنْ قُرَيْشٍ يَنْتَظِرُونَهُ لِيَقْتُلُوهُ بِزَعْمِهِمْ، فَخَرَجَ عَلَيهِمْ رَسُولُ اللهِ ﷺ وَقَدْ حَجَبَهُ اللهُ عَزَّ وَجَلَّ عَنْهُمْ.

Similarly al-Subkī (683-756/1284-1355) said:

169. Truly Allah knows that every goodness in my life which He has bestowed upon me is on account of the Prophet, and that my recourse is to him, and my reliance is upon him in seeking a means to Allah in every matter of mine. Verily he is my means to Allah in this world and the next, and the gifts of Allah I owe to him are too many to count, both the hidden and the visible.

قال شيخ الإسلام التقي السبكي قَدَّسَ اللهُ رُوحَهُ فِي كِتَابٍ سَمَّاهُ (تَنَزُّلُ السَّكِينَةِ عَلَى قَنَادِيلِ المَدِينَةِ) في فتاويه: إِنَّ اللهَ يَعْلَمُ أَنَّ كُلَّ خَيْرٍ أَنَا فِيهِ وَمَنَّ عَلَيَّ بِهِ فَهُوَ بِسَبَبِ النَّبِيِّ ﷺ، وَالْتِجَائِي إِلَيْهِ، وَاعْتِمَادِي فِي تَوَسُّلِي إِلَى اللهِ فِي كُلِّ أُمُورِي عَلَيْهِ، فَهُوَ وَسِيلَتِي إِلَى اللهِ فِي الدُّنْيَا وَالْآخِرَةِ، وَكَمْ لَهُ عَلَيَّ مِنْ نِعَمٍ بَاطِنَةٍ وَظَاهِرَةٍ.

The Egyptian gnostic Abū al-Ḥasan Muḥammad al-Bakrī (d. 952/1545) began his poem on intermediacy (*tawassul*) with the lines:

170. *Never did or will the All-Beneficent send*

any mercy that rises or descends
In the dominion of Allah and His kingdom
of any kind, universal or minute,
But His servant Ṭaha the Elect,
His chosen Prophet and Messenger,
Is its intermediary and its root,
as any that gives thought well knows.[238]

أنشد العارف بالله أبو الحسن محمد البكري رحمه الله في ديوانه (الأنوار ومصباح السرور والأفكار وذكر نور محمّد ﷺ المصطفى المختار):

مَا أَرْسَلَ الرَّحْمٰنُ أَوْ يُرْسِلُ * مِنْ رَحْمَةٍ تَصْعَدُ أَوْ تَنْـــزِلُ
فِي مَلَكُوتِ اللهِ أَوْ مُلْكِــهِ * مِنْ كُلِّ مَا يَخْتَصُّ أَوْ يَشْمُلُ
إِلَّا وَطَهَ الْمُصْطَفَـى عَبْـدُهُ * نَبِيُّـــهُ الْمُخْتَـــارُ الْمُرْسَـــلُ
وَاسِطَةٌ فِيهَــا وَأَصْلٌ لَهَـا * يَعْلَمُ هٰذَا كُـلُّ مَـنْ يَعْقِـلُ

As is clear from the preceding proofs such Prophetic patronage and authority, moreover, begin before time.

His Exalted Status before Adam's Creation and Adam's Request of His Intercession

The fuller wording of the Prophet's—upon him blessings and peace—answer to the Companion Maysarat al-Fajr when he replied "when Adam was still between spirit and body" is none other than the famous hadith of Adam's prayer of repentence through the intercession of the Prophet, and elaborates the meaning of his statement "when Adam was still between spirit and body":

[238] From his *Dīwān* entitled *al-Anwār wa-Miṣbāḥ al-Surūr wal-Afkār wa-Dhikr Nūr Muḥammad al-Muṣṭafā al-Mukhtār* as cited in al-Kattānī, *Maṭāli*ʿ (p. 266-267).

171. I said: "Messenger of Allāh, when did you become a Prophet?" He replied: "When Allāh created the earth and turned to the heavens, arranging them into seven heavens, and He created the Throne, He wrote on the leg of the Throne: **MUḤAMMAD IS THE MESSENGER OF ALLAH AND THE SEAL OF PROPHETS**. Allāh created Paradise in which He made Adam and Ḥawwā' dwell, then He wrote my Name there, on the gates, the tree-leaves, the houses and tents, while Adam was still between the spirit and the body. When Allāh Most High brought him to life, he looked at the Throne and saw my Name, whereupon Allāh Most High informed him: 'He is the liege-lord of your offspring.' When Satan deceived them, they repented and sought intercession with my Name from Him."[239]

قال الحافظ الصالحي في سبل الهدى والرشاد: روى ابن الجوزي بسند جيد لا بأس به:

عَنْ مَيْسَرَةَ قَالَ قُلْتُ: يَا رَسُولَ اللهِ، مَتَى كُنْتَ نَبِيّاً؟ قَالَ لَمَّا خَلَقَ اللهُ تعَالَى الْأَرْضَ، وَاسْتَوَى إِلَى السَّمَاءِ، فَسَوَّاهُنَّ سَبْعَ سَمَوَاتٍ، وَخَلَقَ العَرْشَ، كَتَبَ عَلَى سَاقِ الْعَرْشِ: مُحَمَّدٌ رَسُولُ اللهِ خَاتِمُ الْأَنْبِيَاءِ، وَخَلَقَ اللهُ تَعَالَى الجَنَّةَ الَّتِي أَسْكَنَهَا آدَمَ وَحَوَّاءَ، فَكَتَبَ إِسْمِي عَلَى الْأَبْوَابِ وَالْأَوْرَاقِ وَالْقِبَابِ وَالْخِيَامِ، وَآدَمُ بَيْنَ الرُّوْحِ وَالجَسَدِ، فَلَمَّا أَحْيَاهُ اللهُ تَعَالَى نَظَرَ إِلَى الْعَرْشِ فَرَأى إِسْمِي، فَأَخْبَرَهُ اللهُ تَعَالَى أَنَّهُ سَيِّدُ وَلَدِكَ. فَلَمَّا غَرَّهُمَا الشَّيْطَانُ

[239] The hadith master al-Ṣāliḥī cited it in *Subul al-Hudā wal-Rashād* (Beirut ed. 1:86=Cairo ed. 1:104) from the narration of Ibn al-Jawzī in *al-Wafā* with his chain through the trustworthy *Ḥāfiẓ* Abū al-Ḥusayn ʿAlī b. Muḥammad b. ʿAbd Allāh, known as Ibn Bishrān al-ʿAdl al-Umawī al-Baghdādī al-Muʿaddal (d. 411 or 415) in his *Fawā'id* and said "Its chain is good and there is no harm in it." Aḥmad b. Taymiyya cites the entire wording with the full chain of transmission in his *Majmūʿ al-Fatāwā* (2:150-151). A similar hadith is also narrated with weak chains from (i) ʿUmar by al-Ḥākim in *al-Mustadrak* (2:615) and al-Ṭabarānī in *al-Muʿjam al-Ṣaghīr* (2:82 §992) and *Muʿjam al-Awsaṭ* (6:313-614 §6502) and (ii) Ibn ʿAbbās by al-Khallāl in *al-Sunna* (1:261 §316) and al-Ḥākim in *al-Mustadrak* (2:614-615).

تَابَا وَاسْتَشْفَعَا بِإِسْمِي إِلَيْهِ. فوائد ابن بشران ومن طريقه ابن الجوزي في الوفا.

ويُروى مثله عن عمر وابن عباس رضي الله عنهم.

The Meaning of "Adam Looked at the Throne and Saw My Name" = *And We exalted Your Fame* (Rāzī)

The writing of the Prophet's name everywhere in Paradise and on the Throne of the All-Beneficent[240] is among the marks of honor he received from Allah in illustration of the verses *Of those messengers, We have caused some to excel others, and to one Allah spoke, while one of them He exalted above others in degree* (2:253) and *Did We not exalt your fame?* (94:4), as stated in the vibrant lines of Imam al-Rāzī's (543-606/1148-1209) *Tafsīr*:

> **172.** Among the proofs of the Prophet's superiority to everything else in creation is the saying of Allah Most High: *And did We not exalt your fame?* (94:4). It was explained as referring to His joining the mention of Muḥammad with His own mention in the testimony of faith, in the call to prayer, and in the *tashahhud* inside prayer, while no other Prophet was ever thus honored. ... Know that the verse is comprehensive of everything they mentioned such as his Prophethood, his fame on earth and in the heavens, the fact that his name is written on the Throne, that he is mentioned in *shahāda* and *tashahhud*, that Allah named him in the earlier Scriptures, that his fame has spread everywhere, that Prophethood came to a close with him, that he is mentioned in every *khuṭba*, every call to prayer, and at the opening and closing of letters, that Allah has joined his mention in the Qur'ān with His own – *but Allah, with His messenger, has more right that they should please Him* (9:62); *and whoever obeys Allah and His Messenger* (4:12, 24:52, 33:71, 48:17); *say: obey Allah and obey the Messenger* (24:54) – and He calls him by the names of *Messenger* and *Prophet*,

[240] See more reports to that effect in Abū al-Mawāhib Ja'far b. Idrīs al-Kattānī, *al-Ghayth al-Midrār wal-Sirr al-'Ammār fī-mā Yata'allaq bil-Nabī al-Mukhtār* (Beirut: Dār Ibn Ḥazm; Casablanca: Markaz al-Turāth al-Maghribī, 1428/2007) p. 89-104.

whereas He calls others by their names: *O Mūsā*, *O ʿĪsā*. He has also put him in every heart to the point that they delight in mentioning him, and that is the meaning of *the Beneficent will appoint for them love* (19:96), as if He were saying: I will fill the world with your followers, all of them praising you and blessing you and keeping your Sunna – nay, there is not a single *farḍ* of prayer except there is a *sunna* that goes with it. Thus they follow My order in the *farḍ* and they follow your order in the *sunna*; and I have made obedience to you obedience to Me, and your pledge My pledge: *Whoever obeys the Messenger obeys Allah* (4:80), *Truly those who swear allegiance unto you (Muhammad), swear allegiance only unto Allah* (48:10). Sultans do not scorn to be counted as your followers. Rather, it would be foolish audacity for even the most ignorant of kings to be enthroned as caliph outside of your tribe [Quraysh]. Qur'ān reciters memorize the wordings of your Edict; exegetes explain the meanings of your Criterion; and admonishers convey your admonitions. Nay, scholars and sultans strive to serve you, they humbly greet you from behind the door, they wipe their faces on the dust of your garden, and they ardently hope for your intercession. Your honor endures to the Day of Resurrection.[241]

قال الفخر الرازي في تفسير سورة البقرة الآية 253: مِنْ دَلَائِلِ أَفْضَلِيَّتِهِ عَلَى الْعَالَمِينَ قَوْلُهُ تَعَالَى: ﴿ وَرَفَعْنَا لَكَ ذِكْرَكَ ﴿٤﴾ ﴾ الشرح فَقِيلَ فِيهِ لِأَنَّهُ قَرَنَ ذِكْرَ مُحَمَّدٍ ﷺ بِذِكْرِهِ فِي كَلِمَةِ الشَّهَادَةِ وَفِي الْأَذَانِ وَفِي التَشَهُّدِ وَلَمْ يَكُنْ ذِكْرُ سَائِرِ الْأَنْبِيَاءِ كَذٰلِكَ. ثم قال في تفسير الآية من سورة الإنشراح: إِعْلَمْ أَنَّهُ عَامٌّ فِي كُلِّ مَا ذَكَرُوهُ مِنْ نُبُوَّتِهِ، وَشُهْرَتِهِ فِي الْأَرْضِ وَالسَّمٰوَاتِ، وَأَنَّ اسْمَهُ مَكْتُوبٌ عَلَى الْعَرْشِ، وَأَنَّهُ يُذْكَرُ مَعَهُ فِي الشَّهَادَةِ وَالتَّشَهُّدِ، وَأَنَّهُ تعالَى ذَكَرَهُ

[241] al-Rāzī, *Mafātīḥ al-Ghayb* (*sub* 2:253 and 94:4).

فِي الْكُتُبِ الْمُتَقَدِّمَةِ، وَانْتِشَارِ ذِكْرِهِ فِي الآفَاقِ، وَأَنَّهُ خُتِمَتْ بِهِ النُّبُوَّةُ، وَأَنَّهُ يُذْكَرُ فِي الْخُطَبِ وَالأَذَانِ وَمَفَاتِيحِ الرَّسَائِلِ وَعِنْدَ الْخَتمِ، وَجُعِلَ ذِكْرُهُ فِي الْقُرْآنِ مَقْرُوناً بِذِكْرِهِ: ﴿ وَٱللَّهُ وَرَسُولُهُۥٓ أَحَقُّ أَن يُرْضُوهُ ﴾ الآية. التوبة ﴿ وَمَن يُطِعِ ٱللَّهَ وَرَسُولَهُۥ ﴾ الآية. النساء و﴿ قُلْ أَطِيعُواْ ٱللَّهَ وَأَطِيعُواْ ٱلرَّسُولَ ﴾ الأية. النور. وَيُنَادِيهِ بِإِسْمِ الرَّسُولِ وَالنَّبِيِّ، حِينَ يُنَادِي غَيْرَهُ بِالإِسْمِ: يَا مُوسَى يَا عِيسَى، وَأَيْضاً جَعَلَهُ فِي الْقُلُوبِ بِحَيْثُ يَسْتَطِيبُونَ ذِكْرَهُ وَهُوَ مَعْنَى قَوْلِهِ تَعَالَى ﴿ سَيَجْعَلُ لَهُمُ ٱلرَّحْمَٰنُ وُدًّا ﴾ مريم كَأَنَّهُ تَعَالَى يَقُولُ: أَمْلأُ الْعَالَمَ مِنْ أَتْبَاعِكَ كُلُّهُمْ يُثْنُونَ عَلَيْكَ وَيُصَلُّونَ عَلَيْكَ وَيَحْفَظُونَ سُنَّتَكَ، بَلْ مَا مِنْ فَرِيضَةٍ مِنْ فَرَائِضِ الصَّلَاةِ إِلَّا وَمَعَهُ سُنَّةٌ فَهُمْ يَمْتَثِلُونَ فِي الْفَرِيضَةِ أَمْرِي، وَفِي السُّنَّةِ أَمْرَكَ، وَجَعَلْتُ طَاعَتَكَ طَاعَتِي وَبَيْعَتَكَ بَيْعَتِي ﴿ مَّن يُطِعِ ٱلرَّسُولَ فَقَدْ أَطَاعَ ٱللَّهَ ﴾ الآية. النساء ﴿ إِنَّ ٱلَّذِينَ يُبَايِعُونَكَ إِنَّمَا يُبَايِعُونَ ٱللَّهَ ﴾ الآية. الفتح. لَا تَأْنَفُ السَّلَاطِينُ مِنِ اتِّبَاعِكَ، بَلْ جَرَاءَةٌ لِأَجْهَلِ الْمُلُوكِ أَنْ يُنْصَبَ خَلِيفَةً مِنْ غَيْرِ قَبِيلَتِكَ. فَالْقُرَّاءُ يَحْفَظُونَ أَلْفَاظَ مَنْشُورِكَ، وَالْمُفَسِّرُونَ يُفَسِّرُونَ مَعَانِي فُرْقَانِكَ، وَالْوُعَّاظُ يُبَلِّغُونَ وَعْظَكَ بَلِ الْعُلَمَاءُ وَالسَّلَاطِينُ يَصِلُونَ إِلَى خِدْمَتِكَ، وَيُسَلِّمُونَ مِنْ وَرَاءِ الْبَابِ عَلَيْكَ، وَيَمْسَحُونَ وُجُوهَهُمْ بِتُرَابِ رَوْضَتِكَ، وَيَرْجُونَ شَفَاعَتَكَ، فَشَرَفُكَ بَاقٍ إِلَى يَوْمِ الْقِيَامَةِ. وانظر كلام الدبّاغ الآتي في استطابة ذكره ﷺ.

The Meaning of "I was a Prophet when Adam was still between spirit and body" (Subkī)

The *Ḥāfiẓ*, Qāḍī al-Quḍāt and undisputed Shaykh al-Islām, Taqī al-Dīn al-Subkī commented further on the meaning of the hadith "I was a Prophet when Adam was still between spirit and body" in a treatise titled *al-Ta'ẓīm wal-Minna fī "latu'minunna bihi wa-la-tanṣurunnah"* in which he said:

> **173.** Glory to Allah Who has magnified His Prophet, granted us His favor through him, and guided us to every goodness by connecting our means to his means. To proceed, a look was taken into the explanation of the saying of Allah Most High *When Allah made His Covenant with the Prophets He said: Behold that which I have given you of the Scripture and knowledge. And afterward there will come unto you a Messenger, confirming that which you possess. You shall believe in him and you shall help him. He said: Do you agree, and will you take up My burden (which I lay upon you) in this matter? They answered: We agree. He said: Then bear you witness. I will be a witness with you* (3:81).
>
> The commentators said that the Messenger here is our Prophet Muḥammad—upon him blessings and peace—and that "there is no Prophet but Allah has taken a covenant from him that if Muḥammad were sent in his time he would certainly have to believe in him, assist him, and charge his community to do the same." All this entails high praise of the Prophet—upon him blessings and peace—and obviously emphasizes his high rank. In addition, it shows that if he ever appeared in their own time he would actually be sent to them. So his Prophethood and Message are universal and encompass all creation from the time of Adam to Resurrection; and Prophets and their communities are all part of his Community. Thus his saying "I was sent to all people" (*bu'ithtu ilā al-nāsi kāffa*)[242] is not restricted to the people of his time until Resurrection but rather also includes those before them.

[242] Narrated from Ibn 'Abbās by al-Bukhārī, *Ṣaḥīḥ* (*Ṣalāt, Bāb qawl al-Nabī ju'ilat lī al-arḍ masjidan wa-ṭahūran*); al-Nasā'ī, *Sunan* (*al-Ghusl wal-tayammum, Bāb al-tayammum bil-ṣa'īd*); Aḥmad, *Musnad* (4:471-472 §2742) and others.

This is made clear by the saying of the Prophet: "I was a Prophet while Adam was still between the spirit and the body." Whoever explained it to refer only to the Divine foreknowledge that he was destined to be a Prophet[243] fell short of this understanding, for the Divine foreknowledge encompasses all things, while the description of the Prophet as actually being a Prophet must be understood as a firmly established status for him at that time. That is why Adam saw his name inscribed on the Throne as *Muḥammadun Rasul Allāh.* Hence it is inevitable that such a meaning be firmly established at that time. If only foreknowledge of future destinies were meant then there would be nothing special to single him out as "a Prophet while Adam was still between the spirit and the body," since Allah knows the Prophethood of all Prophets equally at that time and before it also. Rather, there has to be a meaning that is specific to the Prophet himself—upon him blessings and peace—because of which he spoke that hadith in order to inform his Community of his immense worth in the Divine presence, so that great goodness would ensue for them.

If you ask: "I want to understand that added dimension, for Prophethood describes someone that needs to exist in the first place, and only after his fortieth year! So how can he be described by it before his existence and before being sent? For if this is true then it is true of others also."

I reply: it was narrated that Allah created spirits before bodies, and the Prophet's reference in the hadith "I was a Prophet while Adam was still between the spirit and the body" may be to his noble spirit or to some tremendous reality (*ḥaqīqatin min al-ḥaqā'iq*). Our minds fall short of knowing those realities, only their Creator knows them, and also those to whom He extends a divine help (*madad*) of light. After that, Allah brings to existence whichever of these realities He likes in the time that He pleases. As for the reality of the Prophet, Allah may have given it this attribute since before the creation of Adam in the sense that He cre-

[243] He means (i) Ibn Taymiyya, *Majmū' al-Fatāwā* (11:57) and (ii) the author of *al-Nafkh wal-Taswiya*, also known as *al-Maḍnūn al-Ṣaghīr*, *al-Maḍnūn bihi 'alā Ahlih* and *al-Ajwibat al-Ghazāliyya fīl-Masā'il al-Ukhrāwiyya*, attributed to al-Ghazālī but which Ibn al-'Arabī al-Mālikī said was authored by Abū al-Ḥasan 'Alī al-Musaffir al-Sibtī. Sa'īd Fawda in his *Naẓarāt fī Kitāb al-Maḍnūn al-Ṣaghīr* similarly rejects the attribution of its authorship to al-Ghazālī.

ated it fully ready and qualified for this (*khalaqahā mutahayyi'atan li-dhālik*), and outpoured it over it since that time. Thus he was made Prophet, and He inscribed his name on the Throne, and He told about him in the Message so as to inform His angels and others of his immense rank in His Presence; and his reality exists already since that time.[244]

قال شيخ الإسلام قاضي القضاة التقي السبكي رضي الله عنه في تحقيق معنى قوله ﷺ **كُنْتُ نَبِيّاً وَآدَمُ بَيْنَ الرُّوحِ وَالجَسَدِ**: الحَمْدُ لله الَّذِي عَظَّمَ نَبِيَّهُ ﷺ وَمَنَّ عَلَيْنَا بِهِ وَهَدَانَا إِلَى كُلِّ خَيْرٍ إِذْ وَصَلَ سَبَبَنَا بِسَبَبِهِ وَبَعْدُ: فَقَدْ حَصَلَ الْبَحْثُ فِي تَفْسِيرِ قَوْلِهِ تَعَالَى ﴿ وَإِذْ أَخَذَ ٱللَّهُ مِيثَٰقَ ٱلنَّبِيِّـۧنَ لَمَآ ءَاتَيْتُكُم مِّن كِتَٰبٍ وَحِكْمَةٍ ثُمَّ جَآءَكُمْ رَسُولٌ مُّصَدِّقٌ لِّمَا مَعَكُمْ لَتُؤْمِنُنَّ بِهِۦ وَلَتَنصُرُنَّهُۥۚ قَالَ ءَأَقْرَرْتُمْ وَأَخَذْتُمْ عَلَىٰ ذَٰلِكُمْ إِصْرِى ۖ قَالُوٓاْ أَقْرَرْنَا ۚ قَالَ فَٱشْهَدُواْ وَأَنَا۠ مَعَكُم مِّنَ ٱلشَّٰهِدِينَ ﴿٨١﴾ ﴾ آل عمران وَقَوْلُ الْمُفَسِّرِينَ هُنَا أَنَّ الرَّسُولَ هُوَ نَبِيُّنَا مُحَمَّدٌ ﷺ وَأَنَّهُ مَا مِنْ نَبِيٍّ إِلَّا أَخَذَ اللهُ عَلَيْهِ المِيثَاقَ أَنَّهُ إِنْ بُعِثَ مُحَمَّدٌ ﷺ فِي زَمَانِهِ ﴿ لَتُؤْمِنُنَّ بِهِۦ وَلَتَنصُرُنَّهُۥ ﴾ وَيُوصِي أُمَّتَهُ بِذَٰلِكَ وَفِي ذَٰلِكَ مِنَ التَّنْوِيهِ بِالنَّبِيِّ ﷺ وَتَعْظِيمِ قَدْرِهِ الْعَلِيِّ مَا لَا يَخْفَى وَفِيهِ مَعَ ذَٰلِكَ أَنَّهُ عَلَى تَقْدِيرِ مَجِيئِهِ فِي زَمَانِهِمْ يَكُونُ مُرْسَلاً إِلَيْهِمْ فَتَكُونُ نُبُوَّتُهُ وَرِسَالَتُهُ عَامَّةٌ لِجَمِيعِ الخَلْقِ مِنْ زَمَنِ آدَمَ إِلَى يَوْمِ الْقِيَامَةِ وَيَكُونُ الأَنْبِيَاءُ وَأُمَمُهُمْ كُلُّهُمْ مِنْ أُمَّتِهِ وَيَكُونُ قَوْلُهُ **بُعِثْتُ إِلَى النَّاسِ كَافَّةً** (رواه البخاري

[244] Subkī, *Fatāwā* (1:48-50); Suyūṭī, *Ḥāwī* (2:100-101); Qasṭallānī, *Mawāhib* (1:31).

والنسائي وأحمد وغيرهم) لَا يَخْتَصُّ بِهِ النَّاسُ مِنْ زَمَانِهِ إِلَى يَوْمِ الْقِيَامَةِ بَلْ يَتَنَاوَلُ مَنْ قَبْلَهُمْ أَيْضاً وَيَتَبَيَّنُ بِذٰلِكَ مَعْنَى قَوْلِهِ ﷺ **كُنْتُ نَبِيّاً وَآدَمُ بَيْنَ الرُّوحِ وَالْجَسَدِ** (رواه أحمد والترمذي والطحاوي والطبراني وابن سعد عن جمع من الصحابة) وَأَنَّ مَنْ فَسَّرَهُ بِعِلْمِ اللهِ بِأَنَّهُ سَيَصِيرُ نَبِيًّا لَمْ يَصِلْ إِلَى هٰذَا الْمَعْنَى لِأَنَّ عِلْمَ اللهِ مُحِيطٌ بِجَمِيعِ الْأَشْيَاءِ وَوَصْفُ النَّبِيِّ ﷺ بِالنُّبُوَّةِ فِي ذٰلِكَ الْوَقْتِ يَنْبَغِي أَنْ يُفْهَمَ مِنْهُ أَنَّهُ أَمْرٌ ثَابِتٌ لَهُ فِي ذٰلِكَ الْوَقْتِ وَلِهٰذَا رَأَى اسْمَهُ آدَمُ مَكْتُوباً عَلَى الْعَرْشِ **مُحَمَّدٌ رَسُولُ اللهِ** فَلَا بُدَّ أَنْ يَكُونَ ذٰلِكَ مَعْنًى ثَابِتاً فِي ذٰلِكَ الْوَقْتِ وَلَوْ كَانَ الْمُرَادُ بِذٰلِكَ مُجَرَّدَ الْعِلْمِ بِمَا سَيَصِيرُ فِي الْمُسْتَقْبَلِ لَمْ يَكُنْ لَهُ خُصُوصِيَّةٌ بِأَنَّهُ نَبِيٌّ وَآدَمُ بَيْنَ الرُّوحِ وَالْجَسَدِ لِأَنَّ جَمِيعَ الْأَنْبِيَاءِ يَعْلَمُ اللهُ نُبُوَّتَهُمْ فِي ذٰلِكَ الْوَقْتِ وَقَبْلَهُ فَلَا بُدَّ مِنْ خُصُوصِيَّةٍ لِلنَّبِيِّ ﷺ لِأَجْلِهَا أَخْبَرَ بِهٰذَا الْخَبَرِ إِعْلَاماً لِأُمَّتِهِ لِيَعْرِفُوا قَدْرَهُ عِنْدَ اللهِ فَيَحْصُلَ لَهُمُ الْخَيْرُ بِذٰلِكَ. فَإِنْ قُلْتَ: أُرِيدُ أَنْ أَفْهَمَ ذٰلِكَ الْقَدْرَ الزَّائِدَ فَإِنَّ النُّبُوَّةَ وَصْفٌ لَا بُدَّ أَنْ يَكُونَ الْمَوْصُوفُ بِهِ مَوْجُوداً وَإِنَّمَا يَكُونُ بَعْدَ بُلُوغِ أَرْبَعِينَ سَنَةٍ أَيْضاً فَكَيْفَ يُوصَفُ بِهِ قَبْلَ وُجُودِهِ وَقَبْلَ إِرْسَالِهِ؟ فَإِنْ صَحَّ ذٰلِكَ فَغَيْرُهُ كَذٰلِكَ. قُلْتُ: قَدْ جَاءَ أَنَّ اللهَ خَلَقَ الْأَرْوَاحَ قَبْلَ الْأَجْسَادِ فَقَدْ تَكُونُ الْإِشَارَةُ بِقَوْلِهِ **كُنْتُ نَبِيّاً** إِلَى رُوحِهِ الشَّرِيفَةِ ﷺ وَإِلَى حَقِيقَتِهِ، وَالْحَقَائِقُ تَقْصُرُ عُقُولُنَا عَنْ مَعْرِفَتِهَا وَإِنَّمَا يَعْلَمُهَا خَالِقُهَا وَمَنْ أَمَدَّهُ بِنُورٍ إِلٰهِيٍّ. ثُمَّ إِنَّ تِلْكَ الْحَقَائِقَ يُؤْتِي اللهُ كُلَّ حَقِيقَةٍ مِنْهَا مَا يَشَاءُ فِي الْوَقْتِ الَّذِي يَشَاءُ فَحَقِيقَةُ النَّبِيِّ ﷺ قَدْ تَكُونُ مِنْ

قَبْلِ خَلْقِ آدَمَ آتَاهَا اللهُ ذٰلِكَ الْوَصْفَ بِأَنْ يَكُونَ خَلَقَهَا مُتَهَيِّئَةً لِذٰلِكَ وَأَفَاضَهُ عَلَيْهَا مِنْ ذٰلِكَ الْوَقْتِ فَصَارَ نَبِيّاً وَكَتَبَ إِسْمَهُ عَلَى الْعَرْشِ وَأَخْبَرَ عَنْهُ بِالرِّسَالَةِ لِيُعْلِمَ مَلَائِكَتَهُ وَغَيْرَهُمْ كَرَامَتَهُ ﷺ عِنْدَهُ فَحَقِيقَتُهُ مَوْجُودَةٌ مِنْ ذٰلِكَ الْوَقْتِ.

Al-Suyūṭī endorsed the above position and commented: "What al-Subkī concluded is confirmed by the verses of al-Būṣīrī—who died before him—when he said:

> **174.** *And every single sign brought by the noble Prophets*
> *was theirs only as part of his light,*
> *For truly he is a sun of perfection of which they are the moons*
> *bringing its light to people in the midst of darkness.*"[245]

Ibn Marzūq (710-781/1310-1379) commented on al-Būṣīrī's lines:

> **175.** He means that every miracle that every messenger has brought surely was only as an extension of the light of Muḥammad to each one of them. How beautiful is his saying "was theirs only as part of his light" for it suggests that his light has ever been existing in him, and nothing of it was decreased. Had he said "it was from his light," then it could have been imagined that he distributed it to them, and that perhaps nothing of it remained for him. All the signs given to each one of them became theirs only through his light, because he is a sun of excellence, and they are the planets of that sun which convey its lights to humankind in the darkness. The planets are not shining by themselves, but they receive light from the sun, so that when the sun is absent they show the light of the sun. Similarly, the Prophets before his existence used to show his excellence, so that whatever lights appeared at the hands of the

[245] al-Būṣīrī, *Burda* (lines 52-53 p. 288-293) and al-Suyūṭī, *Tazyīn al-Arā'ik fī Irsāl al-Nabī ilā al-Malā'ik* in *al-Ḥāwī lil-Fatāwā* (2:146).

messengers other than him, it was only from his outpouring light and extended help *(madad)*, without decreasing anything of it.[246]

قال الإمام السيوطي رحمه الله:

وَهٰذَا التَّقْرِيرُ الَّذِي قَرَّرَهُ السُّبْكِيُّ قَدْ أَشَارَ إِلَيْهِ الشَّرَفُ البُوصِيرِيُّ – وَقَدْ مَاتَ قَبْلَ مَوْلِدِ السُّبْكِيِّ – بِقَوْلِهِ فِي الْبُرْدَةِ:

وَكُلُّ آيٍ أَتَى الرُّسْلُ الْكِرَامُ بِهَا * فَإِنَّمَا اتَّصَلَتْ مِنْ نُورِهِ بِهِمِ

فَإِنَّهُ شَمْسُ فَضْلٍ هُمْ كَوَاكِبُهَا * يُظْهِرْنَ أَنْوَارَهَا لِلنَّاسِ فِي الظُّلَمِ

وأورد القسطلاني في المواهب شرح ابن مرزوق لهذين البيتين الذي قال فيه:

يَعْنِي أَنَّ كُلَّ مُعْجِزَةٍ أَتَى بِهَا كُلُّ وَاحِدٍ مِنَ الرُّسُلِ فَإِنَّمَا اتَّصَلَتْ بِكُلِّ وَاحِدٍ مِنْهُمْ مِنْ نُورِ مُحَمَّدٍ ﷺ. وَمَا أَحْسَنَ قَوْلَهُ: (فَإِنَّمَا اتَّصَلَتْ مِنْ نُورِهِ بِهِمِ) فَإِنَّهُ يُعْطِي أَنَّ نُورَهُ ﷺ لَمْ يَزَلْ قَائِماً بِهَا وَلَمْ يَنْقُصْ مِنْهُ شَيْءٌ. وَلَوْ قَالَ: فَإِنَّمَا هِيَ مِنْ نُورِهِ، لَتُوُهِّمَ أَنَّهُ وُزِّعَ عَلَيْهِمْ وَقَدْ لَا يَبْقَى مِنْهُ شَيْءٌ. وَإِنَّمَا كَانَتْ آيَاتُ كُلِّ وَاحِدٍ مِنْ نُورِهِ ﷺ لِأَنَّهُ شَمْسُ فَضْلٍ هُمْ كَوَاكِبُ تِلْكَ الشَّمْسِ يُظْهِرْنَ – أَيْ تِلْكَ الْكَوَاكِبُ – أَنْوَارَ تِلْكَ الشَّمْسِ لِلنَّاسِ فِي الظُّلَمِ، فَالْكَوَاكِبُ لَيْسَتْ مُضِيئَةً بِالذَّاتِ وَإِنَّمَا هِيَ مُسْتَمِدَّةٌ مِنَ الشَّمْسِ، فَهِيَ عِنْدَ غَيْبَةِ الشَّمْسِ تُظْهِرُ نُورَ الشَّمْسِ وَكَذٰلِكَ الْأَنْبِيَاءُ قَبْلَ وُجُودِهِ ﷺ كَانُوا يُظْهِرُونَ فَضْلَهُ. فَجَمِيعُ مَا ظَهَرَ عَلَى أَيْدِي الرُّسُلِ سِوَاهُ عَلَيْهِ وعَلَيهِمُ الصَّلَاةُ

[246] In al-Qasṭallānī, *Mawāhib* (2:243).

والسَّلَامُ مِنَ الأَنْوَارِ: فَإِنَّمَا هُوَ مِنْ نُورِهِ الفَائِضِ وَمَدَدِهِ الوَاسِعِ مِنْ غَيرِ أنْ يَنْقُصَ مِنْهُ شَيْءٌ.

The Prophet's Light and His Name Fill Creation (al-Dabbāgh)

The erudite Maghrebine scholar ʿAlī b. Mubārak al-Sijilmāsī (1090-1156/1679-1743) narrated from his teacher the *Ghawth* ʿAbd al-ʿAzīz al-Dabbāgh (1095-1131/1684-1719) the following account heard in the spiritual gathering of the Friends of Allah (*Dīwān al-Awliyā'*) from its *Ghawth* at the time, Aḥmad b. ʿAbd Allāh al-Miṣrī:

176. I once had a *murīd* whom I loved dearly. One day I was describing to him the immense status of the Liegelord of creation—upon him blessings and peace—and I said to him: "My son, were it not for the Light of our liegelord Muḥammad, not a single one of the secrets of the earth would have appeared. Were it not for him, not a single spring would have burst forth and not a single river would have run. His light, my son, permeates all seeds in the month of March three times more than normal, and by his blessings they bear fruit. Were it not for his light they would never bear fruit. My son, truly the one who has the least faith among people sees his faith over him like a mountain, or bigger yet, let alone others. Truly a soul might tire at times of carrying faith, so it tries to cast it aside, whereupon the light of the Prophet pours its fragrance over it, and this helps it to carry faith, and it finds it sweet and delightful." As I was describing to him the Prophet's greatness and listing for him the bounties obtained from him, I went into a trance in the Prophet. When he saw what happened to me he said: "O my master! I ask you by the Honor of that Noble Prophet! Please give me the Secret!" I tried to say no but I saw the Magnificent Honor in front of me, so I satisfied him and gave him the Secret. After he heard it from me he began to reveal it to a large group of people who could not bear it. Not long passed before they prosecuted him and had him killed.[247]

[247] Ibn Mubārak, *Ibrīz* (p. 28, *Faṣl* 2 *fī kayfiyyat tadrījih*).

نقل الشيخ المحقق علي بن مبارك السِّجِلْمَاسي في كتابه (الإبريز من كلام سيدي عبد العزيز) عن القطب الغوث السيد عبد العزيز بن مسعود الدَّبَّاغ رضي الله عنه أنّه حكى عن سيّدي أحمد بن عبد الله المصري الغوث ما نصُّه:

كَانَ لِي مُرِيدٌ وَكُنْتُ أُحِبُّهُ حُبّاً شَدِيداً، فَكُنْتُ ذَاتَ يَوْمٍ أُعَظِّمُ لَهُ أَمْرَ سَيِّدِ الْوُجُودِ ﷺ، فَقُلْتُ لَهُ: يَا وَلَدِي، لَوْلَا نُورُ سَيِّدِنَا مُحَمَّدٍ ﷺ مَا ظَهَرَ سِرٌّ مِنْ أَسْرَارِ الْأَرْضِ، فَلَوْلَا هُوَ مَا تَفَجَّرَتْ عَيْنٌ مِنَ الْعُيُونِ وَلَا جَرَى نَهْرٌ مِنَ الْأَنْهَارِ، وَإِنَّ نُورَهُ ﷺ يَا وَلَدِي يَفُوحُ فِي شَهْرِ مَارِس ثَلَاثَ مَرَّاتٍ عَلَى سَائِرِ الْحُبُوبِ فَيَقَعُ لَهَا الْإِثْمَارُ بِبَرَكَتِهِ ﷺ، وَلَوْلَا نُورُهُ مَا أَثْمَرَتْ. يَا وَلَدِي إِنَّ أَقَلَّ النَّاسِ إِيمَاناً مَنْ يَرَى إِيمَانَهُ عَلَى ذَاتِهِ مِثْلَ الْجَبَلِ وَأَعْظَمَ مِنْهُ، فَأَحْرَى غَيْرُهُ، وَإِنَّ الذَّاتَ تَكِلُّ أَحْيَاناً عَنْ حَمْلِ الْإِيمَانِ، فَتُرِيدُ أَنْ تَرْمِيَهُ، فَيَفُوحُ نُورُ النَّبِيِّ ﷺ عَلَيْهَا فَيَكُونُ مُعِيناً لَهَا عَلَى حَمْلِ الْإِيمَانِ فَتَسْتَحْلِيهِ وَتَسْتَطِيبُهُ. فَبَيْنَمَا أَذْكُرُ لَهُ تَعْظِيمَهُ ﷺ وَأُعَدِّدُ لَهُ الْخَيْرَاتِ الْمُكْتَسَبَةَ مِنْهُ حَتَّى غِبْتُ فِيهِ ﷺ، فَلَمَّا رَآنِي حَصَلَ لِي مَا حَصَلَ، قَالَ: يَا سَيِّدِي قَدَّمْتُ عَلَيْكَ جَاهَ هَذَا النَّبِيِّ الْكَرِيمِ ﷺ إِلَّا مَا أَعْطَيْتَنِي السِّرَّ! فَأَرَدْتُ أَنْ أَمْتَنِعَ فَرَأَيْتُ الْجَاهَ الْعَظِيمَ فَسَاعَفْتُهُ وَأَعْطَيْتُهُ السِّرَّ. فَلَمَّا سَمِعَ مِنِّي السِّرَّ ذَهَبَ وَجَمَعَ عَلَيْهِ جَمَاعَةً وَجَعَلَ يَذْكُرُ هُمُ السِّرَّ فَلَمْ تُطِقْهُ عُقُولُهُمْ فَلَمْ يَبْقَ إِلَّا مُدَّةً قَلِيلَةً وَشَهِدُوا عَلَيْهِ وَقَتَلُوهُ.

Al-Dabbāgh recounted a similar explanation from Muḥammad b. ʿAbd al-Karīm al-Baṣrāwī, a master he described as "the Trustee (*wakīl*) of the *Dīwān*, also known as its Qadi," in explanation of Ibn Mashīsh's reference to the Prophet as "he from whom the secrets were sundered" (*man minhu inshaqqat al-asrār*) in his *Ṣalāt Mashīshiyya*:

177. When Allah desired to bring out the blessings of the earth and its secrets such as its trove of springs, wells, rivers, trees, fruit, and flowers, He sent 70,000 angels to 70,000 angels to 70,000 angels; that is, seventy thousand three times that came down and roamed the earth. The first 70,000 mention the Name of the Prophet, and by that we mean his High Name (*ismahu al-ʿālī*), which is the name that discloses the origin of the named, of what substance it is made, and its benefit, so that merely by hearing the wording of the name the sciences and knowledge connected to it become known. The second 70,000 mention his nearness to Allah Most High and his high rank in His presence. The third 70,000 invoke blessings on him. His light is with all three groups. Thus all things in existence were formed through the blessing of the mention of his Name, its presence among them, and their witnessing of his nearness to His Almighty Lord. So the angels mentioned it over the earth and it settled; over the heavens and they rose; over the joints of human beings and they softened by permission of Allah Most High; and over their eyes, so they were opened wide with the lights they contain. This is the meaning of his phrase *he from whom the secrets were sundered.* I [Ibn Mubārak] said: "So then, this is meaning of the statement in *Dalā'il al-Khayrāt*, 'and by the Name You have placed over night so that it became dark; and over day so that it became illumined; and over the heavens so that they rose; and over the earth so that it settled; and over the mountains so that they were anchored; and over the seas so that they flowed; and over the springs so that they emerged; and over the clouds so that they rained?'" He said: "Yes, and that Name is the Name of our Prophet and Liegelord Muḥammad. By his blessing all creation was formed, and Allah knows best."[248]

[248] Ibn Mubārak, *Ibrīz* (p. 385; *Bāb 7 fī tafsīrih li-baʿḍi mā ushkila ʿalaynā*); *Dalā'il al-Khayrāt*: in *ḥizb yawm al-khamīs* and *ḥizb yawm al-jumuʿa.*

وقال الشيخ علي بن مبارك أيضاً: سمعته رضي الله عنه يقول في شرح قوله (اللّٰهُمَّ صَلِّ عَلَى مَنْ مِنْهُ انْشَقَّتِ الأَسْرَارُ)، حاكياً عن سيدي محمد بن عبد الكريم البصراوي رضي الله عنه وكيل ديوان الأولياء:

إِنَّ اللهَ تَعَالَى لَمَّا أَرَادَ إِخْرَاجَ بَرَكَاتِ الْأَرْضِ وَأَسْرَارِهَا مِثْلَ مَا فِيهَا مِنَ الْعُيُونِ وَالْآبَارِ وَالْأَنْهَارِ وَالْأَشْجَارِ وَالثِّمَارِ وَالْأَزْهَارِ، أَرْسَلَ سَبْعِينَ أَلْفِ مَلَكٍ إِلَى سَبْعِينَ أَلْفِ مَلَكٍ إِلَى سَبْعِينَ أَلْفِ مَلَكٍ، ثَلَاثَ سَبْعِينَاتٍ مِنَ الْأُلُوفِ، فَنَزَلُوا يَطُوفُونَ فِي الْأَرْضِ. فَالسَّبْعُونَ الْأُولَى يَذْكُرُونَ اسْمَ النَّبِيِّ ﷺ، وَمُرَادُنَا بِالْإِسْمِ الإِسْمُ الْعَالِي – وَالإِسْمُ الْعَالِي هُوَ الَّذِي يُشْعِرُ بِأَصْلِ الْمُسَمَّى وَمِنْ أَيِّ شَيْءٍ هُوَ وَبِفَائِدَةِ الْمُسَمَّى، فَيُعْلَمُ مِنْ مُجَرَّدِ سَمَاعِ لَفْظِهِ هٰذِهِ الْعُلُومُ وَالْمَعَارِفُ الْمُتَعَلِّقَةُ بِهِ – وَالسَّبْعُونَ الثَّانِيَةُ يَذْكُرُونَ قُرْبَهُ ﷺ مِنْ رَبِّهِ عَزَّ وَجَلَّ وَمَنْزِلَتَهُ ﷺ مِنْهُ، وَالسَّبْعُونَ الثَّالِثَةُ تُصَلِّي عَلَيْهِ ﷺ، وَنُورُهُ ﷺ مَعَ الطَّوَائِفِ الثَّلَاثِ. فَتَكَوَّنَتِ الْكَائِنَاتُ بِبَرَكَةِ ذِكْرِ اسْمِهِ ﷺ، وَحُضُورِهِ بَيْنَهَا، وَمُشَاهَدَتِهَا قُرْبَهُ ﷺ مِنْ رَبِّهِ عَزَّ وَجَلَّ. قَالَ: وَذَكَرُوهُ عَلَى الْأَرْضِ فَاسْتَقَرَّتْ، وَعَلَى السَّمٰوَاتِ فَاسْتَقَلَّتْ، وَعَلَى مَفَاصِلِ ذَاتِ ابْنِ آدَمَ فَلَانَتْ بِإِذْنِ اللهِ تَعَالَى، وَعَلَى مَوَاضِعِ عَيْنَيْهِ فَفُتِّحَتْ بِالْأَنْوَارِ الَّتِي فِيهَا، فَهٰذَا مَعْنَى قَوْلِهِ: (مِنْهُ انْشَقَّتِ الأَسْرَارُ). فَقُلْتُ – القائل هو الشيخ علي بن مبارك – فَهٰذَا مَعْنَى قَوْلِ دَلَائِلِ الْخَيْرَاتِ: (وَبِالْإِسْمِ الَّذِي وَضَعْتَهُ عَلَى اللَّيْلِ فَأَظْلَمَ، وَعَلَى النَّهَارِ فَاسْتَنَارَ، وَعَلَى السَّمٰوَاتِ فَاسْتَقَلَّتْ، وَعَلَى الْأَرْضِ فَاسْتَقَرَّتْ،

وَعَلَى الْجِبَالِ فَرَسَتْ، وَعَلَى الْبِحَارِ فَجَرَتْ، وَعَلَى الْعُيُونِ فَنَبَعَتْ، وَعَلَى السَّحَابِ فَأَمْطَرَتْ)؟ فَقَالَ رَضِيَ اللهُ عَنْهُ: نَعَمْ، ذٰلِكَ الإِسْمُ هُوَ إِسْمُ نَبِيِّنَا وَمَوْلَانَا مُحَمَّدٍ ﷺ، فَبِبَرَكَتِهِ تَكَوَّنَتِ الْكَائِنَاتُ، وَاللهُ أَعْلَمُ.

The Prophet Intercedes for Hundreds of Billions

Another report from ʿĀ'isha states:

178. The Messenger of Allah spent the night by my side then he rose from bed. I looked for him and did not find him, then I heard his movement as he prayed. I made ablution then stood in prayer behind him. The Messenger of Allah supplicated his fill that night. Then a great light came and illuminated the entire house. It stayed for as long as Allah willed then it disappeared, while the Messenger of Allah continued to supplicate. [Then another great light came and illuminated the entire house.] It stayed for as long as Allah willed [then it disappeared, while the Prophet continued to supplicate]. Then another light came, more powerful than all that preceded, to the point that if I had been searching for a mustard-seed in the house I could have picked it up. Then the Messenger of Allah ended his prayer. I asked, "Messenger of Allah, what was that light I saw?" He said, "Did you see that, ʿĀ'isha?" I said yes. He continued: "I petitioned my Lord regarding my Nation, so He gave me one third of them; so I praised Him and thanked Him. Then I asked him for the rest, so He gave me the second third, and I praised Him and thanked Him. Then I asked Him for the third third, so He gave it to me, and I praised Him and thanked Him."[249]

[249] Abū Nuʿaym, *Ḥilya* (10:130 *sub* Muḥammad b. ʿAmr al-Maghribī).

قَالَتْ عَائِشَةُ رَضِيَ اللهُ عَنْهَا: بَاتَ رَسُولُ اللهِ ﷺ إِلَى جَانِبِي ثُمَّ اسْتَيْقَظَ فَاسْتَوْحَشْتُ لَهُ، فَسَمِعْتُ حِسَّهُ يُصَلِّي، فَتَوَضَّأْتُ ثُمَّ جِئْتُ فَصَلَّيْتُ وَرَاءَهُ، فَدَعَا رَسُولُ اللهِ ﷺ مَا شَاءَ مِنَ اللَّيْلِ، فَجَاءَ نُورٌ حَتَّى أَضَاءَ الْبَيْتَ كُلَّهُ فَمَكَثَ مَا شَاءَ اللهُ، ثُمَّ ذَهَبَ وَرَسُولُ اللهِ ﷺ يَدْعُو، [ثُمَّ جَاءَ نُورٌ حَتَّى أَضَاءَ الْبَيْتَ كُلَّهُ] فَمَكَثَ مَا شَاءَ اللهُ، [ثُمَّ ذَهَبَ وَرَسُولُ اللهِ ﷺ يَدْعُو،] ثُمَّ جَاءَ نُورٌ هُوَ أَشَدُّ مِنْ ذٰلِكَ كُلِّهِ ضَوْءاً حَتَّى لَوْ كَانَ الْخَرْدَلُ فِي بَيْتِي فَشِئْتُ أَنْ أَلْتَقِطَهُ لَلَقَطْتُهُ، ثُمَّ انْصَرَفَ رَسُولُ اللهِ ﷺ فَقُلْتُ: يَا رَسُولَ اللهِ مَا هٰذَا النُّورُ الَّذِي رَأَيْتُ؟ قَالَ: وَقَدْ رَأَيْتِيهِ يَا عَائِشَةُ؟ قُلْتُ نَعَمْ يَا رَسُولَ اللهِ. قَالَ: إِنِّي سَأَلْتُ رَبِّي فِي أُمَّتِي فَأَعْطَانِي الثُّلُثَ مِنْهُمْ، فَحَمِدْتُهُ وَشَكَرْتُهُ ثُمَّ سَأَلْتُهُ الْبَقِيَّةَ فَأَعْطَانِي الثُّلُثَ الثَّانِي، فَحَمِدْتُهُ وَشَكَرْتُهُ ثُمَّ سَأَلْتُهُ الثُّلُثَ الثَّالِثَ فَأَعْطَانِيهِ فَحَمِدْتُهُ وَشَكَرْتُهُ. رواه أبو نعيم

The triple Divine Promise in the above report recurs in a number-specific sound hadith from Abū Umāma:

179. My Lord has promised me to bring 70,000 of my Community into Paradise without any account nor punishment, and with each thousand of them 70,000 more, and three such scoops from the scoops of my Lord.[250]

[250] al-Tirmidhī, *Sunan* (*Ṣifat al-Qiyāma wal-raqā'iq wal-wara'*, *bāb* 11, *ḥasan*); Ibn Mājah, *Sunan* (*Zuhd, ṣifat Ummat Muḥammad*); Aḥmad (36:639 §22303); al-Baghawī, *Sharḥ al-Sunna* (15:164).

عَنْ أَبِي أُمَامَةَ رَضِيَ اللهُ عَنْهُ قَالَ سَمِعْتُ رَسُولَ اللهِ ﷺ يَقُولُ وَعَدَنِي رَبِّي أَنْ يُدْخِلَ الجَنَّةَ مِنْ أُمَّتِي سَبْعِينَ أَلْفاً لَا حِسَابَ عَلَيْهِمْ وَلَا عَذَابَ، مَعَ كُلِّ أَلْفٍ سَبْعُونَ أَلْفاً، وَثَلَاثُ حَثَيَاتٍ مِنْ حَثَيَاتِ رَبِّي الترمذي وحسّنه وابن ماجه وأحمد.

Other authentic versions clarify that the three Divine scoops are *in addition* to the figure of 70x70,000 given above:

180. [Abū Umāma al-Bāhilī:] "Allah has promised me to enter into Paradise 70,000 of my Community without account." Yazīd b. al-Akhnas said: "By Allah, that number in comparison to your Community is like the red fly inside the rest of the flies!" The Messenger of Allah said: "My Lord had promised me 70,000 and with each thousand 70,000, and He increased it for me with three scoops."[251]

عَنْ أَبِي أُمَامَةَ الْبَاهِلِيِّ رَضِيَ اللهُ عَنْهُ أَنَّ رَسُولَ اللهِ ﷺ قَالَ: إِنَّ اللهَ عَزَّ وَجَلَّ وَعَدَنِي أَنْ يُدْخِلَ مِنْ أُمَّتِي الجَنَّةَ سَبْعِينَ أَلْفًا بِغَيْرِ حِسَابٍ. فَقَالَ يَزِيدُ بْنُ الْأَخْنَسِ السُّلَمِيُّ وَاللهِ مَا أُولَئِكَ فِي أُمَّتِكَ إِلَّا كَالذُّبَابِ الْأَصْهَبِ فِي الذِّبَّانِ. فَقَالَ رَسُولُ اللهِ ﷺ كَانَ رَبِّي عَزَّ وَجَلَّ قَدْ وَعَدَنِي سَبْعِينَ أَلْفًا، مَعَ كُلِّ أَلْفٍ سَبْعُونَ أَلْفًا، وَزَادَنِي ثَلَاثَ حَثَيَاتٍ. أحمد وابن أبي عاصم والطبراني والبيهقي.

181. [Abū Sa'īd al-Anmārī, also known as Abū Sa'd al-Khayr al-Anṣārī:] Truly my Lord has promised me that 70,000 of my Community will enter Paradise without account, each thousand of whom will intercede for another 70,000. After that my Lord will scoop up three [additional] scoops with His Hands. Qays al-Kindī

[251] Aḥmad (36:479-480 §22156) and others.

[the *Tābiʿī* sub-narrator] said: "I grabbed Abū Saʿīd by his garment and pulled him to me suddenly, and said: 'My father be sacrificed for you! Did you really hear this from the Messenger of Allah?'" Abū Saʿīd said: "Yes, I heard it with my two ears and my heart preserved it. Then this was computed before the Messenger of Allah and it reached four million and 900,000.[252] He said: "Truly this will cover, if Allah wills, all the emigrants of my Community; and Allah Most High will make up the difference for us from among our bedouins."[253]

عَنْ أَبِي سَعِيدٍ الأَنْمَارِيِّ وَيُعْرَفُ بِأَبِي سَعْدِ الخَيرِ الأَنْصَارِيِّ رَضِيَ اللهُ عَنْهُ أَنَّ رَسُولَ اللهِ ﷺ قَالَ: إِنَّ رَبِّي وَعَدَنِي أَنْ يُدْخِلَ الجَنَّةَ مِنْ أُمَّتِي سَبْعِينَ أَلْفًا بِغَيْرِ حِسَابٍ، وَيَشْفَعُ كُلُّ أَلْفٍ لِسَبْعِينَ أَلْفًا، ثُمَّ يُحْثِي رَبِّي ثَلَاثَ حَثَيَاتٍ بِكَفَّيْهِ قَالَ قَيْسٌ: فَأَخَذْتُ بِتَلَابِيبِ أَبِي سَعِيدٍ فَجَذَبْتُهُ جَذْبَةً وَقُلْتُ: بِأَبِي سَمِعْتَ مِنْ رَسُولِ ﷺ هَذَا؟ قَالَ: نَعَمْ ، بِأُذُنَيَّ وَوَعَاهُ قَلْبِي. فَحُسِبَ ذَٰلِكَ عِنْدَ رَسُولِ اللهِ ﷺ فَبَلَغَ أَرْبَعَ أَلْفِ أَلْفٍ وَتِسْعَ مِائَةِ أَلْفٍ. فَقَالَ رَسُولُ اللهِ ﷺ إِنَّ ذَٰلِكَ يَسْتَوْعِبُ إِنْ شَاءَ اللهُ تَعَالَى مُهَاجِرِي أُمَّتِي وَيُوفِينَا اللهُ تَعَالَى مِنْ أَعْرَابِنَا. ابن أبي عاصم وروى نحوه الطبراني وأبو نعيم. وفي المطبوع فَبَلَغَ أَرْبَعَ مِائَةِ أَلْفِ أَلْفٍ وَتِسْعَ مِائَةِ أَلْفٍ وهو بيّن الخطأ.

182. [ʿUtba b. ʿAbd al-Sulamī:] "Truly my Lord has promised me to enter into Paradise of my Community 70,000 without account, then to let 70,000 more follow each thousand, and then to scoop

[252] The text in Ibn Abī ʿĀṣim has "four hundred million and 900,000" which is contradicted by the rest of the hadith since 70x70,000 = 4,970,000.

[253] Ibn Abī ʿĀṣim, *Sunna* (1:554-556 §835) and *Āḥād* (5:297-298 §1027). A slightly shorter wording is narrated in al-Ṭabarānī's *Kabir* (22:304-305 §771) and *Awsaṭ* (1:128-129 §404), and Abū Nuʿaym's *Maʿrifa* (*sub* Abū Saʿd al-Khayr al-Anmārī).

up with His hand three scoops." 'Umar said: *Allāhu akbar!* The Prophet continued: "He will let the first 70,000 intercede for their fathers and mothers, and I hope that Allah will put my Community in the first of the last two scoops."[254]

عَنْ عُتْبَةَ بْنِ عَبْدٍ السُّلَمِيِّ: قَالَ رَسُولُ اللهِ ﷺ: إِنَّ رَبِّي وَعَدَنِي أَنْ يُدْخِلَ مِنْ أُمَّتِي الجَنَّةَ سَبْعِينَ أَلْفاً بِغَيْرِ حِسَابٍ ثُمَّ يُتْبِعَ كُلَّ أَلْفٍ بِسَبْعِينَ أَلْفاً ثُمَّ يُحْثِي بِكَفِّهِ ثَلَاثَ حَثَيَاتٍ فَكَبَّرَ عُمَرُ، فَقَالَ النَّبِيُّ ﷺ: إِنَّ السَّبْعِينَ أَلْفَ الأُوَلَ يُشَفِّعُهُمْ فِي آبَائِهِمْ وَأُمَّهَاتِهِمْ، وَأَرْجُو أَنْ يَجْعَلَ اللهُ أُمَّتِي أَدْنَى الحَثَوَاتِ الْأَوَاخِرَ. الفسوي في المعرفة والتاريخ والطبراني وابن حبان واللفظ له والبيهقي.

183. [al-Faltān b. 'Āṣim:] We were sitting with the Prophet in the mosque when his gaze fell on a man walking in the mosque. He said: "Abū Fulān!" The man replied: "At your service, Messenger of Allah!" and he would not speak except he said "Messenger of Allah." The Prophet said: "Do you bear witness that I am the Messenger of Allah?" He said: "No." The Prophet said: "Do you read the Torah?" He said yes. "And the *Injīl*?" He said yes. "And the Qur'ān?" He said: "By the One in Whose Hand is my soul, if I wished I would read it." Then the Prophet made him swear and said: "Do you not find me mentioned in the Torah and the *Injīl*?" He replied: "We do find something identical to you, your Community, and your origin; and we were hoping that you would be among us. But when you came out, we feared that it might be you, so we investigated and we concluded that it was not you." The Prophet said: "Why so?" He said: "Because he will have with him 70,000 of his Community who will have no account and no punishment, whereas you only have with you a small group." The Prophet said: "By the One in Whose Hand is my soul, truly I am

[254] Ibn Ḥibbān, *Ṣaḥīḥ* (16:231-232 §7247), al-Fasawī, *al-Ma'rifa wal-Tārīkh* (2:341-342), al-Ṭabarānī, *Kabīr* (17:126-127 §312), al-Bayhaqī, *al-Ba'th* (p. 169-170 §300).

that one, and truly they are my Community, and truly they are more than 70,000, and 70,000, and 70,000!"[255]

عَنِ الْفَلْتَانِ بْنِ عَاصِمٍ رَضِيَ اللهُ عَنْهُ قَالَ كُنَّا قُعُودًا مَعَ النَّبِيِّ ﷺ فِي الْمَسْجِدِ فَشَخَصَ بَصَرُهُ إِلَى رَجُلٍ يَمْشِي فِي الْمَسْجِدِ فَقَالَ: أَبَا فُلاَنٍ! قَالَ: لَبَّيْكَ يَا رَسُولَ اللهِ، وَلاَ يُنَازِعُهُ الْكَلاَمَ إِلَّا قَالَ: يَا رَسُولَ اللهِ. قَالَ: أَتَشْهَدُ أَنِّي رَسُولُ اللهِ؟ قَالَ: لاَ. قَالَ: أَتَقْرَأُ التَّوْرَاةَ؟ قَالَ: نَعَمْ. قَالَ: وَالإِنْجِيلَ؟ قَالَ: نَعَمْ. قَالَ: وَالْقُرْآنَ؟ قَالَ: وَالَّذِي نَفْسِي بِيَدِهِ لَوْ أَشَاءُ لَقَرَأْتُهُ، قَالَ: ثُمَّ نَاشَدَهُ، قَالَ: مَا تَجِدُونِي فِي التَّوْرَاةِ، وَالإِنْجِيلِ؟ قَالَ: نَجِدُ مِثْلَكَ وَمِثْلَ أُمَّتِكَ وَمَخْرَجِكَ، وَكُنَّا نَرْجُو أَنْ تَكُونَ فِينَا، فَلَمَّا خَرَجْتَ تَخَوَّفْنَا أَنْ تَكُونَ أَنْتَ هُوَ، فَنَظَرْنَا فَإِذَا لَسْتَ أَنْتَ هُوَ. قَالَ: وَلِمَ ذَاكَ؟ قَالَ: إِنَّ مَعَهُ مِنْ أُمَّتِهِ سَبْعُونَ أَلْفاً لَيْسَ عَلَيْهِمْ حِسَابٌ وَلاَ عَذَابٌ، وَإِنَّمَا مَعَكَ نَفَرٌ يَسِيرٌ، قَالَ: وَالَّذِي نَفْسِي بِيَدِهِ لَأَنَا هُوَ، وَإِنَّهُمْ لَأُمَّتِي، وَإِنَّهُمْ لَأَكْثَرُ مِنْ سَبْعِينَ أَلْفًا، وَسَبْعِينَ أَلْفًا، وَسَبْعِينَ أَلْفًا. البزار والطبراني وابن حبان واللفظ له والبيهقي.

The astronomical three thirds and three scoops are further confirmed by the following hadith from Anas narrated with strong chains:

184. "Truly Allah has promised me to put in Paradise 400,000 of my Community without any account." Abū Bakr said, "Increase us, O Prophet of Allah!" He said, "And like that," and he gathered up his two hands. Then Abū Bakr said, "Increase us, O Prophet of Allah!" He said, "and like that!" Then ʿUmar said, "Enough, Abū Bakr!" but Abū Bakr said, "Let me be me, ʿUmar! What would

[255] al-Bazzār, *Musnad* (9:144-145 §3700); al-Ṭabarānī, *Kabīr* (18:332-333 §854); Ibn Ḥibbān, *Ṣaḥīḥ* (14:541-542 §6580); al-Bayhaqī, *Dalā'il* (6:273).

you lose if Allah entered all of us into Paradise?" Whereupon ʿUmar exclaimed: "Truly Allah the Exalted, if He wants, will enter all His creation into Paradise with one hand." The Prophet said: "ʿUmar speaks the truth."[256]

عَنْ أَنَسٍ رَضِيَ اللهُ عَنْهُ مَرْفُوعاً: إِنَّ اللهَ عَزَّ وَجَلَّ وَعَدَنِي أَنْ يُدْخِلَ الجَنَّةَ مِنْ أُمَّتِي أَرْبَعَمِائَةِ أَلْفٍ بِلَا حِسَابٍ. فَقَالَ أَبُو بَكْرٍ زِدْنَا يَا رَسُولَ اللهِ. فَقَالَ: وَهٰكَذَا. فَحَثَا بِكَفَّيْهِ وَجَمَعَهَا. فَقَالَ أَبُو بَكْرٍ: زِدْنَا يَا رَسُولَ اللهِ. فَقَالَ: وَهٰكَذَا. فَقَالَ عُمَرُ: دَعْنَا يَا أَبَا بَكْرٍ. فَقَالَ أَبُو بَكْرٍ: وَمَا عَلَيْكَ أَنْ يُدْخِلَنَا اللهُ كُلَّنَا الجَنَّةَ؟ فَقَالَ عُمَرُ: إِنَّ اللهَ عَزَّ وَجَلَّ إِنْ شَاءَ أَدْخَلَ خَلْقَهُ الجَنَّةَ بِكَفٍّ وَاحِدَةٍ. فَقَالَ النَّبِيُّ ﷺ صَدَقَ عُمَرُ. رواه أحمد وعبد الرزاق بإسناد صحيح على شرط الشيخين.

Another version of the above events from Abū Hurayra shows Abū Bakr and ʿUmar in reverse roles:

185. I asked Allah to let me intercede for my Community and He said: "You will have 70,000 who will enter Paradise without account." I said, "O my Lord, increase it for me." He said: "Truly there will be, for each thousand of them, another 70,000 who will enter Paradise without account." I said, "O my Lord, increase it for me." He said: "Truly, you will have this much," and he took one scoop from his front, one from his right, and one from his left. Abū Bakr said: "That is enough for us, Messenger of Allah." Then ʿUmar said: "Abū Bakr, let the Messenger of Allah give us in abundance just as Allah gave us in abundance!" Abū Bakr said:

[256] ʿAbd al-Razzāq, *Muṣannaf* (11:286 §20556); Aḥmad, *Musnad* (19:121-122 §12695); al-Ṭabarānī in *al-Ṣaghīr* (1:124); al-Baghawī, *Sharḥ al-Sunna* (15:163-164 §4335); al-Bayhaqī, *Asmā'* (2:153-154 §721). Abū Nuʿaym in the *Ḥilya* (2:234) narrates it with 100,000 instead of 400,000.

"We are nothing but a handful (*ḥafna*) from the handfuls of Allah Almighty." The Prophet said: "Abū Bakr speaks the truth."[257]

عَنْ أَبِي هُرَيرَةَ رَضِيَ اللهُ عَنْهُ قَالَ رَسُولُ اللهِ ﷺ سَأَلْتُ اللهَ عَزَّ وَجَلَّ الشَّفَاعَةَ لِأُمَّتِي فَقَالَ: لَكَ سَبْعُونَ أَلْفًا يَدْخُلُونَ الجَنَّةَ بِغَيْرِ حِسَابٍ. فَقُلْتُ رَبِّ زِدْنِي. قَالَ: فَإِنَّ لَكَ مَعَ كُلِّ أَلْفٍ سَبْعِينَ أَلْفًا يَدْخُلُونَ الجَنَّةَ بِغَيْرِ حِسَابٍ. فَقُلْتُ: رَبِّ زِدْنِي. قَالَ: فَإِنَّ لَكَ هَكَذَا، فَحَثَى بَيْنَ يَدَيْهِ وَعَنْ يَمِينِهِ وَعَنْ شِمَالِهِ فَقَالَ أَبُو بَكْرٍ رَضِيَ اللهُ عَنْهُ: حَسْبُنَا يَا رَسُولَ اللهِ. فَقَالَ عُمَرُ رَضِيَ اللهُ عَنْهُ: يَا أَبَا بَكْرٍ، دَعْ رَسُولَ اللهِ ﷺ يُكْثِرُ لَنَا كَمَا أَكْثَرَ اللهُ لَنَا. فَقَالَ أَبُو بَكْرٍ: إِنَّمَا نَحْنُ حَفْنَةٌ مِنْ حَفَنَاتِ اللهِ عَزَّ وَجَلَّ. فَقَالَ رَسُولُ اللهِ ﷺ صَدَقَ أَبُو بَكْرٍ. ابن الجعد وهنّاد في الزهد وابن أبي شيبة والآجري والكلاباذي في معاني الأخيار.

A narration from Abū Bakr's son, ʿAbd al-Raḥmān b. Abī Bakr al-Ṣiddīq, reveals ʿUmar repeatedly asking the Prophet to intercede for more:

186. "Truly my Blessed Lord has given me 70,000 of my Community who will enter Paradise without account." ʿUmar said: "Did you not ask Him for more?" The Prophet said: "I did ask Him for more and He gave me for each thousand an additional 70,000." ʿUmar said: "Did you not ask Him for more?" The Prophet said: "I did ask Him for more and He gave me for each man an additional 70,000." ʿUmar said: "Did you not ask Him for more?" The Prophet said: "He gave me this much." Al-Sahmī – Aḥmad b. Ḥanbal's shaykh – spread out his hands and said: "He stretched out his arms," then he gestured in a scooping motion. Hishām b.

[257] Ibn al-Jaʿd, *Musnad* (2:1018-1019 §2951); Hannād, *Zuhd* (p. 135-136 §178); Ibn Abī Shayba, *Muṣannaf* (16:470-471 §32397); al-Ājurrī, *Sharīʿa* (2:1127-1228 §795); al-Kalābādhī, *Baḥr* (1:238-239 §181).

Ḥassān – al-Sahmī's shaykh – said: "This, on the part of Allah, is impossible to compute." [258]

عَنْ عَبْدِ الرَّحْمَنِ بْنِ أَبِي بَكْرٍ رَضِيَ اللهُ عَنْهُمَا أَنَّ رَسُولَ اللهِ ﷺ قَالَ: إِنَّ رَبِّي تَبَارَكَ وَتَعَالَى أَعْطَانِي سَبْعِينَ أَلْفًا مِنْ أُمَّتِي يَدْخُلُونَ الْجَنَّةَ بِغَيْرِ حِسَابٍ، فَقَالَ عُمَرُ رَضِيَ اللهُ عَنْهُ: فَهَلَّا اسْتَزَدْتَهُ؟ قَالَ: قَدِ اسْتَزَدْتُهُ، فَأَعْطَانِي مَعَ كُلِّ – يَعْنِي أَلْفًا – سَبْعِينَ أَلْفًا، فَقَالَ : فَهَلَّا اسْتَزَدْتَهُ؟ قَالَ: قَدِ اسْتَزَدْتُهُ، فَأَعْطَانِي مَعَ كُلِّ رَجُلٍ سَبْعِينَ أَلْفًا، فَقَالَ عُمَرُ رَضِيَ اللهُ عَنْهُ: فَهَلَّا اسْتَزَدْتَهُ، فَقَالَ: أَعْطَانِي هٰكَذَا، وَفَرَّجَ عَبْدُ اللهِ بْنُ بَكْرٍ – السَّهْمِيُّ شيخ أحمد – بَيْنَ يَدَيْهِ وَقَالَ عَبْدُ اللهِ: وَبَسَطَ بَاعَيْهِ، وَحَثَا عَبْدُ اللهِ. و قَالَ هِشَامٌ – أي هِشَامُ بْنُ حَسَّانَ شيخ السَّهمِي – وَهَذَا مِنَ اللهِ لَا يُدْرَى مَا عَدَدُهُ. أحمد وأبو يعلى والطبراني والبزار.

The Sufi hadith master Abū Bakr al-Kalābādhī (d. 380/990) said:

187. There are two meanings in the Prophet's scooping from his right and his left: abundance and admixture (*al-kathra wal-ikhtilāṭ*). This is because someone who scoops up right and left does not make any difference in what he takes; he does not pick and choose or leave something out, but rather takes whatever ends up in his grasp no matter what it is and no matter in what condition.... [259]

قال الكلاباذي رحمه الله في بحر الفوائد: فِي حَثْيَةِ النَّبِيِّ ﷺ عَنْ يَمِينِهِ وَشِمَالِهِ مَعْنَيَانِ: الْكَثْرَةُ وَالإِخْتِلَاطُ، وَذٰلِكَ أَنَّ مَنْ حَثَى عَنْ يَمِينِهِ وَشِمَالِهِ لَا يُمَيِّزُ

[258] Aḥmad, *Musnad* (3:232-233 §1706); al-Bazzār, *Musnad* (6:234 §2268); al-Ṭabarānī, *Musnad al-Shāmiyyīn* (4:382 §3612).
[259] al-Kalābādhī, *Baḥr* (1:239).

وَلَا يَخْتَارُ فَيَأْخُذُ شَيْئاً وَيَدَعُ آخَرَ، وَلَكِنَّهُ يَأْخُذُ مَا حَصَلَ فِي قَبْضَتِهِ مِنْ أَيِّ شَيْءٍ كَانَ، وَعَلَى أَيِّ صِفَةٍ كَانَ، وَمَا كَانَ مِنَ الْعَدُوِّ. فَكَانَ النَّبِيُّ ﷺ أَعْلَمَ بِحَثْيِهِ أَنَّ الَّذِينَ شَفَّعَهُ اللهُ تَعَالَى فِيهِمْ يَجُوزُ الْعَدَدُ كَثْرَةً وَالصِّفَةُ جَمِيعاً، فَكَأَنَّهُ يَقُولُ: شَفَّعَنِي اللهُ تَعَالَى فِي أُمَّتِي بِغَايَةٍ مِنَ الْكَثْرَةِ لَا يُحْصَى عَدَدُهُمْ، وَلَا يُعْرَفُ أَوْصَافُهُمْ مُسِيئِينَ كَانُوا أَوْ مُحْسِنِينَ، أَصْحَابَ صَغَائِرَ كَانُوا أَوْ كَبَائِرَ. يَدُلُّ عَلَى ذَلِكَ قَوْلُهُ ﷺ: **شَفَاعَتِي لِأَهْلِ الْكَبَائِرِ مِنْ أُمَّتِي.**

The first batch of these saved souls will appear on the Resurrection in the form of full moons as narrated fom Abū Hurayra:

188. I petitioned my Lord and He promised me to enter into Paradise, of my Community, 70,000 in the form of the full moon. I asked Him for more, so He gave me more, with each thousand 70,000 more. I said: "O my Lord, what if those are not of the emigrants of my Community?" He said: "In that case I will complete them for you with the Bedouins."[260]

عَنْ أَبِي هُرَيْرَةَ عَنْ رَسُولِ اللهِ ﷺ أَنَّهُ قَالَ سَأَلْتُ رَبِّي عَزَّ وَجَلَّ فَوَعَدَنِي أَنْ يُدْخِلَ مِنْ أُمَّتِي سَبْعِينَ أَلْفًا عَلَى صُورَةِ الْقَمَرِ لَيْلَةَ الْبَدْرِ فَاسْتَزَدْتُ فَزَادَنِي مَعَ كُلِّ أَلْفٍ سَبْعِينَ أَلْفًا فَقُلْتُ أَيْ رَبِّ إِنْ لَمْ يَكُنْ هَؤُلَاءِ مُهَاجِرِي أُمَّتِي قَالَ إِذَنْ أُكْمِلُهُمْ لَكَ مِنَ الْأَعْرَابِ. أحمد وابن الأعرابي في المعجم والبيهقي.

Another wording of the same narration from Abū Hurayra implies that (i) all the batches of 70,000 will be negotiating the Bridge

[260] Aḥmad, *Musnad* (14:326-327 §8707); Ibn al-Aʿrābī, *Muʿjam* 3:401 §1397); al-Bayhaqī, *al-Baʿth* (p. 229 §460).

overpassing Hellfire but (ii) at different speeds and (iii) their light will be protecting them from its blaze:

189. "Truly I will be passing [the Bridge] with a host of 70,000 in the image of the full moon, like lightning." They said: "Messenger of Allah, only 70,000 will enter Paradise?" He said: "With each thousand of them there will be 70,000 more. They will be passing like the wind; then like race horses; then like travelling camels; then like a man running. The last of those who pass over the Bridge will be a man with a thin strand of light on his thumb. The Fire will burn him in places, so they will take him to the River of Life and wash him."[261]

وجاء بلفظ: إِنِّي أَمُرُّ فِي زُمْرَةِ سَبْعِينَ أَلْفاً عَلَى صُورَةِ الْقَمَرِ لَيْلَةَ الْبَدْرِ كَهَيْئَةِ الْبَرْقِ. قَالُوا يَا رَسُولَ الله مَا يَدْخُلُ الجَنَّةَ غَيْرُ سَبْعِينَ أَلْفاً؟ قال: مَعَ كُلِّ أَلْفٍ سَبْعُونَ أَلْفاً ثُمَّ يَمُرُّونَ كَالرِّيحِ وَكَحُضْرِ الْفَرَسِ وَكَأَيْضَاعِ الْبَعِيرِ وَكَشَدِّ الرَّجُلِ ثُمَّ يَكُونُ آخِرُ مَنْ يَمُرُّ عَلَى الصِّرَاطِ رَجُلٌ يَكُونُ عَلَى إِبْهَامِهِ كَشِرَاكِ النَّعْلِ مِنْ نُورٍ فَتُصِيبُ النَّارُ مِنْهُ فَيُنْطَلَقُ بِهِ إِلَى نَهْرِ الحَيَاةِ فَيَغْتَسِلُونَ الدارقطني وأبو نعيم. وفي الباب عَنْ عَامِرِ بْنِ عُمَيْرٍ رَضِيَ اللهُ عَنْهُ قَالَ: لَبِثَ رَسُولُ الله ﷺ ثَلاَثًا لاَ يَخْرُجُ إِلَّا إِلَى صَلاَةٍ مَكْتُوبَةٍ. الحديث رواه الطبراني وابن سعد والبيهقي.

The Companion ʿĀmir b. ʿUmayr narrates something similar in a hadith beginning "The Prophet for three days did not come out except for the obligatory prayer…"[262] This shows that the Prophet

[261] al-Dāraquṭnī, *al-Mu'talif wal-Mukhtalif* (2:846); Abū al-Shaykh, *Ṭabaqāt* (2:351-352 §283).

[262] al-Ṭabarānī, *al-Kabīr* cf. al-Haythamī, *Majma*ʿ (10:410); Ibn Saʿd, *Ṭabaqāt* (9:73 §3761 *sub* ʿAmr b. ʿUmayr); and al-Bayhaqī, *al-Baʿth* (p. 229 §460) cf. al-Būṣīrī, *Itḥāf* (8:248 §7890).

was engaged in a deep Divine negotiation that caused him to absent himself for days as confirmed by the following narration from Abū Ayyūb al-Anṣārī:

190. The Messenger of Allah came out to see them and said: "Truly my Lord gave me the choice between 70,000 who will enter Paradise with complete amnesty, without any account, or, on the other hand, a scoopful [*var.* hidden gift (*khabī'a*)] on his part." A man said: "Messenger of Allah, let your Lord scoop for you!" [*var.* Messenger of Allah, your Lord keeps that hidden?]. Then the Messenger of Allah went back in. He came out again saying *Allāhu akbar!* and he said: "Truly my Lord has given me more, for every thousand 70,000 more will follow, and He will reserve the additional scoop with Him" [*var.* He will keep the hidden gift with Him]. Abū Ruhm [the *Tābi'ī* sub-narrator] said: "Abū Ayyūb, how much do you think the Divine scoop is?" [*var.* What do you think the gift hidden for the Messenger of Allah is?] People chewed him out [*add.* and said: "How dare you ask about the hidden gift of the Messenger of Allah?"] but Abū Ayyūb said: "Leave your friend [*var.* the man] alone. I will inform you about the scoop [*var.* hidden gift] of the Prophet as I think, or rather as I know for sure. The scoop [*var.* hidden gift] of the Prophet is that he will say: "My Lord! Whoever witnesses that there is no god but You, alone, without partner, and that Muḥammad is Your servant and Your Messenger, then his heart confirms what his tongue said, then Paradise is guaranteed for him [*var.* then enter him Paradise]."[263]

عَنْ أَبِي أَيُّوبَ رَضِيَ اللهُ عَنْهُ أَنَّ رَسُولَ اللهِ ﷺ خَرَجَ إِلَيْهِمْ فقَالَ إِنَّ رَبِّي عَزَّ وَجَلَّ خَيَّرَنِي بَيْنَ سَبْعِينَ أَلْفًا يَدْخُلُونَ الجَنَّةَ عَفْوًا بِغَيْرِ حِسَابٍ وَبَيْنَ الحَثْيَةِ عِنْدَهُ. فَقَالَ لَهُ رَجُلٌ يَا رَسُولَ اللهِ يَحْثِي لَكَ رَبُّكَ. فَدَخَلَ رَسُولُ اللهِ ﷺ ثُمَّ خَرَجَ إِلَيْهِمْ وَهُوَ يُكَبِّرُ فَقَالَ: إِنَّ رَبِّي عَزَّ وَجَلَّ زَادَنِي يَتْبَعُ كُلَّ أَلْفٍ سَبْعُونَ

[263] al-Ṭabarānī, *Kabīr* (4:127 §3882); Abū Nu'aym, *Ḥilya* (1:362-363). The variants and addendum are narrated in Aḥmad, *Musnad* (38:491 §23505).

أَلْفًا وَالحَثْيَةُ عِنْدَهُ، قَالَ أَبُو رُهْمٍ: يَا أَبَا أَيُّوبَ، وَمَا تَظُنُّ حَثْيَةَ اللهِ؟ فَأَكَلَهُ النَّاسُ بِأَفْوَاهِهِمْ، فَقَالَ أَبُو أَيُّوبَ: دَعُوا صَاحِبَكُمْ، أُخْبِرُكُمْ عَنْ حَثْيَةِ النَّبِيِّ ﷺ كَمَا أَظُنُّ بَلْ كَالمُسْتَيْقِنِ. حَثْيَةُ النَّبِيِّ ﷺ أَنْ يَقُولَ: رَبِّ مَنْ شَهِدَ أَنْ لَا إِلَهَ إِلَّا أَنْتَ وَحْدَكَ لَا شَرِيكَ لَكَ، وَأَنَّ مُحَمَّدًا عَبْدُكَ وَرَسُولُكَ، ثُمَّ يُصَدِّقُ قَلْبُهُ لِسَانَهُ، وَجَبَتْ لَهُ الجَنَّةُ. أحمد والطبراني وأبو نعيم.

Thus the Prophet interceded and was given two forms of intercession: a number-specific intercession for 70,000 then 70 times that, and an unspecified Divine intercession consisting of one to three scoops.

Similar to that already narrated from his son ʿAbd al-Raḥmān, Abū Bakr's own version cites a number-specific intercession for 70,000[2]:

> **191.** I was given 70,000 who will enter Paradise without account. Their faces will be like the full moon and their hearts will all conform to the heart of a single man. I asked my Lord for more, so He increased me, for each one, 70,000 more. Abū Bakr said: "We considered it to apply to townspeople and include deserts."[264]

عَنْ أَبِي بَكْرٍ الصِّدِّيقِ قَالَ رَسُولُ اللهِ ﷺ أُعْطِيتُ سَبْعِينَ أَلْفًا يَدْخُلُونَ الجَنَّةَ بِغَيْرِ حِسَابٍ وُجُوهُهُمْ كَالْقَمَرِ لَيْلَةَ الْبَدْرِ وَقُلُوبُهُمْ عَلَى قَلْبِ رَجُلٍ وَاحِدٍ، فَاسْتَزَدْتُ رَبِّي عَزَّ وَجَلَّ فَزَادَنِي مَعَ كُلِّ وَاحِدٍ سَبْعِينَ أَلْفًا. قَالَ أَبُو بَكْرٍ رَضِيَ اللهُ عَنْهُ فَرَأَيْتُ أَنَّ ذَلِكَ آتٍ عَلَى أَهْلِ الْقُرَى وَمُصِيبٌ مِنْ حَافَّاتِ الْبَوَادِي.

أحمد وأبو يعلى. وفي الباب عن عمرو بن حزم عند البيهقي.

[264] Aḥmad, *Musnad* (1:203 §22); Abū Yaʿlā, *Musnad* (1:104-105 §112).

The same is narrated from the Companion ʿAmr b. Ḥazm.[265]

In further confirmation of all that preceded al-Kalābādhī and Imam al-Ghazālī (450-505/1058-1111) cited yet another version of the triple light report from ʿĀ'isha:

192. One night I noticed that the Prophet was missing. I looked for him and found him in a small room, praying. I saw three lights over his head. When he finished his prayer he said: "Who is there?" I said: "It is I, ʿĀ'isha, Messenger of Allah." He said: "Did you see the three lights?" I said "Yes, Messenger of Allah." He said: "A visitor from my Lord came and gave me the glad tidings that Allah Most High will bring into Paradise, of my Community, 70,000 without account and without punishment. Then another visitor from my Lord came in the second light and gave me the glad tidings that Allah Most High will bring into Paradise, of my Community, for each one of the 70,000, another 70,000 without account and without punishment. Then another visitor from my Lord came in the third light and gave me the glad tidings that Allah Most High will bring into Paradise, of my Community, for each one of the squared 70,000, another 70,000 without account and without punishment. I said, 'O my Lord, my Community does not reach that number?' He replied: 'They will be completed with the Bedouins, those that neither pray nor fast.'"[266]

عَنْ عَائِشَةَ رَضِيَ اللهُ عَنْهَا قَالَتْ: فَقَدْتُ النَّبِيَّ ﷺ ذَات لَيْلَةٍ فَاتَّبَعْتُهُ – وفي رواية: فَابْتَغَيْتُهُ – فَإِذَا هُوَ فِي مَشْرُبَةٍ يُصَلِّي، فَرَأَيْتُ عَلَى رَأْسِهِ أَنْوَاراً ثَلَاثَةً. فَلَمَّا قَضَى صَلَاتَهُ قَالَ: مَهْيَمْ مَنْ هٰذِهِ؟ قُلْتُ: أَنَا عَائِشَةُ يَا رَسُولَ الله. قَالَ: هَلْ رَأَيْتِ الْأَنْوَارَ الثَّلَاثَةَ؟ فَقُلْتُ: نَعَمْ يَا رَسُولَ الله. فَقَالَ: إِنَّ آتِياً أَتَانِي مِنْ رَبِّي

[265] al-Bayhaqī, *Shuʿab* (1:429 §264).
[266] al-Kalābādhī, *Baḥr* (2:648-649 §756); al-Ghazālī, *Fayṣal* (p. 82-83) cf. Sherman Jackson, *On The Boundaries of Theological Tolerance in Islam: Abū Ḥāmid al-Ghazālī's* Fayṣal al-Tafriqa (Oxford: Oxford University Press, 2002) p. 125-126. Cf. Ibn Ḥajar, *Fatḥ* (11:411 *Riqāq, yadkhul al-Janna sabʿūna alfan bi-ghayri ḥisāb*).

فَبَشَّرَنِي أَنَّ اللهَ تَعَالَى يُدْخِلُ الجَنَّةَ مِنْ أُمَّتِي سَبْعِينَ أَلْفاً بِغَيْرِ حِسَابٍ وَلَا عَذَابٍ . ثُمَّ أَتَانِي فِي النُّورِ الثَّانِي آتٍ مِنْ رَبِّي فَبَشَّرَنِي أَنَّ اللهَ تَعَالَى يُدْخِلُ الجَنَّةَ مِنْ أُمَّتِي، مَكَانَ كُلِّ وَاحِدٍ مِنَ السَّبْعِينَ أَلْفاً، سَبْعِينَ أَلْفاً بِغَيْرِ حِسَابٍ وَلَا عَذَابٍ. ثُمَّ أَتَانِي فِي النُّورِ الثَّالِثِ آتٍ مِنْ رَبِّي فَبَشَّرَنِي أَنَّ اللهَ تَعَالَى يُدْخِلُ الجَنَّةَ مِنْ أُمَّتِي، مَكَانَ كُلِّ وَاحِدٍ مِنَ السَّبْعِينَ أَلْفاً المُضَاعَفَةِ، سَبْعِينَ أَلْفاً بِغَيْرِ حِسَابٍ وَلَا عَذَابٍ. فَقُلْتُ: يَا رَبِّ لَا تَبْلُغُ هٰذَا أُمَّتِي؟ قَالَ: يُكْمَلُونَ لَكَ مِنَ الْأَعْرَابِ، مَنْ لَا يُصَلِّي وَلَا يَصُومُ. رواه الحافظ الكلاباذي في بحر الفوائد وأورده حجة الإسلام الغزالي في كتاب فيصل التفرقة. قال الحافظ ابن حجر في الفتح سنده واه. ومَهْيَمْ كلمة يمانية معناها ما أمركم ما شأنكم؟ نهاية.

Al-Kalābādhī commented:

193. Scholars differed over who is meant by "the *Umma.*" Some said they are the people of the Islamic religion while others said they are everyone the Prophet was sent to and on whom the proof of his call is binding. The latter are of different types: (i) those he was sent to and who were summoned to Islam but did not respond, such as those who belong to the religious communities of the Christians, the Jews, and all the Polytheists. These all *will not enter Paradise until the camel passes through the eye of the needle* (7:40). (ii) Those who were summoned and responded; but they did not follow him with regard to practicing whatever their acceptance made obligatory on them: these are believers who accepted the call to the oneness of God, the Messengership of the Prophet, and the truth of everything he brought, even if they did not put into practice what they were commanded, due to indifference, isolation, or transgression. These are all part of the Community of Summoning and of Responding (*ummat al-daʿwa wal-ijāba*), but not the Community of Following (*ummat al-ittibāʿ*).

(iii) Those who accepted what they were summoned to and practiced what they were commanded. These are of the Community of Summoning, Responding, and Following.[267]

قال الكلاباذي في بحر الفوائد:

إِخْتَلَفَ النَّاسُ فِي الْأُمَّةِ مَنْ هُمْ؟ فَقَالَ قَوْمٌ: أَهْلُ المِلَّةِ؛ وَقَالَ آخَرُونَ: كُلُّ مَبْعُوثٍ إِلَيْهِ وَلَزِمَتْهُ الحُجَّةُ بِالدَّعْوَةِ. وَهٰؤُلَاءِ يَخْتَلِفُ أَحْوَالُهُمْ، فَمِنْهُمْ مَنْ بُعِثَ إِلَيْهِ وَدُعِيَ فَلَمْ يُجِبْ كَأَهْلِ الْأَدْيَانِ مِنْ أَهْلِ الْكِتَابِ وَسَائِرِ الْمُشْرِكِينَ: فَهٰؤُلَاءِ ﴿لَا يَدْخُلُونَ ٱلْجَنَّةَ حَتَّىٰ يَلِجَ ٱلْجَمَلُ فِى سَمِّ ٱلْخِيَاطِ﴾. الآية من سورة الأعراف. وَمِنْهُمْ مَنْ دُعِيَ فَأَجَابَ الدَّعْوَةَ، وَلَمْ يَتَّبِعْ مِنْ جِهَةِ اسْتِعْمَالِ مَا لَزِمَهُ بِالْإِجَابَةِ؛ فَهُوَ مُؤْمِنٌ بِإِجَابَتِهِ إِلَى مَا دُعِيَ إِلَيْهِ مِنْ تَوْحِيدِ اللهِ وَرِسَالَةِ النَّبِيِّ ﷺ وَبِمَا جَاءَ بِهِ أَنَّهُ حَقٌّ وَإِنْ لَمْ يَسْتَعْمِلْ مَا أُمِرَ بِهِ تَشَاغُلاً عَنْهُ وَخَلَاعَةً وَتَجَوُّزاً، فَهُمْ مِنْ أُمَّةِ الدَّعْوَةِ وَالْإِجَابَةِ وَلَيْسُوا مِنْ أُمَّةِ الإِتِّبَاعِ. وَمِنْهُمْ مَنْ أَجَابَ إِلَى مَا دُعِيَ وَاسْتَعْمَلَ مَا أُمِرَ بِهِ: فَهٰؤُلَاءِ مِنْ أُمَّةِ الدَّعْوَةِ وَالْإِجَابَةِ وَالإِتِّبَاعِ.

The basic wording of all the above narrations is narrated in the two *Ṣaḥīḥ*s and *Sunan* through several Companions.[268] The totality of the reports show the following literal scenarios of intercession in ascending order of magnitude:[269]

[267] al-Kalābādhī, *Baḥr al-Fawā'id* (2:649).
[268] al-Bukhārī, *Ṣaḥīḥ* (*Ṭibb, man lam yarqi*; *Libās, al-burūd wal-ḥibara wal-shamla*; and *Riqāq, yadkhulu al-janna sab'una alfan bi-ghayri ḥisāb*); Muslim, *Ṣaḥīḥ* (*Īmān, al-dalīl 'alā dukhūl ṭawā'if min al-muslimīn al-janna bi-ghayr ḥisāb* and *Ṣifat al-Qiyāma, nuzul ahl al-Janna*); etc.
[269] Cf. al-Būṣīrī, *Itḥāf* (8:244-245 *Bāb fī-man yadkhul al-Janna bi-ghayri ḥisāb*).

(i) Intercession for 70,000: narrated from Ibn ʿAbbās, Abū Saʿīd al-Khudrī, ʿImrān b. Ḥuṣayn, Abū Hurayra, Anas b. Mālik, Sahl b. Saʿd al-Sāʿidī, Ḍamḍam b. Zurʿa, Jābir b. ʿAbd Allāh, Rifāʿa b. ʿArāba, Samura b. Jundub and others. This is the most heavily documented and authentic category.

(ii) Intercession for 70,000 x 3 = 210,000: narrated from Faltān b. ʿĀṣim.

(iii) Intercession for 400,000 plus two scoops: Anas.

(iv) Intercession for 70,000 x 70 = 4,900,000 plus one scoop: Abū Ayyūb.

(v) Intercession for 70,000 x 70 = 4,900,000 plus three scoops: narrated from Abū Umāma, Abū Saʿīd al-Anmārī, ʿUtba b. ʿAbd, and Abū Hurayra. This is the second most heavily documented and authentic category.

(vi) intercession for 70,000 x 70,000 = 4,900,000,000 plus one scoop: narrated from Abū Bakr, ʿAbd al-Raḥmān b. Abī Bakr, and ʿAmr b. Ḥazm.

(vii) Intercession for 70,000 x 70,000 x 70,000 = 343 billion: narrated from ʿĀʾisha; likewise intercession for all three thirds of the *Umma*.

"70,000" and Its Multiples Denote Over-Abundance

The Ottoman exegete Abū al-Suʿūd al-ʿImādī (898-982/1492-1574) in his language-oriented commentary of the Qurʾān pointed out that the number seven and its decimal multiples denote abundance and perfection:

194. Usage of seven, 70, 700 etc. is widespread in the sense of unqualified abundance because seven comprises all the numerical subdivisions so it is as if the number par excellence. It was said that it is the most complete of numbers because it encompasses them all in essence and because six is the first perfect number,[270] since it is equal to the integrals that are its divisors, since its half is three, its third is two, and its sixth is one, which totals six. Add one and you get seven, so you get complete perfection, since there is no rank after perfection except perfection. Then 70 is the boundary of perfection – since decimals form the boundaries of units – and 700 is the boundary of the boundary.[271]

قال الإمام المفسّر أبو السُّعُود العِمادي رحمه الله في تفسيره إرشاد العقل السليم إلى مزايا الكتاب الكريم في قول الله تعالى ﴿ ٱسْتَغْفِرْ لَهُمْ أَوْ لَا تَسْتَغْفِرْ لَهُمْ إِن تَسْتَغْفِرْ لَهُمْ سَبْعِينَ مَرَّةً فَلَن يَغْفِرَ ٱللَّهُ لَهُمْ ۚ ذَٰلِكَ بِأَنَّهُمْ كَفَرُوا۟ بِٱللَّهِ وَرَسُولِهِۦ ۗ وَٱللَّهُ لَا يَهْدِى ٱلْقَوْمَ ٱلْفَٰسِقِينَ ﴿٨٠﴾ ﴾:

قَدْ شَاعَ اسْتِعْمَالُ السَّبْعَةِ وَالسَّبْعِينَ وَالسَّبْعِمائَةِ فِي مُطْلَقِ التَكْثِيرِ لِاشْتِمَالِ السَّبْعَةِ عَلَى جُمْلَةِ أَقْسَامِ الْعَدَدِ فَكَأَنَّهَا الْعَدَدُ بِأَسْرِهِ. وَقِيلَ هِيَ أَكْمَلُ الْأَعْدَادِ لِجَمْعِهَا مَعَانِيهَا وَلِأَنَّ السِّتَّةَ أَوَّلُ عَدَدٍ تَامٍّ لِتَعَادُلِ أَجْزَائِهَا الصَّحِيحَةِ إِذْ نِصْفُهَا ثَلَاثَةٌ وَثُلُثُهَا اثْنَانِ وَسُدُسُهَا وَاحِدٌ وَجُمْلَتُهَا سِتَّةٌ وَهِيَ مَعَ الْوَاحِدِ سَبْعَةٌ، فَكَانَتْ كَامِلَةً إِذْ لَا مَرْتَبَةَ بَعْدَ التَّمَامِ إِلَّا الْكَمَالُ. ثُمَّ السَّبْعُونَ غَايَةُ الْكَمَالِ إِذِ الْآحَادُ غَايَتُهَا الْعَشَرَاتُ، وَالسَّبْعُمائَةِ غَايَةُ الْغَايَاتِ.

[270] A perfect number is an integer that is equal to the sum of its divisors such as 6 = 3+2+1. The next three perfect numbers are 496; 8,128; and 33,550,336.

[271] Abū al-Su'ūd, *Irshād al-'Aql al-Salīm* (*sub* 9:80). Cf. "The number 7 has for the Arabs the symbolical significance of perfection, especially in theological matters." Muṣṭafā Ṣādiq al-Rāfi'ī (d. 1356/1937), *I'jāz al-Qur'ān wal-Balāghat al-Nabawiyya*, 9th ed. (Beirut: Dār al-Kitāb al-'Arabī, 1393/1973) p. 68.

The triple flash and Divine Promise in ʿĀ'isha's report also resemble another triple flash and Divine Promise that occurred at the shattering of the rock at the time the Prophet and his Companions were preparing for the Battle of the Trench as narrated by ʿAmr b. ʿAwf al-Muzanī:

195. A white, round rock emerged before us from the trench. It broke our blades and caused hardship. We complained to the Prophet. He took the pick from Salmān and struck the rock, cracking it, whereupon a great light glimmered, illuminating Madina from one boundary-stone to another until it seemed like a light in the midst of a dark night. The Messenger of Allāh exclaimed *Allāhu Akbar!* Then he struck it a second time and cracked it, whereupon a great light glimmered, illuminating Madina from one boundary-stone to another. He exclaimed *Allāhu Akbar!* Then he struck it a third time and shattered it, whereupon a great light glimmered, illuminating al-Madīna from one boundary-stone to another. He exclaimed *Allāhu Akbar!* We said: "Messenger of Allāh, we saw you strike and lightning came out like waves, and we saw you exclaim *Allāhu Akbar!*" He said: "The first time, the palaces of al-Ḥīra and Kisrā's Madā'in were illuminated for me as bright as the canine teeth of a dog, and Jibrīl informed me that my Community would prevail over them. The second time the palaces of the red in Byzantine lands were illuminated for me as bright as the canine teeth of a dog, and Jibrīl informed me that my Community would prevail over them. The third time the palaces of Ṣan'ā' were illuminated for me as bright as the canine teeth of a dog, and Jibrīl informed me that my Community would prevail over them. So receive the glad tidings of victory!" Hearing this, the hypocrites said: "Muḥammad is telling you that he is seeing the palaces of al-Ḥīra and al-Madā'in from Yathrib and that you will conquer them and here you are entrenching yourselves, unable to have the upper hand!" At that time was revealed *And When the hypocrites, and those in whose hearts is a disease, were saying: Allah and His Messenger promised us nothing but delusion* (33:12).[272]

[272] Ibn Saʿd, *Ṭabaqāt* (4:83); *Tafsīr*s of al-Ṭabarī, Ibn Abī Ḥātim, al-Wāḥidī, al-Thaʿlabī, and al-Baghawī (*sub* 33:12); al-Ṭabarī, *Tārīkh* (2:568-570); al-Bayhaqī, *Dalā'il* (3:418-419); and *mursal* from Qatāda by al-Ṭabarī in his *Tafsīr* (21:133) cf. Ibn Hishām, *Sīra*, (3/4:55-56) and Ibn Kathīr, *Bidāya* (4:101).

عَنْ عَمْرِو بْنِ عَوْفٍ الْمُزَنِيِّ رَضِيَ اللهُ عَنْهُ قَالَ خَرَجَتْ لَنَا مِنَ الْخَنْدَقِ صَخْرَةٌ بَيْضَاءُ مُدَوَّرَةٌ فَكَسَرَتْ حَدِيدَنَا وَشَقَّتْ عَلَيْنَا فَشَكَوْنَا إِلَى رَسُولِ اللهِ ﷺ فَأَخَذَ الْمِعْوَلَ مِنْ سَلْمَانَ فَضَرَبَ الصَّخْرَةَ ضَرْبَةً صَدَعَهَا وَبَرَقَتْ مِنْهَا بَرْقَةٌ أَضَاءَ مَا بَيْنَ لَابَتَيِ الْمَدِينَةِ حَتَّى لَكَأَنَّ مِصْبَاحاً فِي جَوْفِ لَيْلٍ مُظْلِمٍ فَكَبَّرَ رَسُولُ اللهِ ﷺ ثُمَّ ضَرَبَهَا الثَّانِيَةَ فَصَدَّهَا وَبَرَقَ مِنْهَا بَرْقَةٌ أَضَاءَ مَا بَيْنَ لَابَتَيْهَا فَكَبَّرَ ثُمَّ ضَرَبَهَا الثَّالِثَةَ فَكَسَرَهَا وَبَرَقَ مِنْهَا بَرْقَةٌ أَضَاءَ مَا بَيْنَ لَابَتَيْهَا فَكَبَّرَ فَقُلْنَا يَا رَسُولَ اللهِ قَدْ رَأَيْنَاكَ تَضْرِبُ فَيَخْرُجُ بَرْقٌ كَالْمَوْجِ وَرَأَيْنَاكَ تُكَبِّرُ فَقَالَ أَضَاءَ لِي فِي الْأُولَى قُصُورُ الْحِيرَةِ وَمَدَائِنُ كِسْرَى كَأَنَّهَا أَنْيَابُ الْكِلَابِ فَأَخْبَرَنِي جِبْرَئِيلُ أَنَّ أُمَّتِي ظَاهِرَةٌ عَلَيْهَا وَأَضَاءَ لِي فِي الثَّانِيَةِ قُصُورُ الْحُمْرِ مِنْ أَرْضِ الرُّومِ كَأَنَّهَا أَنْيَابُ الْكِلَابِ فَأَخْبَرَنِي جِبْرَئِيلُ أَنَّ أُمَّتِي ظَاهِرَةٌ عَلَيْهَا وَأَضَاءَ لِي فِي الثَّالِثَةِ قُصُورُ صَنْعَاءَ كَأَنَّهَا أَنْيَابُ الْكِلَابِ فَأَخْبَرَنِي جِبْرَئِيلُ أَنَّ أُمَّتِي ظَاهِرَةٌ عَلَيْهَا فَأَبْشِرُوا بِالنَّصْرِ فَقَالَ الْمُنَافِقُونَ يُخْبِرُكُمْ مُحَمَّدٌ أَنَّهُ يُبْصِرُ مِنْ يَثْرِبَ قُصُورَ الْحِيرَةِ وَمَدَائِنَ كِسْرَى وَأَنَّهَا تُفْتَحُ لَكُمْ وَأَنْتُمْ تَحْفُرُونَ الْخَنْدَقَ وَلَا تَسْتَطِيعُونَ أَنْ تَبْرُزُوا فَنَزَلَ ﴿وَإِذْ يَقُولُ ٱلْمُنَٰفِقُونَ وَٱلَّذِينَ فِى قُلُوبِهِم مَّرَضٌ مَّا وَعَدَنَا ٱللَّهُ وَرَسُولُهُۥٓ إِلَّا غُرُورًا ۝١٢﴾ رواه ابن سعد والواحدي في أسباب النزول والطبري وابن أبي حاتم والثعلبي والبغوي جميعهم في التفسير والطبري أيضا في التاريخ والبيهقي

Another version from Salmān states:

196. I was digging in one corner of the trench at which time one rock gave me difficulty. The Messenger of Allāh came near and saw my predicament. He came down and took the pick from my hands. Then he struck and a great spark flashed under the pick. He struck again and another spark flashed. He struck a third time and a third spark flashed. I said to him: "My father and mother be ransomed for you, Messenger of Allāh! What is that I saw flashing under the pick as you were striking?" He said: "Did you see it, Salmān?" I said yes. He continued: "The first time, Allāh opened Yemen for me; the second time, He opened al-Shām and al-Maghrib for me; and the third time, he opened the East."[273]

قَالَ ابْنُ إِسْحَاقَ حُدِّثْتُ عَنْ سَلْمَانَ رَضِيَ اللهُ عَنْهُ قَالَ ضَرَبْتُ فِي نَاحِيَةٍ مِنَ الخَنْدَقِ فَغَلُظَتْ عَلَيَّ صَخْرَةٌ فَعَطَفَ عَلَيَّ رَسُولُ اللهِ ﷺ وَهُوَ قَرِيبٌ مِنِّي فَلَمَّا رَآنِي أَضْرِبُ وَرَأَى شِدَّةَ المَكَانِ عَلَيَّ نَزَلَ فَأَخَذَ المِعْوَلَ مِنْ يَدِي فَضَرَبَ بِهِ ضَرْبَةً فَلَمَعَتْ تَحْتَ المِعْوَلِ بَرْقَةٌ ثُمَّ ضَرَبَ ضَرْبَةً أُخْرَى فَلَمَعَتْ تَحْتَهُ بَرْقَةٌ أُخْرَى ثُمَّ ضَرَبَ الثَّالِثَةَ فَلَمَعَتْ تَحْتَهُ بَرْقَةٌ أُخْرَى فَقُلْتُ يَا رَسُولَ اللهِ بِأَبِي أَنْتَ وَأُمِّي مَا هٰذَا الَّذِي رَأَيْتُ يَلْمَعُ تَحْتَ المِعْوَلِ وَأَنْتَ تَضْرِبُ بِهِ فَقَالَ أَوَقَدْ رَأَيْتَ ذٰلِكَ يَا سَلْمَانُ فَقُلْتُ نَعَمْ فَقَالَ أَمَّا الأُولَى فَإِنَّ اللهَ عَزَّ وَجَلَّ فَتَحَ عَلَيَّ بِهَا اليَمَنَ وَأَمَّا الثَّانِيَةُ فَإِنَّ اللهَ عَزَّ وَجَلَّ فَتَحَ عَلَيَّ بِهَا الشَّامَ وَالمَغْرِبَ وَأَمَّا الثَّالِثَةُ فَإِنَّ اللهَ فَتَحَ عَلَيَّ بِهَا المَشْرِقَ ابن هشام والبيهقي.

[273]Narrated through Ibn Isḥāq by Ibn Hishām, *Sīra* (3/4:175-176) and al-Bayhaqī, *Dalā'il* (3:417-418) cf. Suyūṭī, *Khaṣā'iṣ* (1:378) and Ibn Kathīr, *Bidāya* (4:99-101).

VII

His Light Overpowers All Lights

"The Prophet Had No Shadow That Could Be Seen"

A consequence of the Prophet's aspect of light was his shadowlessness, a miraculous phenomenon that many scholars highlighted and documented, not only in the *Sīra* and "special exclusive characteristics" (*khaṣā'iṣ*) genres but also in other genres such as *fiqh*.[274]

Ibn al-Jawzī in the chapter devoted to the beauty of the Prophet in *al-Wafā* cited from Ibn ʿAbbās the following report:

> **197.** The Prophet did not have a shadow. When he stood in the sun his light would always overcome the light of the sun and when he stood near a candle his light would overcome its light.

قال ابن الجوزي في الوفا الباب التاسع والعشرون في ذكر حسنه ﷺ **عَنِ ابْنِ عَبَّاسٍ رَضِيَ اللهُ عَنْهُمَا قَالَ: لَمْ يَكُنْ لِرَسُولِ اللهِ ﷺ ظِلٌّ، وَلَمْ يَقُمْ مَعَ شَمْسٍ قَطُّ إِلَّا غَلَبَ ضَوْؤُهُ ضَوْءَ الشَّمْسِ، وَلَمْ يَقُمْ مَعَ سِرَاجٍ قَطُّ إِلَّا غَلَبَ ضَوْؤُهُ عَلَى ضَوْءِ السِّرَاجِ**

Al-Suyūṭī said:

[274] Ibn al-Jawzī, *Wafā* (p. 412 §664 *fī dhikri ḥusnih*); ʿIyāḍ, *Shifā* I.iv.28 (p. 462 §1126 *mā ẓahara min al-āyāt ʿinda mawlidih*); Ibn al-Mulaqqin, *Khaṣā'iṣ* (p. 213); al-Suyūṭī, *Khaṣā'iṣ* (1:116 and 1:122) and *Unmūdhaj al-Labīb* (p. 88); al-Qasṭallāni, *Mawāhib* (2:71 *wa-ammā mashyuhu maʿa aṣḥābih*); al-Qārī, *Sharḥ al-Shifā* (1:505); al-Ṣāliḥī, *Subul al-Hudā* (2:12); al-Zurqānī, *Sharḥ al-Mawāhib* (4: 253-254 *Shamā'il, wa-lam yakun lahu ẓill*); and al-Nabhānī, *Ḥujjat Allāh* (p. 686). For *fiqh* sources see further down.

198. Ḥakīm al-Tirmidhī (d. 320/932) narrated from Dhakwān[275] that one could see no shadow to the Messenger of Allāh whether in sunlight or moonlight. Ibn Sabʿ (440?-520?/1048-1126) said: "Among his characteristics is that his shadow did not cast itself on the ground and that he was a light – so that, when he walked in sunlight or moonlight, one could not see any shadow to him." A scholar said that what witnesses to the truth of this is his supplication "... and make me a light." Razīn (d. 524/1130) explained it by the fact that his lights overcame all other lights.[276]

قال السيوطي في الخصائص الكبرى والصغرى: أَخْرَجَ الحَكِيمُ التِّرْمِذِيُّ عَنْ ذَكْوَانٍ أَنَّ رَسُولَ الله ﷺ لَمْ يَكُنْ يُرَى لَهُ ظِلٌّ فِي شَمْسٍ وَلَا قَمَرٍ. قَالَ ابْنُ سَبُعٍ: مِنْ خَصَائِصِهِ أَنَّ ظِلَّهُ كَانَ لَا يَقَعُ عَلَى الْأَرْضِ وَأَنَّهُ كَانَ نُوراً فَكَانَ إِذَا مَشَى فِي الشَّمْسِ أَوِ الْقَمَرِ لَا يُنْظَرُ لَهُ ظِلٌّ. قَالَ بَعْضُهُمْ: وَيَشْهَدُ لَهُ حَدِيثُ قَوْلِهِ ﷺ فِي دُعَائِهِ **وَاجْعَلْنِي نُوراً**. وَقَالَ رَزِينٌ: لِغَلَبَةِ أَنْوَارِهِ. ابن سبع بضم الباء وإسكانها وهو الإمام الخطيب أبو الربيع سليمان بن سبع السَّبْتي صاحب (شفاء الصدور) والعنوان الكامل للكتاب – كما ذكره المؤلف في مختصره (الخصائص): (شفاء الصدور في إيضاح البيان عن كشف حقائق البرهان في أعلام نبوة الرسول محمد بن عبد الله وخصائصه).

Al-Zurqānī (d. 1122/1710) mentioned all the above – adding Ibn al-Mubārak as a third primary source – then commented:

275 "I.e. Abū Ṣāliḥ al-Sammān al-Zayyāt al-Madanī or Abū ʿAmr al-Madanī Mawlā ʿĀ'isha; both are trustworthy Successors. Thus the report is *mursal* (missing the Companion-reporter) but confirmed by the report of Ibn ʿAbbās." al-Zurqānī, *Sharḥ al-Mawāhib* (4: 253-254 *Shamā'il, wa-lam yakun lahu ẓill*).

276 Al-Suyūṭī, *Khaṣā'iṣ* (1:116 and 1:122) and *Unmūdhaj al-Labīb* (p. 88).

199. Light does not have a shadow, and this makes the proof ironclad.[277]

200. The Prophet's shadowlessness was also mentioned among his unique aspects in the *fiqh* books of the Shāfiʿī and Ḥanbalī schools.[278]

جاء في شرح الزرقاني على المواهب عند الكلام على مشي النبي ﷺ: وَنَفْيُ أَنْ يَكُونَ لَهُ ظِلٌّ رَوَاهُ الْحَكِيمُ التِّرْمِذِيُّ عَنْ ذَكْوَانَ مَوْلَى عَائِشَةَ وَرَوَاهُ ابْنُ الْمُبَارَكِ وَابْنُ الْجَوْزِيِّ عَنِ ابْنِ عَبَّاسٍ. وَقَوْلُهُ ﷺ فِي دُعَائِهِ **وَاجْعَلْنِي نُوراً**، وَالنُّورُ لَا ظِلَّ لَهُ، وَبِهِ يَتِمُّ الْإِسْتِشْهَادُ. اهـ وأورده مجموع فتاوى الأزهر من أجوبة وفتاوى لشهر مايو 1997. وفي كتب الفقه: كَانَ إِذَا مَشَى ﷺ فِي الشَّمْسِ أَوِ الْقَمَرِ لَا يَظْهَرُ لَهُ ظِلٌّ، وَيَشْهَدُ لِذَلِكَ أَنَّهُ سَأَلَ اللهَ أَنْ يَجْعَلَ فِي جَمِيعِ أَعْضَائِهِ وَجِهَاتِهِ نُوراً، وَخَتَمَ بِقَوْلِهِ **وَاجْعَلْنِي نُوراً** اهـ. من أسنى المطالب في شرح روض الطالب لشيخ الإسلام زكريا الأنصاري. ومثله في الغرر البهية في شرح البهجة الوردية له، وفي حاشية الجمل على شرح المنهج لشيخ الإسلام. وقال غيرهما: لَمْ يَكُنْ لَهُ ﷺ فَيْءٌ أَيْ ظِلٌّ فِي الشَّمْسِ وَالْقَمَرِ لِأَنَّهُ نُورَانِيٌّ وَالظِّلُّ نَوْعُ ظُلْمَةٍ ذَكَرَهُ ابْنُ عَقِيلٍ وَغَيْرُهُ وَيَشْهَدُ لَهُ أَنَّهُ سَأَلَ اللهَ أَنْ يَجْعَلَ فِي جَمِيعِ أَعْضَائِهِ وَجِهَاتِهِ نُورًا وَخَتَمَ بِقَوْلِهِ **وَاجْعَلْنِي نُورًا**. اهـ. من كَشَّاف الْقِنَاع عن متن الإقناع لِلبُهُوتِي ومثله في الإنصاف للمَرْدَاوِي ومَطالب أُولِي النُّهَى في شرح غاية المُنْتَهَى لِلرُّحَيْبَانِي.

---

[277] al-Zurqānī, *Sharḥ al-Mawāhib* (4: 253-254 *Shamāʾil, wa-lam yakun lahu ẓill*).
[278] Shaykh al-Islām Zakariyyā al-Anṣārī, *Asnā al-Maṭālib* (ʿIlmiyya, 2001 ed. 3:107) and *al-Ghurar al-Bahiyya* (ʿIlmiyya, 1997 ed. 4:91); al-Jamal, *Ḥāshiyat Manhaj al-Ṭullāb* (ʿIlmiyya, 1996 ed. 4:115); al-Buhūtī, *Kashshāf al-Qināʿ* (ʿĀlam al-Kutub, 1997 ed. 5:31); al-Mardāwī, *Inṣāf* (Fiqqī 1995 ed. 8:43); and al-Ruḥaybānī, *Maṭālib Ulī al-Nuhā* (al-Maktab al-Islāmī, 1961 ed. 5:41).

This miraculous phenomenon is mentioned three times in the Qur'ān in relation to the hand of the Prophet Mūsā (20:22, 27:12, 28:32) as narrated by al-Baghawī from Ibn ʿAbbās and Mujāhid:

> **201.** On His saying *And thrust your hand within your wing, it will come forth white without hurt* (20:22) Mujāhid said it means "Thrust your hand under your armpit, it will come out full of shining light with radiance like the light of the sun without defect." "Hurt" here means leprosy. Ibn ʿAbbās said: "His hand shone with a blazing light night and day similar to the light of the sun and the moon."[279]

قال البغوي في معالم التنزيل: قَوْلُهُ تَعَالَى ﴿وَٱضْمُمْ يَدَكَ إِلَىٰ جَنَاحِكَ﴾ أَيْ إِبْطِكَ، قَالَ مُجَاهِدٌ: تَحْتَ عَضُدِكَ، وَجَنَاحُ الإِنْسَانِ عَضُدِهِ إِلَى أَصْلِ إِبْطِهِ. ﴿تَخْرُجْ بَيْضَآءَ﴾ نَيِّرَةً مُشْرِقَةً وَلَهَا شُعَاعٌ كَضَوْءِ الشَّمْسِ ﴿مِنْ غَيْرِ سُوٓءٍ﴾ مِنْ غَيْرِ عَيْبٍ، وَالسُّوءُ هَاهُنَا بِمَعْنَى الْبَرَصِ. قَالَ ابْنُ عَبَّاسٍ رَضِيَ اللهُ عَنْهُمَا: كَانَ لِيَدِهِ نُورٌ سَاطِعٌ يُضِيءُ بِاللَّيْلِ وَالنَّهَارِ كَضَوْءِ الشَّمْسِ وَالْقَمَرِ.

The Sun and the Moon Obeyed Him

Other allusions (*ishārāt*) to the Prophet's overwhelming light can be inferred from the miracles of his controlling the sun and the moon.

The Companions al-Ḥusayn b. ʿAlī and Asmā' bint ʿUmays narrated:

> **202.** The Messenger of Allah was resting his head in ʿAlī's lap and he was receiving revelation. When it lifted from him he asked: "ʿAlī, did you pray the *ʿaṣr* prayer?" He said no. The Prophet said: "O Allah, truly You know that he was serving Your cause and the cause of Your Messenger; therefore turn back the sun for him." He turned it back so that he prayed, then the sun set.[280]

[279] al-Baghawī, *Maʿālim* (*sub* 20:22 and 28:32).
[280] From al-Ḥusayn: al-Khaṭīb, *Talkhīṣ al-Mutashābih* (1:225 §353 under Ibrāhīm b.

عن فاطمة الصغرى ابنة الحسين عن الحسين بن علي رضي الله عنهم، قال:

كَانَ رَأْسُ رَسُولِ اللهِ ﷺ فِي حِجْرِ عَلِيٍّ وَكَانَ يُوحَى إِلَيْهِ فَلَمَّا سُرِّيَ عَنْهُ قَالَ يَا عَلِيُّ صَلَّيْتَ الْعَصْرَ؟ قَالَ لَا قَالَ اللّٰهُمَّ إِنَّكَ تَعْلَمُ أَنَّهُ كَانَ فِي حَاجَتِكَ وَحَاجَةِ رَسُولِكَ فَرُدَّ عَلَيْهِ الشَّمْسَ فَرَدَّهَا عَلَيْهِ فَصَلَّى وَغَابَتِ الشَّمْسُ.

أخرجه الخطيب في تلخيص المتشابه والدولابي في الذرّيّة الطاهرة. ورواه عن أسماء بنت عميس: الطبراني في الكبير والطحاوي في شرح مشكل الآثار وغيرهما. قال السيوطي في اللآلئ: وقفت على جزء مستقل في جمع طرق هذا الحديث تخريج أبي الحسن شاذان الفضلي ثم ساقه. وقد رد هذا الحديث طائفة من المتأخرين كابن الجوزي والمزي وأحمد بن تيمية والذهبي وابن القيم وابن كثير. لكن صححه السلف كالحافظ الفريابي في دلائل النبوة والحافظ أحمد بن صالح وقال القاضي عياض في الشفا قال الطحاوي وهذان الحديثان ثابتان ورواتهما ثقات. وحكى الطحاوي أن أحمد بن صالح كان يقول لا ينبغي لمن سبيلُه العلم التخلُّف عن حفظ حديث أسماء لأنه من علامات النبوة. اهـ. من كتاب الشفا. وكذا صححه الولي العراقي في طرح التثريب والسيوطي في رسالته (كشف اللَّبْس في حديث رد الشمس)، وجاء نحوه عن جابر بسند حسن كما في مجمع الزوائد والفتح. وأنشد الحافظ ابن حجر في ديوانه:

وَعَيْنُ الشَّمْسِ رُدَّتْ بَعْدَ حَجْبٍ ❋ لِذِي الْحَسَنَيْنِ مِنْهُ بِالدُّعَاءِ

وقال عبد الرحيم البرعي:

نَبِيٌّ مَا رَأَتْهُ الشَّمْسُ إِلَّا ❋ وَكَلَّتْ مِنْ مَحَاسِنِهِ حَيَاءَ

Ḥayyān) and al-Dūlābī in *al-Dhurriyyat al-Ṭāhira* (p. 91-93 §164). From Asmā': al-Ṭabarānī, *al-Muʿjam al-Kabīr* (24:144-151 §382, 390-391) and al-Ṭaḥāwī, *Sharḥ Mushkil al-Āthār* (3:92-95 §1067-1068). Cf. al-Haythamī, *Majmaʿ* (8:297) and ʿIyāḍ, *Shifā* (p. 347-348 §684).

Another hadith reveals the Prophet showing that superstellar ability to ʿAlī himself:

203. I went out with the Prophet until we reached the Kaʿba whereupon he told me to crouch. He then climbed on my shoulders and I tried to stand but he noticed some weakness in me. He climbed down and crouched for me then said, "Climb on my shoulders." I climbed on his shoulders then he stood and <u>I felt as if I could touch the top of the sky if I wanted</u>. Then I climbed on top of the House and there was a yellow copper statue which I began to budge right and left, front and back until I dislodged it. The Messenger of Allah told me to throw it down. I threw it down and it broke into pieces just like a glass vessel. I climbed down and we sprinted away between the houses lest anyone see us.[281]

عَنْ عَلِيٍّ رَضِيَ اللهُ عَنْهُ قَالَ انْطَلَقَ بِي رَسُولُ اللهِ ﷺ حَتَّى أَتَى بِي الْكَعْبَةَ فَقَالَ لِي إِجْلِسْ فَجَلَسْتُ إِلَى جَنْبِ الْكَعْبَةِ وَصَعِدَ رَسُولُ اللهِ ﷺ عَلَى مِنْكَبَيَّ ثُمَّ قَالَ لِي إِنْهَضْ بِي فَنَهَضْتُ بِهِ فَلَمَّا رَأَى ضَعْفِي تَحْتَهُ قَالَ إِجْلِسْ فَجَلَسْتُ فَنَزَلَ عَنِّي وَجَلَسَ لِي ثُمَّ قَالَ يَا عَلِيُّ إِصْعَدْ عَلَى مَنْكِبَيَّ فَصَعِدْتُ عَلَى مَنْكِبَيْهِ ثُمَّ نَهَضَ بِي رَسُولُ اللهِ ﷺ فَلَمَّا نَهَضَ بِي خُيِّلَ إِلَيَّ أَنِّي لَوْ شِئْتُ نِلْتُ أُفُقَ السَّمَاءَ وَصَعِدْتُ عَلَى الْكَعْبَةِ وَتَنَحَّى رَسُولُ اللهِ ﷺ فَقَالَ لِي أَلْقِ صَنَمَهُمُ الْأَكْبَرَ صَنَمَ قُرَيْشٍ وَكَانَ مِنْ نُحَاسٍ وَكَانَ مَوْتُوداً بِأَوْتَادٍ مِنْ حَدِيدٍ إِلَى الْأَرْضِ فَقَالَ لِي رَسُولُ اللهِ ﷺ عَالِجْهُ فَجَعَلْتُ أُعَالِجُهُ وَرَسُولُ اللهِ ﷺ

---

[281] Narrated with a fair chain cf. al-Haythamī, *Majmaʿ* (6:23): by Aḥmad, *Musnad* (2:73-74 §644 and 2:430 §1302); al-Ṭabarī with three chains, *Tahdhīb al-Āthār* (p. 236-240 §31-33); Ibn Abī Shayba without the last sentence, *Muṣannaf* (20:470-471 §38062); al-Bazzār, *Musnad* (3:21-22 §769); Abū Yaʿlā, *Musnad* (1:251-252 §292; see Asad's correctives to ʿAwwāma's statements); al-Ḥākim, *Mustadrak* through two chains (2:366-367); and al-Nasāʾī in *Khaṣāʾiṣ ʿAlī* (p. 22).

يَقُولُ إِيهْ إِيهْ فَلَمْ أَزَلْ أُعَالِجُهُ حَتَّى اسْتَمْكَنْتُ فَقَالَ اقْذِفْهُ فَقَذَفْتُهُ وَنَزَلْتُ

رواه أحمد وابن أبي شيبة والبزار وأبو يعلى والطبري وعندهم جميعاً إلا ابن أبي شيبة زيادة: فَانْطَلَقْتُ أَنَا وَرَسُولُ اللهِ ﷺ نَسْتَبِقُ حَتَّى تَوَارَيْنَا بِالْبُيُوتِ خَشْيَةَ أَنْ يَلْقَانَا أَحَدٌ مِنَ النَّاسِ.

204. It was also narrated from many Companions that about five years before the Hijra the Prophet was challenged by the Meccans to produce a miracle, whereupon he called upon them to bear witness that the moon had split in two, each of its two halves on the two sides of the mountain of Ḥirā' overlooking Mecca, following which they claimed he had bewitched them.[282]

عَنْ أَنَسِ بْنِ مَالِكٍ رَضِيَ اللهُ عَنْهُ أَنَّ أَهْلَ مَكَّةَ سَأَلُوا رَسُولَ اللهِ ﷺ أَنْ يُرِيَهُمْ آيَةً فَأَرَاهُمُ الْقَمَرَ شِقَّتَيْنِ حَتَّى رَأَوْا حِرَاءً بَيْنَهُمَا رواه البخاري وهذا لفظه ومسلم والترمذي وأحمد وغيرهم وفي الباب عن علي وابن مسعود قَالَ انْشَقَّ الْقَمَرُ وَنَحْنُ مَعَ النَّبِيِّ ﷺ فَصَارَ فِرْقَتَيْنِ فَقَالَ لَنَا اشْهَدُوا اشْهَدُوا وحذيفة وجبير بن مطعم بزيادة فَقَالُوا سَحَرَنَا مُحَمَّدٌ فَقَالَ بَعْضُهُمْ لَئِنْ كَانَ سَحَرَنَا فَمَا يَسْتَطِيعُ أَنْ يَسْحَرَ النَّاسَ كُلَّهُمْ وابن عمر وابن عباس. وعدّه جماعة من المتواتر. وتدلّى له القمر لمّا كان في المهد صبيّاً لتسليته كما رواه أصحاب السِّيَر وإليه الإشارة في إنشادهم:

مَنْ دَنَا لَهُ الْقَمَرْ ❋ وَنَزَلْ سَلَّمْ عَلَيْه

[282] al-Bukhārī, *Ṣaḥīḥ* (*Manāqib, su'āl al-mushrikīn an yuriyahum al-Nabī āya*); Muslim, *Ṣaḥīḥ* (*Ṣifat al-qiyāma, inshiqāq al-qamar*); al-Tirmidhī, *Sunan* (*Tafsīr, Sūrat al-Qamar*). Narrated from Anas, Ibn Mas'ūd, Jubayr b. Muṭ'im, Ibn 'Umar, Ibn 'Abbās, Ḥudhayfa, and 'Alī. The *Sīra* authors also narrate that the moon would descend and play with the Prophet as he lay in his cradle to entertain him. This is the reference meant in the *mawlid* line: "He whom the moon approached and greeted."

Invocations of Blessings by His Light as the Source of All Lights

In light of such abundant evidence it is not surprising to find that the generations that followed Ḥassān b. Thābit and al-ʿAbbās viewed the primal light of the Prophet as the greatest of all the themes of panegyric poetry and devotional expressions, for example the *Ṣalāt Mashīshiyya* or *Bashīshiyya* – also known as *Ṣalāt Baḥr al-Ḥaqā'iq wal-ʿUlūm* – attributed to the "Spiritual Pole" (*Quṭb*) ʿAbd al-Salām b. Mashīsh or Bashīsh (559-626/1163-1228):

[*Ṣalāt al-Asrār wal-Anwār (Mashīshiyya)*:]

205. *O Allah! Send blessings upon him from whom the secrets were sundered and the lights broke forth! In him the realities rose up and Adam's sciences descended until he made all creatures helpless, and minds capitulated so that none of us can reach him, from the first to the last!...*

في الصلاة المشيشية لسيدي عبد السلام بن مشيش رضي الله عنه:

اللّٰهُمَّ صَلِّ عَلَى مَنْ مِنْهُ انْشَقَّتِ الأَسْرَارُ وَانفَلَقَتِ الأَنْوَارُ. وَفِيهِ ارْتَقَتِ الْحَقَائِقُ. وَتَنَزَّلَتْ عُلُومُ آدَمَ فَأَعْجَزَ الْخَلائِقَ. وَلَهُ تَضَاءَلَتِ الْفُهُومُ فَلَمْ يُدْرِكْهُ مِنَّا سَابِقٌ وَلَا لَاحِقٌ. نرويها عن الشيخ الوَقور رَمزي عَجَم التونسي.

Similar meanings are found in the *Ṣalāt Nūrāniyya* attributed to another Moroccan *Quṭb*, Aḥmad al-Badawī (596-675/1200-1276):

[*Ṣalāt Nūrāniyya*:]

206. *O Allah! Bless, greet and sanctify our master and liegelord Muḥammad, the Tree of Original Light, the Sparkle of the Handful of Divine Mercy, the Best of All Humankind, the Noblest of Physical Frames, the Vessel of the Lord's Secrets and Storehouse of the Sciences of the Elect, the Possessor of the Original Divine Grasp, Resplendent Grace and Uppermost Rank, under whose flag line up all the Prophets, so that they are from him and point* *to him. Bless, greet and sanctify him and his Family and Companions, to the number of all that You have ever created, sustained, caused to die, and caused to live again, to the Day You resurrect those You reduced to dust, and greet him with an abundant and endless greeting. Glory and praise belong to Allah, the Lord of the worlds!*

الصلاة النورانية لسيدي أحمد البدوي رضي الله عنه:

اللّٰهُمَّ صَلِّ وَسَلِّمْ وَبَارِكْ عَلَى سَيِّدِنَا وَمَوْلَانَا مُحَمَّدٍ شَجَرَةِ الْأَصْلِ النُّورَانِيَّةِ
وَلَمعَةِ الْقَبْضَةِ الرَّحْمَانِيَّةِ وَأَفْضَلِ الْخَلِيقَةِ الْإِنْسَانِيَّةِ وَأَشْرَفِ الصُّورَةِ الْجُسْمَانِيَّةِ
وَمَعْدَنِ الْأَسْرَارِ الرَّبَّانِيَّةِ وَخَزَائِنِ الْعُلُومِ الْإِصْطِفَائِيَّةِ صَاحِبِ الْقَبْضَةِ
الْأَصْلِيَّةِ وَالْبَهْجَةِ السَّنِيَّةِ وَالرُّتْبَةِ الْعَلِيَّةِ مَنِ انْدَرَجَتِ النَّبِيُّونَ تَحْتَ لِوَائِهِ
فَهُمْ مِنْهُ وَإِلَيْهِ وَصَلِّ وَسَلِّمْ وَبَارِكْ عَلَيْهِ وَعَلَى آلِهِ وَصَحْبِهِ عَدَدَ مَا خَلَقْتَ
وَرَزَقْتَ وَأَمَتَّ وَأَحْيَيْتَ إِلَى يَوْمِ تَبْعَثُ مَنْ أَفْنَيْتَ وَسَلِّمْ تَسْلِيماً كَثِيراً
وَالْحَمْدُ لله رَبِّ الْعَالَمِينَ تلقّيناها عن قرة أعيننا الشيخ محمد هشام القباني حفظه الله.

The Egyptian Khalwatī rhetorician, jurist and exegete Aḥmad al-Ṣāwī (1175-1241/1761-1825) said in his explanation of the above text:

207. Concerning *the Sparkle of the Handful of Divine Mercy*: the handful (*qabḍa*) attributed to the All-Beneficent is an allusion (*ishāra*) to its being the vastest of all Divine bounties – how much and how – as the All-Beneficent alone is the Bestower of tremendous bounties in quantity, quality, and essence. *The Sparkle of the Handful* is its source, which was used as the substance of all the created worlds. Its form (*ṣūra*) was honored as shown by the perfection of his physique, the beauty of his countenance, and the proportion of his frame. "I was a hidden treasure and I loved to be known, so I created creation, then they knew me through Me (*fa-bī ʿarafūnī*)."[283] Know that Allah was unknown in His pre-eternity since there was no one created that might know Him. He loved to be known, so He seized a handful of His Light (*qabaḍa qabḍatan min nūrihi*), that is, He seized it Himself (*ay bi-dhātihi*). So "of" (*min*) here stands for "with" (*bi*), the light stands for the Essence, and the construct is explicative (*lil-bayān*). It means He caused it to appear without the intermediary of any materia. That which He seized is what is known as the Muḥammadan Light, the Soul of Souls, the Muḥammadan Secret, the Greater Throne of Allah, the First Adam, the Greater Forefather, and the Perfect Man. This is the gist of the saying of Ibn al-Fāriḍ (576-632/1180-1235):

Though outwardly Adam's descendant, truly I have,
in essence, a witness to my begetting him.

It is also known as the Secret of Secrets, the Pupil of the Eye of Existence, the Tree of Origins, and other names that are familiar to the gnostics. After that, Allah poured down over that reality the most tremendous bounties with His Attribute of All-Beneficent (*al-Raḥmān*), and the most subtle of them with His Attribute of Most Merciful (*al-Raḥīm*), and out of it He supplied all the created worlds, as witnessed to by the hadith of Jābir.[284]

قال الإمام الصاوي رحمه الله في شرح الصلوات الدرديرية:

نِسْبَةُ الْقَبْضَةِ لِلرَّحْمٰنِ إِشَارَةٌ إِلَى أَنَّهَا أَجَلُّ النِّعَمِ كَمّاً وَكَيْفًا لِأَنَّ الرَّحْمٰنَ هُوَ الْمُنْعِمُ
بِجَلَائِلِ النِّعَمِ كَمّاً وَكَيْفاً وَمَعْنىً. (لَمْعَةُ الْقَبْضَةِ) نَشْأَتُهَا الَّتِي جُعِلَتْ مَادَّةً

[283] Most versions of this saying have "so they knew me through it [i.e. creation] (*fa-bihi ʿarafūnī*)." al-Qārī in *al-Asrār al-Marfūʿa* said it has no known chain "but its meaning is nevertheless true and is inferred from the saying of Allah Most High, *I created the Jinns and humankind only that they may worship Me* (51:56), meaning 'that they may know Me' as Ibn ʿAbbās explained it." Also Ibn Jurayj cf. *Tafsīr*s of Ibn Kathīr and Ibn Abī Ḥātim; al-Ḍaḥḥāk cf. al-Māwardī, *Nukat*; and Mujāhid cf. al-Baghawī, al-Qurṭubī, al-Thaʿlabī, and al-Alūsī, all under verse 51:56, the latter explaining the hidden treasure as a metonymy *(majāz mursal)*.

[284] al-Ṣāwī, *Sharḥ al-Ṣalawāt al-Dardīriyya* (p. 33).

لِلْعَوَالِمِ كُلِّهَا وَشَرَّفَ صُورَتَهَا بِاعْتِبَارِ مَا قَامَ بِهَا مِنْ كَمَالِ الْخِلْقَةِ وَحُسْنِ الطَّلْعَةِ وَاعْتِدَالِ الْقَامَةِ. كُنْتُ كَنْزاً مَخْفِيّاً فَأَحْبَبْتُ أَنْ أُعْرَفَ فَخَلَقْتُ الْخَلْقَ فَبِي عَرَفُونِي. إِعْلَمْ أَنَّ اللهَ كَانَ فِي أَزَلِهِ لَمْ يُعْرَفْ لِعَدَمِ وُجُودِ مَنْ يَعْرِفُهُ فَأَحَبَّ أَنْ يُعْرَفَ فَقَبَضَ قَبْضَةً مِنْ نُورِهِ أَيْ بِذَاتِهِ. فَـ(مِنْ) بِمَعْنَى الْبَاءِ، وَالنُّورُ بِمَعْنَى الذَّاتِ، وَالْإِضَافَةُ لِلْبَيَانِ، وَالْمُرَادُ: أَبْرَزَهُ بِقُدْرَتِهِ مِنْ غَيْرِ وَاسِطَةِ مَادَّةٍ. وَهَذَا الْمَقْبُوضُ هُوَ الْمُسَمَّى بِالنُّورِ الْمُحَمَّدِيِّ وَبِرُوحِ الْأَرْوَاحِ وَبِالسِّرِّ الْمُحَمَّدِيِّ وَبِعَرْشِ اللهِ الْأَكْبَرِ وَبِآدَمَ الْأَوَّلِ وَبِالْأَبِ الْأَكْبَرِ وَبِالْإِنْسَانِ الْكَامِلِ. وَمِنْ ذَلِكَ قَوْلُ ابْنِ الْفَارِضِ:

وَإِنِّي وَإِنْ كُنْتُ ابْنَ آدَمَ صُورَةً * فَلِي فِيهِ مَعْنًى شَاهِدٌ بِأُبُوَّتِي

وَبِسِرِّ الْأَسْرَارِ وَبِإِنْسَانِ عَيْنِ الْوُجُودِ وَبِشَجَرَةِ الْأَصْلِ وَغَيْرِ ذَلِكَ مِنَ الْأَسْمَاءِ الْمَشْهُورَةِ بَيْنَ الْعَارِفِينَ. ثُمَّ أَفَاضَ اللهُ عَلَى تِلْكَ الْحَقِيقَةِ جَلَائِلَ النِّعَمِ بِوَصْفِ الرَّحْمَنِ وَدَقَائِقَهَا بِوَصْفِ الرَّحِيمِ، وَأَمَدَّ مِنْهَا الْعَوَالِمَ كُلَّهَا كَمَا يَشْهَدُ لَهُ حَدِيثُ جَابِرٍ.

Similar invocations of blessings related from the *Awliyā* state:

[*Ṣalāt Nūr al-Abṣār (Ṭibbiyya)*:]

208. *O Allah! Bless and greet our liegelord Muḥammad the medicine of hearts and their treatment, the health of bodies and their cure, the light of eyesights and heartsights and their illumination, the soul of souls and their food, and upon his Family and Companions.*

ومن أوراد السيد أحمد الرفاعي وكثير من الأولياء:

اللّٰهُمَّ صَلِّ عَلَى سَيِّدِنَا مُحَمَّدٍ طِبِّ الْقُلُوبِ وَدَوَائِها، وَعَافِيَةِ الأَبْدَانِ وَشِفَائِهَا، وَنُورِ الأَبْصَارِ وَالْبَصَائِرِ وَضِيَائِهَا، وَرُوحِ الأَرْوَاحِ وَغِذَائِها، وَعَلَى آلِهِ وَصَحْبِهِ وَسَلِّمْ. روينا هذا اللفظ عن البركة المعمّر الشيخ محمد سليم الحمّامي الدمشقي وحثّنا على ذكر لفظ وَالْبَصَائِرِ زيادة على ما تعهده الناس أكرمه الله.

All the three texts cited above were explained by al-Ṣāwī in his commentary on the *Ṣalawāt al-Dardīriyya* entitled *al-Asrār al-Rabbāniyya wal-Fuyūḍāt al-Raḥmāniyya.*

[*Ṣalāt Nūrika al-Sārī*]

209. *O Allah! Bless and greet our liegelord Muḥammad, Your Light that permeates all things and Your assistance that circulates in all things, and reunite me with him in all my stages, and upon his Family and Companions, O Light!*

ولبعضهم أيضاً: اللّٰهُمَّ صَلِّ وَسَلِّمْ عَلَى سَيِّدِنَا مُحَمَّدٍ نُورِكَ السَّارِي وَمَدَدِكَ الْجَارِي وَاجْمَعْنِي بِهِ فِي كُلِّ أَطْوَارِي وَعَلَى آلِهِ وَصَحْبِهِ يَا نُور.

[*Ṣalāt Nūr al-Nūr*]

210. *O Allah! Bless and greet our liegelord the Light of lights, the Beloved of Allah the Forgiver and the Bestower of thanks, our Intercessor on the Day of Resurrection and Gathering, and upon his Family and Companions.*

وللشيخ سليم أيضاً: اللّٰهُمَّ صَلِّ عَلَى سَيِّدِنَا مُحَمَّدٍ نُورِ النُّورِ وَحَبِيبِ اللهِ الْغَفُورِ الشَّكُورِ وَشَفِيعِنَا يَوْمَ الْبَعْثِ وَالنُّشُورِ وَعَلَى آلِهِ وَصَحْبِهِ وَسَلِّمْ.

The gnostic of Ḥamā, Shaykh Ḥusayn al-Ḥamawī al-Ṭaybānī, narrated from al-Khiḍr:

[*Ṣalāt al-Nūr al-Awwal (Ṭaybāniyya Khaḍiriyya)*:]

211. *O Allah,bless and greet the Essence formed of Your First Light, which You have made to be the one who is depended on, and whom You have sent with a Revealed Book. Join me with him awake and in my sleep, O First, O Last, O Outward, O Inward, O Allah!*

وبالسند إلى العارف بالله الشيخ حسين الحموي الطيباني قدس الله سره، عن سيدنا الخضر عليه السلام، قال:

اللّٰهُمَّ صَلِّ وَسَلِّمْ عَلَى الذَّاتِ المُكَوَّنَةِ مِنْ نُورِكَ الْأَوَّلِ، الَّذِي جَعَلْتَ عَلَيْهِ المُعَوَّل، وَأَرْسَلْتَهُ بِكِتَابٍ مُنْزَل. إِجْمَعْ بَيْنِي وَبَيْنَهُ يَقَظَةً وَمَنَاماً، يَا أَوَّلُ يَا آخِرُ، يَا ظَاهِرُ يَا بَاطِنُ، يَا اللهُ.

The *Ṣalāt Tāziyya*, also known by its dot-corrupted name of *Nāriyya* (نارية → تازية),[285] also known as the *Kāmila*, is transmitted from Abū al-Mawāhib ʿAbd al-Wahhāb al-Tāzī (1099-1206 or 1213/1688-1792 or 1798):

[*Ṣalāt al-Kāmila (Tāziyya=Nāriyya)*]

212. *O Allah, bless with a perfect blessing and greet with a complete greeting our Liegelord Muḥammad by whom difficulties are solved, troubles are lifted, needs are fulfilled, desires and excellent endings are reached, by whose noble face the rain-prayer rises to the clouds, and upon his Family and Companions in every glimpse and breath by the number of all everything You know.*

[285] Cf. al-Nabhānī, *Saʿādat al-Dārayn* (p. 376).

أمّا الصلاة التازيّة وتعرف بالناريّة وتعرف بالكاملة فبالسند إلى الحافظ محمد بن علي السنوسي، عن الإمام سيدي أحمد بن إدريس، عن سيدي أبي المواهب أحمد التازي، قال:

اللّٰهُمَّ صَلِّ صَلاةً كَامِلَةً وَسَلِّمْ سَلَاماً تَامّاً عَلَى سَيِّدِنَا مُحَمَّدٍ الَّذِي تَنْحَلُّ بِهِ الْعُقَدُ وَتَنْفَرِجُ بِهِ الْكُرَبُ وَتُقْضَى بِهِ الْحَوَائِجُ وَتُنَالُ بِهِ الرَّغَائِبُ وَحُسْنُ الْخَوَاتِمِ وَيُسْتَسْقَى الْغَمَامُ بِوَجْهِهِ الْكَرِيمِ وَعَلَى آلِهِ وَصَحْبِهِ فِي كُلِّ لَمْحَةٍ وَنَفَسٍ بِعَدَدِ كُلِّ مَعْلُومٍ لَكَ.

The *Ṣalāt al-ʿĀẓīmiyya* or Invocation of Magnificence is narrated from the *Quṭb* Aḥmad b. Idrīs (1163-1253/1750-1837):

[*Ṣalāt Nūr Wajhillāh (ʿĀẓīmiyya)*:]

213. *O Allah, I ask you by the Light of the Magnificent Countenance of Allah that fills the foundations of the Magnificent Throne of Allah and by which the worlds of Allah Almighty subsist, to bless our liegelord Muḥammad who holds the Magnificent Rank and the Family of the Prophet of Allah Almighty, to the extent of the Magnificence of the Essence of Allah Almighty in every glimpse and breath, to the number of what lies within the knowledge of Allah Almighty, a perpetual blessing by the eternity of Allah Almighty, in exaltation of your immense right, O our liegelord, O Muḥammad, O possessor of a magnificent character! And greet him and his Family likewise! And join me to him as You have joined together spirit and life, outwardly and inwardly, awake and in my sleep, and make him, O my Lord, the soul of my being in every aspect, in this world before the next, O Almighty!*

وأمّا الصلاة العظيمية لإمام الطريقة الإدريسية السنوسية سيدي أبي العباس صفي الدين أحمد بن إدريس الفاسي العرائشي الأثري دفين صبيا باليمن الملقب بشفاء رضي الله عنه: فبالسند إليه قال رضي الله عنه:

اللّٰهُمَّ إِنِّي أَسْأَلُكَ بِنُورِ وَجْهِ اللهِ الْعَظِيمِ الَّذِي مَلَأَ أَرْكَانَ عَرْشِ اللهِ الْعَظِيمِ وَقَامَتْ بِهِ عَوَالِمُ اللهِ الْعَظِيمِ أَنْ تُصَلِّيَ عَلَى مَوْلَانَا مُحَمَّدٍ ذِي الْقَدْرِ الْعَظِيمِ وَعَلَى آلِ نَبِيِّ اللهِ الْعَظِيمِ بِقَدْرِ عَظَمَةِ ذَاتِ اللهِ الْعَظِيمِ فِي كُلِّ لَمْحَةٍ وَنَفَسٍ عَدَدَ مَا فِي عِلْمِ اللهِ الْعَظِيمِ صَلَاةً دَائِمَةً بِدَوَامِ اللهِ الْعَظِيمِ تَعْظِيماً لِحَقِّكَ يَا مَوْلَانَا يَا مُحَمَّدُ يَا ذَا الْخُلُقِ الْعَظِيمِ وَسَلِّمْ عَلَيْهِ وَعَلَى آلِهِ مِثْلَ ذٰلِكَ وَاجْمَعْ بَيْنِي وَبَيْنَهُ كَمَا جَمَعْتَ بَيْنَ الرُّوحِ وَالنَّفْسِ ظَاهِراً وَبَاطِناً يَقَظَةً وَمَنَاماً وَاجْعَلْهُ يَا رَبِّ رُوحاً لِذَاتِي مِنْ جَمِيعِ الْوُجُوهِ فِي الدُّنْيَا قَبْلَ الْآخِرَةِ يَا عَظِيمُ.

[*Ṣalāt Tājiyya*:]

214. *O Allah, bless and greet our liegelord Muḥammad the Owner of the Crown and the Ascent, of the Burāq and the Flag, the Repeller of affliction and plague and sickness and pain! His body is pure and purified, filled with light, his name is written, raised, and placed on the Tablet and the Pen. He is the sun of mid-morning, the full moon in the deepest night, the forefront of height, the light of guidance, the lamp in the darkness, Abu al-Qāsim, the liegelord of the two universes and intercessor of humankind and jinn, our master Muḥammad, upon him and his Family blessings and peace, the liegelord of Arabs and non-Arabs, the Prophet of the Two Sanctuaries, the one who is beloved in the presence of the Lord of the Two Easts and the Two Wests! You who long to behold his beauty, bless him and greet him with an abundant greeting.*

ورُوِّينا مناولةً عن الحبيب حمزة بن علي بن محسن في جاكرتا عن جده الشيخ أبي بكر بن سالم با علوي رضي الله عنه:

اللّٰهُمَّ صَلِّ وَسَلِّمْ عَلَى سَيِّدِنَا مُحَمَّدٍ صَاحِبِ التَّاجِ وَالْمِعْرَاجِ وَالْبُرَاقِ وَالْعَلَمِ، دَافِعِ الْبَلَاءِ وَالْوَبَاءِ [في رواية زيادة: وَالْقَحْطِ] وَالْمَرَضِ وَالْأَلَمِ،

جِسْمُهُ طَاهِرٌ مُطَهَّرٌ مُعَطَّرٌ مُنَوَّرٌ [في رواية زيادة: فِي البَيتِ وَالْحَرَمِ]، مَنْ إِسْمُهُ مَكْتُوبٌ مَرْفُوعٌ مَوْضُوعٌ عَلَى [فِي] اللَّوْحِ وَالْقَلَمِ، [في رواية زيادة: سَيِّدِ الْعَرَبِ وَالْعَجَمِ،] شَمْسِ الضُّحَى، بَدْرِ الدُّجَى، صَدْرِ الْعُلَا، نُورِ الهُدَى، [في رواية زيادة: كَهْفِ الْوَرَىٰ،] مِصْبَاحِ الظُّلَمِ، [في رواية زيادة: جَمِيلِ الشِّيَمِ، الخ] أَبِي الْقَاسِمِ سَيِّدِ الْكَوْنَيْنِ وَشَفِيعِ الثَّقَلَيْنِ سَيِّدِنَا مُحَمَّدٍ ﷺ وَآلِهِ سَيِّدِ الْعَرَبِ وَالْعَجَمِ نَبِيِّ الحَرَمَينِ، مَحْبُوبٌ عِنْدَ رَبِّ المَشْرِقَينِ وَالمَغْرِبَينِ، فَيَا أَيُّهَا المُشْتَاقُونَ إِلَى رُؤْيَةِ جَمَالِهِ صَلُّوا عَلَيْهِ وَسَلِّمُوا تَسْلِيماً.

Recitations of *al-Mawlid al-Dayba'ī* sometimes include a poem that contains the lines:

215. *My Lord has created Ṭaha from light, sanctifying him;*
He called him: Come, my Elect, you are trustworthy!
Bless the one with dazzling lights, the source of Certainty.
He called him: Come, my Elect, you are trustworthy!

رَبِّي خَلَقْ طٰهَ مِـنْ نُورْ   فِيـهِ احْتِرَامْ
نَادَاهُ أَقْبِلْ يَـــا مُخْتَارْ   أَنْتَ الأَمِينْ
صَلِّ عَلَى بَاهِي الأَنْوَارْ   عَينِ الْيَقِيـنْ
نَادَاهُ أَقْبِلْ يَـــا مُخْتَارْ   أَنْتَ الأَمِينْ

"Every version has its own angels reciting back on you *Ṣalawāt* from Allah.... and taking you through the seven heavens to the Throne."[286]

[286] Shaykh Hisham Kabbani, *Ṣuḥba* of 28 April 2012, Burton, Michigan (USA). http://sufilive.com/The_Fragrance_that_Penetrates_the_Heavens_to_The_Throne_of_al_Rahman-4272.html from Muḥammad al-Mahdī al-Fāsī's *Maṭāli' al-Masarrāt bi-*

The Unfathomability of the Prophet's Rank I

Such expressions reached their apex of craftsmanship in the works of the Egyptian poet Sharaf al-Dīn al-Būṣīrī, teacher to some of the greatest scholars of his time,[287] who was eulogized in glowing terms by the Egyptian then Meccan leader of the Shāfiʿī school in his time, Ibn Ḥajar al-Haytamī (909-973/1503-1565) in the latter's introduction to his commentary on al-Būṣīrī's *Hamziyya*:

216. Truly among the most eloquent of the works of praise of the Prophet in brilliant, highly literate poetry; the most beautiful in showing many of his attributes in peerlessly concise prosody; the most comprehensive of poems in describing his great deeds, special attributes, and miracles; and the most chaste of odes pointing to the wonders of his perfections, is what was chiselled like the purest gold and refined like pearls and jewels by the verifying, erudite, singularly accomplished shaykh, imam, and gnostic, meticulous orator and man of letters, leader of poets, most poetry-imbued of scholars, most eloquent of the speakers of pure Arabic, chastest of the speakers of wisdom: Shaykh Sharaf al-Dīn Abū ʿAbd Allāh Muḥammad b. Saʿīd b. Ḥammād b. Muḥsin b. ʿAbd Allāh b. Ṣinhāj b. Hilāl al-Ṣunhājī al-Dalāṣīrī, then he became famous by the name of al-Būṣīrī.[288]

قال الإمام الهيتمي رحمه الله في مقدّمة كتابه (المِنَح المكيّة في شرح الهمزية):

وَإِنَّ مِنْ أَبْلَغِ مَا مُدِحَ بِهِ النَّبِيُّ ﷺ مِنَ النَّظْمِ الرَّائِقِ البَدِيعِ، وَأَحْسَنِ مَا كَشَفَ عَنْ كَثِيرٍ مِنْ شَمَائِلِهِ مِنَ الْوَزْنِ الْفَائِقِ المَنِيعِ، وَأَجْمَعِ مَا حَوَتْهُ قَصِيدَةٌ مِنْ مَآثِرِهِ وَخَصَائِصِهِ وَمُعْجِزَاتِهِ، وَأَفْصَحِ مَا أَشَارَتْ إِلَيْهِ مَنْظُومَةٌ مِنْ

Jalā' Dalā'il al-Khayrāt (1309/1892 ed. p. 38) cf. al-Quḥḥī's *Talkhīṣ al-Maʿārif.*

[287] Such as the exegete Abū Ḥayyān, the historian Ibn Sayyid al-Nās, and the jurist al-ʿIzz Ibn Jamāʿa.

[288] al-Haytamī, *Minaḥ* (1:105).

بَدَائِعِ كَمَالَاتِهِ، مَا صَاغَهُ صَوْغَ التِّبْرِ الْأَحْمَرِ وَنَظَمَهُ نَظْمَ الدُّرِّ وَالْجَوْهَرِ، الشَّيْخُ الإِمَامُ الْعَارِفُ الْهُمَامُ الْكَامِلُ الْمُفَنَّنُ الْمُحَقِّقُ، وَالْبَلِيغُ الْأَدِيبُ الْمُدَقِّقُ، إِمَامُ الشُّعَرَاءِ وَأَشْعَرُ الْعُلَمَاءِ، وَبَلِيغُ الْفُصَحَاءِ، وَأَفْصَحُ الْحُكَمَاءِ، الشَّيْخُ شَرَفُ الدِّينِ أَبُو عَبْدِ اللهِ مُحَمَّدُ بْنُ سَعِيدِ بْنِ حَمَّادِ بْنِ مُحْسِنِ بْنِ عَبْدِ اللهِ بْنِ صِنْهَاجِ بْنِ هِلَالٍ الصُّنْهَاجِيُّ الدَّلَاصِيرِيُّ، ثُمَّ اشْتَهَرَ بِالْبُوصِيرِيِّ.

Sufi masters past and present who spoke of the immense rank of the Prophet typically rely on al-Būṣīrī to illustrate their points.

Al-Ṣāwī commented thus on Ibn Mashīsh's supplication quoted above:

217. By him everything hidden was made clear and the gate of sensory and spiritual lights was thrown open. In him the realities of all things became manifest, so he is like the sky in which realities are like the stars. And all the sciences that descended on Adam descended on the Elect One as well, who also obtained knowledge of the realities of all things named. He left all creatures helpless, including angels and others, even Adam, as Adam's knowledge left only the angels helpless while his knowledge left all creatures from beginning to end helpless. The comprehension of creatures dwindles long before it can attain the reality of the Prophet. That is the meaning of al-Būṣīrī's saying:

Creation failed to comprehend his true self and none is seen near him or far from him except they all fall short.[289]

Hence he [Ibn Mashīsh] followed it up with the explanation that *none of us can reach him, from the first to the last.* That is, none of us who were ever created from the beginning of time to the end. *None* can comprehend his reality in this world! As for the

[289] al-Būṣīrī, *Burda* (line 46 p. 278).

next world, his reality can be reached because the veil will be lifted from creatures. Al-Būṣīrī said:

They but describe your attributes for rational beings
only as much as water can describe the stars.[290]

He further said in the *Burda*:

And how can his reality be apprehended in this world
by a drowsy folk distracted away from him by dreams?[291]

قال الإمام الصاوي رحمه الله في شرح الصلاة المشيشية ضمن شرحه للصلوات الدرديرية:

اِتَّضَحَ بِهِ كُلُّ مَا كَانَ خَفِيّاً وَانْفَتَحَ بَابُ الأَنْوَارِ الْحِسِّيَّةِ وَالمَعْنَوِيَّةِ وَفِيهِ ظَهَرَتْ حَقَائِقُ الأَشْيَاءِ، فَهُوَ بِمَنْزِلَةِ السَّمَاءِ وَالْحَقَائِقُ بِمَنْزِلَةِ الْكَوَاكِبِ. وَجَمِيعُ الْعُلُومِ الَّتِي نَزَلَتْ عَلَى آدَمَ نَزَلَتْ عَلَى الْمُصْطَفَى ﷺ وَزَادَ عِلْمُ حَقَائِقِ الْمُسَمَّيَاتِ. فَأَعْجَزَ جَمِيعَ الْخَلَائِقِ أَيِ الْمَخْلُوقَاتِ: مَلَائِكَةً وَغَيْرَهُمْ حَتَّى آدَمَ، فَعِلْمُ آدَمَ لَمْ يُعْجِزْ إِلَّا الْمَلَائِكَةَ، وَعِلْمُهُ ﷺ أَعْجَزَ الأَوَّلِينَ وَالآخِرِينَ. وَتَصَاغَرَتْ أَفْهَامُ الْخَلَائِقِ عَنْ إِدْرَاكِ حَقِيقَةِ النَّبِيِّ ﷺ وَهٰذَا مَعْنَى قَوْلِ الْبُوصِيرِيِّ:

أَعْيَا الْوَرَى فَهْمُ مَعْنَاهُ فَلَيْسَ يُرَى * فِي الْقُرْبِ وَالْبُعْدِ فِيهِ غَيْرُ مُنْفَحِمِ

وَلِذٰلِكَ عَلَّلَهُ بِقَوْلِهِ (فَلَمْ يُدْرِكْهُ مِنَّا سَابِقٌ وَلَا لَاحِقٌ) أَيْ مَعْشَرُ الْمَخْلُوقِينَ مِنْ أَوَّلِ الزَّمَانِ إِلَى آخِرِهِ، فَلَمْ يَقِفْ لَهُ أَحَدٌ عَلَى حَقِيقَةِ الدُّنْيَا، أَمَّا فِي الْآخِرَةِ فَتُدْرَكُ حَقِيقَتُهُ لِكَشْفِ الْحِجَابِ عَنِ الْخَلَائِقِ؛ قَالَ الْبُوصِيرِيُّ:

[290] al-Būṣīrī, *Hamziyya* (line 3, 1:133-135).
[291] al-Būṣīrī, *Burda* (line 50, p. 284); al-Ṣāwī, *Sharḥ al-Mashīshiyya*, f° 1a-b cf. his *Sharḥ al-Ṣalawāt al-Dardīriyya* (p. 35-36).

إِنَّمَا مَثَّلُوا صِفَاتِكَ لِلنَّاسِ * كَمَا مَثَّلَ النُّجُومَ الْمَاءُ

وَقَالَ فِي الْبُرْدَةِ:

وَكَيفَ يُدْرِكُ فِي الدُّنْيَا حَقِيقَتَهُ * قَوْمٌ نِيَامٌ تَسَلَّوا عَنْهُ بِالْحُلُمِ

Ibn ʿAjība said in his commentary on Ibn al-Bannā al-Marrākushī's (d. 721/1321) poem on *taṣawwuf* entitled *al-Mabāḥith al-Aṣliyya*:

218. Allah has singled out the Messenger of Allah—upon him blessings and peace—with unique attributes which no one shared with him. Whoever looks at his worship finds it impossible to bear; whoever looks at his inward character finds it impossible to attain; whoever looks at his gnosis finds it impossible to match. No one even comes near his sanctuary. Thus he possesses a station that is unattainable, unmatchable, and unknowable. Consider the statement of Shaykh ʿAbd al-Salām b. Mashīsh—Allah be well-pleased with him: *In him the realities rose up and Adam's sciences descended until he made all creatures helpless, and minds capitulated so that none of us can reach him, from the first to the last.* None of the scholars, the devotees, and the Sufis will obtain any of the Prophet's knowledge, his deeds, or his character except a drop or a sprinkle. May Allah well reward al-Būṣīrī in his poem of praise, the *Burda*, in which he says:

And all of them humbly seek from the Messenger of Allah
a scoop from the ocean or a sip from the rains.
And they all stop before him at their assigned limits:
one point of knowledge or a glimpse of wisdom.[292]

قال ابن عجيبة في شرح المباحث الأصلية لابن البَنَّا:

[292] al-Būṣīrī, *Burda* (lines 39-40, p. 248-259) and Ibn ʿAjība, *Futūḥāt* (p. 59).

قَدْ خَصَّ اللهُ تَعَالَى رَسُولَ اللهِ ﷺ بِخَصَائِصَ لَمْ يُشَارِكْهُ أَحَدٌ فِيهَا، فَمَنْ نَظَرَ فِي عِبَادَتِهِ وَجَدَهُ لَا يُطَاقُ، وَمَنْ نَظَرَ فِي أَخْلَاقِهِ الْبَاطِنَةِ وَجَدَهُ لَا يُدْرَكُ، وَمَنْ نَظَرَ فِي مَعْرِفَتِهِ وَجَدَهُ لَا يُلْحَقُ، ولَا يَقْرُبُ أَحَدٌ حَوْلَ حِمَاهُ، فَكَانَ ﷺ عَلَى مَقَامٍ لَا يُدْرَكُ وَلَا يُلْحَقُ وَلَا يُعْرَفُ.

وَانْظُرْ قَوْلَ الشَّيْخِ الْقُطْبِ ابْنِ مَشِيشٍ رَضِيَ اللهُ عَنْهُ: «وَفِيهِ ارْتَقَتِ الْحَقَائِقُ. وَتَنَزَّلَتْ عُلُومُ آدَمَ فَأَعْجَزَ الْخَلَائِقَ. وَلَهُ تَضَاءَلَتِ الْفُهُومُ فَلَمْ يُدْرِكْهُ مِنَّا سَابِقٌ وَلَا لَاحِقٌ.» وَلَنْ يَنَالَ أَحَدٌ مِنَ الْعُلَمَاءِ وَالْعُبَّادِ وَالصُّوفِيَّةِ مِنْ عِلْمِهِ ﷺ أَوْعَمَلِهِ أَوْ خُلُقِهِ إِلَّا رَشْفَةً أَوْ رَشَّةً، وَللهِ دَرُّ الْبُوصِيرِيِّ حَيْثُ يَقُولُ:

وَكُلُّهُمْ مِنْ رَسُولِ اللهِ مُلْتَمِسٌ * غَرْفاً مِنَ الْبَحْرِ أَوْ رَشْفاً مِنَ الدِّيَمِ
وَوَاقِفُونَ لَدَيهِ عِنْدَ حَدِّهِمُ * مِنْ نُقْطَةِ الْعِلْمِ أَوْ مِنْ شَكْلَةِ الحِكَمِ

Al-Būṣīrī said in the opening of his masterpiece, the *Hamziyya*:

219. *How can Prophets ascend such as your Ascent*
O Heaven no heaven can surpass?
They cannot even match you in your heights when, long before,
too great a light bars them from you, and loftiness.
They only describe your attributes for rational beings
as much as water can describe the stars.
You are the Lamp of every merit, hence lights
can never issue from other than your Light.
To you belongs the essence of sciences pouring from the Knower
of the unseen and thence, to Adam, knowledge of the Names.
From the origins, in the most secret places of creation,
your mothers and forefathers were chosen for you.

No empty interval between Divine Messengers passed
except Prophets gave their people joy, reminding them of you.
The times (here and hereafter) boast of you, rising aloft
with you, one towering summit then another.
And you dawned on the world, a Most Honorable One
from a most honorable one issued from honorable sires,
A lineage that, for its dazzling brilliance, you would take
for Gemini (al-Jawzā') garlanding with its stars the firmaments!
O lovely and beloved the jewelled necklace of lordship and pride
of which you are the most unique and flawless Pearl!
And the Face of brightness like the sun that you are,
from which a radiant night has lifted up its veil![293]

قال الشرف البوصيري رحمه الله في أول قصيدته الهمزية:

كَيْفَ تَرْقَى رُقِيَّكَ الْأَنْبِيَاءُ * يَا سَمَاءً مَا طَاوَلَتْهَا سَمَاءُ
لَمْ يُسَاوُوكَ فِي عُلَاكَ وَقَدْ حَا * لَ سَنًى مِنْكَ دُونَهُمْ وَسَنَاءُ
إِنَّمَا مَثَّلُوا صِفَاتِكَ لِلنَّاسِ * كَمَا مَثَّلَ النُّجُومَ الْمَاءُ
أَنْتَ مِصْبَاحُ كُلِّ فَضْلٍ فَمَا تَصْـ * ـدُرُ إِلَّا عَنْ ضَوْئِكَ الْأَضْوَاءُ
لَكَ ذَاتُ الْعُلُومِ مِنْ عَالِمِ الْغَيْـ * ـبِ وَمِنْهَا لِآدَمَ الْأَسْمَاءُ
لَمْ تَزَلْ فِي ضَمَائِرِ الْكَوْنِ تُخْتَا * رُ لَكَ الْأُمَّهَاتُ وَالْآبَاءُ
مَا مَضَتْ فَتْرَةٌ مِنَ الرُّسْلِ إِلَّا * بَشَّرَتْ قَوْمَهَا بِكَ الْأَنْبِيَاءُ
تَتَبَاهَى بِكَ الْعُصُورُ وَتَسْمُو * بِكَ عَلْيَاءُ بَعْدَهَا عَلْيَاءُ
وَبَدَا لِلْوُجُودِ مِنْكَ كَرِيمٌ * مِنْ كَرِيمٍ آبَاؤُهُ كُرَمَاءُ
نَسَبٌ تَحْسَبُ الْعُلَا بِحُلَاهُ * قَلَّدَتْهَا نُجُومَهَا الْجَوْزَاءُ

[293] al-Būṣīrī, *Hamziyya* (lines 1-12) in al-Haytamī, *Minaḥ* (1:115-173).

حَبَّذَا عِقْدُ سُؤْدَدٍ وَفَخَارٍ * أَنْتَ فِيهِ الْيَتِيمَةُ الْعَصْمَاءُ

وَمُحَيّاً كَالشَّمْسِ مِنْكَ مُضِيءٌ * أَسْفَرَتْ عَنْهُ لَيْلَةٌ غَرَّاءُ

Al-Haytamī commented on the lines *You are the lamp of every merit, hence lights can never issue from other than your light*:

220. It means you are the lamp of every merit and every perfection that ever existed for others, because you are the supreme Vicegerent who assists everything in existence (*al-khalīfat al-akbar al-mumidd li-kulli mawjūd*). In witness to this the authentic hadiths state "Adam and everyone after him and under my flag;"[294] "Allah is the Giver and I am the Distributor,"[295] "Were Mūsā alive he would have no choice but be my follower,"[296] and "Truly Ibrāhīm said: 'I was only an Intimate Friend from behind two remotes (*min warā'a warā'*).'"[297] … The torchlight (*miṣbāḥ*) from which lamps (*aḍwā'*) are derived is a metaphor for our Prophet because all perfections are derived from him. The import of the comparison is that his light causes inner meanings to appear like the light of insights (*nūr al-baṣā'ir*), while the light of a torchlight causes physical things to appear like the light of eyesights (*nūr al-abṣār*). He preferred it above the comparison to the sun and moon

[294] See above, note 40.

[295] al-Bukhārī, *Ṣaḥīḥ* (*'Ilm, man yurid Allāh bihi khayran yufaqqihhu fīl-Dīn*; *Farḍ al-khumus, qawl Allāh Ta'ālā: fa-inna lillāhi khumusahu wa-lil-Rasūl*; *al-I'tiṣām bil-Kitāb wal-Sunna, qawl al-Nabī lā tazāl ṭā'ifatun min ummatī ẓāhirīn 'alā al-ḥaqq*); Muslim, *Ṣaḥīḥ* (*Zakāt, al-nahy 'an al-masala*; *Ādāb, al-nahy 'an al-takannī bi-Abī al-Qāsim* without the last sentence) from Mu'āwiya. Its full wording is "Whoever Allah intends immense good for, He grants them superlative understanding of the Religion. Allah is the Giver and I am the Distributor. This Community will never cease to hold sway over their opponents until the final command of Allah comes while they have the upper hand."

[296] al-Dārimī, *Sunan* (*Muqaddima, mā yuttaqā min tafsīr ḥadīth al-Nabī*) from Jābir; and Aḥmad, *Musnad* (23:349 §15156) from 'Abd Allāh b. Thābit.

[297] Muslim, *Ṣaḥīḥ* (*Īmān, adnā ahl al-janna manzilatan fīhā*) from Abū Hurayra and Ḥudhayfa. Spoken by way of humbleness to refer to the intermediacy of Jibrīl and the preferred status of Mūsā to Ibrāhīm, since the latter continues: "But go to Mūsā, to whom Allah spoke without intermediary," and the second mention of *warā'* is an allusion to the Prophet Muḥammad, who was given both interlocutorship and sight, as if to say "I am behind Mūsā who is behind Muḥammad." Al-Ḥifnī, marginalia on al-Būṣīrī's *Hamziyya* (Cairo: al-Maṭba'at al-'Āmira, 1292/1875) p. 19.

because (i) lights are easily lit from it, and these derivative lights remain after it; and (ii) *ḍaw'* is higher than *nūr* as proved by the verse *He has made the sun a* ḍiyā' *and the moon a* nūr (10:5). Thus *your ḍaw'* stands for the attributes of perfection as an explicit comprehensive metaphor (*isti'āratan muṣarraḥatan bi-jāmi'*) that both the light of inner meanings and the physical lights guide one to the goal, and also that spiritual perfections enlighten both the outward person and their inward being.[298]

قال الإمام الهيتمي في المِنَح المكّية شارحاً قول البوصيري **أَنْتَ مِصْبَاحُ كُلِّ فَضْلٍ فَمَا تَصْدُرُ إِلَّا عَنْ ضَوْئِكَ الْأَضْوَاءُ:**

أَنْتَ مِصْبَاحُ كُلِّ فَضْلٍ وَكَمَالٍ بَرَزَ لِغَيْرِكَ فِي الْوُجُودِ، لِأَنَّكَ الخَلِيفَةُ الْأَكْبَرُ الْمُمِدُّ لِكُلِّ مَوْجُودٍ. وَشَاهِدُهُ مَا صَحَّ مِنْ خَبَرِ **آدَمُ فَمَنْ دُونَهُ تَحْتَ لِوَائِي وَلَا فَخْرَ** رواه أحمد عن ابن عباس وهذا لفظه والترمذي عن أبي سعيد وقال حديث حسن صحيح وَخَبَرِ **إِنَّمَا أَنَا الْقَاسِمُ وَاللهُ الْمُعْطِي** متفق عليه. وَخَبَرِ **لَوْ كَانَ مُوسَى حَيّاً مَا وَسِعَهُ إِلَّا اتِّبَاعِي** رواه أحمد والدارمي. وَخَبَرِ **فَيَقُولُ إِبْرَاهِيمُ: إِنَّمَا كُنْتُ خَلِيلاً مِنْ وَرَاءَ وَرَاءَ** رواه مسلم. ... وَاسْتِعَارَةُ السِّرَاجِ الَّذِي يُستَمَدُّ مِنْهُ الْأَضْوَاءُ لِنَبِيِّنَا ﷺ لِأَنَّهُ الَّذِي يُسْتَمَدُّ مِنْهُ الْكَمَالَاتُ بِأَسْرِهَا، وَآثَرَ التَّشْبِيهَ بِالسِّرَاجِ عَلَى الْقَمَرَيْنِ لِأَنَّهُ يُقْتَبَسُ مِنْهُ الْأَنْوَارُ بِسُهُولَةٍ وَتَخْلُفُهُ فُرُوعُهُ فَتَبْقَى بَعْدَهُ. وَالضَّوْءُ الَّذِي هُوَ أَعْلَى مِنَ النُّورِ بِدَلِيلِ ﴿ جَعَلَ ٱلشَّمْسَ ضِيَآءً وَٱلْقَمَرَ نُورًا ﴾ الآية. يونس. لِصِفَاتِ الْكَمَالِ اسْتِعَارَةً مُصَرَّحَةً[299] بِجَامِعِ أَنْ

[298] al-Haytamī, *al-Minaḥ al-Makkiyya* (1:138-141). The metaphor is explicit because the vehicle (light) to which the tenor (the Prophet) is being compared to is explicited.

[299] الاستعارة المصرَّحة هي ما صُرِّحَ فيها بالمستعار منه، نحو: هو على نورٍ من ربّه. أي على هدىً كالنور في

كُلًّا مِنَ الضَّوْئَيْنِ المَعْنَوِيِّ وَالحِسِّيِّ يَهْدِي إِلَى المَقْصُودِ، وَأَيْضاً الكَمَالَاتُ
الدِّينِيَّةُ تُنَوِّرُ الظَّاهِرَ وَالْبَاطِنَ.

The Unfathomability of the Prophet's Rank II

When the verse was revealed *Allah and His angels shower blessings on the Prophet. O you who believe! Invoke blessings on him and salute him with abundant salutations* (33:56) the Companion Bashīr b. Sa'd al-Anṣārī asked in what manner they should invoke blessings. The Prophet paused for a long time then he said:

221. Say: "O Allah, bless Muḥammad and the Household of Muḥammad just as you blessed the Household of Ibrāhīm; and grant grace to Muḥammad and the Household of Muḥammad just as you graced the Household of Ibrāhīm over all creation. Truly You are All-Praiseworthy, All-Glorious!" As for salutation (*al-salām*), you already know it.[300]

لَمَّا نَزَلَتْ ﴿ إِنَّ ٱللَّهَ وَمَلَٰٓئِكَتَهُۥ يُصَلُّونَ عَلَى ٱلنَّبِيِّۚ يَٰٓأَيُّهَا ٱلَّذِينَ ءَامَنُواْ صَلُّواْ عَلَيْهِ وَسَلِّمُواْ تَسْلِيمًا ﴿٥٦﴾ ﴾ قَالَ بَشِيرُ بْنُ سَعْدٍ رَضِيَ اللهُ عَنْهُ: أَمَرَنَا اللهُ تَعَالَى أَنْ نُصَلِّيَ عَلَيْكَ يَا رَسُولَ اللهِ، فَكَيْفَ نُصَلِّي عَلَيْكَ؟ فَسَكَتَ رَسُولُ اللهِ ﷺ حَتَّى تَمَنَّيْنَا أَنَّهُ لَمْ يَسْأَلْهُ. ثُمَّ قَالَ رَسُولُ اللهِ ﷺ قُولُوا: اللَّهُمَّ صَلِّ عَلَى مُحَمَّدٍ وَعَلَى آلِ مُحَمَّدٍ كَمَا صَلَّيْتَ عَلَى آلِ إِبْرَاهِيمَ. وَبَارِكْ عَلَى مُحَمَّدٍ وَعَلَى آلِ مُحَمَّدٍ كَمَا بَارَكْتَ عَلَى آلِ إِبْرَاهِيمَ فِي الْعَالَمِينَ. إِنَّكَ حَمِيدٌ مَجِيدٌ. وَالسَّلَامُ كَمَا قَدْ عَلِمْتُمْ. رواه التسعة وفي الباب عن كعب بن عُجْرَة وأبي حُمَيدٍ

الظهور والوضوح؛ فقد صُرِّحَ فيها بالمستعار منه، وهو النور. اهـ. من (البيان) لكرم البستاني ص ٦٦.

[300] Mass-transmitted through fourteen Companions in the Nine Books.

الساعِدِي وأبي سعيد الخدري وأبي مسعود الأنصاري وطلحة بن عبيد الله وعلي وبريدة الأسلمي وزيد بن خارجة ويقال ابن جارية وأبي هريرة وسهل بن سعد الساعدي ورويفع بن ثابت وجابر وابن عباس والنعمان بن أبي عياش.

The Divine command that we bless him is in reality a command that we invoke further Divine blessings on him. Thus we invoke not our own blessings but the blessings of Allah on the Prophet. The Moroccan scholar-poet Muḥammad al-Ṭāhir al-Kattānī (1299-1347/1881-1928) wrote in commentary of the above hadith:

> **222.** If every hair in our body invoked blessings on the Prophet, praised him, and thanked him, it would still not repay one tenth of a drop in the sea of his blessings; hence we have been ordered to ask Allah Himself to bless and greet him on our behalf, with His abundant bounty in recompensing him. For no one is able to recompense or repay the Prophet except His Almighty Lord.[301]

قال الإمام محمد الطاهر الكتاني في كتاب مطالع السعادة في اقتران كَلِمَتَي الشهادة:

لَوْ كَانَ فِي كُلِّ مَنْبَتِ شَعْرَةٍ مِنَّا لِسَانٌ يُصَلِّي عَلَيهِ ﷺ وَيُثْنِي عَلَيْهِ وَيَشْكُرُهُ، لَمَا وَفَى بِعُشْرِ قَطْرَةٍ مِنْ بَحْرِهِ الدَّافِقِ التَّيَّارِ، المُتَلَاطِمِ الأَمْوَاجِ. وَلِأَجْلِ هٰذَا أُمِرْنَا أَنْ نَسْأَلَ اللهَ تَعَالَى أَنْ يُصَلِّيَ وَيُسَلِّمَ عَلَيْهِ نِيَابَةً عَنَّا، بِفَضْلِهِ فِي مُكَافَاتِهِ، إِذْ لَا يَقْدِرُ عَلَى مُكَافَاتِهِ وَمُجَازَاتِهِ إِلَّا رَبُّهُ تَبَارَكَ وَتَعَالَى.

A further confirmation of the boundless nature of the Divine exaltation of the Prophet is the fact that for each single one of our invocations of blessings we make, we receive an infinitely disproportionate reward of ten to seventyfold blessings from Allah Himself:

301 al-Kattānī, *Maṭāliʿ al-Saʿāda* (p. 270).

223. Whoever invokes blessings on me once, Allah Most High blesses him ten times.[302]

عَنْ أَبِي هُرَيْرَةَ رَضِيَ اللهُ عَنْهُ مَرْفُوعاً: مَنْ صَلَّى عَلَيَّ وَاحِدَةً صَلَّى اللهُ عَلَيْهِ بِهَا عَشْراً. رواه مسلم وأحمد والثلاثة وفي الباب عن أبي الدرداء وعلي وأنس وعبد الله بن عمرو بن العاص وأبي طلحة رضي الله عنهم.

224. Abū al-Mawāhib al-Shādhilī (9th/15th c.) asked the Prophet in vision or in dream: "Messenger of Allah, is this [only] for someone who has presence of heart?" He replied: "Nay, but for anyone who invokes blessings on me, even if his heart is elsewhere; and Allah shall give him angels the like of mountains, praying for him and asking forgiveness for him." "And if he has presence of heart?" He replied: "Then no one but Allah knows how much reward he will get."[303]

وقال العارف أبو المواهب الشاذلي رضي الله عنه: **رَأَيْتُ رَسُولَ اللهِ ﷺ فَقُلْتُ: يَا رَسُولَ اللهِ صَلَاةُ اللهِ تَعَالَى عَشْراً عَلَى مَنْ صَلَّى عَلَيْكَ مَرَّةً وَاحِدَةً، هَلْ ذٰلِكَ إِنْ كَانَ حَاضِرَ الْقَلْبِ؟ فَقَالَ ﷺ بَلْ لِكُلِّ مُصَلٍّ عَلَيَّ وَلَوْ كَانَ غَافِلَ الْقَلْبِ وَيُعْطِيهِ اللهُ أَمْثَالَ الْجِبَالِ مِنَ الْمَلَائِكَةِ تَدْعُو لَهُ وَتَسْتَغْفِرُ لَهُ فَقَالَ وَإِذَا كَانَ حَاضِرَ الْقَلْبِ؟ قَالَ: فَلا يَعْلَمُ ذٰلِكَ إِلَّا اللهُ تَعَالَى** ذكره القطب عبد الوهاب الشعراني الشافعي في الطبقات الكبرى ويلقّب بالحنفي لأنه من نسل محمد ابن الحنفية رضي الله عنه. ونقله عنه السيد أحمد زيني دحلان في كتاب (تقريب الأصول لتسهيل الوصول لمعرفة الله والرسول).

[302] Muslim, *Ṣaḥīḥ* (*Ṣalāt, al-ṣalāt ʿalā al-Nabī*); al-Nasāʾī, *Sunan* (*Sahū, faḍl al-ṣalāt ʿalā al-Nabī*); al-Tirmidhī, *Sunan* (*Ṣalāt/Witr, taṭawwuʿ/mā jāʾ fī faḍl al-ṣalāt ʿalā al-Nabī*); Abū Dāwūd, *Sunan* (*Ṣalāt, istighfār*); Aḥmad, *Musnad* (14:444 §8854) etc.

[303] Cited by al-Shaʿrānī, *Ṭabaqāt* (2:67-68 *sub* Muḥammad Abū al-Mawāhib al-Shādhilī) and Sayyid Aḥmad b. Zaynī Daḥlān in his book *Taqrīb al-Uṣūl*.

ʿAbd Allah b. ʿAmr b. al-ʿĀṣ said:

225. Whoever invokes blessings on the Messenger of Allah once, Allah and His angels bless him seventy times; therefore let each servant do as little or as much of that as he wants.[304]

عَنْ عَبْدِ اللهِ بْنِ عَمْرِو بْنِ الْعَاصِ رَضِيَ اللهُ عَنْهُمَا قَالَ: مَنْ صَلَّى عَلَى رَسُولِ اللهِ ﷺ صَلَاةً صَلَّى اللهُ عَلَيْهِ وَمَلَائِكَتُهُ سَبْعِينَ صَلَاةً فَلْيُقِلَّ عَبْدٌ مِنْ ذٰلِكَ أَوْ لِيُكْثِرْ. رواه أحمد موقوفاً بسند جيد. وحكمه حكم المرفوع إذ لا يقال من باب الرأي.

In a similar vein Ibn ʿAbbās narrated that the Prophet said:

226. Whoever says: "May Allah recompense Muḥammad on our behalf as he deserves," he has exhausted seventy [angelic] scribes for 1,000 mornings.[305]

وَعَنِ ابْنِ عَبَّاسٍ رَضِيَ اللهُ عَنْهُمَا قَالَ: قَالَ رَسُولُ اللهِ ﷺ: مَنْ قَالَ جَزَى اللهُ مُحَمَّدًا عَنَّا مَا هُوَ أَهْلُهُ، أَتْعَبَ سَبْعِينَ كَاتِبًا أَلْفَ صَبَاحٍ. رواه الطبراني وابن شاهين والخطيب وأبو نعيم.

The abundance of such reward has led scholars to view the invoking of blessings on the Prophet as higher in merit than the Pillar of *zakāt*:

227. Al-Raṣṣāʿ said in *Tuḥfat al-Akhyār* that one of the scholars was asked in the Great Mosque of Damascus whether the invocation of blessings on the Prophet was better or the obligatory charity. The scholar replied the invocation of blessings is better.

[304] A saying of ʿAbd Allāh b. ʿAmr which has the status of a Prophetic hadith. Narrated by Aḥmad, *Musnad* (11:178 §6605 and 11:366 §6754) with a good chain cf. al-Haythamī, *Majma*ʿ (10:248 §17283) and al-Būṣīrī, *Itḥāf* (6:496 §6276).

[305] al-Ṭabarānī, *Kabīr* (11:206 §11509), *Awsaṭ* (1:180 §237), and *Musnad al-Shāmiyyīn* (3:196-197 §2070); Ibn Shāhīn, *Targhīb* (1:87 §15); al-Khaṭīb, *Tārīkh* (8:338-339); and Abū Nuʿaym, *Ḥilya* (3:206) and *Akhbār Aṣbahān* (2:230).

The questioner said: "How can it be said that the invocation of blessings is better than the obligatory charity that concerns property?" He replied: "There is a big difference between, on the one hand, the *farḍ* which Allah mentioned, in which He Himself invoked blessings, which His angels performed, and which He commanded His servants to do, and, on the other hand, the *farḍ* which He only made obligatory on His servants."[306]

قال الرَّصَّاع في تحفة الأخيار: سُئِلَ بَعْضُ الْعُلَمَاءِ بِجَامِعِ دِمَشْقَ عَنْ صَلَاةِ الْعَبْدِ عَلَى نَبِيِّهِ ﷺ هَلْ هِيَ أَفْضَلُ مِنْ صَدَقَةِ الْفَرْضِ أَمْ أَنَّ صَدَقَةَ الْفَرْضِ أَفْضَلُ؟ فَقَالَ: الصَّلَاةُ عَلَى النَّبِيِّ ﷺ أَفْضَلُ مِنْ صَدَقَةِ الْفَرْضِ. فَقَالَ السَّائِلُ: كَيْفَ يُقَالُ أَنَّ الصَّلَاةَ عَلَى النَّبِيِّ ﷺ أَفْضَلُ مِنْ صَدَقَةِ الْفَرْضِ الْوَاجِبِ فِي المَالِ؟ فَقَالَ: لَيْسَ الْفَرْضُ الَّذِي ذَكَرَهُ اللهُ تَعَالَى، وَصَلَّى فِيهِ بِنَفْسِهِ ، وَأَتَتْ بِهِ مَلَائِكَتُهُ، وَأَمَرَ بِهِ عَبْدَهُ: كَالْفَرْضِ الَّذِي أَوْجَبَهُ عَلَى عَبْدِهِ وَحْدَهُ. نقله عنه الشيخ يوسف النبهاني في سعادة الدارين.

All of the above reports confirm the doctrine that the Prophet is beyond emulation and that no one truly knows the Prophet except Allah Himself, as expressed by Ibn Mashīsh ("minds capitulated so that none of us can reach him, from the first to the last"), Ibn ʿAjība ("he possessed a station that is unattainable, unmatchable, and unknowable") and Sukayrij ("He came to know his own reality in a way none other than him has ever been able to know"). Ibn Ḥajar al-Haytamī said in commentary of al-Būṣīrī's statement,

228. *Whatever trait of his you begin with, you find that it reunites all the news of his immense merits from the start:*[307]

[306] In al-Nabhānī, *Saʿādat al-Dārayn* (p. 39).
[307] al-Būṣīrī, *Hamziyya* (line 125, *Minaḥ* 2:569-570).

قال البوصيري رحمه الله في الهمزية:

كُلُّ وَصْفٍ لَهُ ابْتَدَأْتَ بِهِ اسْتَوْ   عَبَ أَخْبَارَ الْفَضْلِ مِنْهُ ابْتِدَاءُ

229. You also have to believe that part of the perfection of faith in him is to believe that Allah created his noble body in a form the like of which was never seen before or after in any human being. The secret of this is that the beautiful aspects of a person point to what is hidden inwardly of their superlative manners and qualities, in which our Prophet has reached an unprecedented and unparalleled perfection. Hence he said in *Burdat al-Madīḥ*:

He is the one whose essence and form were made perfect,
  then the Creator of life chose him for His beloved,
Exempt of any partner in his beautiful traits
  so that the jewel of beauty was, in him, undivided.
Avoid whatever the Christians said about their Prophet
  then say whatever praise of him you like and do your best![308]

How well one of them spoke when he said: "The totality of his beauty was not revealed to us. If it had, our eyes would not have been able to look at him."

قال الهيتمي رحمه الله في شرح الهمزية:

يَجِبُ عَلَيْكَ أَنْ تَعْتَقِدَ أَيْضاً أَنَّ مِنْ تَمَامِ الإِيمَانِ بِهِ ﷺ الإِيمَانَ بِأَنَّ اللهَ تَعَالَى أَوْجَدَ خَلْقَ بَدَنِهِ الشَّرِيفِ عَلَى وَجْهٍ لَمْ يَظْهَرْ قَبْلَهُ وَلَا بَعْدَهُ فِي آدَمِيٍّ مِثْلِهِ. وَسِرُّ ذَلِكَ أَنَّ مَحَاسِنَ الذَّاتِ دَلِيلٌ عَلَى مَا بَطَنَ فِيهَا مِنْ بَدَائِعِ الأَخْلَاقِ وَجَلَائِلِ الصِّفَاتِ، وَنَبِيُّنَا ﷺ قَدْ بَلَغَ الْغَايَةَ الَّتِي لَمْ يَصِلْ إِلَيْهَا غَيْرُهُ فِي كُلٍّ مِنْ ذَيْنِكَ. وَمِنْ ثَمَّ قَالَ النَّاظِمُ فِي بُرْدَةِ الْمَدِيحِ:

---

[308] al-Būṣīrī, *Burda* (lines 41-43, *ʿUmda* p. 260-267).

فَهْوَ الَّذِي تَمَّ مَعْنَاهُ وَصُورَتُـــهُ * ثُمَّ اصْطَفَـــاهُ حَبِيباً بَارِئُ النَّسَـــمِ
مُنَزَّهٌ عَنْ شَرِيكٍ فِي مَحَاسِنِــــهِ * فَجَوْهَرُ الحُسْـــنِ فِيهِ غَيْرُ مُنْقَسِـــمِ
دَعْ مَا ادَّعَتْهُ النَّصَارَى فِي نَبِيِّهِمِ * وَاحْكُمْ بِمَا شِئْتَ مَدْحاً فِيهِ وَاحْتَكِمِ

وَمَا أَحْسَنَ قَولَ بَعْضِهِمْ: لَمْ يَظْهَرْ لَنَا تَمَامُ حُسْنِهِ ﷺ، وَإِلَّا لَمَا أَطَاقَتْ اَعْيُنُنَا النَّظَرَ إِلَيهِ.

VIII

The Light of the Prophetic Inheritors

The Three Types of Progeny in the Verse *alastu bi-Rabbikum*

Al-Tustarī (d. 283/896) in his Sufi exegesis of the Qur'ān glossed "their progeny" (*dhurriyyatahum*) in the verse *And when your Lord brought forth from Adam's Children, from their reins, their progeny, and made them testify of themselves: Am I not your Lord? They said: Yes, truly. We testify. That was lest you should say on the Day of Resurrection: Truly of this we were unaware* (7:172) in three senses:

230. The first sense of *dhurriyyatahum* is Muḥammad—upon him blessings and peace—because when Allah Most High wanted to create Muḥammad, He caused a light to appear out of h/His light (*aẓhara min nūrihi nūran*); when he reached the Veil of Magnificence he went into a great prostration to Allah. Allah then created out of his prostration a tremendous pillar like glass made of light, that is, both its inward and its outward contain Muḥammad himself (*bāṭinuh wa-ẓāhiruh fīhi ʿaynu Muḥammadin*). Then he stood before the Lord of the worlds in service for a million years with the indelible markers (*ṭabāʾiʿ*) of belief, namely, the eye-witnessing of faith, the uncovering of certainty, and the sighting of the Lord. Hence Allah Most High honored him with sight [of Him] before the beginning of creation by a million years.

The second sense is Ādam—upon him blessings and peace. He created him out of light, and He created Muḥammad's body out of Adam's clay.

The third sense is Adam's progeny. Truly Allah Most Glorious has created the seekers (*al-murīdīn*) from the light of Adam, and He has created the sought ones (*al-murādīn*) from the light of Muḥammad. The generality of creatures live in the mercy of the People of Nearness (*ahl al-qurb*), and the People of Nearness live in the mercy of the One Brought Near (*al-muqarrab*). *Their light will run before them and on their right hands* (66:8).[309]

قَالَ سَهْلُ التُّسْتَرِيُّ رَضِيَ اللهُ عَنْهُ فِي تَفْسِيرِ ﴿ وَإِذْ أَخَذَ رَبُّكَ مِنۢ بَنِىٓ ءَادَمَ مِن ظُهُورِهِمْ ذُرِّيَّتَهُمْ وَأَشْهَدَهُمْ عَلَىٰٓ أَنفُسِهِمْ أَلَسْتُ بِرَبِّكُمْ ۖ قَالُوا۟ بَلَىٰ ۛ شَهِدْنَآ ۛ ﴾ الآية الأعراف: وَالذُّرِّيَّةُ ثَلَاثٌ: أَوَّلٌ وَثَانٍ وَثَالِثٌ. فَالْأَوَّلُ: مُحَمَّدٌ ﷺ؛ لِأَنَّ اللهَ تَعَالَى لَمَّا أَرَادَ أَنْ يَخْلُقَ مُحَمَّداً ﷺ أَظْهَرَ مِنْ نُورِهِ نُوراً فَلَمَّا بَلَغَ حِجَابَ الْعَظَمَةِ سَجَدَ لله سَجْدَةً فَخَلَقَ سُبْحَانَهُ مِنْ سَجْدَتِهِ عَمُوداً عَظِيماً كَالزُّجَاجِ مِنَ النُّورِ أَيْ بَاطِنُهُ وَظَاهِرُهُ فِيهِ عَيْنُ مُحَمَّدٍ ﷺ فَوَقَفَ بَينَ يَدَيْ رَبِّ الْعَالَمِينَ بِالخِدْمَةِ أَلْفَ أَلْفِ عَامٍ بِطَبَائِعِ الإِيمَانِ وَهُوَ مُعَايَنَةُ الإِيمَانِ وَمُكَاشَفَةُ الْيَقِينِ وَمُشَاهَدَةُ الرَّبِّ فَأَكْرَمَهُ اللهُ تَعَالَى بِالْمُشَاهَدَةِ قَبْلَ بَدْءِ الخَلْقِ بِأَلْفِ أَلْفِ عَامٍ... الثاني: آدَمُ صَلَوَاتُ اللهِ عَلَيْهِ خَلَقَهُ مِنْ نُورٍ، قَالَ عَلَيْهِ السَّلَامُ: وَخَلَقَ مُحَمَّداً ﷺ يَعْنِي جَسَدَهُ، مِنْ طِينِ آدَمَ عَلَيْهِ السَّلَامُ. وَالثَّالِثُ: ذُرِّيَّةُ آدَمَ. وَإِنَّ اللهَ عَزَّ وَجَلَّ خَلَقَ الْمُرِيدِينَ مِنْ نُورِ آدَمَ وَخَلَقَ الْمُرَادِينَ مِنْ نُورِ مُحَمَّدٍ ﷺ فَالْعَامَّةُ مِنَ الْخَلْقِ يَعِيشُونَ فِي رَحْمَةِ أَهْلِ الْقُرْبِ، وَأَهْلُ الْقُرْبِ يَعِيشُونَ فِي رَحْمَةِ الْمُقَرَّبِ ﴿ نُورُهُمْ يَسْعَىٰ بَيْنَ أَيْدِيهِمْ وَبِأَيْمَـٰنِهِمْ ﴾. تفسير التستري.

[309] al-Tustarī, *Tafsīr* (p. 152-153).

Prophets and *Awliyā* drank deepest from his light (Dabbāgh)

Ibn Mubārak heard his teacher al-Dabbāgh give the following description of the creation of all things out of the light of the Prophet in commentary of Ibn Mashīsh's statement "*and from whom the lights broke forth*":

231. The first thing that Allah Most High created is the light of our liegelord Muḥammad. Then He created out of it the Pen, the Seventy Veils, and their angels. Then He created the Tablet and, before the latter was completed and formalized, He created the Throne, the souls, Paradise, and the interval world (*barzakh*). As for the Throne, He created it from His Light, that most honored light which is the light of our Prophet and liegelord Muḥammad. … Then Allah Most High created the angels of the earths from the Prophet's light, and He ordered them to worship Him there; and He created the angels of the heavens from his light, and He ordered them to worship Him there. As for souls and Paradise, but for some parts, they were also created from a light which itself was created out of his light. As for the *Barzakh*, its upper half is from his light. The upshot is that the Pen, the Tablet, half of the *Barzakh*, the Seventy Veils and all their angels, and all the angels of the [seven] heavens and the [seven] earths were created of the light of the Prophet without intermediary, while the Throne, water, Paradise, and souls were created from a light that was created out of his light. All these creations also drank from his light after that. … As for Prophets and all the believers from this and past communities they were given to drink from it eight times, the third of them on the Day of Promises, when all their souls drank from his light, but some drank much and some drank little, hence the disparity among the believers and the reason some of them are *awliyā'* and others not.[310]

قال الشيخ علي بن مبارك نقلاً عن القطب الغوث عبد العزيز الدَّبَّاغ في شرح قول القطب ابن مشيش (وَانْفَلَقَتِ الأَنْوَارُ):

[310] Ibn Mubārak, *Ibrīz* (p. 387-389).

إِنَّ أَوَّلَ مَا خَلَقَ اللهُ تَعَالَى نُورُ سَيِّدِنَا مُحَمَّدٍ ﷺ ثُمَّ خَلَقَ مِنْهُ الْقَلَمَ وَالْحُجُبَ السَّبْعِينَ وَمَلَائِكَتَهَا، ثُمَّ خَلَقَ اللَّوْحَ، ثُمَّ قَبْلَ كَمَالِهِ وَانْعِقَادِهِ خَلَقَ الْعَرْشَ وَالْأَرْوَاحَ وَالْجَنَّةَ وَالْبَرْزَخَ. أَمَّا الْعَرْشُ فَإِنَّهُ خَلَقَهُ اللهُ تَعَالَى مِنْ نُورِهِ، وَخَلَقَ ذٰلِكَ النُّورَ مِنَ النُّورِ الْمُكَرَّمِ، وَهُوَ أَيْ النُّورُ الْمُكَرَّمُ نُورُ نَبِيِّنَا وَمَوْلَانَا مُحَمَّدٍ ﷺ. ... ثُمَّ إِنَّ اللهَ تَعَالَى خَلَقَ مَلَائِكَةَ الْأَرَضِينَ مِنْ نُورِهِ ﷺ وَأَمَرَهُمْ أَنْ يَعْبُدُوهُ عَلَيْهَا وَخَلَقَ مَلَائِكَةَ السَّمٰوَاتِ مِنْ نُورِهِ ﷺ وَأَمَرَهُمْ أَنْ يَعْبُدُوهُ عَلَيْهَا. وَأَمَّا الْأَرْوَاحُ وَالْجَنَّةُ إِلَّا مَوَاضِعُ مِنْهَا، فَإِنَّهَا أَيْضاً خُلِقَتْ مِنْ نُورٍ، وَخُلِقَ ذٰلِكَ النُّورُ مِنْ نُورِهِ ﷺ. وَأَمَّا الْبَرْزَخُ فَنِصْفُهُ الْأَعْلَى مِنْ نُورِهِ ﷺ. **فَخَرَجَ مِنْ هٰذَا أَنَّ الْقَلَمَ، وَاللَّوْحَ، وَنِصْفَ الْبَرْزَخِ، وَالْحُجُبَ السَّبْعِينَ، وَجَمِيعَ مَلَائِكَتِهَا، وَجَمِيعَ مَلَائِكَةِ السَّمٰوَاتِ وَالْأَرَضِينَ، كُلَّهَا خُلِقَتْ مِنْ نُورِهِ ﷺ بِلَا وَاسِطَةٍ؛ وَأَنَّ الْعَرْشَ، وَالْمَاءَ، وَالْجَنَّةَ، وَالْأَرْوَاحَ، خُلِقَتْ مِنْ نُورٍ خُلِقَ مِنْ نُورِهِ ﷺ. ثُمَّ بَعْدَ هٰذَا، فَلِهٰذِهِ الْمَخْلُوقَاتِ أَيْضاً سُقْيٌ مِنْ نُورِهِ** ﷺ. ... وَأَمَّا الْأَنْبِيَاءُ عَلَيْهِمُ الصَّلَاةُ وَالسَّلَامُ وَكَذَا سَائِرُ الْمُؤْمِنِينَ مِنَ الْأُمَمِ الْمَاضِيَةِ وَمِنْ هٰذِهِ الْأُمَّةِ فَإِنَّهُمْ سُقُوا ثَمَانِ مَرَّاتٍ، الثَّالِثَةُ يَوْمَ أَلَسْتُ بِرَبِّكُمْ فَإِنَّ كُلَّ مَنْ أَجَابَ اللهَ تَعَالَى مِنْ أَرْوَاحِ الْمُؤْمِنِينَ وَالْأَنْبِيَاءِ عَلَيْهِمُ الصَّلَاةُ وَالسَّلَامُ سُقِيَ مِنْ نُورِهِ ﷺ لٰكِنْ مِنْهُمْ مَنْ سُقِيَ كَثِيراً، وَمِنْهُمْ مَنْ سُقِيَ قَلِيلاً، فَمِنْ هُنَا وَقَعَ التَّفَاوُتُ بَيْنَ الْمُؤْمِنِينَ حَتَّى كَانَ مِنْهُمْ أَوْلِيَاءُ وَغَيْرُهُمْ.

The Visible Light of the *Awliyā* Here and Hereafter

"The People of Nearness" (*ahl al-qurb*) and "the One Brought Near" (*al-muqarrab*) in al-Tustarī's text are references to the Friends of Allah in relation to the Seal of Prophets, beginning with the rest of the Prophets followed by the Companions, concerning whom the swordsman-Companion Burayda al-Aslamī related from the Prophet:

232. Any of my Companions that dies in a certain land will be their light and their leader on the Day of Resurrection.[311]

مَنْ مَاتَ مِنْ أَصْحَابِي بِأَرْضٍ كَانَ نُورَهُمْ وَقَائِدَهُمْ يَوْمَ الْقِيَامَةِ. الترمذي وأبو نعيم وابن بِشران وتمّام الرازي والخطيب والبغوي والسِلَفي وابن عساكر.

Reports that witness to the visible light of the Companions in their lifetime abound. Among them:

233. [Anas:] Usayd b. Ḥuḍayr and ʿAbbād b. Bishr left the house of the Prophet late one dark night. The tip of the staff of one of them lit up like a lamp and they were able to see as they walked. When they parted ways, the tip of the other staff lit up as well.[312]

234. Usayd is the one who related he witnessed angels appearing in the night sky in the forms of lights because of his melodious Qur'ān recitation.[313]

[311] al-Tirmidhī, *Sunan*, (*Manāqib, Bāb man sabba aṣḥāb al-Nabī*); Tammām, *Fawā'id* (*Rawḍ* 4:355 §1528); Ibn Bishrān, *Amālī* (1:53 §69); Abū Nuʿaym, *Maʿrifat al-Ṣaḥāba* (1:17 §42); al-Khaṭīb, *Tārīkh Baghdād* (1:127-128); al-Baghawī, *Sharḥ al-Sunna* (14:72 §3862, *ḥasan gharīb*), *al-Anwār* (2:775 §1241) and *Tafsīr* (*sub* 58:29); Ibn ʿAsākir, *Tārīkh* (2:416).

[312] al-Bukhārī, *Ṣaḥīḥ* (*Manāqib, manqabat Usayd b. Ḥuḍayr wa-ʿAbbād b. Bishr*); al-Nasā'ī, *al-Sunan al-Kubrā* (7:346-347 §8188) and others.

[313] al-Bukhārī, *Ṣaḥīḥ* (*Faḍā'il al-Qur'ān, nuzūl al-sakīna wal-malā'ika ʿinda qirā'at al-Qur'ān*); Muslim, *Ṣaḥīḥ* (*Ṣalāt al-musāfirīn, nuzūl al-sakīna li-qirā'at al-Qur'ān*); al-Nasā'ī, *al-Sunan al-Kubrā* (7:257-258 §7962).

عَنْ أَنَسٍ رَضِيَ اللهُ عَنْهُ أَنَّ رَجُلَيْنِ خَرَجَا مِنْ عِنْدِ النَّبِيِّ ﷺ فِي لَيْلَةٍ مُظْلِمَةٍ وَإِذَا نُورٌ بَيْنَ أَيْدِيهِمَا حَتَّى تَفَرَّقَا فَتَفَرَّقَ النُّورُ مَعَهُمَا وَقَالَ مَعْمَرٌ عَنْ ثَابِتٍ عَنْ أَنَسٍ إِنَّ أُسَيْدَ بْنَ حُضَيْرٍ وَرَجُلًا مِنَ الْأَنْصَارِ وَقَالَ حَمَّادٌ أَخْبَرَنَا ثَابِتٌ عَنْ أَنَسٍ كَانَ أُسَيْدُ بْنُ حُضَيْرٍ وَعَبَّادُ بْنُ بِشْرٍ عِنْدَ النَّبِيِّ ﷺ رواه البخاري وجاء بلفظ فَخَرَجَا مِنْ عِنْدِهِ فَأَضَاءَتْ عَصَا أَحَدِهِمَا مِثْلَ السِّرَاجِ وَكَانَا يَمْشِيَانِ بِضَوْئِهَا فَلَمَّا أَرَادَا أَنْ يَتَفَارَقَا إِلَى مَنَازِلِهِمَا أَضَاءَتْ لَهُمَا عَصَوَاهُمَا. قال البوصيري في الإتحاف: رواه أبو داود الطيالسي ومحمد بن يحيى بن أبي عُمَر والنسائي في الكبرى. وأُسَيد هو الذي نزلت الملائكة لقراءته القرآن، قال: مِثْلَ الظُّلَّةِ فِيهَا أَمْثَالُ الْمَصَابِيحِ. متفق عليه.

235. [Abū Hurayra:] We were praying the *ʿishā'* prayer with the Prophet. Whenever the Prophet prostrated al-Ḥasan and al-Ḥusayn climbed onto his back. Whenever he raised his head he would gently reach for them behind him and put them on the ground. When he went back into prostration they would climb up again. When he finished praying he sat them on his thighs. I went up to him and asked him, "Messenger of Allah, shall I take them to their mother?" Then a light flashed in the sky, whereupon he said: "Go to your mother." The light remained until they went in.[314]

عَنْ أَبِي هُرَيْرَةَ قَالَ كُنَّا نُصَلِّي مَعَ رَسُولِ اللهِ ﷺ الْعِشَاءَ فَإِذَا سَجَدَ وَثَبَ الْحَسَنُ وَالْحُسَيْنُ عَلَى ظَهْرِهِ فَإِذَا رَفَعَ رَأْسَهُ أَخَذَهُمَا بِيَدِهِ مِنْ خَلْفِهِ أَخْذًا

[314] Aḥmad, *Musnad* (16:386 §10659); al-Ṭabarānī, *Kabīr* (3:45 §2659 and [al-Ḥusayn alone] 3:45-46 §2660); al-Bazzār, *Musnad* cf. al-Haythamī, *Kashf* (3:227 §2629); al-Ḥākim, *Mustadrak* (3:167); al-Bayhaqī, *Dalā'il* (5:76); and Ibn ʿAsākir, *Tārīkh* (14:159).

رَفِيقًا وَيَضَعُهُمَا عَلَى الْأَرْضِ فَإِذَا عَادَ عَادَا حَتَّى إِذَا قَضَى صَلَاتَهُ أَقْعَدَهُمَا عَلَى فَخِذَيْهِ قَالَ فَقُمْتُ إِلَيْهِ فَقُلْتُ يَا رَسُولَ اللهِ أَرُدُّهُمَا؟ فَبَرَقَتْ بَرْقَةٌ فَقَالَ لَهُمَا أَلْحِقَا بِأُمِّكُمَا. قَالَ: فَمَكَثَ ضَوْءُهَا حَتَّى دَخَلَا. أحمد والطبراني والبزار والحاكم والبيهقي وابن عساكر.

236. [Anas b. Mālik:] I accompanied the Prophet from his house to the mosque where a group of people, hands raised, were supplicating. He said: "Do you see in their hands what I see?" "What is in their hands?" I asked. "In their hands there is light," he replied. I said: "Ask Allah Most High to show it to me." He supplicated and showed it to me then he sped and we raised our hands too. [*Var.* He supplicated to Allah then I saw it and he said: "Hurry up and stretch your hands with the group." We sped and stretched our hands with the group.][315]

عَنْ أَنَسِ بْنِ مَالِكٍ خَرَجْتُ مَعَ النَّبِيِّ ﷺ مِنَ الْبَيْتِ إِلَى الْمَسْجِدِ وَقَوْمٌ فِي الْمَسْجِدِ رَافِعُو أَيْدِيهِمْ يَدْعُونَ. قَالَ: تَرَى بِأَيْدِيهِمْ مَا أَرَى؟ فَقُلْتُ: وَمَا بِأَيْدِيهِمْ؟ قَالَ: بِأَيْدِيهِمْ نُورٌ. قُلْتُ: أُدْعُ اللهَ أَنْ يُرِيَنِيهِ. فَدَعَا فَأَرَانِيهِ فَأَسْرَعَ فَرَفَعْنَا أَيْدِينَا. البخاري في التاريخ الكبير والبيهقي في الدلائل. وجاء بلفظ فَدَعَا اللهَ فَرَأَيْتُهُ فَقَالَ: أَسْرِعْ حَتَّى تَنْشُرَ يَدَكَ مَعَ الْقَوْمِ. فَأَسْرَعْنَا فَنَشَرْنَا أَيْدِينَا مَعَ الْقَوْمِ. العقيلي في الضعفاء.

237. [Ṭufayl b. ʿAmr:] The poet and regal leader of Abū Hurayra's tribe, al-Ṭufayl b. ʿAmr al-Dawsī, known as Dhūl-Nūr because of this miracle, asked the Prophet to supplicate for a sign to show to

[315] al-Bukhārī, *al-Tārīkh al-Kabīr* (*sub* Khaṭṭāb b. ʿUmar); al-Bayhaqī, *Dalāʾil* (5:197). The variant is in al-ʿUqaylī, *Ḍuʿafāʾ* (*sub* Khattāb b. ʿUmayr al-Thawrī).

his tribesmen, whereupon the Prophet supplicated for him and he left. As he emerged from the mountain pass overlooking their [Daws's] watering-place, a light shone between his two eyes like a lamp. He supplicated, "O Allah, other than in my face, I fear they might think it a disfigurement!" The light moved to the tip of his whip and people saw it there like a hanging lantern.[316]

عَنِ الطُّفَيلِ بْنِ عَمْرٍو الدَّوْسِيِّ ذِي النُّورِ رَضِيَ اللهُ عَنْهُ أَنَّهُ قَدِمَ مَكَّةَ فَأَسْلَمَ وَقَالَ: يَا رَسُولَ اللهِ إِنِّي امْرُؤٌ مُطَاعٌ فِي قَوْمِي وَإِنِّي رَاجِعٌ إِلَيْهِمْ وَدَاعِيهِمْ إِلَى الْإِسْلَامِ فَادْعُ اللهَ أَنْ يَجْعَلَ لِي آيَةً تَكُونُ عَوْناً عَلَيْهِمْ فَقَالَ: اللّٰهُمَّ اجْعَلْ لَهُ آيَةً فَخَرَجْتُ حَتَّى إِذَا كُنْتُ بِثَنِيَّةٍ تُطْلِعُنِي عَلَى الحَاضِرِ وَقَعَ نُورٌ بَيْنَ عَيْنَيَّ مِثْلَ المِصْبَاحِ فَقُلْتُ: اللّٰهُمَّ فِي غَيْرِ وَجْهِي، وَأَخْشَى أَنْ يَظُنُّوا بِي أَنَّهَا مُثْلَةٌ. فَتَحَوَّلَ فَوَقَعَ فِي رَأْسِ سَوْطِي فَجَعَلَ الحَاضِرُونَ يَرَوْنَ ذٰلِكَ النُّورَ فِي سَوْطِي كَالْقِنْدِيلِ المُعَلَّقِ. ابن سعد وابن هشام وأبو نعيم والبيهقي والماوردي في أعلام النبوة وهذا لفظه. وابن عساكر.

Al-Ṭufayl b. ʿAmr al-Dawsī declaimed about the Prophet:

238. *I saw proofs that convinced me*
that his path leads to the best goal,
And that Allah has transfigured him with beauty
and has raised his destiny above all destinies.
So I triumphed through what Allah placed in my heart
and Muḥammad triumphed with my purest love.[317]

[316] Ibn Saʿd, *Ṭabaqāt* (4:224-225); Ibn Hishām, *Sīra* (1/2:383); Abū Nuʿaym, *Maʿrifa* (*sub* al-Ṭufayl b. ʿAmr al-Dawsī) and *Dalāʾil* (p. 238-239 §191); al-Māwardī, *Aʿlām al-Nubuwwa* (p. 104); al-Bayhaqī, *Dalāʾil* (5:360-361); Ibn ʿAsākir (25:18); cf. Fayrūzābādī, *Qāmūs* (*sub al-nūr*); Ibn Ḥajar, *Iṣāba* (*sub* al-Ṭufayl b. ʿAmr) and *Fatḥ* (*Maghāzī, qiṣṣat Daws wal-Ṭufayl b. ʿAmr*).

[317] al-Marzubānī in his *Muʿjam al-Shuʿarāʾ* cf. al-Ṣāliḥī, *Subul al-Hudā* (2:549-550)

أَنْشَدَ الطُّفَيلُ بْنُ عَمْرٍو الدَّوْسِيُّ:

رَأَيْتُ لَهُ دَلَائِلَ أَنْبَأَتْنِي * بِأَنْ سَبِيلَهُ يَهْدِي لِقَصْدِ
وَأَنَّ اللهَ جَلَّلَهُ بَهَاءً * وَأَعْلَى جَدَّهُ فِي كُلِّ جَدِّ
فَفُزْتُ بِمَا حَبَاهُ اللهُ قَلْبِي * وَفَازَ مُحَمَّدٌ بِصَفَاءِ وُدِّي

مما ذكره الحافظ الصالحي في سبل الهُدى والرَّشاد

As for the light of the *Umma* on Resurrection it is affirmed in the Qur'ān – *the day when Allah will not abase the Prophet and those who believe with him. Their light will run before them and on their right hands: they will say: Our Lord! Perfect our light for us* (66:8) – and the Prophetic Sunna as related from Abū Dharr and Abū al-Dardā':

239. I shall certainly know my Community among all others on the Day of Resurrection. I shall know them because they will be given their records with the right hand; I shall know them because *their signs will be in their faces from the marks of prostration* (48:29); and I shall know them by *their light that will run before them* (66:8).[318]

﴿ يَوْمَ تَرَى ٱلْمُؤْمِنِينَ وَٱلْمُؤْمِنَٰتِ يَسْعَىٰ نُورُهُم بَيْنَ أَيْدِيهِمْ وَبِأَيْمَٰنِهِم بُشْرَىٰكُمُ ٱلْيَوْمَ جَنَّٰتٌ تَجْرِى مِن تَحْتِهَا ٱلْأَنْهَٰرُ خَٰلِدِينَ فِيهَا ۚ ذَٰلِكَ هُوَ ٱلْفَوْزُ ٱلْعَظِيمُ ﴿١٢﴾ ﴾ الحديد. ﴿ يَوْمَ لَا يُخْزِى ٱللَّهُ ٱلنَّبِىَّ وَٱلَّذِينَ ءَامَنُوا۟ مَعَهُۥ ۖ نُورُهُمْ يَسْعَىٰ بَيْنَ أَيْدِيهِمْ وَبِأَيْمَٰنِهِمْ يَقُولُونَ رَبَّنَآ أَتْمِمْ لَنَا نُورَنَا

and Ibn Sayyid al-Nās, *Minaḥ* (p. 139).
318 Aḥmad, *Musnad* (36:66 §21740) and al-Ḥākim, *Mustadrak* (2:478).

وَٱغۡفِرۡ لَنَآۖ إِنَّكَ عَلَىٰ كُلِّ شَيۡءٖ قَدِيرٞ ﴿٨﴾ التحريم. عَنْ أَبِي ذَرٍّ وَأَبِي الدَّرْدَاءِ أَنَّ رَسُولَ اللهِ ﷺ قَالَ إِنِّي لَأَعْرِفُ أُمَّتِي يَوْمَ الْقِيَامَةِ مِنْ بَيْنِ الْأُمَمِ قَالُوا يَا رَسُولَ اللهِ وَكَيْفَ تَعْرِفُ أُمَّتَكَ قَالَ أَعْرِفُهُمْ يُؤْتَوْنَ كُتُبَهُمْ بِأَيْمَانِهِمْ وَأَعْرِفُهُمْ بِسِيمَاهُمْ فِي وُجُوهِهِمْ مِنْ أَثَرِ السُّجُودِ وَأَعْرِفُهُمْ بِنُورِهِمْ يَسْعَى بَيْنَ أَيْدِيهِمْ. رواه أحمد والحاكم.

The Prophet thus revealed that this light was specific to his Community. Furthermore, he connected that light to ablution and prostration as narrated from Abū Hurayra and ʿAbd Allah b. Busr respectively:

240. The Prophet came to the graveyard and greeted the graveyard saying: "Peace upon you, Abode of the believing folk! Truly we will, if Allah wills, join up with you." Then he said: "Would that we saw our brothers." They said: "Messenger of Allah, are we not your brothers?" He said: "You are my Companions, and my brothers are those who will come after me; and I am your forerunner at the Pond." They said: "Messenger of Allah, how will you recognize those of your Community that have not appeared yet?" He said: "Consider a man that has horses, some of them sabino piebalds (*ghurrun muḥajjala*) and the rest plain dark. Can he not tell the first from the rest?" They said yes. He continued: "They will come on the Day of Resurrection with spots of light on their faces and limbs from the mark of ablutions."[319]

عَنْ أَبِي هُرَيْرَةَ رَضِيَ اللهُ عَنْهُ عَنِ النَّبِيِّ ﷺ أَنَّهُ أَتَى الْمَقْبَرَةَ فَسَلَّمَ عَلَى الْمَقْبَرَةِ. فَقَالَ: السَّلَامُ عَلَيْكُمْ دَارَ قَوْمٍ مُؤْمِنِينَ! وَإِنَّا، إِنْ شَاءَ اللهُ تَعَالَى، بِكُمْ لَاحِقُونَ. ثُمَّ قَالَ: لَوَدِدْنَا أَنَّا قَدْ رَأَيْنَا إِخْوَانَنَا. قَالُوا: يَا رَسُولَ اللهِ أَوَلَسْنَا

[319] Ibn Mājah, *Sunan* (*Zuhd, dhikr al-ḥawḍ*).

إِخْوَانَكَ؟ قَالَ: أَنْتُمْ أَصْحَابِي، وَإِخْوَانِي الَّذِينَ يَأْتُونَ مِنْ بَعْدِي. وَأَنَا فَرَطُكُمْ عَلَى الْحَوْضِ. قَالُوا: يَا رَسُولَ اللهِ كَيْفَ تَعْرِفُ مَنْ لَمْ يَأْتِ مِنْ أُمَّتِكَ؟ قَالَ: أَرَأَيْتُمْ لَوْ أَنَّ رَجُلاً لَهُ خَيْلٌ غُرٌّ مُحَجَّلَةٌ بَيْنَ ظَهْرَانَيْ خَيْلٍ دُهْمٍ بُهْمٍ، أَلَمْ يَكُنْ يَعْرِفُهَا؟ قَالُوا: بَلَى. قَالَ فَإِنَّهُمْ يَأْتُونَ يَوْمَ الْقِيَامَةِ غُرّاً مُحَجَّلِينَ، مِنْ أَثَرِ الْوُضُوءِ. ابن ماجه.

A variant wording from Anas states:

241. "When will I meet my beloved ones (*aḥbābī*)?" They said: "Messenger of Allah, are we not your beloved ones?" He said: "You are my Companions, but my beloved ones are a folk that never saw me and yet they believed in me, and I long for them."[320]

عَنْ أَنَسٍ رَضِيَ اللهُ عَنْهُ مَرْفُوعاً مَتَى أَلْقَى أَحْبَابِي؟ فَقَالَ أَصْحَابُهُ: بِأَبِينَا أَنْتَ وَأُمِّنَا أَوَلَسْنَا أَحْبَابَكَ؟ قَالَ أَنْتُمْ أَصْحَابِي؛ أَحْبَابِي قَوْمٌ لَمْ يَرَوْنِي وَآمَنُوا بِي وَأَنَا إِلَيْهِمْ بِالْأَشْوَاقِ أبو الشيخ في الثواب كما في كنز العُمّال وتصحيحه من القشيرية

242. [ʿAbd Allāh b. Busr:] My Community on the Day of Resurrection will be marked with light due to prostration and on their foreheads and limbs due to ablution.[321]

وَعَنْ عَبْدِ اللهِ بْنِ بُسْرٍ رَضِيَ اللهُ عَنْهُ عَنِ النَّبِيِّ ﷺ قال: أُمَّتِي يَوْمَ الْقِيَامَةِ غُرٌّ مِنَ السُّجُودِ مُحَجَّلُونَ مِنَ الْوُضُوءِ. الترمذي وقال حديث حسن صحيح.

[320] Abū al-Shaykh in *al-Thawāb* cf. al-Muttaqī al-Hindī, *Kanz* (14:51-52 §37913) and al-Qushayrī, *Risāla* (*sub Ṣuḥba*).
[321] al-Tirmidhī, *Sunan* (*Jumuʿa, mā dhukira min sīmā hādhihi al-Umma yawma al-Qiyāma, ḥasan ṣaḥīḥ*).

The great Successor Sālim b. ʿAbd Allāh b. ʿUmar (d. 106/725) said:

243. A man recounted his dream in a gathering in which Kaʿb al-Aḥbār was present, saying: "I saw in a dream that all the Communities were gathered up. Every Prophet had two lights and every follower in each of their Communities had one light. Lo and behold! Muḥammad had as many lights as there were hairs on his head and body, and every follower in his Community had two lights!" Kaʿb said: "By the One Who revealed the Torah to Mūsā and the Furqān to Muḥammad! I certainly find in the Torah the mission of the Prophets and their Communities and the mission of Muḥammad just as you have described."[322]

عَنْ سَالِمِ بْنِ عَبْدِ اللهِ بْنِ عُمَرَ رَضِيَ اللهُ عَنْهُمْ أَنَّ رَجُلاً حَدَّثَ قَوْماً كَانَ فِيهِمْ كَعْبٌ قَالَ رَأَيْتُ كَأَنَّ الْأُمَمَ جُمِعَتْ فَكَانَ لِكُلِّ نَبِيٍّ نُورَانِ وَلِمَنْ مَعَهُ مِنْ أُمَّتِهِ نُوراً وَاحِداً وَإِذَا مُحَمَّدٌ لِكُلِّ شَعْرَةٍ مِنْ رَأْسِهِ وَجَسَدِهِ نُورٌ وَلِمَنْ مَعَهُ مِنْ أُمَّتِهِ نُورَانِ نُورَانِ فَقَالَ كَعْبٌ وَالَّذِي أَنْزَلَ التَّوْرَاةَ عَلَى مُوسَى عَلَيهِ السَّلامُ وَالْفُرْقَانَ عَلَى مُحَمَّدٍ ﷺ إِنِّي أَجِدُ فِي التَّوْرَاةِ بَعْثَ الْأَنْبِيَاءِ وَأُمَمِهِمْ وَبَعْثَ مُحَمَّدٍ ﷺ كَمَا رَأَيْتَ. رواه الحافظ ابن حجر في كتاب نزهة السامعين فى رواية الصحابة عن التابعين بإسناد صحيح.

The Prophet's Definition of the *Awliyā*

The Companions asked the Prophet to define the "friends of Allāh" *(awliyā')* and, at other times, to recommend who they should keep company with. Ibn ʿAbbas, ʿAmr b. al-Jamūḥ and others narrated that he replied to those questions thus:

[322]Narrated by Ibn Ḥajar in *Nuzhat al-Sāmiʿīn* (p. 98) with a sound chain.

244. The *awliyā'* of Allah are those who, when you see them, you are reminded of Allāh.[323]

245. My *awliyā'* among My servants, and My beloved among My creatures are those who are are remembered with My remembrance, and I am remembered with their remembrance.[324]

عَنِ ابْنِ عَبَّاسٍ رَضِيَ اللهُ عَنْهُمَا قَالَ: قَالَ رَجُلٌ: يَا رَسُولَ اللهِ مَنْ أَوْلِيَاءُ اللهِ؟ قَالَ: الَّذِينَ إِذَا رُؤُوا ذُكِرَ اللهُ. رواه وابن المبارك النسائي في الكبرى والطبراني والبزار بسند جيد وأبو نعيم. وفي الباب عن عبد الله بن عمرو وأنس وابن مسعود وأبي مالك الأشعري وأسماء بنت يزيد وابن عمر وعُبادة بن الصامت وسعد بن أبي وقاص رضي الله عنهم. **وَعَنْ عَمْرِو بْنِ الجَمُوحِ رَضِيَ اللهُ عَنْهُ مَرْفُوعاً إِنَّ أَوْلِيَائِي مِنْ عِبَادِي وَأَحِبَّائِي مِنْ خَلْقِي الَّذِينَ يُذْكَرُونَ بِذِكْرِي وَأُذْكَرُ بِذِكْرِهِمْ** أحمد، ورواه الطبراني عن عمرو بن الحَمِق رضي الله عنه.

"*Awliyā* are the very purpose of all that exists" (Ibn al-Jawzī)

Since remembrance of Allah and worship of Him is the reason for creation, and since seeing a Friend of Allah reminds one of Him, it is not surprising that in the preface to his biographical dictionary of the Sufis entitled *Ṣifat al-Ṣafwa* Ibn al-Jawzī said:

[323] al-Nasā'ī, *al-Sunan al-Kubrā* (10:124 §11171), al-Bazzār, *Musnad* (11:251 §5034, cf. Ibn Ḥajar's *Mukhtaṣar* 2:394-395 §2083 and al-Haythamī, *Majma'* 10:78), al-Ṭabarī, *Tafsīr* (11:131), al-Ṭabarānī in *al-Kabīr* (12:13 §12325), Ibn al-Mubārak in *al-Zuhd* (p. 72 §218), Abū Nu'aym in *Akhbār Aṣbahān* (1:231); also narrated from 'Abd Allāh b. 'Amr, Anas, Ibn Mas'ūd, Abū Mālik al-Ash'arī, Asmā' bint Yazīd, Ibn 'Umar, 'Ubāda b. al-Ṣāmit, Sa'īd b. Jubayr, 'Abd al-Raḥmān b. Ghanm al-Ash'arī, and Ṭāwūs b. Kaysān.

[324] Aḥmad, *Musnad* (24:316-317 §15549); also from 'Amr b. al-Ḥamiq by al-Ṭabarānī, *al-Mu'jam al-Awsaṭ* (1:203 §651).

246. The Friends of Allah and the Righteous are the very purpose of all that exists (*al-awliyā' wal-ṣāliḥūn hum al-maqṣud min al-kawn*). They are those who learned and practiced with the reality of knowledge. ... 'Aṭā' b. Yasār related that Mūsā said: "O my Lord! Who are Your People that are truly Your People, and whom You will shade under Your Throne?" Allah said: "They are those with innocent hands and pure hearts who love one another in My Majesty; those who, when I am remembered, they are remembered, and when they are remembered, I am remembered through their remembrance." … Ibn 'Uyayna said: "At the mention of the Righteous mercy descends." Muḥammad b. Yūnus said: "I never saw a more beneficial act for the heart than to mention the Righteous."[325]

قال ابن الجوزي رحمه الله في باب ذكر فضل الأولياء والصالحين من مقدمة صِفَة الصَفْوَة:

الأَوْلِيَاءُ وَالصَّالِحُونَ هُمُ المَقْصُودُ مِنَ الكَونِ، وَهُمُ الَّذِينَ عَلِمُوا فَعَمِلُوا بِحَقِيقَةِ الْعِلْمِ. ... وَعَنْ عَطَاءِ بْنِ يَسَارٍ: قَالَ مُوسَى عَلَيْهِ السَّلَامُ: يَا رَبِّ مَنْ أَهْلُكَ الَّذِينَ هُمْ أَهْلُكَ، الَّذِينَ تَظِلُّهُمْ فِي عَرْشِكَ؟ قَالَ: هُمُ الْبَرِيئَةُ أَيْدِيهِمْ، الطَّاهِرَةُ قُلُوبُهُمْ، الَّذِينَ يَتَحَابُّونَ بِجَلَالِي، الَّذِينَ إِذَا ذُكِرْتُ ذُكِرُوا وَإِذَا ذُكِرُوا ذُكِرْتُ بِذِكْرِهِمْ ... وَعَنْ سُفْيَانَ بْنِ عُيَيْنَةَ قَالَ: عِنْدَ ذِكْرِ الصَّالِحِينَ تَنْزِلُ الرَّحْمَةُ . وَقَالَ مُحَمَّدُ بْنُ يُونُسَ: مَا رَأَيْتُ لِلْقَلْبِ أَنْفَعَ مِنْ ذِكْرِ الصَّالِحِينَ.

Such Divine remembrance is also the implied meaning of the lines attributed to the *Quṭb* 'Abd Allāh b. 'Alawī al-Ḥaddād (1044-1132/ 1634-1720) describing Tarīm in the Ḥaḍramawt valley, Yemen:

[325] Ibn al-Jawzī, *Ṣifat al-Ṣafwa* (1:17-20).

247. *The abodes of the best masters*
leaders to all people!
To love them means bliss
and to see them is worship.

يروى عن الإمام قطب الدعوة والإرشاد السيد عبدالله بن علوي الحداد رضي الله عنه:

مَنَازِلْ خَيرِ سَادَةْ * لِكُلِّ النَّاسِ قَادَةْ

مَحَبَّتُهُمْ سَعَادَةْ * وَرُؤْيَتُهُمْ عِبَادَةْ

The Syrian *Ghawth* or "Arch-Helper" Bahā' al-Dīn al-Rawwās (1220-1287/1805-1870) in his *Dīwān* of poetry describes the arch-saints (*aqṭāb*) or major *Awliyā* in ineffable terms as "those who make visible the particles of Ṭaha (i.e. the Prophet) in creatures":

248. *The host of the unseen hailed from the unseen worlds*
guarding our sanctuary with Signs of the invisible.

Dispelling the darkness of griefs away from our secrets,
high energies put up the pillars of loftiness.

The revival of the unseen has dawned,
greeting the core of what is and will be.

Allah accustomed us to every beauty. Even before
He sewed existence, He exalted us in His Unseen;

And He appointed us leaders of His gnostics,
bestowing upon us the subtleties of immense help.

We are, among the folk of heavenly ascents, a Kaʿba:
they circumambulate us, seeking the light of our guidance.

We are the Signs of the One God in His creation:
we rise up to uncover His symbols like a Criterion.

We represent the Prophet: our state is from his state.

With the perfection of the secret of his Gnoses he adorns us.

We have become the supports of his science in his House.
We have increased the types of his multitudes in faith.

We confer on the walī his honorific gifts; and truly
whoever fights us meets Allah in the worst state.

Spiritual Opening is our lovers' share everlastingly,
and infinite bounty flows for those who support us....

Thus you see hearts – even if some hold back
out of envy – always extolling our reality.

Have any piloted the droves of purling hearts to their Lord
after unrighteousness had sullied them but us?

Look well! You will see the Honored Purifier is our sire,
and the well-pleasing one – the Lion among men – our father.

Is there, here and now, of Ṭaha's particles in creation
anything still seen of his human nature besides us?

Utter dependency on the All-Beneficent has cloaked us,
without disgrace; His knowledge has made us sufficient.

Great men die on the dais of their wild claims,
but Allah gave us Life in His Reality.

Therefore shelter in us; keep our pacts straight and pure.
There is no door to the Prophet here besides us.[326]

وقال القطب الغوث بهاء الدين الرَّوَّاس رضي الله عنه في ديوانه (فائدة الهِمَم من مائدة الكَرَم):

[326] al-Rawwās, *Fā'idat al-Himam* (p. 23-24).

حِزْبُ الْغُيُوبِ مِنَ الْغُيُوبِ أَتَانَا ❊ فَحَمَى بِآيَاتِ الْغُيُوبِ حِمَانَـا
وَجَلَا ظَلَامَ الْهَمِّ عَنْ أَسْرَارِنَـا ❊ هِمَمٌ أَقَامَتْ لِلْعُـلَا أَرْكَانَـا
وَالنَّهْضَةُ الْغَيْبِيَّةُ انْبَلَجَـتْ وَقَـدْ ❊ حَيَّتْ بِمَعْنَى مَا يَكُونُ وَكَانَا
اللهُ عَوَّدَنَا الْجَمِيلَ وَقَبْـلَ أَنْ ❊ نَسَجَ الْوُجُودَ بِغَيْبِهِ أَعْلَانَـا
وَأَقَامَنَـا لِلْعَـارِفِينَ أَئِمَّـةً ❊ وَلَطَائِفَ الْمَدَدِ الْعَظِيمِ حَبَانَا
فَلَنَحْنُ فِي أَهْـلِ الْمَعَارِجِ كَعْبَةٌ ❊ طَافُوا بِنَا يَبْغُونَ نُورَ هُدَانَـا
وَلَنَحْـنُ آيَـاتُ الْإِلَـٰهِ بِكَوْنِهِ ❊ قُمْنَا لِكَشْفِ رُمُوزِهِ فُرْقَانَـا
نُبْنَا النَّبِيَّ فَحَالُنَـا مِنْ حَالِـهِ ❊ وَكَمَالَ سِـرٍّ فُهُومِهِ حَلَّانَـا
صِرْنَا دَعَائِـمَ عِلْمِـهِ فِي بَيْتِـهِ ❊ زِدْنَا صُنُوفَ صُفُوفِهِ إِيمَانَـا
نُوْلِي الْوَلِيَّ الْمَكْرُمَاتِ وَإِنَّـهُ ❊ بِالسُّوءِ يَلْقَى اللهَ مَنْ عَادَانَـا
فَالْفَتْحُ سَهْمُ مُحِبِّينَا أَبَدَ الْمَـدَى ❊ وَالْخَيْرُ مَبْذُولٌ لِمَـنْ وَالَانَـا....
فَتَرَى الْقُلُوبَ وَإِنْ تَلَكَّأَ بَعْضُهَـا ❊ حَسَداً تُعَظِّمُ دَائِماً مَعْنَانَـا
هَلْ سَاقَ زَمْزَمَةَ الْقُلُوبِ لِرَبِّهَـا ❊ بَعْدَ انْحِرَافٍ مَسَّهَـا إِلَّانَـا؟
فَانْظُرْ تَرَ الطُّهْرَ الْمُكَرَّمَ جَدَّنَـا ❊ وَالْمُرْتَضَى أَسَدَ الرِّجَالِ أَبَانَـا
<u>هَلْ ثَمَّ مِنْ أَجْزَاءِ طَهَ فِي الْوَرَى ❊ شَيْءٌ يُرَى نَاسُوتُهُ لَوْلَانَـا؟</u>
أَلْفَقْرُ لِلرَّحْمَـٰنِ جَلْبَبَنَا بِـلَا ❊ ذُلٍّ وَعِلْمُ اللهِ قَدْ أَغْنَانَـا
مَاتَ الرِّجَالُ عَلَى بِسَاطِ زُعُومِهِمْ ❊ وَاللهُ بِالتَّحْقِيقِ قَدْ أَحْيَانَـا
فَالْجَأْ لَنَا وَاحْفَظْ صَمِيمَ عُهُودِنَا ❊ مَا ثَمَّ بَابٌ لِلنَّبِيِّ سِوَانَـا

The Hadith of the *Awliya* on Pulpits of Lights

Many Prophetic narrations and *qudsī* hadiths related from a number of Companions describe their glorious position on the Day of Judgment as an object of longing even for Prophets:

249. [Muʿādh b. Jabal:] Those who love one another for the sake of My Majesty shall have pulpits of light and the Prophets and martyrs shall yearn to be in their position.[327]

عَنْ مُعَاذِ بْنِ جَبَلٍ رَضِيَ اللهُ عَنْهُ قَالَ سَمِعْتُ رَسُولَ اللهِ ﷺ يَقُولُ قَالَ اللهُ عَزَّ وَجَلَّ الْمُتَحَابُّونَ فِي جَلَالِي لَهُمْ مَنَابِرُ مِنْ نُورٍ يَغْبِطُهُمُ النَّبِيُّونَ وَالشُّهَدَاءُ.

رواه الترمذي وقال حسن صحيح والطبراني.

The above hadith is narrated from Muʿādh by the *Tābiʿī* Abū Muslim al-Khawlānī (ʿAbd Allāh b. Thuwab), one of the greatest Yemeni *Awliyā'*, whom the *dajjāl* and pseudo-prophet al-Aswad al-ʿAnsī unsuccessfully tried to burn in a huge furnace, after which Abū Bakr and ʿUmar would call Abū Muslim "the Ibrāhīm of this *Umma*."[328]

A longer version reconstitutes the context of Abū Muslim's first meeting with Muʿādh:

250. I entered the great mosque of Ḥimṣ. Lo and behold, there were thirty mature Companions of the Prophet there! Among them was a young man, kohl-eyed, with lightning-white teeth, who kept silent. Whenever the group was in doubt of something they would consult him. I asked my friend who this was and he said: "Muʿādh b. Jabal." I immediately felt love for him. I stayed

[327] al-Tirmidhī, *Sunan (Zuhd, mā jā'a fil-ḥubb bil-Lāh, ḥasan ṣaḥīḥ)*; al-Ṭabarānī in *al-Kabīr* (20:168 §358).
[328] Ibn Ḥibbān, *Ṣaḥīḥ* (2:339-340). He is buried in Dārayya, Syria and one of those listed by Abū Nuʿaym and others as "The Eight Ascetics": ʿĀmir b. ʿAbd Qays al-Ḥaḍramī, Abū Muslim al-Khawlānī, Uways al-Qaranī, al-Rabīʿ Ibn Khathyam, al-Aswad b. Yazīd, Masrūq, Sufyān al-Thawrī, and al-Ḥasan al-Baṣrī – mostly Yemenis and Iraqis.

with them until they dispersed then went back into the mosque. There Mu'ādh b. Jabal was, praying opposite a pillar. I prayed then sat down and wrapped myself in my cloak. I kept quiet and did not address him, and he kept quiet and did not address me. Then I said: "I swear by Allah that I do love you!" He said: "For what reason do you love me?" I said: "For Allah." He seized me by the cloak, pulled me gently to himself and said: "Be happy if you speak the truth! I heard the Messenger of Allah say: 'Those who love one another for the majesty of Allah are on pulpits of light. Prophets and martyrs will long to be in their position.'"[329]

وَعَنْ أَبِي مُسْلِمٍ الخَوْلَانِيِّ قَالَ: دَخَلْتُ مَسْجِدَ حِمْصٍ، فَإِذَا فِيهِ نَحْوٌ مِنْ ثَلَاثِينَ كَهْلاً مِنْ أَصْحَابِ النَّبِيِّ ﷺ وَإِذَا فِيهِمْ شَابٌّ أَكْحَلُ الْعَيْنَيْنِ بَرَّاقُ الثَّنَايَا، سَاكِتٌ لَا يَتَكَلَّمُ، فَإِذَا امْتَرَى الْقَوْمُ (أي ارتاب) فِي شَيْءٍ أَقْبَلُوا عَلَيْهِ فَسَأَلُوهُ، فَقُلْتُ لِجَلِيسٍ لِي: مَنْ هٰذَا؟ قَالَ: مُعَاذُ بْنُ جَبَلٍ. فَوَقَعَ لَهُ فِي نَفْسِي حُبٌّ؛ فَكُنْتُ مَعَهُمْ حَتَّى تَفَرَّقُوا، ثُمَّ هَجَرْتُ إِلَى الْمَسْجِدِ، فَإِذَا مُعَاذُ بْنُ جَبَلٍ قَائِمٌ يُصَلِّي إِلَى سَارِيَةٍ، فَصَلَّيْتُ ثُمَّ جَلَسْتُ وَاحْتَبَيْتُ بِرِدَائِي، فَسَكَتُّ لَا أُكَلِّمُهُ، وَسَكَتَ لَا يُكَلِّمُنِي، ثُمَّ قُلْتُ: وَاللهِ إِنِّي لَأُحِبُّكَ. قَالَ: فِيمَ تُحِبُّنِي؟ قُلْتُ: فِي اللهِ. فَأَخَذَ بِحَبْوَتِي فَجَذَبَنِي إِلَيْهِ هُنَيَّةً، ثُمَّ قَالَ: **أَبْشِرْ إِنْ كُنْتَ صَادِقاً! فَإِنِّي سَمِعْتُ رَسُولَ اللهِ ﷺ يَقُولُ: الْمُتَحَابُّونَ فِي جَلَالِ اللهِ عَلَى مَنَابِرَ مِنْ نُورٍ، يَغْبِطُهُمُ النَّبِيُّونَ وَالشُّهَدَاءُ.** رواه أحمد وأبو نعيم وابن حبان.

329 Aḥmad, *Musnad* (399-400 §22080); Ibn Ḥibbān, *Ṣaḥīḥ* (2:338 §577); Abū Nu'aym, *Ḥilya* (2:131).

251. [Abū Umāma:] Truly Allāh has servants whom He shall seat on pulpits of light, and their faces shall be completely covered in light until Allāh finishes with the sins of creatures."³³⁰

عَنْ أَبِي أُمَامَةَ رَضِيَ اللهُ عَنْهُ قَالَ: قَالَ رَسُولُ اللهِ ﷺ إِنَّ لِلَّهِ عِبَاداً يُجْلِسُهُمْ يَوْمَ الْقِيَامَةِ عَلَى مَنَابِرَ مِنْ نُورٍ يَغْشَى وُجُوهَهُمُ النُّورُ حَتَّى يَخْلُوَ مِنْ نَجَاسَةِ الْخَلَائِقِ رواه الطبراني بسند جيد وهذا لفظه في المعجم الكبير. وأما في مسند الشاميين فبلفظ يَغْشَى وُجُوهَهُمُ النُّورُ وَيُلْقَى عَنْهُمُ السَّيِّئَاتُ حَتَّى يَفْرَغَ اللهُ مِنْ حِسَابِ الْخَلَائِقِ.

252. [Abū Hurayra:] Truly there are those, among the servants of Allah, that are not Prophets but whom the Prophets and martyrs yearn to resemble." Someone asked: "Who are they so that we may love them?" He said: "They are a folk who loved one another with the light of Allāh, without kinship nor affiliation [*var.* "without business or kinship"]. <u>Their faces are light on pulpits of light</u>. They shall not fear when all people fear, nor shall they grieve when all people grieve." Then he recited: *The Friends of Allāh! Truly no fear shall there be for them, nor shall they grieve* (10:62).³³¹

عَنْ أَبِي هُرَيْرَةَ رَضِيَ اللهُ عَنْهُ قَالَ قَالَ رَسُولُ اللهِ ﷺ إِنَّ مِنْ عِبَادِ اللهِ عِبَاداً لَيْسُوا بِأَنْبِيَاءَ يَغْبِطُهُمُ الأَنْبِيَاءُ وَالشُّهَدَاءُ. قِيلَ: مَنْ هُمْ لَعَلَّنَا نُحِبُّهُمْ؟ قَالَ: هُمْ قَوْمٌ تَحَابُّوا بِنُورِ اللهِ مِنْ غَيْرِ أَرْحَامٍ وَلاَ انْتِسَابٍ، وُجُوهُهُمْ نُورٌ عَلَى

---

³³⁰ al-Ṭabarānī, *al-Muʿjam al-Kabīr* (8:112 §7527) and *Musnad al-Shāmiyyīn* (2:10 §826) with a good chain according to al-Haythamī, *Majmaʿ* (10:492 §18001).
³³¹ Abū Yaʿlā, *Musnad* (10:495 §6110); Ibn Abī al-Dunyā, *al-Ikhwān* (p. 45 §5); al-Tabarī, *Tafsīr* (sub 10:62); Ibn Ḥibbān, *Ṣaḥīḥ* (2:332-334 §573); al-Nasāʾī, *al-Sunan al-Kubrā* (10:124 §11172); al-Bayhaqī, *Shuʿab* (11:314-315 §8584). Also thus narrated from ʿUmar b. al-Khaṭṭāb by Abū Dāwūd, *Sunan* (*Ijāra, bāb fīl-rahn*).

مَنَابِرَ مِنْ نُورٍ، لاَ يَخَافُونَ إِذَا خَافَ النَّاسُ وَلاَ يَحْزَنُونَ إِذَا حَزِنَ النَّاسُ. ثُمَّ قَرَأَ ﴿ أَلَآ إِنَّ أَوْلِيَآءَ ٱللَّهِ لَا خَوْفٌ عَلَيْهِمْ وَلَا هُمْ يَحْزَنُونَ ﴾ يونس. رواه ابن حبان بسند صحيح وأبو يعلى وابن أبي الدنيا والبيهقي وغيرهم ورواه النسائي في الكبرى بلفظ تَحَابُّوا بِرَوْحِ اللهِ عَلَى غَيْرِ أَمْوَالٍ وَلَا أَنْسَابٍ وبلغ عدد رواته من الصحابة العشرة فهو متواتر. ومنها: رواية أبي داود في سننه عن عمر بن الخطاب رضي الله عنه بسند صحيح.

253. [Abū Mālik al-Ash'arī:] One day, when the Prophet finished his prayer, he turned to face the people and said: "People! Listen to this, understand it, and know it. Allah has servants who are neither Prophets nor martyrs and whom the Prophets and martyrs yearn to resemble due to their seat and proximity in relation to Allah." One of the Bedouin Arabs who came from among the most isolated of people twisted his hand at the Prophet and said: "Messenger of Allah! People from humankind who are neither Prophets nor martyrs and yet the Prophets and the martyrs yearn to be like them due to their seat and proximity in relation to Allah? Describe them for us!" The face of the Prophet showed delight at the question and he said: "They are strangers from here and there. They frequent this tribe or that without belonging to any of them. They do not have family connections with each other. They love one another for the sake of Allah. They are of pure intent towards one another. On the Day of Resurrection Allah shall place for them pedestals of light upon which He shall seat them, and He will turn their faces and clothes into light. On the Day of Resurrection the people will be terrified but not those. They are *the Friends of Allah upon whom fear comes not, nor do they grieve* (10:62)."[332]

[332] Aḥmad, *Musnad* (37:540-542 §22906); Ibn al-Mubārak, *Zuhd* (p. 248-249 §714); Ibn Abī al-Dunyā, *al-Ikhwān* (p. 47 §6); al-Baghawī, *Sharḥ al-Sunna* (13:50 §3464); al-Ṭabarī, *Tafsīr* (*sub* 10:62); and others.

عَنْ أَبِي مَالِكٍ الأَشْعَرِيِّ قَالَ: إِنَّ رَسُولَ اللهِ ﷺ لَمَّا قَضَى صَلاَتَهُ أَقْبَلَ إِلَى النَّاسِ بِوَجْهِهِ فَقَالَ: يَا أَيُّهَا النَّاسُ اِسْمَعُوا! وَاعْقِلُوا! وَاعْلَمُوا أَنَّ للهِ عَزَّ وَجَلَّ عِبَادًا لَيْسُوا بِأَنْبِيَاءَ وَلَا شُهَدَاءَ يَغْبِطُهُمُ الأَنْبِيَاءُ وَالشُّهَدَاءُ عَلَى مَجَالِسِهِمْ وَقُرْبِهِمْ مِنَ اللهِ فَجَاءَ رَجُلٌ مِنَ الأَعْرَابِ مِنْ قَاصِيَةِ النَّاسِ – وفي رواية ابن أبي أسامة: قَالَ: وَكَانَ يُعْجِبُنَا أَنْ يَكُونَ فِينَا الأَعْرَابِيُّ إِذَا شَهِدْنَا رَسُولَ اللهِ ﷺ، لِأَنَّهُمْ يَجْتَرِئُونَ أَنْ يَسْأَلُوهُ وَلَا نَجْتَرِئُ – **وَأَلْوَى بِيَدِهِ إِلَى نَبِيِّ اللهِ ﷺ فَقَالَ يَا نَبِيَّ اللهِ نَاسٌ مِنَ النَّاسِ لَيْسُوا بِأَنْبِيَاءَ وَلاَ شُهَدَاءَ يَغْبِطُهُمُ الأَنْبِيَاءُ وَالشُّهَدَاءُ عَلَى مَجَالِسِهِمْ وَقُرْبِهِمْ مِنَ اللهِ؟ إِنْعَتْهُمْ لَنَا! يَعْنِي صِفْهُمْ لَنَا. فَسُرَّ وَجْهُ رَسُولِ اللهِ ﷺ لِسُؤَالِ الأَعْرَابِيِّ** – وفي رواية أبي يعلى: **فَرَأَيْنَا وَجْهَ رَسُولِ اللهِ ﷺ يَتَهَلَّلُ**، وفي رواية معمر **فَرَأَيْتُ وَجْهَ رَسُولِ اللهِ ﷺ أَبْشَرَ**، وفي رواية الطبراني **فَرَأَيْتُ وَجْهَ رَسُولِ اللهِ ﷺ يَنْتَشِرُ**، وفي رواية شُعَب الإيمان **فَرَأَيْتُ فِي وَجْهِ رَسُولِ اللهِ ﷺ الْبُشْرَ** – **فَقَالَ رَسُولُ اللهِ ﷺ هُمْ نَاسٌ مِنْ أَفْنَاءِ النَّاسِ وَنَوَازِعِ الْقَبَائِلِ لَمْ تَصِلْ بَيْنَهُمْ أَرْحَامٌ مُتَقَارِبَةٌ تَحَابُّوا فِي اللهِ وَتَصَافَوْا، يَضَعُ اللهُ لَهُمْ يَوْمَ الْقِيَامَةِ مَنَابِرَ مِنْ نُورٍ فَيُجْلِسُهُمْ عَلَيْهَا فَيَجْعَلُ وُجُوهَهُمْ نُورًا وَثِيَابَهُمْ نُورًا، يَفْزَعُ النَّاسُ يَوْمَ الْقِيَامَةِ وَلاَ يَفْزَعُونَ وَهُمْ أَوْلِيَاءُ اللهِ الَّذِينَ** ﴿ لَا خَوْفٌ عَلَيْهِمْ وَلَا هُمْ يَحْزَنُونَ ﴾ رواه أحمد وهٰذا لفظه وأبو يعلى والطبراني ورجالهم ثقات إلا شهر بن حوشب وهو حسن الحديث، والطبري وغيرهم.

Thus the Prophet described the *Awliyā* as those at the sight of whom one is reminded of Allah, who love one another with His Light and for His Majesty, servants who are neither Prophets nor martyrs, unrelated and unaffiliated with one another, strangers from here and there. In the following Prophetic hadith from ʿAbd Allāh b. ʿAmr b. al-ʿĀṣ he also calls them the poor among those who left their lands:

254. "Blessed are the strangers!" It was asked: "Who are they, Messenger of Allah?" He said: "Righteous people who are few among many evil people; those who disobey them outnumber those who obey them." One day we were with him when the sun was rising and he said: "A people will come to Allah on the Day of Resurrection, their light like that of the sun." Abū Bakr asked: "Are we those people, Messenger of Allah?" He said: "No, and you will have immense goodness; but these are the poor emigrants. Bad things are averted through them. Each of them dies with his worldly need unfulfilled [lit. "with his need stuck in his chest"]. They will be resurrected from the four corners of the world.[333]

عَنْ عَبْدِ اللهِ بْنِ عَمْرِو بْنِ الْعَاصِ رَضِيَ اللهُ عَنْهُمَا: قَالَ لِي النَّبِيُّ ﷺ: طُوبَى لِلْغُرَبَاءِ. قِيلَ: وَمَنِ الْغُرَبَاءُ يَا رَسُولَ اللهِ؟ قَالَ: نَاسٌ صَالِحُونَ قَلِيلٌ فِي نَاسِ سُوءٍ كَثِيرٍ، مَنْ يَعْصِيهِمْ أَكْثَرُ مِمَّنْ يُطِيعُهُمْ. وَقَالَ: كُنَّا يَوْماً عِنْدَ رَسُولِ اللهِ ﷺ، فَطَلَعَتِ الشَّمْسُ فَقَالَ رَسُولُ اللهِ ﷺ: يَأْتِي اللهَ عَزَّ وَجَلَّ فِي يَوْمِ الْقِيَامَةِ قَوْمٌ نُورُهُمْ كَالشَّمْسِ. فَقَالَ أَبُو بَكْرٍ: نَحْنُ هُمْ يَا رَسُولَ اللهِ؟ قَالَ: لَا، وَلَكُمْ خَيْرٌ كَثِيرٌ، وَلَكِنَّهُمْ فُقَرَاءُ الْمُهَاجِرِينَ. تُتَّقَى بِهِمُ الْمَكَارِهُ، يَمُوتُ أَحَدُهُمْ وَحَاجَتُهُ فِي صَدْرِهِ. يُحْشَرُونَ مِنْ أَقْطَارِ الْأَرْضِ. رواه يعقوب بن سفيان الفَسَوي في المعرفة والتاريخ.

[333] al-Fasawī, *al-Maʿrifa wal-Tārīkh* (2:517-518).

"The *walī* is a light from the light of Allah"

Ibn ʿAjība (d. 1224/1809) after his gloss of *There has come to you from Allah a Light and a manifest Book* (5:15) states:

255. The allusion in this verse is that Allah has informed the possessors of spiritual knowledge (*ʿulamāʾ al-bāṭin*) of the spiritual stations of the possessors of external knowledge (*ʿulamāʾ al-ẓāhir*), their states, and most of their spiritual diseases, especially those that used to be external scholars then moved on to inward knowledge such as al-Ghazālī, Ibn ʿAbbād, and others. Al-Ghazālī argued with the scholars of external knowledge and exposed many of their ills in the opening of the *Iḥyāʾ*[334]. Ibn ʿAbbād did the same in the commentary on the *Ḥikam*, and they forgave much, for truly they are at the foot of the Messenger of Allah and they are the elite of his inheritors because they have obtained his inheritance in its entirety, as in the *Mabāḥith*:

The scholar follows him in speech
and the ascetic devotee in deeds,
While the Sufi competes in both
but adds high character.[335]

Hence the *walī* is a light from the light of Allah and a secret from among His secrets, by which He brings those for whom Divine help is foreordained out of the dark layers of veiling and into the light of witnessing, and by which He guides those whom He selected for His Presence on the path of arrival to Him. Success is by Allah![336]

قال ابن عجيبة في تفسير البحر المديد:

[334] I.e. Book of Knowledge, where he defines *ʿilm* as spiritual knowledge, not *fiqh*.
[335] Ibn al-Bannā al-Saraqusṭī, *al-Mabāḥith al-Aṣliyya* (verses 62-63), cf. Ibn ʿAjība, *Futūḥāt* (p. 59).
[336] Ibn ʿAjība, *al-Baḥr al-Madīd* (*sub* 5:15).

الإِشَارَةُ فِي آيَة ﴿قَدْ جَآءَكُم مِّنَ ٱللَّهِ نُورٌ وَكِتَٰبٌ مُّبِينٌ﴾: قَدْ أَطْلَعَ اللهُ عُلَمَاءَ الْبَاطِنِ عَلَى مَقَامَاتِ عُلَمَاءِ الظَّاهِرِ وَأَحْوَالِهِمْ وَجُلِّ مَسَاوِئِهِمْ وَلَا سِيَّمَا مَنْ كَانَ عَالِمًا بِالظَّاهِرِ ثُمَّ انْتَقَلَ إِلَى عِلْمِ الْبَاطِنِ كَالْغَزَالِيِّ وَابْنِ عَبَّادٍ وَغَيْرِهِمَا فَقَدْ تَكَلَّمَ الْغَزَالِيُّ فِي صَدْرِ الْإِحْيَاءِ [كتاب العلم] مَعَ عُلَمَاءِ الظَّاهِرِ فَفَضَحَ كَثِيراً مِنْ مَسَاوِئِهِمْ وَكَذَٰلِكَ ابْنُ عَبَّادٍ فِي شَرْحِ الحِكَمِ وَعَفَوا عَنْ كَثِيرٍ فَهُمْ عَلَى قَدَمِ رَسُولِ اللهِ ﷺ وَخَوَاصُّ وَرَثَتِهِ لِأَنَّهُمْ حَازُوا الْوِرَاثَةَ كُلَّهَا كَمَا فِي (المَبَاحِثِ):

تَبِعَهُ الْعَالِمُ فِي الْأَقْوَالِ * وَالْعَابِدُ الزَّاهِدُ فِي الْأَفْعَالِ
وَفِيهِمَا الصُّوفِيُّ فِي السِّبَاقِ * لَكِنَّهُ قَدْ زَادَ بِالْأَخْلَاقِ

فَالْوَلِيُّ نُورٌ مِنْ نُورِ اللهِ وَسِرٌّ مِنْ أَسْرَارِهِ يُخْرِجُ بِهِ مَنْ سَبَقَتْ لَهُ الْعِنَايَةُ مِنْ ظُلُمَاتِ الحِجَابِ إِلَى نُورِ الشُّهُودِ وَيَهْدِي بِهِ مَنِ اصْطَفَاهُ لِحَضْرَتِهِ تَعَالَى طَرِيقَ الْوُصُولِ إِلَيْهِ. وَبِاللهِ التَّوْفِيقُ.

IX: Epilogue

My heart nearly flies off with unbearable longing (ʿAlī al-Ḥabshī)

256. *My heart nearly flies off with unbearable longing*
for the Beloved whose love has settled within me.

When, when will the Lord allow us to travel and visit
the Best of creation, the Elect, Ṭaha, the Bringer of good news?

We will visit his grave and scent ourselves with that Perfume.
Allah will open for us the Door of immense gifts.

We will visit in peace, every hardship for us turns to ease.
We will visit with our children, the old and the young.

It will be such a visit with the great help of my Beloved!
We will look at that face so radiant, so full of light!

We will behold his beauty, our eyes will finally exult.
O Leader of the Messengers, under your door a poor seeker

Asks for your gifts by which all else is erased
and with which the servant attains everything he pines for.

I want nothing other than meet the light-giving lamp.
Always his image is with me, at home or on the road.

O Allah, by his honor, protect us from the heat of Hellfire
and forgive us every mistake, and erase everything,

And catch us with Your Mercy by which skies turn to rain.[337]

[337] ʿAlī al-Ḥabshī, *Simṭ al-Durar* (p. 228-230).

أنشد الحبيب علي بن محمد الحبشي رضي الله عنه:

يَكَادُ مِنْ شِدَّةِ أَشْوَاقِي فُؤَادِي يَطِيرْ
إِلَى الحَبِيبِ الَّذِي حُبُّهْ سَكَنْ فِي الضَّمِيرْ

مَتَى مَتَى يَأْذَنُ المَوْلَى لَنَا بِالمَسِيرْ
نَزُورْ خَيْرَ الْوَرَى الْمُخْتَارْ طٰهٰ الْبَشِيرْ

نَزُورْ قَبْرَهْ وَنَتَعَطَّرْ بِذَاكَ الْعَبِيرْ
وَيَفْتَحُ اللهْ لَنَا بَابَ الْعَطَايَا الْكَبِيرْ

نَزُورْ فِي عَافِيَهْ يَسْهُلْ عَلَيْنَا الْعَسِيرْ
نَزُورْ بِأَوْلَادِنَا كَبِيرِهِمْ وَالصَّغِيرْ

تَقَعْ زِيَارَهْ مَدَدْهَا مِنْ حَبِيبِي كَثِيرْ
نَنْظُرْ إِلَى ذٰلِكَ الْوَجْهِ الصَّبِيحِ النَّوِيرْ

نَشْهَدْ جَمَالَهْ وَيُمْسِي الطَّرْفُ مِنَّا قَرِيرْ
يَا سَيِّدَ الرُّسُلْ تَحْتَ الْبَابْ طَالِبْ فَقِيرْ

يَبْغَى كَرَامَاتْ يُمْحَى كُلُّ مَا فِي النَّظِيرْ
وَيُدْرِكُ الْعَبْدُ مِنْكَ كُلَّ مَا فِي الضَّمِيرْ

مَا لِي طَلَبْ غَيرُ لُقْيَا السِّرَاجِ الْمُنِيرْ
دَايِمْ خَيَالُهْ مَعِي فِي مَقْعَدِي وَالمَسِيرْ

يَا اللهْ بِجَاهِهْ تَقِينَا حَرَّ نَارِ السَّعِيرْ

وَاغْفِرْ لَنَا كُلَّ زَلَّهْ وَامْحُ مَا فِي النَّظِيرْ

وَادْرِكْ بِرَحْمَتِكْ يُمْسِي الجَوُّ مِنْهَا مَطِيرْ

تمّ بحمد الله

كتاب النور المحمّدي ﷺ يوم المولد المبارك غرة رجب المرجّب سنة ١٤٣٣ بعد هجرة أكمل أهل الأرض والسمٰوات الموافق آخر الشهر الخامس من سنة 2012م على يد أحقر العباد جبريل فؤاد حداد الراجي عفو ربّه ومغفرته والمتوسّل برسوله ﷺ والحمد لله ربّ العالمين أولاً وأخيراً ظاهراً وباطناً.

وَجُدْ لِي بِفَضْلِ الجَمْعِ فَضْلاً وَمِنَّةً * وَدَاوِ بِوَصْلِ الْوَصْلِ رُوحِي مِنَ الضَّنَا

وَصَلِّ وَسَلِّمْ سَيِّدِي كُلَّ لَمْحَةٍ * عَلَى الْمُصْطَفَى خَيْرِ الْبَرَايَا نَبِيِّنَا

Bibliography

ʿAbd al-Razzāq b. Hammām al-Ṣanʿānī. *Tafsīr al-Qurʾān*. Ed. Muṣṭafā Muslim Muḥammad. 3 vols. Riyadh: Maktabat al-Rushd, 1410/1989.

Abū Bakr al-Ṣiddīq. *Dīwān Abī Bakr al-Ṣiddīq*. Ed. Muḥammad Sharād Ḥassānī and Ḥaydar Kāmil Farḥān al-Zurqānī. Beirut: Dār wa-Maktabat al-Hilāl and Dār al-Biḥār, 2006.

Abū Dāwūd Sulaymān b. al-Ashʿath al-Azdī al-Sijistānī. *Sunan*. Ed. Muḥammad ʿAwwāma. 5 vols. 2nd ed. Jeddah: Dār al-Qibla lil-Thaqāfat al-Islāmiyya; Beirut: Muʾassasat al-Rayyān, 1425/2004.

Abū Ḥayyān al-Andalusī, Muḥammad b. Yūsuf. *Tafsīr al-Baḥr al-Muḥīṭ*. Ed. ʿĀdil Aḥmad ʿAbd al-Mawjūd et al. 8 vols. Beirut: Dār al-Kutub al-ʿIlmiyya, 1413/1993.

Abū al-Layth al-Samarqandī, see al-Samarqandī.

Abū Nuʿaym al-Aṣbahānī, Aḥmad b. ʿAbd Allāh b. Aḥmad. [*al-Muntakhab min*] *Dalāʾil al-Nubuwwa*. Ed. Muḥammad Rawwās Qalʿahjī and ʿAbd al-Barr ʿAbbās. 2 vols. in 1. 2nd ed. Beirut: Dār al-Nafāʾis, 1419/1999.

———. *Ḥilyat al-Awliyāʾ wa-Ṭabaqāt al-Aṣfiyāʾ*. 10 vols. Cairo: Maṭbaʿat al-Saʿāda, 1399/1979. Repr. Beirut: Dār al-Kutub al-ʿIlmiyya, 1409/1988.

———. *Kitāb Dhikr Akhbār Iṣbahān*. 2 vols. Leiden : E.J. Brill, 1931. Rept. Beirut: Dār al-Kitāb al-Islāmī, n.d.

———. *Maʿrifat al-Ṣaḥāba*. Ed. ʿĀdil b. Yūsuf al-ʿAzāzī. 7 vols. Dār al-Waṭan lil-Nashr, 1419/1998.

Abū Saʿd al-Naysābūrī, see al-Kharkūshī.

Abū al-Shaykh al-Asbahānī, Abū Muḥammad ʿAbd Allāh b. Muḥammad b. Jaʿfar b. Ḥayyān. *Kitāb al-ʿAẓama*. Ed. Riḍāʾ Allāh b. Muḥammad Idrīs al-Mubārakfūrī. 5 vols. Riyadh: Dār al-ʿAṣima, 1408/1988.

———. *Ṭabaqāt al-Muḥaddithīn bi-Aṣbahān wal-Wāridīn ʿalayhā*. Ed. ʿAbd al-Ghafūr ʿAbd al-Ḥaqq Ḥusayn al-Balūshī. 4 vols. Beirut: Muʾassasat al-Risāla, 1412/1992.

Abū al-Suʿūd al-ʿImādī, Muḥammad b. Muḥammad b. Muṣṭafā. *Tafsīr Abī al-Suʿūd, aw, Irshād al-ʿAql al-Salīm ilā Mazāyā al-Kitāb al-Karīm*. Ed. ʿAbd al-Qādir Aḥmad ʿAṭā. 5 vols. Riyadh: Maktabat al-Riyāḍ al-Ḥadītha, [1391/1971].

Abū Yaʿlā al-Mawṣilī al-Tamīmī, Aḥmad b. ʿAlī b. al-Muthannā. *al-Mafārīd ʿan Rasūl Allāh*. Ed. ʿAbd Allāh b. Yūsuf al-Judayyiʿ. Kuwait: Maktabat Dār al-Aqṣā, 1405/1985.

———. *Musnad*. Ed. Ḥusayn Salīm Asad. 14 vols. 2nd ed. Damascus: Dār al-Maʾmūn lil-Turāth, 1410/1989-1990.

Abū Zahra, Muḥammad b. Aḥmad Muṣṭafā. *Zahrat al-Tafāsīr*. 10 vols. Cairo: Dār al-Fikr al-ʿArabī, 1987.

Aḥmad b. Muḥammad b. Ḥanbal. *Kitāb Faḍā'il al-Ṣaḥāba* Ed. Waṣiy Allāh b. Muḥammad ʿAbbās. 2 vols. Mecca: Jāmiʿat Umm al-Qurā, 1403/1983.

———. *Kitāb al-ʿIlal wa-Maʿrifat al-Rijāl.* Ed. Waṣiy Allāh b. Muḥammad ʿAbbās. 4 vols. Riyadh: 2nd ed. Dār al-Khānī, 1422/2001.

———. *al-Musnad.* Ed. Shuʿayb al-Arnāʾūṭ et al. 50 vols. Beirut: Muʾassasat al-Risāla, 1999-2001.

al-ʿAjlūnī al-Jarrāḥī, Ismāʿīl b. Muḥammad b. ʿAbd al-Hādī. *Kashf al-Khafā' wa-Muzīl al-Albās ʿammā Ishtahar min al-Aḥādīth ʿalā Alsinat al-Nās.* Ed. Yūsuf b. Maḥmūd al-Ḥājj Aḥmad. 2 vols. Damascus: Editor, 1422/2001.

al-Ājurrī, Abū Bakr Muḥammad b. al-Ḥusayn. *Kitāb al-Sharīʿa.* Ed. ʿAbd Allāh b. ʿUmar b. Sulaymān al-Dumayjī. 6 vols. Riyadh: Dār al-Waṭan, 1418/1997.

al-Ālūsī, Abū al-Faḍl Shihāb al-Dīn al-Sayyid Maḥmūd b. ʿAbdallāh. *Rūḥ al-Maʿānī fī Tafsīr al-Qurʾān al-ʿAẓīm wal-Sabʿ al-Mathānī.* 30 vols. in 15. Cairo: Idārat al-Ṭibāʿat al-Munīriyya, 1345/1926. Repr. Beirut: Dār Iḥyāʾ al-Turāth al-ʿArabī, [1970?].

al-Aṣfahānī, Abū al-Faraj ʿAlī b. al-Ḥusayn b. Muḥammad al-Qurashī. *Kitāb al-Aghānī.* Ed. Aḥmad al-Shinqīṭī. 25 vols. Cairo: Maṭbaʿat al-Taqaddum, 1323/1905.

al-Azharī, Abū Manṣūr Muḥammad b. Aḥmad. *Tahdhīb al-Lugha.* Ed. ʿAbd al-Salām Muḥammad Hārūn et al. 15 vols. Cairo: al-Dār al-Miṣriyya lil-Ta'līf wal-Tarjama, 1966.

al-Baghawī, Muḥyī al-Sunna Abū Muḥammad al-Ḥusayn b. Masʿūd al-Farrā'. *al-Anwār fī Shamā'il al-Nabī al-Mukhtār.* Ed. Ibrāhīm al-Yaʿqūbī. 2 vols. Beirut: Dār al-Ḍiyā', 1409/1989.

———. *Sharḥ al-Sunna.* Ed. Shuʿayb al-Arnā'ūṭ. 16 vols. 2nd ed. Beirut: al-Maktab al-Islāmī, 1403/1983.

———. *Tafsīr al-Baghawī al-Musammā Maʿālim al-Tanzīl.* Ed. ʿAbd al-Razzāq al-Mahdī. 5 vols. Beirut: Dār Iḥyāʾ al-Turāth al-ʿArabī, 1420/2000.

al-Bājūrī, Ibrāhīm. *Ḥāshiyat al-Isʿād ʿalā Bānat Suʿād.* In the margins of Abū Muḥammad Jamāl al-Dīn ʿAbd Allāh b. Hishām al-Anṣārī, *Sharḥ ʿalā Qaṣīdat Bānat Suʿād.* [Cairo: s.n.], 1302/1885. Rept. Bombay: Molvi Mohammed b. Gulamrasul Surtis Sons, n.d.

al-Bayḍāwī, Nāṣir al-Dīn Abū Sa'īd ʿAbd Allāh b. ʿUmar. *Tafsīr al-Bayḍāwī al-Musammā Anwār al-Tanzīl wa-Asrār al-Taʾwīl.* 3 vols. Ed. Muḥammad Ṣubḥī b. Ḥasan Ḥallāq and Maḥmūd Aḥmad al-Aṭrash. Damascus: Dār al-Rashīd; Beirut: Muʾassasat al-Īmān, 2000.

al-Bayhaqī, Abū Bakr Aḥmad b. al-Ḥusayn. *al-Asmāʾ wal-Ṣifāt.* Ed. ʿAbd Allāh b. Muḥammad al-Ḥāshidī. 2 vols. Riyadh: Maktabat al-Sawādī, 1413/1993.

———. *Dalā'il al-Nubuwwa wa-Ma'rifat Aḥwāl Ṣāḥib al-Sharī'a*. Ed. 'Abd al-Mu'ṭī Amīn Qal'ajī. 7 vols. Beirut: Dār al-Kutub al-'Ilmiyya, 1405/1985.

———. *Kitāb al-Ba'th wal-Nushūr*. Ed. Abū Hājar Muḥammad al-Sa'īd b. Basyūnī Zaghlūl. Beirut: Mu'assasat al-Kutub al-Thaqāfiyya, 1408/1988.

———. [*Shu'ab al-Īmān*]. *al-Jāmi' li-Shu'ab al-Īmān*. Ed. 'Abd al-'Alī 'Abd al-Ḥamīd Ḥāmid. 14 vols. Riyadh: Maktabat al-Rushd, 1423/2003.

———. *al-Sunan al-Kubrā*. With Ibn al-Turkmānī's *al-Jawhar al-Naqy*. 10 vols. Hyderabad, Deccan: Maṭba'at Majlis Dā'irat al-Ma'ārif al-'Uthmāniyya, 1355/1937.

———. *al-Sunan al-Ṣughrā*. Ed. Bahjat Yūsuf Ḥamad Abū al-Ṭayyib. 4 vols. Beirut: Dār al-Jīl, 1415/1995.

al-Bazzār, Abū Bakr Aḥmad b. 'Umar b. 'Abd al-Khāliq al-'Utaykī. [*Musnad*.] *al-Baḥr al-Zakhkhār al-Ma'rūf bi-Musnad al-Bazzār*. Ed. Maḥfūẓ al-Raḥmān Zayn Allāh and 'Ādil b. Sa'd. 15 vols. Beirut: Mu'assasat 'Ulūm al-Qur'ān and Madina: Maktabat al-'Ulūm wal-Ḥikam, 1409-1427/1988-2006.

al-Biqā'ī, Burhān al-Dīn Abū al-Ḥasan Ibrāhīm b. 'Umar. *Naẓm al-Durar fī Tanāsub al-Āyāt wal-Suwar*. 22 vols. Cairo: Dār al-Kitāb al-Islāmī, 1404/1984.

al-Bukhārī, Abū 'Abd Allāh Muḥammad b. Ismā'īl b. Ibrāhīm b. al-Mughīra al-Ju'fī. *al-Adab al-Mufrad*. Ed. Muḥammad Fu'ād 'Abd al-Bāqī. 3rd ed. Beirut: Dār al-Bashā'ir al-Islāmiyya, 1989.

———. *al-Jāmi' al-Ṣaḥīḥ: wa-Huwa al-Jāmi' al-Musnad al-Ṣaḥīḥ al-Mukhtaṣar min Umūr Rasūl Allāh ṣallā Allāh 'alayh wa-sallam wa-Sunanih wa-Ayyāmih*. Ed. Muḥammad al-Zuhrī al-Ghamrāwī. 8 vols. in 3. 2nd ed. Būlāq: al-Maṭba'at al-Kubrā al-Amīriyya, 1314/1896. Rept. Cairo: al-Maṭba'at al-Maymūniyya [Muṣṭafā Bābā al-Ḥalabī et al.], 1323/1905.

———. *al-Tārīkh al-Awsaṭ* [= *al-Tārīkh al-Ṣaghīr*]. Ed. Muḥammad b. Ibrāhīm al-Luḥaydān. 2 vols. Riyadh: Dār al-Ṣumay'ī, 1418/1998.

———. *al-Tārīkh al-Kabīr*. 8 vols. in 4. Hyderabad Deccan: Dā'irat al-Ma'ārif al-'Uthmāniyya, 1361/1942. Rept. Beirut: Dār al-Kutub al-'Ilmiyya, n.d.

al-Būṣīrī, Sharaf al-Dīn Muḥammad b. Sa'īd b. Ḥammād. *al-Burda*. See al-Haytamī, *al-'Umda fī Sharḥ al-Burda*.

———. *al-Hamziyya*. See al-Haytamī, *al-Minaḥ al-Makkiyya fī Sharḥ al-Hamziyya*.

al-Būṣīrī al-Kinānī, Shihāb al-Dīn Abū al-'Abbās Aḥmad b. Abū Bakr b. Ismā'īl. *Kitāb Itḥāf al-Khiyarat al-Mahara bi-Zawā'id al-Masānīd al-'Ashara*. Ed. Abū Tamīm Yāsir Ibrāhīm et al. 9 vols. Riyadh: Dār al-Waṭan lil-Nashr, 1420/1999.

———. *Miṣbāḥ al-Zujāja fī Zawā'id Ibn Mājah*. Ed. 'Awaḍ b. Aḥmad al-Shahrī. 2 vols. Madina: al-Jāmi'a al-Islāmiyya, 1425/2004.

Daḥlān, Aḥmad b. Zaynī. *Taqrīb al-Uṣūl li-Tas-hīl al-Wuṣūl li-Ma'rifat Allāh wal-Rasūl*. Beirut: Mu'assasat al-Kutub al-Thaqāfiyya, 1999.

al-Dāraquṭnī, Abū al-Ḥasan 'Alī b. 'Umar b. Aḥmad b. Mahdī. *Kitāb al-Ru'ya*. Ed. Ibrāhīm Muḥammad al-'Alī and Aḥmad Fakhrī al-Rifā'ī. al-Zarqā' (Jordan): Maktabat al-Manār, 1411/1990.

———. *al-Mu'talif wal-Mukhtalif*. Ed. Muwaffaq b. 'Abd Allāh b. 'Abd al-Qādir. 5 vols. Beirut: Dār al-Gharb al-Islāmī, 1406/1986.

———. *Sunan*. With Muḥammad Shams al-Ḥaqq al-'Aẓīm Ābādī's *al-Ta'līq al-Mughnī*. Ed. Al-Sayyid 'Abd Allāh Hāshim Yamānī al-Madanī. 4 vols. in 2. Beirut: Dār al-Ma'rifa, 1966. Repr. Beirut: Dār Iḥyā' al-Turāth al-'Arabī, 1993.

al-Dārimī, Abū Muḥammad 'Abd Allāh b. 'Abd al-Raḥmān b. al-Faḍl b. Bahrām. *Sunan al-Dārimī*. Ed. Muṣṭafā Dīb al-Bughā. 2 vols. Damascus: Dār al-Qalam, 1412/1991.

al-Dhahabī, Shams al-Dīn Muḥammad b. Aḥmad b. 'Uthmān. *Mīzān al-I'tidāl fī Naqd al-Rijāl*. Ed. 'Alī Muḥammad Mu'awwaḍ and 'Ādil Aḥmad 'Abd al-Mawjūd. 8 vols. Beirut: Dār al-Kutub al-'Ilmiyya, 1416/1995.

———. *Tadhkirat al-Ḥuffāẓ*. 4 vols. in 2. Ed. 'Abd al-Raḥmān b. Yaḥyā al-Mu'allimī. A fifth volume, titled *Dhayl Tadhkirat al-Ḥuffāẓ*, consists in al-Ḥusaynī's *Dhayl Tadhkirat al-Ḥuffāẓ*, Muḥammad b. Fahd al-Makkī's *Lahẓ al-Alḥāẓ bi-Dhayl Tadhkirat al-Ḥuffāẓ*, al-Suyūṭī's *Dhayl Ṭabaqāt al-Ḥuffāẓ*, and Aḥmad Rāfi' al-Ḥusaynī al-Ṭahṭāwī's *al-Tanbīh wal-Īqāẓ li-mā fī Dhuyūl Tadhkirat al-Ḥuffāẓ*. Ed. Muḥammad Zāhid b. Ḥasan b. 'Alī al-Kawtharī. Beirut: Dār Iḥyā' al-Turāth al-'Arabī, n.d. Rept. of the 1376-77/1956-58 Hyderabad 3rd edition.

al-Dūlābī, *al-Dhurriyyat al-Ṭāhira al-Nabawiyya*. Ed. Sa'd al-Mubārak al-Ḥasan. Kuwait: al-Dār al-Salafiyya, 1407/1986.

al-Fasawī, Abū Yūsuf Ya'qūb b. Sufyān. *al-Ma'rifa wal-Tārīkh*. Ed. Akram Ḍiyā' al-'Umarī. 4 vols. Madina: Maktabat al-Dār, 1410/1990.

al-Fayrūzābādī, Muḥammad b. Ya'qūb. *al-Qāmūs al-Muḥīṭ*. 4 vols. 3rd ed. Cairo: al-Maṭba'at al-Amīriyya, 1301/1884. Rept. Cairo: al-Hay'at al-Miṣriyya lil-Kitāb, 1400/1980.

al-Ghazālī, Abū Ḥāmid Muḥammad b. Muḥammad b. Muḥammad. *Fayṣal al-Tafriqa bayn al-Islām wal-Zandaqa*. Ed. Maḥmūd Bījū. Damascus: s.n., 1413/1993.

al-Ḥabshī, 'Alī b. Muḥammad b. Ḥusayn. *Simṭ al-Durar fī Akhbār Mawlid Khayr al-Bashar wa-Mā lahu min Akhlāq wa-Awṣāf wa-Siyar*. With an anthology of his poetry. Ed. Aḥmad b. 'Alawī b. 'Alī al-Ḥabshī. Solo (Indonesia): Masjid Riyadh, 1410/1990.

Haddad, Gibril Fouad. *The Excellence of Syro-Palestine – al-Shām – and Its People: Forty Hadiths*. Damascus: Maktabat al-Aḥbāb, 1422/2002.

———. *The Four Imams and Their Schools: Abu Hanifa, Malik, al-Shafi'i, Ahmad b. Hanbal*. Oxford: Muslim Academic Trust, 2007.

———. *Sunna Notes: Studies in Hadith and Doctrine I. Hadith History and Principles. With Ibn Hajar al-ʿAsqalānī's* Nukhbat al-Fikar. Trans. Musa Furber. Birmingham: Aqsa Publications; Hellenthal (Germany): Warda Publications, 1426/2005.

al-Ḥākim al-Naysābūrī, Abū ʿAbd Allāh Muḥammad b. ʿAbd Allāh b. al-Bayyiʿ. *Maʿrifat ʿUlūm al-Ḥadīth wa-Kammiyyat Ajnāsih.* Ed. Aḥmad b. Fāris al-Salūm. Beirut: Dār Ibn Ḥazm, 1424/2003.

———. *al-Mustadrak ʿalā al-Ṣaḥīḥayn.* With al-Dhahabī's *Talkhīṣ al-Mustadrak.* 5 vols. Indices by Yūsuf ʿAbd al-Raḥmān al-Marʿashlī. Beirut: Dār al-Maʿrifa, 1986. Repr. of the 1334/1916 Hyderabad edition.

Hannād b. al-Sarī al-Kūfī. *Kitāb al-Zuhd.* Ed. ʿAbd al-Raḥmān b. ʿAbd al-Jabbār al-Faryawāʾī. Kuwait: Dār al-Khulafāʾ lil-Kitāb al-Islāmī, 1406/1985.

Ḥaqqī Burūsawī, Ismāʿīl. *Tafsīr Rūḥ al-Bayān.* Ed. Ḥāfiẓ Muḥammad Khayrī and Aḥmad Rifʿat. 10 vols. Istanbul: al-Maṭbaʿat al-ʿUthmāniyya, 1330/1912.

Ḥassān b. Thābit, *Dīwān Ḥassān b. Thābit al-Anṣārī.* Ed. ʿAbd Allāh Sandah. 2nd ed. Beirut: Dār al-Maʿrifa, 1429/2008.

al-Haytamī, Abū al-Faḍl Aḥmad b. Muḥammad b. Ḥajar. *al-Minaḥ al-Makkiyya fī Sharḥ al-Hamziyya.* With al-Būṣīrī's *Hamziyya.* Ed. Bassām Muḥammad Bārūd. 3 vols. Abū Dhabī: al-Mujammaʿ al-Thaqāfī and Beirut: Dār al-Ḥāwī, 1418/1998.

———. *al-ʿUmda fī Sharḥ al-Burda.* With al-Būṣīrī's *al-Burda.* Ed. Bassām Muḥammad Bārūd. United Arab Emirates: Dār al-Faqīh, 1426/2005.

al-Haythamī, Nūr al-Dīn ʿAlī b. Abī Bakr. *Bughyat al-Bāḥith ʿan Zawāʾid Musnad al-Ḥārith.* Ed. Ḥusayn Aḥmad Ṣāliḥ al-Bākirī. 2 vols. Madina: al-Jāmiʿa al-Islāmiyya, 1413/1992.

———. *Majmaʿ al-Zawāʾid wa-Manbaʿ al-Fawāʾid.* 10 vols. Cairo: Dār al-Rayyān lil-Turāth, 1407/1987.

———. *Mawārid al-Ẓamʾān ilā Zawāʾid Ibn Ḥibbān.* Ed. Ḥusayn Salīm Asad al-Dārānī and ʿAbduh ʿAlī al-Kawshak. 9 vols. Damascus: Dār al-Thaqāfa al-ʿArabiyya, 1411/1990.

Ibn ʿAbd al-Barr al-Namarī al-Qurṭubī, Abū ʿUmar Yūsuf b. ʿAbd Allāh b. Muḥammad. *al-Istīʿāb fī Maʿrifat al-Aṣḥāb.* Ed. ʿĀdil Murshid. Amman: Dār al-Aʿlām, 1423/2002.

———. *al-Istidhkār al-Jāmiʿ li-Madhāhib Fuqahāʾ al-Amṣār wa-ʿUlamāʾ al-Aqṭār fī-mā Taḍammanahu al-Muwaṭṭaʾ min Maʿānī al-Raʾy wal-Āthār wa-Sharḥ Dhālik Kullih bil-Ījāz wal-Ikhtiṣār.* Ed. ʿAbd al-Muʿṭī Amīn Qalʿajī. 30 vols. Damascus and Beirut: Dār Qutayba; Aleppo and Cairo: Dār al-Waʿy, 1414/1993.

———. *al-Tamhīd li-mā fīl-Muwaṭṭa' min al-Ma'ānī wal-Asānīd*. Ed. Mūṣṭafā b. Aḥmad al-'Alawī and Muḥammad 'Abd al-Kabīr al-Bakrī. 26 vols. Rabat: al-Maṭba'at al-Malakiyya, 1387/1967.

Ibn 'Abd al-Salām al-Sulamī, 'Izz al-Dīn 'Abd al-'Azīz. *Bidāyat al-Sūl fī Tafḍīl al-Rasūl*. Ed. Iyād Khālid al-Ṭabbā'. Beirut and Damascus: Dār al-Fikr, 1995.

———. *Tafsīr al-'Izz b. 'Abd al-Salām Ikhtiṣār al-Nukat lil-Māwardī*. Ed. 'Abd Allāh b. Ibrāhīm al-Wahbī. Beirut: Dār Ibn Ḥazm, 1416/1996.

Ibn Abī 'Āṣim al-Shaybānī, Abū Bakr Aḥmad b. 'Amr b. al-Ḍaḥḥāk. *Al-Āḥād wal-Mathānī*. Ed. Bāsim Fayṣal Aḥmad al-Jawābira. 6 vols. Riyadh: Dār al-Rāya, 1411/1991.

———. *al-Sunna*. Ed. Bāsim b. Fayṣal al-Jawābira. 2 vols. Riyadh: Dār al-Ṣumay'ī, 1419/1998.

Ibn Abī al-Dunyā, Abū Bakr 'Abd Allāh b. Muḥammad. *al-Ikhwān*. Ed. Muṣṭafā 'Abd al-Qādir 'Aṭā. Beirut: Dār al-Kutub al-'Ilmiyya, 1409/1988.

———. *Kitāb al-Muḥtaḍarīn*. Ed. Muḥammad Khayr Ramaḍān Yūsuf. Beirut: Dār Ibn Ḥazm, 1417/1997.

———. *Kitāb al-Mutamannīn*. Muḥammad Khayr Ramaḍān Yūsuf. Beirut: Dār Ibn Ḥazm, 1418/1997.

Ibn Abī Ḥātim al-Rāzī, 'Abd al-Raḥmān b. Muḥammad b. Idrīs al-Ḥanẓalī. *Tafsīr al-Qur'ān al-'Aẓīm Musnadan 'an Rasūl Allāh Ṣallā Allāh 'Alayh wa-Sallam wal-Ṣaḥāba wal-Tābi'īn*. Ed. As'ad Muḥammad al-Ṭayyib. 14 vols. Makka and Riyadh: Maktabat Nizār Muṣṭafā al-Bāz, 1417/1997.

Ibn Abī Jamra al-Umawī al-Mursī, Abū al-'Abbās Aḥmad b. 'Abd al-Malik b. Mūsā. *Bahjat al-Nufūs wa-Taḥallīha bi-Ma'rifat Mā Lahā wa-Mā 'Alayhā*. Ed. Ismā'īl b. 'Abd Allāh al-Maghribī al-Ṣāwī et al. 4 vols. Cairo: Maṭba'at al-Ṣidq al-Khayriyya, 1355/1936.

Ibn Abī Shayba al-'Absī al-Kūfī, Abū Bakr 'Abd Allāh b. Muḥammad. *al-Muṣannaf*. Ed. Muḥammad 'Awwāma. 26 vols. Jeddah: Dār al-Qila lil-Thaqāfat al-Islāmiyya; Damascus: Mu'assasat 'Ulūm al-Qur'ān, 1427/2006.

Ibn 'Ādil al-Dimashqī al-Ḥanbalī, Abū Ḥafṣ 'Umar b. 'Alī. *al-Lubāb fī 'Ulūm al-Kitāb*. Ed. 'Ādil Aḥmad 'Abd al-Mawjūd et al. 20 vols. Beirut: Dār al-Kutub al-'Ilmiyya, 1419/1998.

Ibn 'Ajība al-Fāsī, Abū al-'Abbād Aḥmad b. Muḥammad b. al-Mahdī. *al-Baḥr al-Madīd fī Tafsīr al-Kitāb al-Majīd*. 8 vols. 2nd ed. Beirut: Dār al-Kutub al-'Ilmiyya, 1423/2002.

———. *al-Futūḥāt al-Ilāhiyya fī Sharḥ al-Mabāḥith al-Aṣliyya*. Ed. 'Abd al-Raḥmān Ḥasan Maḥmūd. Cairo: 'Ālam al-Fikr, n.d.

Ibn al-'Arabī al-Ishbīlī al-Ma'āfirī al-Mālikī, Abū Bakr Muḥammad b. 'Abd Allāh b. Muḥammad. *'Āriḍat al-Aḥwadhī bi-Sharḥ Sunan al-Tirmidhī*. Cairo: Dār al-'Ilm al-Jāmi', 1350/1931. 13 vols. in 7. Rept. Beirut, Dār al-Kutub al-'Ilmiyya, n.d.

Ibn al-Aʿrābī, Abū Saʿīd Aḥmad b. Muḥammad. *Kitāb al-Muʿjam*. Ed. ʿAbd al-Muḥsin b. Ibrāhīm al-Ḥusaynī. 3 vols. Dammam: Dār Ibn al-Jawzī, 1418/1997.

Ibn ʿAsākir, Abū al-Qāsim ʿAlī b. al-Ḥasan b. Hibat Allāh b. ʿAbd Allāh. *Muʿjam al-Shuyūkh*. Ed. Wafā' Taqī al-Dīn. 3 vols. Damascus: Dār al-Bashā'ir, 1421/2000.

———. *Tārīkh Madīnat Dimashq*. Ed. Muḥibb al-Dạn Abū Saʿīd ʿUmar b. Gharāma al-ʿAmrawī. 80 vols. Beirut: Dār al-Fikr, 1415-1421/1995-2001.

Ibn ʿĀshūr, Muḥammad al-Ṭāhir. *Tafsīr al-Taḥrīr wal-Tanwīr*. 30 vols. Tunis: al-Dār al-Tūnisiyya lil-Nashr, 1984.

Ibn al-Athīr al-Jazarī, Majd al-Dīn Abū al-Saʿādāt al-Mubārak b. Muḥammad. *al-Nihāya fī Gharīb al-Ḥadīth wal-Athar*. Ed. Ṭāhir Aḥmad al-Zāwī and Maḥmūd Muḥammad al-Ṭanāḥī. 5 vols. Beirut: Dār Iḥyā' al-Turāth al-ʿArabī, n.d.

Ibn Bābūyah al-Qummī, Abū Jaʿfar Muḥammad b. ʿAlī b. al-Ḥusayn. *Maʿānī al-Akhbār*. Tehran: Maktabat al-Ṣadūq, 1379/1959.

Ibn al-Bannā al-Saraqusṭī, *al-Mabāḥith al-Aṣliyya*. See Ibn ʿAjība, *Futūḥāt*.

Ibn Baṭṭa al-ʿUkbarī, Abū ʿAbd Allāh ʿUbayd Allāh b. Muḥammad. *al-Ibāna ʿan Sharīʿat al-Firqat al-Nājiya wa-Mujānabat al-Firaq al-Madhmūma*. Ed. Riḍā b. Naʿsān Muʿṭī. 8 vols. in 6. 2nd ed. Riyadh: Dār al-Rāya, 1415/1994.

Ibn Bishrān, Abū al-Qāsim ʿAbd al-Malik b. Muḥammad b. ʿAbd Allāh. *al-Amālī*. Ed. Abū ʿAbd al-Raḥmān ʿĀdil b. Yūsuf al-ʿAzāzī. 2 vols. Riyadh: Dār al-Waṭan, 1418/1997.

Ibn Bishrān al-Muʿaddal, Abū al-Ḥusayn ʿAlī b. Muḥammad b. ʿAbd Allāh. *al-Fawā'id*. In Ibn Mandah, *Fawā'id*. Ed. Khalāf Maḥmūd ʿAbd al-Samīʿ. 2 vols. Beirut: Dār al-Kutub al-ʿIlmiyya, 1423/2002. 1:188-245.

Ibn Diḥya al-Balansī,Majd al-Dīn Abū al-Khaṭṭāb ʿUmar b. al-Ḥasan b. ʿAli. *Nihāyat al-Sūl fī Khaṣā'iṣ al-Rasūl*. Ed. Ma'mūn al-Ṣāgharjī and Muḥammad Adīb al-Jābir. Damascus: Dār al-Bashā'ir, 1420/1999.

Ibn Ḥajar al-ʿAsqalānī, Abū al-Faḍl Aḥmad b. ʿAlī. *al-Amālī al-Muṭlaqa*. Ed. Ḥamdī ʿAbd al-Majīd al-Salafī. Beirut: al-Maktab al-Islāmī, 1416/1995.

———. *Fatḥ al-Bārī bi-Sharḥ Ṣaḥīḥ al-Bukhārī*. Ed. Muḥammad Fu'ād ʿAbd al-Bāqī and Muḥibb al-Dīn al-Khaṭib. 14 vols. Beirut: Dār al-Maʿrifa, 1379/1959.

———. *al-Iṣāba fī Tamyīz al-Ṣaḥāba*. 8 vols. Cairo: al-Maṭbaʿat al-Sharafiyya, 1327/1909. Rept. Beirut: Dār al-Kutub al-ʿIlmiyya, n.d.

———. *al-Maṭālib al-ʿĀliya bi-Zawā'id al-Masānīd al-Thamāniya*. Ed. Khālid b. ʿAbd al-Raḥmān b. Sālim al-Bikr and Saʿd b. Nāṣir b. ʿAbd al-ʿAzīz al-Shathrī. 19 vols. Riyadh: Dār al-ʿĀṣima and Dār al-Ghayth, 1420/2000.

———. *Mukhtaṣar Zawā'id Musnad al-Bazzār*. Ed. Ṣabrī 'Abd al-Khāliq Abū Dharr. 2 vols. Beirut: Mu'assasat al-Kutub al-Thaqāfiyya, 1412/1992.

———. *Nuzhat al-Sāmi'īn fī Riwāyat al-Ṣaḥāba 'an al-Tābi'īn* ed. Ṭāriq Muḥammad al-'Umūdī, Ryadh: Dār al-Hijra, 1995.

Ibn Ḥanbal, see Aḥmad b. Muḥammad b. Ḥanbal.

Ibn Ḥibbān al-Bustī, Abū Ḥātim Muḥammad b. Ḥibbān b. Aḥmad. *Ṣaḥīḥ Ibn Ḥibbān bi-Tartīb Ibn Balbān*. Ed. Shu'ayb al-Arnā'ūṭ. 2nd ed. 18 vols. Beirut: Mu'assasat al-Risāla, 1414/1993.

Ibn Hishām, Abū Muḥammad 'Abd al-Malik. *al-Sīrat al-Nabawiyya*. Ed. Muṣṭafā al-Saqqā, Ibrāhīm al-Abyārī, and 'Abd al-Ḥafīẓ Shalabī. 4 vols. in 2. 2nd ed. Beirut: Dār al-Wifāq, 1375/1955.

Ibn al-Ja'd b. 'Ubayd al-Jawharī, Abū al-Ḥasan 'Alī. *Musnad*. Ed. 'Abd al-Mahdī b. 'Abd al-Qādir b. 'Abd al-Hādī. 2 vols. Kuwait: Maktabat al-Falāḥ, 1405/1995.

Ibn al-Jawzī al-Qurashī al-Baghdādī, Abū al-Faraj Jamāl al-Dīn 'Abd al-Raḥmān b. 'Alī b. Muḥammad. *al-Mawḍū'āt min al-Aḥādīth al-Marfū'āt*. Ed. Nūr al-Dīn Shukrī 'Alī Būyājīlār. 4 vols. Riyadh: Aḍwā' al-Salaf, 1418/1997.

———. *Muthīr al-Gharām al-Sākin ilā Ashraf al-Amākin*. Ed. Muṣṭafā Muḥammad Ḥusayn al-Dhahabī. cairo : Dār al-Ḥadīth, 1415/1995.

———. *Ṣifat al-Ṣafwa*. Ed. Ibrāhīm Ramaḍān and Sa'īd al-Laḥḥām. 4 vols. in 2. Beirut: Dār al-Kutub al-'Ilmiyya, 1409/1989.

———. *al-Wafā bi-Aḥwāl al-Muṣṭafā*. Ed. Muṣṭafā 'Abd al-Qādir 'Aṭā. Beirut: Dār al-Kutub al-'Ilmiyya, 1408/1988.

———. *Zād al-Masīr fī 'Ilm al-Tafsīr*. 9 vols. 3rd ed. Beirut: al-Maktab al-Islāmī, 1404/1984.

Ibn Kathīr, 'Imād al-Dīn Abū al-Fidā' Ismā'īl b. 'Umar al-Qurashī al-Dimashqī. *al-Bidāya wal-Nihāya*. Ed. 'Abd Allāh b. 'Abd al-Muḥsin al-Turkī et al. 21 vols. Cairo: Dār Hajar, 1418/1998.

———. *al-Sīra al-Nabawiyya*. Ed. Muṣṭafā 'Abd al-Wāḥid. 4 vols. 2nd ed. Cairo: 'Īsā al-Bābī al-Ḥalabī, 1396/1976.

———. *Tafsīr al-Qur'ān al-'Aẓīm*. Ed. Muṣṭafā al-Sayyid Muḥammad et al. 15 vols. Jīza: Mu'assasat Qurṭuba, 1421/2000.

Ibn Kīrān, al-Ṭayyib b. 'Abd al-Majīd. *Sharḥ al-Ṣalāt al-Mashīshiyya*. Ed. Bassām Muḥammad Bārūd. Abū Dhabī: al-Mujamma' al-Thaqāfī, 1420/1999.

Ibn Mājah, Abū 'Abd Allāh Muḥammad b. Yazīd. *Sunan Ibni Mājah bi-Sharḥ al-Imām Abī al-Ḥasan al-Ḥanafī al-Ma'rūf bil-Sindī*. Ed. Khalīl Ma'mūn Shīḥā. 5 vols. Beirut: Dār al-Ma'rifa, 1416/1996.

Ibn Manẓūr, Abū al-Faḍl Jamāl al-Dīn Muḥammad b. Mukarram. *Lisān al-'Arab*. 15 vols. Beirut: Dār Ṣādir, 1410/1990.

Ibn al-Mubārak b. Wāḍiḥ al-Marwazī al-Ḥanẓalī, Abū 'Abd al-Raḥmān 'Abd Allāh. *Kitāb al-Zuhd*. With his *Kitāb al-Raqā'iq*. Ed. Ḥabīb al-

Raḥmān al-A'ẓamī. Malegaon (Maharashtra State, India): Majlis Iḥyā' al-Ma'ārif, 1386/1966. Rept. Beirut: Dār al-Kutub al-'Ilmiyya, n.d.

Ibn Mubārak al-Bakrī al-Sijilmāsī al-Lamṭī, Aḥmad. *al-Ibrīz min Kalām Sayyidī 'Abd al-'Azīz al-Dabbāgh.* Ed. Muḥammad Bashīr Ḥasan al-Hāshimī. 2nd ed. Beirut: Dār Ṣādir, 1427/2006.

Ibn al-Mulaqqin, Sirāj al-Dīn Abū Ḥafṣ 'Umar b. 'Alī b. Aḥmad. *Kitāb Khaṣā'iṣ al-Nabī.* Ed. al-Sayyid Yūsuf Aḥmad. Beirut: Dār al-Kutub al-'Ilmiyya, 2008.

Ibn al-Najjār al-Baghdādī, Muḥibb al-Dīn Abū 'Abd Allāh Muḥammad b. Maḥmūd b. al-Ḥasan. *al-Durrat al-Thamīna fī Tārīkh al-Madīna.* Ed. Muḥammad Zaynuhum Muḥammad 'Azb. Port Sa'īd: Maktabat al-Thaqāfat al-Dīniyya, 1415/1995.

Ibn Qayyim al-Jawziyya, Shams al-Dīn Abū 'Abd Allāh Muḥammad b. Abī Bakr al-Zur'ī. *Hidāyat al-Ḥayārā fī Ajwibat al-Yahūd wal-Naṣārā.* Ed. Aḥmad Ḥijāzī Saqqā. 4th ed. Cairo: al-Maktabat al-Qayyima, 1407/1987.

———. *al-Rūḥ.* Ed. Yūsuf 'Alī Budaywī. 3rd ed. Damascus and Beirut: Dār Ibn Kathīr, 1419/1998.

Ibn Qutayba al-Dīnawarī, Abū Muḥammad 'Abd Allāh b. Muslim. *Kitāb 'Uyūn al-Akhbār.* 2nd ed. 4 vols. in 2. Cairo: Dār al-Kutub al-Miṣriyya, 1996.

Ibn Rajab, Zayn al-Dīn Abū al-Faraj 'Abd al-Raḥmān b. Aḥmad. *Laṭā'if al-Ma'ārif fī-mā lil-Mawāsim min Waẓā'if.* Ed. Yāsīn Muḥammad al-Sawwās. 5th ed. Damascus and Beirut: Dār Ibn Kathīr, 1420/1999.

Ibn Sa'd b. Manī' al-Zuhrī, Muḥammad. *al-Ṭabaqāt al-Kubrā..* Ed. 'Alī Muḥammad 'Umar. 11 vols Cairo: Maktabat al-Khānjī, 1421/2001.

Ibn Sayyid al-Nās, Abū al-Fatḥ Fatḥ al-Dīn Muḥammad b. Muḥammad b. Muḥammad. *Minaḥ al-Madḥ.* Ed. 'Iffat Wiṣāl Ḥamza. Damascus: Dār al-Fikr, 1407/1987.

Ibn Shāhīn al-Ẓāhirī, Abū Ḥafṣ 'Umar b. Aḥmad b. 'Uthmān. *al-Targhīb fī Faḍā'il al-A'māl wa-Thawāb Dhālik.* Ed. Ṣāliḥ Aḥmad Muṣliḥ al-Wa'īl. Dammam: Dār Ibn al-Jawzī, 1415/1995.

Ibn Taymiyya al-Ḥarrānī, Taqī al-Dīn Abū al-'Abbās Aḥmad b. 'Abd al-Ḥalīm. *Majmū' al-Fatāwā.* Ed. 'Āmir al-Jazzār and Anwar al-Bāz. 37 vols. 3rd ed. al-Manṣūra: Dār al-Wafā', 1426/2005.

al-'Imrānī al-Sarghīnī, 'Abd al-Salām b. al-Mu'ṭī. *al-Lu'lu'at al-Fāshiya fil-Riḥlat al-Ḥijāziyya.* Ed. Nūr al-Hudā 'Abd al-Raḥmān al-Kattānī. Casablanca: Markaz al-Turāth al-Thaqāfī al-Maghribī; Beirut: Dār Ibn Ḥazm, 1431/2010.

'Iyāḍ b. Mūsā al-Yaḥṣubī. *al-Shifā bi-Ta'rīf Ḥuqūq al-Muṣṭafā.* Ed. 'Abduh 'Alī Kawshak. Damascus: Maktabat al-Ghazālī; Beirut: Dār al-Fayḥā', 1420/2000.

al-Jurrāwī al-Tādilī, Abū al-ʿAbbās Aḥmad b. ʿAbd al-Salām. *al-Ḥamāsat al-Maghribiyya*. Ed. Muḥammad Riḍwān al-Dāya. 2nd ed. Damascus: Dār al-Fikr, 1426/2005.

al-Kalābādhī al-Bukhārī, Abū Bakr Muḥammad b. Ibrāhīm b. Yaʿqūb. *Baḥr al-Fawā'id al-Mashhūr bi-Maʿānī al-Akhbār*. Ed. Wajīh Kamāl al-Dīn Zakī. 2 vols. Cairo: Dār al-Salām, 1429/2008.

al-Kattānī, Abū al-Jamāl Muḥammad al-Ṭāhir b. al-Ḥasan. *Maṭāliʿ al-Saʿāda fī Iqtirān Kalimatay al-Shahāda*. Ed. Muḥammad Ḥamza al-Kattānī. Beirut: Dār al-Kutub al-ʿIlmiyya, 1428/2007.

Kayyāl, Hudā bint ʿAbd Allāh. *Yawm wa-Layla maʿ Rasūl Allāh*. Beirut: al-Shafaq lil-Ṭibāʿa wal-Nashr wal-Tawzīʿ, [2006].

al-Khallāl. Abū Bakr Aḥmad b. Muḥammad b. Hārūn. *al-Sunna*. Ed. ʿAṭiyya al-Zahrānī. 7 vols. in 3. Riyadh: Dār al-Rāya, 1410/1989.

al-Kharā'iṭī, Abū Bakr Muḥammad b. Jaʿfar b. Sahl. *Makārim al-Akhlāq wa-Maʿālīhā wa-Maḥmūd Ṭarā'iqihā*. Ed. ʿAbd Allāh b. Bijāsh al-Ḥimyarī. 4 vols. Riyadh: Maktabat al-Rushd, 1427/2006.

al-Kharkūshī al-Naysābūrī, Abū Saʿd ʿAbd al-Malik b. Abī ʿUthmān Muḥammad b. Ibrāhīm. [*Sharaf al-Muṣṭafā*.] *Manāḥil al-Shifā wa-Manāhil al-Ṣafā bi-Taḥqīq Kitāb Sharaf al-Muṣṭafā*. Ed. Abū ʿĀṣim Nabīl b. Hāshim al-Ghamrī Āl Bā ʿAlawī. 5 vols. Beirut: Dār al-Bashā'ir al-Islāmiyya, 1424/2003.

al-Khaṭīb, ʿAbd al-Laṭīf. *Muʿjam al-Qirā'āt*. 11 vols. Damascus: Dār Saʿd al-Dīn, 1422/2002.

al-Khaṭīb al-Baghdādī, Abū Bakr Aḥmad b. ʿAlī b. Thābit. *Tālī Talkhīṣ al-Mutashābih*. Ed. Abū ʿUbayda Mashhūr Ḥasan Salmān and Abū Ḥudhayfa Aḥmad al-Shuqayrāt. Dammam: Dār al-Ṣumayʿī, 1417/1997.

———. *Tārīkh Baghdād aw Madīnat al-Salām*. 14 vols. Cairo: Maktabat al-Khānjī, 1931. Rept. 15 vols. Beirut: Dār al-Kitāb al-ʿArabī, [1966?] and Dār al-Kutub al-ʿIlmiyya, n.d.

al-Laknawī, Abū al-Ḥasanāt Muḥammad ʿAbd al-Ḥayy. *al-Āthār al-Marfūʿa fil-Akhbār al-Mawḍūʿa*. Ed. Muḥammad b. Basyūnī Zaghlūl. Beirut: Dār al-Kutub al-ʿIlmiyya, 1984.

Majmūʿ Mushtamil ʿalā Mawlid al-Nabī ṣallā Allāh ʿalayhi wa-Sallam lil-Barzanjī wal-Daybaʿ wal-ʿAzb. Cairo: Muṣṭafā al-Bābī, 1342/1923.

Makkī b. Abī Ṭālib al-Qaysī, Abū Muḥammad. *al-Hidāya ilā Bulūgh al-Nihāya*. Ed. al-Shāhid al-Būshaykhī et al. 13 vols. Sharjah: Kulliyyat al-Dirāsāt al-ʿUlyā, Jāmiʿat al-Shāriqa, 1429/2008.

al-Maqdisī, Ḍiyā' al-Dīn Muḥammad b. ʿAbd al-Wāḥid b. Aḥmad. *al-Aḥādīth al-Mukhtāra*. Ed. ʿAbd al-Mālik b. ʿAbd Allāh b. Duhaysh. 13 vols. 3rd ed. Makka: Maktabat al-Nahḍat al-Ḥadītha; Beirut: Dār Khaḍir, 1420/2000.

al-Māturīdī al-Samarqandī, Abū Manṣūr Muḥammad b. Muḥammad. *Ta'wīlāt Ahl al-Sunna: Tafsīr al-Qur'ān.* Ed. Majdī Bāsallūm. 10 vols. Beirut: Dār al-Kutub al-'Ilmiyya, 1426/2005.

al-Māwardī, Abū al-Ḥasan 'Alī b. Muḥammad b. Ḥabīb. *A'lām al-Nubuwwa.* Beirut: Dār al-Kutub al-'Ilmiyya, 1406/1986.

———. *al-Nukat wal-'Uyūn: Tafsīr al-Māwardī.* Ed. Sayyid b. 'Abd al-Maqṣūd b.'Abd al-Raḥīm. 6 vols. Beirut: Dār al-Kutub al-'Ilmiyya, 1992.

al-Mizzī, Jamāl al-Dīn Abū al-Ḥajjāj Yūsuf b. al-Zakī 'Abd al-Raḥmān b. Yūsuf. *Tahdhīb al-Kamāl fī Asmā' al-Rijāl.* Ed. Bashshār 'Awwād Ma'rūf. 35 vols. 2nd ed. Beirut: Mu'assasat al-Risāla, 1403/1983.

Mughulṭāy b. Qalīj b. 'Abd Allāh, 'Alā' al-Dīn. *Sharḥ Sunan Ibn Mājah.* [*al-I'lām bi-Sunnatih 'alayh al-Ṣalāt wal-Salām.*] Ed. Kāmil 'Uwayḍa. 6 vols. Mecca and Riyadh: Maktabat Nizār Muṣṭafā al-Bāz, 1419/1999.

Mujāhid b. Jabr al-Makhzūmī. *Tafsīr al-Imām Mujāhid b. Jabr.* Ed. Muḥammad 'Abd al-Salām Abū Nabīl. Cairo: Dār al-Fikr al-Islāmī al-Ḥadītha, 1410/1989.

Muqātil b. Sulaymān. *Tafsīr Muqātil b. Sulaymān.* Ed. Aḥmad Farīd Mazyadī. 3 vols. Beirut: Dār al-Kutub al-'Ilmiyya, 1424/2003.

Muslim b. al-Ḥajjāj b. Muslim al-Qushayrī al-Naysābūrī, Abū al-Ḥusayn. *al-Jāmi' al-Ṣaḥīḥ.* [*al-Musnad al-Ṣaḥīḥ al-Mukhtaṣar min al-Sunan bi-Naql al-'Adl 'an al-'Adl ilā Rasul Allāh ṣallā Allah 'alayh wa-sallam.*] 8 vols. [Istanbul]: al-Maṭba'at al-'Āmira, 1334/1916.

al-Muttaqī al-Hindī al-Burhānfūrī, 'Alā' al-Dīn 'Alī al-Muttaqī b. Ḥusām al-Dīn. *Kanz al-'Ummāl fī Sunan al-Aqwāl wal-Af'āl.* Ed. Bakrī Ḥayyānī and Ṣafwat al-Saqqā. 18 vols. 5th ed. Beirut: Mu'assasat al-Risāla, 1405/1985.

al-Nabhānī, Yūsuf b. Ismā'īl. *Ḥujjat Allāh 'alā al-Ālamīn bi-Mu'jizāt Sayyid al-Mursalīn.* Beirut: al-Maṭba'at al-Adabiyya, 1316/1898.

———. *Sa'ādat al-Dārayn fīl-Ṣalāt 'alā Sayyid al-Kawnayn.* [Beirut:] s.n., 1318/1900.

al-Naḥḥās, Abū Ja'far Aḥmad b. Muḥammad b. Ismā'īl. *Ma'ānī al-Qur'ān al-Karīm.* Ed. Muḥammad 'Alī al-Ṣābūnī. 6 vols. Mecca: Jāmi'at Umm al-Qurā, 1409/1988.

al-Nasā'ī, Abū 'Abd al-Raḥmān Aḥmad b. Shu'ayb b. 'Alī. *Khaṣā'iṣ Amīr al-Mu'minīn 'Alī b. Abī Ṭālib.* Ed. Aḥmad Mīrīn al-Balūshī. Kuwait: Maktabat al-Mu'allā, 1406/1986.

———. *Kitāb al-Sunan al-Kubrā.* Ed. Ḥusayn 'Abd al-Mun'im Shalabī. 12 vols. 1421/2001.

———. *Sunan al-Nasā'ī bi-Sharḥ al-Ḥāfiẓ Jalāl al-Dīn al-Suyūṭī wa-Ḥāshiyat al-Imām al-Sindī.* 8 vols. [Cairo]: al-Maṭba'at al-Miṣriyya, 1348/1930. Repr. 8 vols. in 4. Beirut: Dār Iḥyā' al-Turāth al-'Arabī, n.d.

al-Nawawī, Muḥyī al-Dīn Abū Zakariyyā Yaḥyā b. Sharaf. *Tahdhīb al-Asmā' wal-Lughāt.* 3 vols. Cairo: Idārat al-Ṭibā'at al-Munīriyya, [1927?].

al-Nuwayrī, Shihāb al-Dīn Aḥmad b. ʿAbd al-Wahhāb. *Nihāyat al-Arab fī Funūn al-ʿArab*. Ed. Mufīd Qumayḥa et al. 33 vols. Beirut: Dār al-Kutub al-ʿIlmiyya, 1424/2004.

al-Qārī, Mullā ʿAlī b. Sulṭān Muḥammad. *al-Asrār al-Marfūʿa fīl-Akhbār al-Mawḍūʿa al-Maʿrūf bil-Mawḍūʿāt al-Kubrā*. Ed. Muḥammad Luṭfī al-Ṣabbāgh. 2nd ed. Beirut and Damascus: al-Maktab al-Islāmī, 1406/1986.

———. *Mirqāt al-Mafātīḥ Sharḥ Mishkāt al-Maṣābīḥ*. Ed. Jamāl ʿĪtānī. 12 vols. Beirut: Dār al-Kutub al-ʿIlmiyya, 1422/2011.

———. *Sharḥ al-Shifā*. 2 vols. Istanbul: al-Maṭbaʿat al-ʿUthmāniyya, 1319/1901. Rept. Beirut: Dār al-Kutub al-ʿIlmiyya, n.d.

al-Qasṭallānī, Shihāb al-Dīn Abū al-ʿAbbās Ahmad b. Muḥammad b. Abī Bakr. *al-Mawāhib al-Ladunniyya bil-Minaḥ al-Muḥammadiyya*. Ed. Ma'mūn b. Muḥyī al-Dīn al-Jannān. 3 vols. Beirut: Dār al-Kutub al-ʿIlmiyya, 1416/1996.

al-Qurashī, Abū Zayd Muḥammad b. Abī al-Khaṭṭāb. *Jamharat Ashʿār al-ʿArab fīl-Jāhiliyya wal-Islām*. Ed. ʿAlī Muḥammad al-Bijāwī. Cairo: Nahḍat Miṣr, 1981.

al-Qurṭubī, Abū ʿAbd Allāh Muḥammad b. Aḥmad. *al-Jāmiʿ li-Aḥkām al-Qurʾān wal-Mubayyin li-mā Taḍammanahu min al-Sunna wa-Āy al-Furqān*. Ed. ʿAbd Allāh b. ʿAbd al-Muḥsin al-Turkī and Muḥammad Riḍwān ʿAraqsūsī. 24 vols. Beirut: Muʾassasat al-Risāla, 1427/2006.

al-Qushayrī, Zayn al-Islām Abū al-Qāsim ʿAbd al-Karīm b. Hawzān b. ʿAbd al-Mālik al-Naysābūrī. *Laṭā'if al-Ishārāt: Tafsīr Ṣūfī Kāmil lil-Qurān*. Ed. Ibrāhīm Bayyūnī. 6 vols. Cairo: al-Hay'at al-Miṣriyya al-ʿĀmma lil-Ta'līf wal-Nashr, 1390/1971.

———. *al-Risāla*. With Zakariyyā al-Anṣārī's *Ḥāshiya*. Cairo: Dār al-Ṭibāʿa al-ʿĀmira, 1287/1870.

al-Rawwās al-Ṣayyādī, Bahā' al-Dīn Muḥammad Mahdī Āl Khizām. *Fā'idat al-Himam min Mā'idat al-Karam*. Maʿarrat al-Nuʿmān (Syria): Ṣubḥī Ismāʿīl al-Ṣabbūḥ, 1321/1903.

al-Rāzī al-Bakrī, Fakhr al-Dīn Abū ʿAbd Allāh Muḥammad b. ʿUmar b. al-Ḥasan b. al-Ḥusayn. *Tafsīr al-Fakhr al-Rāzī al-Mushtahar bil-Tafsīr al-Kabīr wa-Mafātīḥ al-Ghayb*. 32 vols. Beirut: Dār al-Fikr, 1401/1981.

Rūzbahān b. Abī Naṣr al-Baqlī al-Shīrāzī, Abū Muḥammad Ṣadr al-Dīn. *Tafsīr ʿArā'is al-Bayān fī Ḥaqā'iq al-Qur'ān*. Ed. Ahmad Farīd al-Mazyadī. 3 vols. Beirut: Dār al-Kutub al-ʿIlmiyya, 1429/2008.

al-Ṣāliḥī, Muḥammad b. Yūsuf. *Subul al-Hudā wal-Rashād fī Sīrat Khayr al-ʿIbād*. Ed. Muṣṭafā ʿAbd al-Wāḥid. 12 vols. Cairo: Lajnat Iḥyā' al-Turāth al-Islāmī, 1418/1997.

al-Samarqandī, Abū al-Layth Naṣr b. Muḥammad b. Ibrāhīm. *Tafsīr al-Samarqandī al-Musammā Baḥr al-ʿUlūm*. Ed. ʿAlī Muḥammad Muʿawwaḍ et al. 3 vols. Beirut: Dār al-Kutub al-ʿIlmiyya, 1993.

al-Sarrāj al-Thaqafī, Abū al-ʿAbbās Muḥammad b. Isḥāq. *Ḥadīth al-Sarrāj*. Ed. Abū ʿAbd Allāh Ḥusayn b. ʿUkāsha b. Ramaḍān. 4 vols. Cairo: al-Fārūq al-Ḥadītha lil-Ṭibāʿa wal-Nashr, 1425/2004.

al-Ṣāwī al-Khalwatī, Aḥmad b. Muḥammad. [*Sharḥ al-Ṣalawāt al-Dardīriyya.*] *Kitāb al-Asrār al-Rabbāniyya wal-Fuyūḍāt al-Raḥmāniyya ʿalā al-Ṣalawāt al-Dardīriyya*. With his *Sharḥ Manẓūmat Asmāʾ Allāh al-Ḥusnā lil-Dardīr*. Cairo: Maṭbaʿat Muḥammad Riḍwān Shaʿrāwī, 1281/1864.

———. *Sharḥ al-Ṣalawāt al-Mashīshiyya*. Princeton University Manuscript Collection. Islamic Manuscripts, Garrett no. 5585Y.

al-Shāfiʿī, Abū Bakr Muḥammad b. ʿAbd Allāh b. Ibrāhīm. [*Ghaylāniyyāt.*] *Kitāb al-Fawāʾid al-Mashhūr bil-Ghaylāniyyāt*. Ed. Ḥilmī Kāmil Asʿad ʿAbd al-Hādī. 2 vols. Dammam: Dār Ibn al-Jawzī, 1997.

al-Shahrastānī, Abū al-Fatḥ Muḥammad b. ʿAbd al-Karīm. *al-Milal wal-Niḥal*. Ed. Aḥmad Fahmī Muḥammad. 3 vols. Maktabat al-Ḥusayn al-Tijāriyya, 1368/1948. Rept. Beirut: Dār al-Surūr, n.d.

al-Shaʿrānī, Abū Muḥammad ʿAbd al-Wahhāb b. Aḥmad b. ʿAlī. *al-Ṭabaqāt al-Kubrā: Lawāqiḥ al-Anwār fī Ṭabaqāt al-Akhyār*. 2 vols. Cairo: al-Maṭbaʿat al-ʿĀmira al-Sharafiyya, 1315/1897.

al-Shawkānī, Muḥammad b. ʿAlī b. Muḥammad. *Fatḥ al-Qadīr al-Jāmiʿ bayna Fannay al-Riwāya wal-Dirāya min ʿIlm al-Tafsīr*. Ed. ʿAbd al-Raḥmān ʿUmayra. 6 vols. al-Manṣūra: Dār al-Wafāʾ, 1415/1994.

al-Silafī, Abū Ṭāhir Aḥmad b. Muḥammad. *Muʿjam al-Safar*. Ed. ʿAbd Allāh ʿUmar al-Bārūdī. Beirut: Dār al-Fikr, 1414/1993.

Sirāj al-Dīn, ʿAbd Allāh. *Shahādatu Lā Ilāha Illā Allāh Muḥammadun Rasūl Allāh*. Aleppo: Maktabat Dār al-Falāḥ, n.d.

al-Subkī, Abū al-Ḥasan Taqī al-Dīn ʿAlī b. ʿAbd al-Kāfī. *Fatāwā*. 2 vols. Cairo: Maktabat al-Qudsī, 1355-1356/1936-1937.

al-Ṣufūrī, ʿAbd al-Raḥmān b. ʿAbd al-Salām. *Nuzhat al-Majālis wa-Muntakhab al-Nafāʾis*. 2 vols. in 1. Cairo: al-Maṭbaʿat al-Azhariyya, 1346/1928.

al-Suhrawardī, Abū Ḥafṣ Shihāb al-Dīn ʿUmar b. Muḥammad b. ʿAbd Allāh al-Tamīmī al-Bakrī. *Kitāb ʿAwārif al-Maʿārif*. Cairo: al-Maktabat al-ʿAlāmiyya, 1358/1939.

Sukayrij, Abū al-ʿAbbās Aḥmad b. al-ʿAyyāshī. *al-Shaṭaḥāt al-Sukayrijiyya*. Cairo: Maṭbaʿat al-Ṣidq al-Khayriyya, 1352/1933.

al-Sulamī, Abū ʿAbd al-Raḥmān Muḥammad b. al-Ḥusayn b. Mūsā al-Azdī. *Tafsīr al-Sulamī wa-Huwa Ḥaqāʾiq al-Tafsīr*. Ed. Sayyid ʿImrān. 3 vols. Beirut: Dār al-Kutub al-ʿIlmiyya, 1421/2001.

al-Suyūṭī, Abū al-Faḍl Jalāl al-Dīn ʿAbd al-Raḥmān b. Abī Bakr. *al-Durr al-Manthūr fīl-Tafsīr bil-Maʾthūr*. Ed. ʿAbd Allah b. ʿAbd al-Muḥsin al-Turkī. 17 vols. Cairo: Markaz Hajar lil-Buḥūth, 1424/2003.

———. *al-Ḥāwī lil-Fatāwā*. 2 vols. Cairo: Idārat al-Ṭibā'at al-Munīriyya, 1352/1933. Rept. Beirut: Dār al-Kutub al-'Ilmiyya, 1402/1982.

———. *al-Khaṣā'iṣ al-Kubrā aw Kifāyat al-Ṭālib al-Labīb fī Khaṣā'iṣ al-Ḥabīb*. 2 vols. Hyderabad, Deccan: Dā'irat al-Ma'ārif al-Niẓāmiyya, 1901-1903. Rept. Beirut: Dār al-Kutub al-'Ilmiyya, 1985.

———. *al-La'āli' al-Maṣnū'a fīl-Aḥādīth al-Mawḍū'a*. 3 vols. Beirut: Dār al-Kutub al-'Ilmiyya, 1996.

———. *Masālik al-Ḥunafā fī Wāliday al-Muṣṭafā*. Ed. Muḥammad Zaynuhum Muḥammad 'Azb. Cairo: Dar al-Amīn, 1414/1993.

———. *al-Nahjat al-Sawiyya fīl-Asmā' al-Nabawiyya*. Ed. Aḥmad 'Abd Allāh Bājūr. Cairo: al-Dār al-Miṣriyya al-Lubnāniyya, 1421/2001.

———. *al-Riyāḍ al-Anīqa fī Sharḥ Asmā' Khayr al-Khalīqa*. Ed. Abū Hājar Muḥammad al-Sa'īd b. Basyūnī Zaghlūl. Beirut: Dār al-Kutub al-'Ilmiyya, 1405/1985.

———. *Unmūdhaj al-Labīb fī Khaṣā'iṣ al-Ḥabīb*. Ed. 'Abbās Aḥmad Ṣaqr al-Ḥusaynī. Madina: Dār al-Madīnat al-Munawwara, 1416/1995.

al-Ṭabarānī, Abū al-Qāsim Sulaymān b. Aḥmad. *al-Aḥādīth al-Ṭiwāl*. Ed. Ḥamdī 'Abd al-Majīd al-Salafī. 2nd ed. Beirut: al-Maktab al-Islāmī, 1419/1998.

———. *al-Du'ā'*. Ed. Muḥammad Sa'īd b. Muḥammad Ḥasan al-Bukhārī. 3 vols. Beirut: Dār al-Bashā'ir al-Islāmiyya, 1407/1987.

———. *al-Mu'jam al-Awsaṭ*. Ed. Ṭāriq b. 'Awaḍ Allāh b. Muḥammad and 'Abd al-Muḥsin b. Ibrāhīm al-Ḥusaynī. 10 vols. Cairo: Dār al-Ḥaramayn, 1415/1995.

———. *al-Mu'jam al-Kabīr*. Ed. Ḥamdī 'Abd al-Majīd al-Salafī. 25 vols. 2nd ed. Baghdad: Wizārat al-Awqāf, 1984-1990. Rept. Cairo: Maktabat Ibn Taymiyya, n.d.

———. *Musnad al-Shāmiyyīn*. Ed. Ḥamdī 'Abd al-Majīd al-Salafī. 4 vols. Beirut: Mu'assasat al-Risāla, 1409/1989.

al-Ṭabarī, Abū Ja'far Muḥammad b. Jarīr. *Tafsīr al-Ṭabarī: Jāmi' al-Bayān 'an Ta'wīl Āy al-Qur'ān*. Ed. 'Abd Allāh b. 'Abd al-Muḥsin al-Turkī et al. 26 vols. Cairo: Dār Hajar, 1422/2001.

———. *Tahdhīb al-Āthār: Musnad 'Alī b. Abī Ṭālib*. Ed. Maḥmūd Muḥammad Shākir. Cairo: Maṭba'at al-Madanī, [1402?/1982?].

———. *Tārīkh al-Ṭabarī: Tārīkh al-Rusul wal-Mulūk*. Ed. Muḥammad Abū al-Faḍl Ibrāhīm. 2nd ed. 11 vols. Cairo: Dār al-Ma'ārif, 1960-1977.

al-Ṭaḥāwī, Abū Ja'far Aḥmad b. Muḥammad b. Salāma al-Azdī al-Ḥajarī. *Sharḥ Mushkil al-Āthār*. Ed. Shu'ayb al-Arnā'ūṭ. 16 vols. Beirut: Mu'assasat al-Risāla, 1415/1994.

al-Ṭā'ī, Abū Tammām Ḥabīb b. Aws. *Dīwān al-Ḥamāsa*. Ed. Aḥmad Ḥasan Basaj. Beirut: Dār al-Kutub al-'Ilmiyya, 1418/1998.

Tammām al-Rāzī, Abū al-Qāsim. [*al-Fawā'id*.] *al-Rawḍ al-Bassām bi-Tartīb wa-Takhrīj Fawā'id Tammām*. By Abū Sulaymān Jāsim b.

Sulaymān al-Fuhayd al-Dawsarī. 5 vols. Beirut: Dār al-Bashā'ir al-Islāmiyya, 1408/1987.

al-Taymī al-Aṣbahānī, Qawwām al-Sunna Abū al-Qāsim Ismā'īl b. Muḥammad b. al-Faḍl. *Dalā'il al-Nubuwwa*. Ed. Musā'id b. Sulaymān al-Rāshid al-Ḥumayd. Riyadh: Dār al-'Āṣima, 1412/1992.

al-Tha'ālibī, Abū Manṣūr 'Abd al-Malik b. Muḥammad b. Ismā'īl. *al-Tamthīl wal-Muḥāḍara*. Ed. 'Abd al-Fattāḥ Muḥammad al-Ḥilū. Cairo: Dār Iḥyā' al-Kutub al-'Arabiyya, 1961.

———. *Yatīmat al-Dahr fī Maḥāsin Ahl al-'Aṣr*. Ed. Mufīd Muḥammad Qumayḥa. 5 vols. Beirut: Dār al-Kutub al-'Ilmiyya, 1403/1983.

al-Tha'labī al-Naysābūrī, Abū Isḥāq Aḥmad b. Muḥammad b. Ibrāhīm. *al-Kashf wal-Bayān al-Ma'rūf bi-Tafsīr al-Tha'labī*. Ed. Abū Muḥammad Ibn 'Āshūr and Naẓīr al-Sā'idī. 10 vols. Beirut: Dār Iḥyā' al-Turāth al-'Arabī, 1422/2002.

al-Tirmidhī, Abū 'Īsā Muḥammad b. 'Īsā. *al-Jāmi' al-Ṣaḥīḥ*. Ed. Aḥmad Muḥammad Shākir et al. 5 vols. 2nd ed. Cairo: Muṣṭafā Bābī al-Ḥalabī, 1398/1978.

———. *al-Shamā'il al-Muḥammadiyya*. With al-Bājūrī's *al-Mawāhib al-Ladunniyya 'alā al-Shamā'il al-Muḥammadiyya*. Ed. Muḥammad 'Awwāma. [Madina?: s.n.], 1422/2001.

al-Tustarī, Abū Muḥammad Sahl b. 'Abd Allāh b. Yūnus. *Tafsīr al-Qur'ān al-'Aẓīm*. Ed. Ṭaha 'Abd al-Ra'ūf Sa'd and Sa'd Ḥasan Muḥammad 'Alī. Cairo: Dār al-Ḥaram lil-Turāth, 2004/1425.

al-'Uqaylī, Abū Ja'far Muḥammad b. 'Amr. *Kitāb al-Ḍu'afā' wa-Man Nusiba ilāl-Kadhib wa-Waḍ' al-Ḥadīth*. Ḥamdī al-Salafī. 4 vols. Riyadh: Dār al-Ṣumay'ī, 1420/2000.

al-Wāḥidī al-Naysābūrī, Abū al-Ḥasan 'Alī b. Aḥmad. *al-Wajīz fī Tafsīr al-Kitāb al-'Azīz*. Ed. Ṣafwān 'Adnān Dāwūdī. 2 vols. Damascus: Dār al-Qalam; Beirut: al-Dār al-Shāmiyya, 1995.

———. *al-Wasīṭ fī Tafsīr al-Qur'ān al-Majīd*. Ed. Aḥmad 'Ādil 'Abd al-Mawjūd et al. 5 vols. Beirut: Dār al-Kutub al-'Ilmiyya, 1415/1994.

al-Zamakhsharī, Jār Allāh Abū al-Qāsim Maḥmūd b. 'Umar. *al-Kashshāf 'an Ḥaqā'iq Ghawāmiḍ al-Tanzīl wa-'Uyūn al-Aqāwīl fī Wujūh al-Ta'wīl*. Ed. 'Ādil Aḥmad 'Abd al-Mawjūd et al. 6 vols. Riyadh: Maktabat al-'Ubaykān, 1418/1998.

———. *Rabī' al-Abrār wa-Nuṣūṣ al-Akhbār*. Ed. 'Abd al-Amīr Muhannā. 5 vols. Beirut: Mu'assasat al-A'lamī lil-Maṭbū'āt, 1412/1992.

al-Zurqānī, Muḥammad b. 'Abd al-Bāqī b. Yūsuf. *Sharḥ al-Mawāhib al-Lāduniyya*. Ed. Ibrāhīm 'Abd al-Ghaffār al-Dusūqī et al. 8 vols. Cairo: Khedive of Egypt Ismā'īl b. Ibrāhīm b. Muḥammad, 1291/1874.

www.ingramcontent.com/pod-product-compliance
Lightning Source LLC
Chambersburg PA
CBHW030305080526
44584CB00012B/442
* 9 7 8 1 9 3 8 0 5 8 0 0 4 *